106923

ADMINISTRATION
OF
CONTINUING
EDUCATION

A Guide for Administrators

EDITORIAL COMMITTEE

NAPCAE is dedicated to the improvement and expansion of publicly supported education for adults. Its goals are to extend and enrich the opportunities for continuing adult education provided by publicly supported adult education agencies. In pursuit of these goals, it works with administrators and teachers of adult education programs in encouraging state and federal legislation which favors the educational needs of adults as well as of children, continuing program evaluation and action research, professional development, systematic data collection and information dissemination, and experimentation with innovative projects. As means of communicating with its membership, it conducts an annual conference and issues periodic newsletters and special publications.

ADMINISTRATION OF CONTINUING EDUCATION

A Guide for Administrators

Edited by
Nathan C. Shaw

Director, New Programs and Community Services, Montgomery Junior College
Rockville and Takoma Park, Maryland

NATIONAL ASSOCIATION FOR PUBLIC CONTINUING AND ADULT EDUCATION
Washington, D. C. • 1969

Single copy: paperbound, $6 (Stock No. 758-01060). Discounts on
quantity orders: 10-29 copies, 10%; 50-99 copies, 15%; 100 or more
copies, 20%. Orders accompanied by payment will be sent post-
paid. Shipping and handling charges will be added to billed orders.
All orders of $10 or less must be accompanied by payment. Order
from Customer Service, National Education Association, 1201
Sixteenth Street, N.W., Washington, D.C. 20036.

FOREWORD

Events which have transpired during the eight years since the first printing of this book in 1969 attest to the rapidity and completeness of change within the field of adult and continuing education. At the Galaxy Conference of Adult Education organizations held in Washington, D.C., in December of 1969 our membership voted unanimously to adopt sweeping changes in our constitution, one of the most visible being our new name — the National Association for Public Continuing and Adult Education — which became effective January 1, 1970. Robert Finch and Clyde Weinhold were the presidents during whose terms of office most of the work on this book was carried out, and Mark Hanna served during that same period of time as chairman of the Publications Committee. All three of these outstanding adult educators are now retired. Robert Luke, our executive secretary from 1952-1969, resigned his NAPCAE position and now holds a full-time adult education post with the National Education Association.

Whereas we were for many years a subsidized department of the NEA, and then a national affiliate, we no longer receive any direct financial support from the NEA. For the first seventeen years of our existence our constitution limited our membership to those who held a functional relationship to a public school adult education program. As a result of our new name and our broadened mandate, our constituency now includes people across the entire gamut of public continuing and adult education.

Even our focus of service has changed, and — in addition to our ongoing program of publications, conferences and committee activities — we are carrying out a variety of specialized services across the country: state and local program evaluations, formulation of professional development plans, on-site consultations, pre- and in-service training programs, and such other activities as are requested by our membership. The NAPCAE headquarters staff has been enlarged in order that we may meet the demands of our expanding roles.

In our role as your legislative advocate in Washington, we continue to carry out what we hope is an active, aggressive and responsible lobbying effort. In the spirit of the continuous change which seems to characterize our field, we are proud to present this third printing of *Administration of Continuing Education*. May it prove to be informative, useful, and stimulating.

James R. Dorland
Executive Director
NAPCAE

MEMBERSHIP PUBLICATIONS

NAPCAE's three newsletters

- PULSE (8 issues a year) is a newsletter of current events to keep you up to date on the most recent developments in state and federal legislation, and features "Names in the News" of personalities and events in adult education.

- SWAP SHOP (6 issues a year) is the "how-to" publication for adult education administrators. Recent issues have emphasized federal legislation and its impact on local programs, best use of local resources, and latest methods of staff development.

- TECHNIQUES (8 issues a year) is the "how-to" publication designed specifically for *Teachers* of adults. Recent issues have concentrated on telling the teaching technology story the way it is, the role of the teaching-learning process in deciding on course objectives, designing learning experiences, and evaluation of student performance, as well as research resources and the practical application of these by teachers of adults. It is reported to be the most useful teacher aid for teachers of adults today.

. . . and a yearly almanac

- PUBLIC CONTINUING & ADULT EDUCATION ALMANAC

  New, revised NAPCAE yearbook. Includes Membership Directory; report on federal legislation; names of NAPCAE officers, board members, committee chairmen; NAPCAE Awards recipients; up-to-date statistical information on adult education enrollments, expenditures, and support at the state level, as well as other useful resource information. Single copy free to Active and Institutional Members and Subscribers at time of publication; $8 to Associate Members; $15 to nonmembers.

NAPCAE MEMBERSHIPS

- ACTIVE MEMBERSHIP

Members of staffs of publicly supported adult education programs (present or former) and anyone who supports the purpose of the Association, which is to give leadership to the development and implementation of public continuing and adult education, may become active members. Includes subscriptions to PULSE, SWAP SHOP, and TECHNIQUES.

- ASSOCIATE MEMBERSHIP

Membership designed specifically for TEACHERS of adults to acquaint and affiliate them with the Association.

- SUBSCRIPTION SERVICE

Includes subscriptions to all publications and services received by Active Members, except the right to vote and hold office. Anyone may subscribe.

- EMERITUS MEMBERSHIP

Open only to former Active Members who have retired. Emeritus Members may attend the annual conference without payment of a registration fee and receive all newsletters, as well as other rights and privileges of the Association except that of holding office.

- INSTITUTIONAL MEMBERSHIP

Includes two sets of all regular publications, and a complimentary copy of each new publication. Each Institutional Member is entitled to designate one individual to represent the Institution as an Active Member of the Association.

- GRADUATE STUDENT MEMBERSHIP

Open to full-time adult education graduate students. Includes same privileges as active membership.

For further information, write to NAPCAE, 1201 Sixteenth Street, N.W., Washington, D.C. 20036.

CONTENTS

FOREWORD, James R. Dorland v

INTRODUCTION, Robert E. Finch 1

SECTION I   THE ORGANIZATION AND ADMINISTRATION OF CONTINUING EDUCATION

CHAPTER 1 The Development of Public Support
for Adult Education 12
Robert A. Luke

CHAPTER 2 Continuing Education in Community Schools 28
Peter L. Clancy

CHAPTER 3 Roles and Interrelationships
of Continuing Education Institutions 46
Russell J. Kleis and Donald G. Butcher

CHAPTER 4 The Evolving Role of the Adult Education Director 76
William S. Griffith

CHAPTER 5 Finance and Budget Development. 102
William J. Johnston

CHAPTER 6 The Impact of Legislation on Adult Education. 118
James R. Dorland

SECTION II   PROGRAM DEVELOPMENT AND OPERATION

CHAPTER 7 Identification of Needs and Resources 138
Samuel E. Hand

CHAPTER 8 Planning a Balanced Curriculum. 160
Raymond T. McCall and Robert F. Schenz

CHAPTER 9 Major Curriculum Areas and Program Concerns 180
Carl E. Minich

CHAPTER 10 Community Relations, Promotion, and Publicity 200
David B. Rauch

SECTION III   THE ADULT PARTICIPANT

CHAPTER 11 Adult Motivation and Recruitment. 218
D. Ray Ferrier

CHAPTER 12 Counseling and Guidance Services. 236
Golden I. Langdon

CHAPTER 13 Expanding Facilities for Adult Learners 264
Floyd N. Peters

SECTION IV   IMPROVEMENT OF INSTRUCTION

CHAPTER 14   Selection of Teachers, Leaders,
and Other Supportive Staff.................................... 280
James A. Sheldon and Gordon B. Wasinger

CHAPTER 15   Teacher Training and Supervision 298
R. Curtis Ulmer

CHAPTER 16   Methods and Materials for Adult Learners 316
Monroe C. Neff

SECTION V   RESEARCH AND EVALUATION

CHAPTER 17   Research for Action Programs 344
George F. Aker and Wayne L. Schroeder

CHAPTER 18   Continuous Program Evaluation 368
Alan B. Knox

A LOOK AHEAD — PATTERNS AND TRENDS 392

APPENDIX

A   Footnote References 394

B   Selected Readings 410

C   Bibliography for Further Reading 423

D   Index 435

INTRODUCTION

Robert E. Finch

The whole socioeconomic makeup of our cities has changed radically, but public education in our cities has not changed. With the exception of a few scattered federal programs superimposed on the public education establishment, there has been no major change in public education in our cities in the past 40 years.

Public education in the cities is in trouble, real trouble, because educators themselves are resistant to change, and the dwindling affluent minority still living within the city limits insists that "quality" education for their college-bound children be maintained.

Why have the public schools, both in cities and rural areas, largely ignored the socioeconomic changes of the past 10 years? Archaic state educational codes for public high schools were written when men and boys were laying railroad ties by hand and girls were operating manual switchboards. In those days there was a place for the high school dropout in the economy.

Public education, as it has from the days of the Latin grammar school in colonial America, sees the preparing of children for college as its major function. Forty years ago, vocational courses were added to the strictly college preparatory high schools of the nation as a means of "taking care of" students not going on to college. But, the major purpose of the comprehensive city high school has been and still remains essentially the preparation of pupils for higher education.

Big cities are no longer college preparatory communities. Most of the affluent who can afford to send their children to college have moved to

Robert E. Finch is director of the Division of Continuing Education, Cincinnati Public Schools, Cincinnati, Ohio.

the suburbs, but public education in the cities is still trying to operate on the same basis that it did 40 years ago. Less than a third of youth in the cities will ever see the front door of a college, and half of those who do will be weeded out there. A third are simply "giving up the ghost" and quitting high school before graduation. The others are either taking watered-down college preparatory courses that prepare neither for a job nor for college or are taking outdated shop courses.

Today, a high school education plus a marketable skill have become the minimum job requirement, but two-thirds of the youth who enter the ninth grade in the typical metropolitan high school will not meet this minimum requirement. Ten years ago, personnel management could say, "Send us more high school dropouts to sort our checks, run our elevators, and do other jobs requiring no training," but it is now a well publicized fact that routine, repetitive jobs are gone. Education must change accordingly or admit failure in its purpose to serve "all the people."

Nine years ago, the U. S. Department of Labor was warning that by 1970 the demand for unskilled labor would be virtually nonexistent. In 1960, it also warned of the economic migrations to the cities of millions of people ill prepared educationally to adjust to the changes of urban technology. As predicted, the postwar baby boom now in the high schools has been coupled with an after-Sputnik demand for higher academic achievement. This combination alone has intensified the "measure up or get out" philosophy which now permeates both secondary and higher education.

More than any other factor, the increasing sweep of technological change has doubled the educational gap for millions of youth and adults with less than a high school education. It has created a manpower imbalance that is shaking our whole economic and social structure. For the man struggling to understand fractions and how to use a ruler, our new world of electronics, with its minimal mathematics requirement of trigonometry, is as far away as the moon. He sees enticing full-page advertisements for electronic workers, draftsmen, and hundreds of other unobtainable jobs. Without the education to secure these jobs he feels cheated, and rightly so.

Tragically, one out of every four persons on the street does not have a high school education. There is no such thing as a "quickie" eight-week course to make up eight years of schooling. Nationally, we are trying to solve the problem with gimmicks, social panaceas, and lengthy committee reports.

Why shouldn't we give every person the opportunity to make up the education our society has failed to provide? What right do we have to deny any citizen the opportunity for learning because of his age? If the opportunity for an education and a job ends at age 18 as it does in many communities, the battle for job opportunities will be fought in the streets.

Education has become a national problem. It's no longer a local community problem. The majority of children no longer enter kindergarten and graduate from high school in the same community. The quality of educational opportunities in rural areas and in small towns is vital to the economy of the nation simply because so many young people are migrating to the urban, industrial centers of the nation.

Many educators consider their sole responsibility to be the education of children until they either drop out of school or graduate from the twelfth grade. They consider the youth standing on street corners saying, "What'll we do now?" to be a responsibility of community agencies, not of public education. But the time for talk is over. As a nation we either move immediately to educate millions of our people and give them the opportunity for jobs, dignity, and self-respect, or we must reconcile ourselves to unrest in our cities, costly lifetime doles, and waste of potentially skilled manpower in our economy.

Public education does not operate in a vacuum — it is a perfect image of the society it serves. Traditionally, public schools are implementers of, or persuaders for, social change. Most educators have never seen themselves as leaders or makers of social change but rather have viewed themselves as followers of social change.

Until the majority of people decide that public education must provide (a) basic elementary education for all, including the millions of adults who have never gone beyond the fifth grade; (b) the same emphasis on preparation for the world of work as is now placed on preparation for college; and (c) the opportunity for high school dropouts, both youth and adults, to have a second chance to complete a high school education, acquire a marketable skill, or upgrade obsolete skills, no major change is going to take place in public education in our nation.

It is this third dimension — continuing education for out-of-school youth and adults — which lies at the core of our national crisis. Education has always been the key to a good job and the money for decent housing, adequate food, and the other advantages commonly known as the American way of life.

The basic question facing our society today is, Does the majority of Americans really want to offer an educational opportunity to the one-fourth of the black and white population of our country who are now in virtual economic bondage? More specifically, Are the majority willing to educate a black man to operate an engine lathe in the next aisle, a stenographer to work at the next desk, or does the majority want to hold a minority of blacks and whites in a position of servitude and reliance on welfare subsistence, a guaranteed income, or some other type of financial holding action? Unrest in the cities is not a new problem. It is a question which has faced most societies since the dawn of civilization.

The federal government has been making sporadic attempts to educate both unemployed youth and adults for the job openings available. Even though 75 percent of those completing training under the Manpower Development and Training Act are getting and holding good jobs, there is considerable resistance to those federal programs by those who want "quality education" reserved for the "selected few."

In most states today, including the industrial North, the average amount of schooling completed by adults is between 9 and 10 years. Education has historically been reserved as a special privilege for those who could afford to pay for it. The United States has come as close as any society in offering an equal educational opportunity for all, but the socioeconomic changes of the past 10 years have caused it to fall short. It is time for a major change in public education.

In 1856, when the Cincinnati Public Schools opened their first evening high school, the Board of Education pointed out that "the perpetuation of our superior form of government depends upon an intelligent and informed citizenry. If this is not looked to, power will gradually pass from the many to the few and in the lapse of time this great fabric of government will find a common grave of all the great republics of history." Because of the loss of two operating levies in 1966, the Cincinnati Board of Education for the first time was forced to charge a resident tuition fee of $48 for adults in its day and evening adult high school courses. Enrollment in the adult high schools and pre-employment classes for high school dropouts dropped nearly in half from the normal enrollment of 7,000 youth and adults. People who need education the most can least afford to pay for it. The Board of Education eliminated the tuition fee, but Cincinnati is the only city in Ohio that does not charge a tuition fee for dropouts who want a second chance to earn a high school diploma and acquire a marketable skill.

Surprisingly, the majority of educators want tuition fees. Unfortunately, many people feel that any youth or adult who was unable to adjust to the academic curriculum of the regular school or who was deprived of an opportunity for an education—even an elementary one —should not be given a second chance for an education or should at least pay for it.

In the United States today, with a few notable exceptions, there is a deep void between publicly supported high schools and publicly supported colleges and universities. Millions of frustrated youth and adults are caught in this educational void. Too many legislators and Congress-men, as evidenced in Congressional hearings, think of adult education as it may exist in their affluent suburban communities—classes in bridge, gourmet cooking, and recreational classes offered on a strictly self-supporting basis. It's adult education of another world from that of the inner city. It is one of the paradoxes of our society. Suburbanites, with the exception of senior citizens, need adult courses to learn how to relax from the stresses of employment while many youth and adults of the inner city have too much leisure.

Adults who have been deprived of the opportunity for an elementary education are not necessarily stupid. Many adults in federally sup-ported basic education classes (elementary 1-8) are achieving two grade levels in 150 hour classes. Many arrive at the adult centers before classes open just for the opportunity of a few minutes' talk with the teacher. The hunger for education on the part of adults who have only two or three years of schooling is almost inconceivable to the suburbanite.

Public school systems with the courage to break with educational traditionalism and to offer programs especially designed for youth and adults are enrolling thousands of students. In Indianapolis, one out of every six graduates of the adult program is a day school dropout who became a drop-in. In Los Angeles, it's one out of eight; Cincinnati, one out of ten.

Throughout the country, public school classrooms, shops, and labora-tories are largely unused in the late afternoons, evenings, Saturdays, and during the summer months. At the same time, a fourth of the popu-lation in the cities is desperately lacking in education. In many instances the Office of Economic Opportunity has been forced to open ill equipped training classes in dirty, abandoned buildings, while boards of educa-tion keep their buildings dark and concentrate on less controversial federal programs such as Head Start and the equipping of school libraries. When boards of education in the 1800's did turn on their school building lights to educate the foreign born, it was the beginning of a night school spirit which appears to have been lost in many communities.

Indeed, public education cannot work in a vacuum—it must co-sponsor educational programs with public welfare departments, metropolitan housing authorities, state employment services, and Neighborhood Youth Corps; and it must work directly with business, industry, and labor. In-plant educational courses for employees, a long established practice in a few cities, is a double-barrelled effort to meet America's educational backlog. The schools, business, and industry are logical partners in educational action programs. Business and industry can help educators develop curriculum, loan teachers for adult vocational evening classes, advise on the type of instructional equipment needed, and refer students for training. Most cities have only scratched the surface in business-education partnerships.

Again, one basic question, Are the majority of people willing to give a black and white minority opportunity for a second chance in education, encourage them to take advantage of the opportunity, and offer opportunity for the better job on a truly equal basis? The fabric of our whole society has been built on equal opportunity. Not all will take advantage of the opportunity; but if we believe in our system, then it is our moral obligation to give every youth and every adult repeated opportunity during his lifetime to achieve our goal of dignity and self-respect for the individual, which in turn strengthens our society and helps each and every one of us.

An action-now program might well consider the following priorities:

1. High schools in the cities must now equitably balance the attention they give to preparation for work with that for college. This means giving equal status to the world of work through vocational-technical programs, not simply using vocational programs as the place to put the noncollege-bound student. It means a willingness on the part of boards of education to spend the necessary funds to update obsolete vocational courses. On the other side of the coin, if local taxpayers don't provide the funds to do the educational job, public education in the city will simply disintegrate. It means the updating of teacher training institutions in preparing teachers and counselors for the world of work. It means that teachers from middle-class families who have never been closer to a ghetto than their car must develop an understanding and appreciation of children and youth in big cities where most of the people now live.

2. Continuing education for out-of-school youth and adults must become a vital part of every public educational system on the same tuition-free basis as elementary and secondary education. It must become a third dimension—a vital part of the school system—and not a supplement or appendage to it.

This means opening up high school buildings in the late afternoons, in the evenings, and on Saturdays plus holding adult basic education classes (grades 1-8) in churches, community centers, and other familiar locations in the neighborhoods where the people live. It means encouraging local taxpayers, state legislators, and Congress to provide the funds to give to one-fourth of our youth and adult population *the opportunity* to complete an elementary or a high school education; to acquire marketable skills either for initial employment or upgrading in employment; and to take short-term general education courses to teach people how to utilize effectively their incomes as well as how to earn a livelihood. It means that the federal government must regain faith in public education as the best means of educating all the people. It means that teacher training institutions must offer professional courses in the instruction of adults.

3. The federal government must abandon its on-again – off-again programs of expediency in attacking the problem of educating the poor. Pilot projects by the thousands have flickered and died over the past five years. Now is the time to light the main burner and develop a comprehensive national manpower plan. The balance of power arrangement among the U. S. Departments of Labor and Health, Education, and Welfare and the U. S. Office of Economic Opportunity has created confusion, duplication, and a spinning of wheels in the cities. The time is past for political gestures and federal programs which expend most of their grants in administrative overhead and carpetbagging rather than helping people.

4. The role and financial responsibility of the states should be clearly defined. Too many states are merely the legal funnel for federal grants between Washington and the local community. Every state must have the same financial responsibility for educating out-of-school youth and adults that it has for educating children and high school youth up to the compulsory school age of 16 or 18 years.

5. Education must take advantage of the new individualized instruction machines and materials, which can dispense facts and help the student correct his own errors and move successfully at his own rate of speed. The new role of the teacher is that of an analyzer of each student's learning progress. Individualized instruction under programed learning appeals to both the able student and the slower student because the emphasis is upon success. Furthermore, responsibility for learning is where it belongs – on the individual. Learning is an individual matter. No one can learn for the student – least of all the teacher. With individualized programed learning instruction, more time can be given to problem solving based on the facts as learned through efficient mechanical devices and other new methods. The traditional classroom methods are no longer practical from the standpoint of available teaching staff, the number of persons who must be served, and the cost of educating millions of people who must be educated, reeducated, and retrained.

6. The evaluative criteria of the regional accrediting associations

which serve as the base for most state high school standards and graduation requirements must be revised. Many of these state standards are based on the assumption that all youth finish high school and go on to college. In many cities there are more people with less than a fifth-grade education than there are college graduates. It's time for a change in an educational world of unreality. A start has been made by the North Central Association of Secondary Schools and Colleges in the establishment of separate evaluative criteria in high school completion programs for out-of-school youth and adults.

7. Overall plans of continuing education must be developed to solve the problem of displacement of our manpower resources. (a) The functional illiterate must acquire, within his capacity, the basic education and the fundamental skills to reach the first rung of the economic ladder. (b) Out-of-school youth and adults with two or three years of high school, who are now filling jobs on the first rung of the ladder, must be encouraged to acquire the necessary high school academic and vocational-technical skills to reach the second rung of the economic ladder. Unless this is accomplished, there will be few job opportunities for the men and women trying to reach the first rung. (c) High school and college graduates must be encouraged to keep up with rapidly changing job requirements and to acquire a higher level of academic, technical, and professional skill to reach the third rung of the economic ladder. The upgrading of the entire labor force has a direct relationship to the number of entry jobs available in the labor market.

A solution to the many problems resulting from the merging social and economic factors of the "second industrial revolution" must be found. It is now recognized that education on all levels — from kindergarten to university graduate work — holds the key to many of these problems.

On a strictly dollar basis, continuing education for out-of-school youth and adults is one of the least expensive actions our economy can generate — to say nothing of the added dignity and self-respect of the individuals involved. There is no pill to take for an instant education, but the vast majority of our people do want the dignity and self-respect of earning their own livelihoods. The fact that an increasing number of out-of-school youth and adults in many cities are seeking under their own *initiative* to improve themselves is one of the most encouraging signs of our times. The economic rewards to the individual for self-improvement remain, as they must, a prime factor in our economy. The fact that millions of adults in the United States are discovering for themselves that *learning never ends* and that *it is never too late to learn* may answer many of the problems — provided public education has the insight, the imagination, and the courage to provide the opportunities for learning.

Age in itself is a relatively unimportant barrier to learning. Of greater significance is the combination of motivation, experience, energy, and capacity to learn. The "time for learning" is no longer considered a prerogative of school-age children.

The change in education, however, will not come in nice, neat packages carefully labeled and tied with blue ribbon. One thing is certain: Change, and radical change, must be made in public education. Until all the people have the opportunity for an education, there can be no such thing as equal opportunity for all as we claim. It becomes simply a matter of attempting to hold a restive minority under physical control.

Do we have the courage to sift the strictly political from the educational values? As a society, do we have the soul to help people help themselves?

SECTION *I*

THE ORGANIZATION AND ADMINISTRATION OF CONTINUING EDUCATION

CHAPTER 1

THE DEVELOPMENT OF PUBLIC SUPPORT FOR ADULT EDUCATION

Robert A. Luke

INTRODUCTION

Adult education today is a mixture of many forces and a collection of many items — antique as well as modern. Its content can run from literature to literacy, from community action to philosophical reflection, from the study of external forces that drive society to the study of internal forces that drive individuals.

Adult education can as easily include classes in furniture refinishing and navigation and speed reading as it can classes in effective speaking or elementary English or community orchestra or intercultural relations or typing. It can take in science . . . political as well as natural. It can examine the world . . . and the test tube. Its aim may be better jobs, increased understanding, more civic participation, better health, or wiser consumer buying.

The "education" in adult education includes the basic subjects normally taught in elementary and high school — reading, writing, and calculus as well as art, modern dance, and conversational Spanish.

Also included are the advanced technology needed today for adult vocations and the recreational and personal development instruction needed by all kinds of individuals, whether jobless manual laborers or overworked executives.

Robert A. Luke is executive secretary of the National Association for Public School Adult Education and director of the Division of Adult Education Service, National Education Association, Washington, D. C.

ADULT EDUCATION AGENCIES

The "adult" in adult education includes the recent high school dropout and the Job Corps enrollee. While not an adult in years, such a person has adult needs for a job, an income, the ability to meet adult responsibilities. "Adult" also includes the scholar, the technician, the housewife, and the retiree who want to learn a new skill or explore a new subject interest. Adult education today can include practically everything and nearly everyone.

Programs of adult education are offered to the community by an incredibly wide range of groups and agencies—churches, local public school systems, land grant colleges, state universities, community colleges, libraries—and all the myriad organizations, institutions, and agencies that claim education as a part or all of their mission.

No one of these sponsors can claim a greater importance than any other or aspire to meet a more essential need. While each program agency may interdepend with others within the total structure of adult education, each has its own history, its own clientele, its own administrative pattern, and—to some extent—its own professional society.

PUBLIC ADULT EDUCATION

Along with the others, the public education authority—local school districts primarily responsible for the education of boys and girls—has had a long and significant part to play in the historical development of adult education. Recently, the programs traditionally offered by the public schools—the well known K-12 administrative pattern—have been augmented by the educational offerings for adults made available by the community colleges. Together, public schools and community colleges represent the bulk of the adult education currently referred to in the nomenclature of the profession as "public adult education." It is that history to which this chapter is directed.

The writer of this chapter has relied heavily on George C. Mann's "The Development of Public School Education," written in 1956 for the first edition of *Public School Adult Education: A Guide for Administrators,* published by NAPSAE. At that time Dr. Mann was chief of the Bureau of Adult Education of the California State Department of Education. An equally important source has been a monograph written by Malcolm Knowles, professor of adult education at Boston University, entitled *The Role of Adult Education in the Public Schools,* which was published in 1962 as No. 4 of Vol. 144 of the Boston University's School of Education *Journal of Education.*

The writer has also had access to two manuscripts awaiting publication. The first is the chapter on adult education as a service of state departments of education written by John Holden, dean of the Graduate School of the U.S. Department of Agriculture, for a two-volume history of state departments of education to be published in 1969 by the Council of Chief State School Officers. The writer has also received permission to quote material appearing in a manuscript he has prepared for the article on the history of the National Association for Public School Adult Education for the forthcoming *Encyclopedia of Education,* to be published by the Macmillan Company.

EARLY HISTORY

Development of Adult Education in the Cities

When adult education began three centuries ago in the United States, it was aimed primarily at helping young industrial workers learn enough to find and keep a better job. Many jobs were different then. There was more emphasis on muscle and less on brain. However, only a minimum amount of schooling was needed for young men who wanted to get ahead. Evening schools catered to their needs.

"In Colonial times," writes Dr. Mann in his chapter on the history of public school adult education, "evening schools existed as private undertakings conducted for profit." As early as 1661, he reports, such schools — with both a vocational and a cultural emphasis — were to be found in New York State. Later, similar schools were opened in Boston (1724), Philadelphia (1734), and Charleston, South Carolina (1744). Through the ensuing years, such privately run schools have steadily grown along with the public adult schools, which started somewhat later.

Massachusetts, which is credited with other notable achievements in education, may have also been the first state to support adult education financially when in 1823 the state appropriated $75 to at least partially support an evening school. By 1854 the state's aid had increased to such an extent that the school could be entirely supported by public funds.

Although Providence, Rhode Island, is credited with opening evening schools in 1810, these were private schools. City-operated evening schools in Providence did not exist before 1850.

New York City opened a public evening program in 1833, but it was discontinued five years later for the lack of funds and was not reestablished until 1847 when the state provided $6,000 "to conduct evening schools for males." About 3,000 boys and men enrolled in the six evening schools established that year in New York. The next year the state appropriation was increased to $15,000, and women were also allowed to enroll. By 1857 New York City was operating 25 schools five evenings a week.

But well before the New York evening schools were successfully reestablished, a number of other cities had undertaken the lead. In 1834 the city council of Louisville, Kentucky, began an evening school for apprentices. In 1836 Boston used half the proceeds from its city hay scales to support evening schools. In 1839 Baltimore opened evening courses for 12- to 21-year-old males unable to attend day schools. The age limit of 17 years was later extended to 30.

Dr. Knowles reports in his monograph on public school adult education that Cincinnati, Ohio, opened three evening elementary schools in 1840 "in response to a law requiring 'the Trustees to provide a suitable number of evening schools for the benefit of young men over 12 years of age who are, by the nature of their occupations, prevented from attending day schools.'" In 1856 Cincinnati became the first sizable city to open an evening high school, and in their annual report for 1857 school officials were able to report that "this school has succeeded much beyond our expectations, not only in the proficiency of the pupils in their studies, the attendance being much more regular than had prevailed in the most successful of the District Night Schools, but especially in the increased numbers attracted to these latter mentioned schools, and the evident zeal for improvement excited among the youth by the opening of a higher course of education."

Mann adds that the big cities were responsible for the growth. "From 1847 to 1869 the major cities of Massachusetts opened evening schools," he writes. "Cities in other states followed the example of Massachusetts and New York. Pittsburgh and San Francisco established evening schools in 1856, St. Louis in 1859, Chicago in 1862, and Philadelphia in 1869. By 1870 there were more than 100 evening schools in the United States. By 1900, 165 major cities of the United States had established evening schools whose major purpose was to meet the educational needs of adults."

State Recognition of the Need for Adult Education

The states generally lagged behind the cities in recognizing the need for adult education. Much of the early state legislation was only permissive in that it allowed cities to establish evening classes if they wished but generally offered no financial support.

Massachusetts, the first state known to give financial aid to evening schools, was also the first—in 1883—to require that evening classes be provided in every city of 10,000 or more population.

California, which provided permissive legislation in 1879, waited until 1893 before the legislature ordered that both special day and evening elementary classes "shall be open for the admission of all children over 16 years of age residing in the district and for the admission of adults."

College and University Support of Adult Education

In a number of states, college and university extension divisions took over the development of adult education when state departments of education failed to create programs. This occurred in Texas, in North

Carolina, in Virginia, and at the University of Wyoming. In Ohio, much of the leadership provided in some states by the state department of education was carried on by the Bureau of Adult Education at Ohio State University.

Enrollment and Curriculum Expansion

During the last quarter of the nineteenth century, enrollments in adult programs expanded, the age level rose (because state compulsory attendance laws were, by then, keeping more of the young students in school), and the subjects offered by evening schools increased.

But it didn't happen all at once. Knowles writes —

> The curriculum of the early evening schools was limited almost entirely to the basic subjects in the primary grades. There is little evidence that the curriculum broadened significantly until close to the turn of the century when four directions of change can be identified: (1) expansion of "Americanization" programs for immigrants, (2) expansion of vocational courses, especially in trade and commercial subjects, (3) extension into secondary and college level subjects with the opening of evening high schools, and (4) experimental sorties into informal adult education.

COMMUNITY AND JUNIOR COLLEGE GROWTH

In recent years the rapid growth of community junior colleges has offered one of the most dramatic new opportunities for the extension and expansion of adult education programs.

The first publicly supported junior college was established in 1901. By 1930 there were 400. By 1952 the number had increased to 597. Since then more than 200 additional junior colleges have opened. If the present rate of expansion continues, it is estimated that in 1970 there will be more than 1,000 junior colleges serving more than 2 million students.

The adult education activities of the community college — frequently called the "community services" program — included all of the educational, cultural, and recreational programs offered in addition to the other general grouping of offerings: two years of college work that can usually be transferred for credit to senior colleges and special occupational programs that prepare students for a semiprofessional or technical career. Approximately one-third of all community college students are adults.

Factors of interdependencies between the adult education programs of community colleges and schools operating under the K-12 administrative structure vary widely. In some states few guidelines differentiating the program ideas of the two have been developed, and similarity of function has emerged. In other states, guidelines have been developed which tend to differentiate their functions. Generally speaking, such guidelines, rather than rigidly demarcating specific instructional roles, tend to take into account the availability of facilities, past histories, and other factors, which together will account for the widest possible program of service to the community offered in a manner that makes maximum use of existing facilities and trained personnel. As will be discussed more fully later in this chapter, in at least two states the responsibility for elementary and secondary education for adults has been transferred to the publicly supported junior colleges.

In addition to the development of the comprehensive community college, there is a trend toward building technical institutes which have as their sole purpose the training of persons at the subprofessional level. New York, Ohio, Michigan, and the District of Columbia illustrate this new development.

ENROLLMENT STATISTICS AND CHARACTERISTICS OF ADULT EDUCATION

Enrollment statistics for the early years of adult education are hard to come by. However, estimates of the number of adults in public school programs ranged up to 1 million in 1924 and up to 1.5 million in 1934. *Volunteers for Learning: A Study of the Educational Pursuits of American Adults,* published in 1965, projected a figure of merely 2 million adults enrolled in programs offered by "elementary and secondary schools." Data for this part of the study were collected in 1962 and, therefore, do not reflect recent rapid growth of adult education or community service programs in community colleges or the rise in enrollments in adult basic education (functional, job-oriented, literacy education) that resulted from the passage of the adult education provisions of the Economic Opportunity Act in 1964. According to the U.S. Office of Education, more than 400,000 individuals were enrolled in federally supported adult basic education classes in 1966-67. It is probably safe to estimate that in 1968 at least 6 million individuals were enrolled in adult education programs offered by elementary-secondary schools and community colleges.

More to the point, however, are the changes in constituency that are reflected in the enrollment figures. In *Volunteers For Learning* the typical adult education student is described as follows: "He is just as often a she; is typically under 40; has completed high school or better; enjoys an above-average income; works full-time and most often in a 'white collar' occupation; is typically white and Protestant; is married and is a parent; lives in an urbanized area, and more likely in suburbs than a large city; and is found in all parts of the country." Today, however, the rapidly changing emphasis of many publicly supported adult education programs reflects on the part of the public schools a much greater enrollment of the seriously undereducated adult residing in the center of the nation's cities, and in community colleges a substantial number of adults are seeking advanced vocational or technical retraining as a means of upgrading their service in their present job or of preparing for new jobs.

TRENDS IN FISCAL SUPPORT

State Aid

While local school districts have always provided the bulk of the adult education funds, the states have gradually increased their appropriations. In his chapter "Financing Adult Education" in the second edition of NAPSAE's *Public School Adult Education*, Homer Kempfer indicates that—

> State aid is distributed to local districts on a reimbursement basis according to three general plans. Several states use average daily attendance (ADA) as the base. Some states allocate funds on an instructional hour basis. A few states allocate money on the basis of local expenditures.
> The three plans exert somewhat different influence on local programs. The ADA basis of distribution normally encourages large classes and high attendance. State education department regulations in California and elsewhere prohibit counting attendance at certain large group meetings. The instructional hour basis of distribution usually requires maintenance of a minimum ADA. It encourages the operation of many classes of reasonable size. Neither this nor the ADA method aid the nonclass type of activity such as tutoring, correspondence instruction, educational radio programs, activities involving the broader community, and program consultation service.

In Dr. Holden's study for the Council of Chief State School Officers, he reports that—

> At present some of the states providing the greatest amount of financial support are New York, California, and Florida. California, Michigan, and Rhode Island are three states having funds for adult education included in the foundation program, and not as a separate appropriation. The Ohio Legislature, in August 1967, included $115,000 for adult education in its school appropriation bill as a part of school moneys.

Dr. Holden also reports that New Jersey has a unique formula for state aid in which it awards a local district three-fourths of the salary of a director. It gives no money for teachers' salaries, but instead provides money for administrative leadership. Connecticut has a general adult education program with a three-stage scale of support providing for free education for adults through high school and for older persons and the handicapped.

However, of the 50 states, the District of Columbia, and Puerto Rico, 25 do not provide any state funds for general adult education (as distinguished from adult vocational education) aside from adult basic education programs. All but three of the states which provide funds restrict their use in some way, if only by requiring they be used for classes which are primarily educational, not recreational. On the other hand, the necessity of providing matching funds for participation in federal funds for adult basic education has stimulated nearly every state which was lagging in financial support for adult education to contribute at least a minimum amount of funds and to begin to build a state supervisory staff. There already is evidence that this action will gradually result in permanent provision for adult education in these states.

Federal Support

As will be pointed out more fully in Chapter 6, "The Impact of Legislation on Adult Education," the federal government has been involved in adult programs for half a century. It is only within the last several years, however, that the federal infusion of funds for general education has become such a tide that it has washed out state money as the second most important source of funds. Local money is still of prime importance but, according to Dr. Holden, federal appropriations now rank second with state spending in third place.

Strenuous efforts are now being made by the National Association for Public School Adult Education and others to extend federal support to high school equivalency and high school diploma programs for adults. There is considerable evidence to indicate that, in time, the Congress will round out the now lacking balance in many programs by offering financial encouragement in the program areas of consumer, health, civic, and family life education; in the arts and sciences; and in other of the commonly accepted subject areas of the secondary school curriculum.

State Fiscal Trends

At the state level, two fiscal trends are apparent. One is the recent action of several state legislatures—notably those of Michigan and

Ohio — in modifying the legislation relating to secondary education in such a way that state funds become available to reimburse local districts for educational programs for all students enrolled in secondary education programs irrespective of the age of the student. This has had the effect of removing tuition barriers while at the same time greatly accelerating enrollments.

A second legislative trend — heavily influenced by fiscal considerations — is evidenced in Washington and North Carolina where all educational programs for adults, including those at the elementary and secondary levels, are mandated to the jurisdiction of the community colleges. This trend developed, in part, as a result of the interaction of soaring costs for elementary secondary education for boys and girls and the creation of new taxing authorities for the community college. This trend reflects the understandable wishes of many boards of education and school administrations to retain their available tax resources for the education of children; and the equally understandable desire of new community college districts to offer as wide and as comprehensive a program as possible out of the new tax bases becoming available to them.

On the other hand, a number of legislatures resist this change on the basis that the general level of the community college work should be postsecondary and that the K-12 school system should continue to offer programs at this level, whatever the age of the student.

Student Fees

Overall, the influence of state and federal aid on adult education cannot be overemphasized. Over and over it has been demonstrated that such aid is essential to the encouragement of the growth of public adult education. Increasing state and federal support in public education has been a key factor in reducing the vicious influence of the fee system on adult education. As stated by the author of this chapter in the second edition of *Public School Adult Education* —

> The hard core of adult education activities cannot be supported out of fees. The mayor is not going to pay a fee for consultation on enriching the educational potential of a community conference on housing. Individuals are going to look at a televised course in learning to read the English language whether they pay for it or not. It would be absurd to think of attaching a price tag to neighborhood conferences on education. By imposing a fee on adult students wishing to complete elementary or secondary education — or a wage earner seeking to upgrade his vocational skills — the very ones most in need may be denied an opportunity.

THE DEVELOPMENT OF PROFESSIONAL LEADERSHIP

In the all important area of professional leadership, the same slow but steady assumption of responsibility at the state and national levels can also be observed.

When local school districts initially undertook to begin adult education programs, it was to meet a specific educational need existing within the community — the demand of out-of-school youths for the continuation of their education. Except in rare instances, however, little attention was paid to the fact that the psychological and learning needs of these young adults differed from those of children. The only difference between regular school and adult school was that the latter was held during the evening hours. The term *standard evening high school* came into being as a means of underscoring that the program for out-of-school youth was no different than the one for children.

Experience soon demonstrated, however, that different administrative procedures and different instructional patterns were needed. Gradually a few specialists in the education of adults began to emerge at the local level. One of the greatest of these was Emily Griffith, who in 1915 began working out the specialized programs which resulted in the founding of the Emily Griffith Opportunity School in Denver, Colorado — the first full-time, round-the-clock, tuition-free school for adults.

Evolving Leadership at the State Level

It was well into the second decade of the new century before the states began to provide the much needed professional leadership that would both encourage local districts to begin programs for adults and to exchange useful experiences with each other. In 1917 Connecticut created within its state department of education a division with a full-time supervisor devoted entirely to evening and continuation schools. Two years later, the state created a division of Americanization. Both divisions were later consolidated into one.

In 1918 the State of New York named a special supervisor for immigrant education as did Delaware in 1919. California initiated the first separate state office of adult education in 1920.

In 1956 the Fund for Adult Education, an independent agency created by the Ford Foundation, provided a series of grants to NAPSAE, which enabled it to undertake programs of considerable magnitude designed to extend and strengthen full-time leadership for adult education programs offered under public auspices. Among the most significant results was the establishment of professional training programs for state and local directors of adult education and demonstration programs on the effectiveness of full-time adult education personnel on the staffs of local school districts and state departments of education. In 1958 five of the 17 states having a full-time consultant on the staff of the chief state school officer were employed as a result of the FAE-NAPSAE grants.

One of the many new strengths that the Adult Basic Education Title of the Economic Opportunity Act brought to publicly supported adult education was its provision that professional leadership be installed within the state education department in every state administering the program. Today, therefore, all states but one have an adult education person on the staff of the chief school officer. Although a number of these are restricted to providing professional leadership in adult basic education, it is proving to provide a foundation from which a more comprehensive program of state leadership can emerge.

U. S. Office of Education Reorganization

Unrelated but equally effective action at the federal level was the reorganization of the U.S. Office of Education in July of 1965, which established an associate commissioner for a newly created Bureau of Adult and Vocational Education (later renamed Bureau of Adult, Vocational, and Library Programs). One of the "divisions" within the new bureau was a Division of Adult Education Programs with subordinate positions established for the administration of specifically authorized federal programs in the areas of civil defense, adult basic education, and adult education at the university extension level. This reorganization at the federal level, placing the administration of adult education at the associate commissioner level, has been reflected in a general upgrading of the administrators of state and local programs, until many of them now also report directly to the chief administrator of the state or local school authority.

Need for Local Leadership

As noted earlier, one of the significant advances was made in New Jersey in 1964 when a state aid bill for adult education was passed authorizing the state to subsidize local districts for two-thirds of the salary of full-time directors. In other words, rather than reimbursing the districts on the basis of the number of students enrolled, it reimbursed on the effort made by the local community to establish full-time local leadership.

One of the most important impacts of the adult basic education program has been its effect on teacher training. Passage by Congress of the

Adult Education Title of the Economic Opportunity Act immediately created a pressing need for trained personnel. During the first year of the Act's operation, federal funds were not available for this purpose. Therefore, during the summer of 1965, "trainer of trainers" institutes were held at the Universities of Washington, New Mexico, and Maryland through the aid of a grant from the Ford Foundation.

Since 1966, federal funds have been advanced for teacher training in adult basic education. Following the three Ford Foundation financed institutes in 1965, nine "trainer of trainers" institutes were held — one in each of the HEW-USOE administrative regions — in 1966. In 1967 the number of institutes was increased to 19, with half being primarily concerned with the training of teachers and half with meeting the training needs of the administrators of these programs. In 1968, 27 institutes were scheduled to be held — two-thirds of them following the 1967 pattern and the remainder devoted, by and large, primarily to the training needs of special or regional groups.

The Adult Education Act of 1966 also provided funds for experimental and innovative projects. The first series of grants was made under this provision in 1967. Since the projects were largely long-range in their scope and implications, it is impossible to make an assessment of them at this time.

Influence of Regional Accrediting Associations

An important force for setting and maintaining standards in elementary and secondary education has been the regional accrediting associations whose force is now beginning to be felt in adult education. In 1968 the North Central Association adopted separate criteria for the evaluation of high school programs for adults. As these criteria become operational, they will have the effect of stimulating increased flexibility in the construction of curriculums for students over the compulsory school age wishing to secure a high school diploma.

A survey made by the Division of Vocational and Adult Education of the Richmond, Virginia, Public Schools in 1962 indicated extreme variations in policies and procedures among the various states as to the nature, extent, and conditions surrounding the granting of a diploma to adults who wish to complete their high school work. Increasingly, all state and local school systems will be forced to make provision for specialized diploma programs for high school dropouts who return to school and seek a high school diploma. (The use of the General Educational Development test as a basis of awarding high school equivalency certificates is widespread. According to the Richmond survey, all of the 50 states except Ohio, Delaware, Massachusetts, and

Wisconsin use this test as a basic instrument for measuring educational achievement in terms of high school equivalency.)

PROFESSIONAL ASSOCIATIONS

While governments were playing their part in the development of adult education, so were adult educators themselves. In 1921 the National Education Association added the Department of Immigrant Education to the roster of professional groups under its umbrella. Three years later the name of the new department was changed to the Department of Adult Education, reflecting its broader aim and broader membership—"All those educators who instruct adults, from beginning English classes to evening high school and general evening classes in special subjects, all under public auspices." In 1926 the American Association for Adult Education was formed as an umbrella organization for teachers, administrators, librarians, college professors, and all others interested in adult education. In 1951 the two organizations—the NEA's Department of Adult Education and the American Association for Adult Education—merged as the Adult Education Association of the U.S.A.

In the essay on the National Association for Public School Adult Education prepared by the author of this chapter for the forthcoming *Encyclopedia of Education*, the further development of the Adult Education Association is described as follows:

> An important constitutional provision of the new organization provided for the organization of sub-organizations composed of members of occupational interest or geographical groups . . . It was under this authorization that the National Association for Public School Adult Education was founded in East Lansing, Michigan, in 1952, as an affiliate of the Adult Education Association of the U.S.A. As one means of assuring the development of specialized services for a single occupational group, membership was restricted to adult education workers in public schools.
>
> With the dissolution in 1951 in the Department of Adult Education of the NEA, any official affiliation of a voluntary association within the structure of the National Education Association also ceased to exist. In 1953, therefore, the membership of NAPSAE voted to again seek affiliation with the NEA. This was granted by the NEA Representative Assembly in 1956, after the three-year waiting period prescribed by NEA By-Laws.
>
> The regranting of departmental status of NAPSAE as a semi-autonomous organizational affiliate within the NEA structure was, in large measure, an organizational formality and did not, in any way, affect the full and complete support that not only NAPSAE had enjoyed from NEA since its inception, but also its predecessor organization.

As an organizational affiliate of NEA since 1921, both the Department of Immigrant Education and the Department of Adult Education had had a place on NEA convention programs, access to consultation from NEA staff members, and opportunities to have information about its activities carried in NEA's communication to its members.

Neither of these early groups, however, had a member of the professional staff of the NEA assigned to work with it until 1945, when the Division of Adult Education Service was established by the NEA and Leland P. Bradford appointed as director. One of Dr. Bradford's duties was to serve as executive secretary of the Department of Adult Education. With the foundation of NAPSAE, the Division's assistant director, Robert A. Luke, was asked by NEA to serve as the executive secretary of NAPSAE.

In 1952, Dr. Bradford was asked to head a newly created unit of the NEA, the National Training Laboratory. Mr. Luke was named director of the Adult Education Division and asked to continue staff services to NAPSAE.

In 1963, in recognition of the continuing interdependent program relationships that had developed between AEA and NAPSAE, and in equal recognition of the different organizational goals and structure that had also developed, the AEA Delegate Assembly voted to discontinue the NAPSAE-AEA organizational affiliation.

Although, as has been previously noted, several states mandated much of the adult education programs to the community colleges, the American Association of Junior Colleges did not have an organizational unit directly concerned with providing technical assistance in the area of community services until 1968. At that time, through a grant made to the Association by the W. K. Kellogg Foundation, the Association began a three-year program to assist two-year colleges to develop community service programs. The new activity had been preceded by a six-month study of community service programs in community colleges supported by the Alfred P. Sloane Foundation.

SUMMARY

Adult education today is a natural outgrowth from what adult education was yesterday. It is a confusing mixture of both raw and well worn programs, of separate and overlapping programs, of programs that work together and programs that work at cross-purposes. It is a mixture of adults who are scarcely students and of students who are scarcely adults. It is a mixture of education for jobs that are disappearing and for jobs yet to appear. All this may appear to be a swirling maelstrom through which the adult educator can pick his way only with difficulty. Certain strengths, however, are emerging from this mixture.

First, adult educators now talk less about operating on a "fourth level" of education that is unrelated to elementary, secondary, and higher education and, instead, strive to closely coordinate their educational efforts with those of their colleagues on other levels of education. Increasingly, the goal is to build programs which provide useful educational experiences for a continuation onward from whatever level at which the adult may have discontinued formal schooling.

Second, there is a steadily increasing awareness on the part of both school authorities and the general public that a closer relationship must exist between the school dropout and his opportunities for a second chance education. What was once an "it's too bad it has to happen" attitude on the part of schoolmen and community leaders toward the dropout has, over the years, changed first to a serious endeavor to improve the holding power of the school and then broadened to include cooperative programing on the part of secondary school officials and of adult education in behalf of both the potential and actual dropout.

Translated into curriculum terms this means that our present concept of literacy is being revised; it is generally understood within the education profession and among members of the general public as a capability of an individual to become a responsible member of the community, a productive worker, and a successful participant in family life experiences. In most cases, this modern literacy level is understood to be at least a high school education or its equivalent.

CHAPTER 2

CONTINUING EDUCATION
IN COMMUNITY SCHOOLS

Peter L. Clancy

HISTORICAL ROLE OF ADULT EDUCATION
IN THE PUBLIC SCHOOLS

When the public school system of any American community could serve the needs of that community by operating essentially as an academy for its young, there were few people indeed who ever thought about the system's capacity to serve the needs of adults. Public schools in pre-Sputnik America stood as little citadels of learning within their communities to offer the basic educational skills to all and, to those bright enough and motivated enough to make the grade, preparation for college. Each public school building, in spite its being located for the convenience of the most people, nevertheless existed as something of an island fortress in its neighborhood. A drawbridge for children descended for the regular school day and was promptly hauled up at the close of the day. Now and then it was lowered for special occasions, but essentially the school was a fortress of formal learning for children. The principal was the King of the Castle and the custodian was the Lord High Chamberlain who really owned and ran the castle.

Education began with kindergarten or first grade and, for some, was thought to end logically when the student had learned to "read, write, and cipher to the rule of three," or had outgrown the seats. For others it was thought to end with a high school diploma, or whatever amount of education beyond the eighth grade represented enough preparation for a particular vocation. For a select few—a very select few—it was finally completed with a college diploma. But to nearly all, education was an *ending* thing; it had a *beginning* and a definite *ending*.

Peter L. Clancy is associate superintendent for the Mott Program of the Flint Board of Education, Flint, Michigan.

Thus, the role of the public school was clearly defined. In America, it had the glorious mission of providing every mother's child the opportunity to become literate. For those who had the ambition and the ability to meet its standards, it was willing to allow them to pick further from its potpourri of learning. The public school took custodial responsibility at least (provided behavior rules were adhered to) up to the age of compulsory attendance. It offered further services up to the completion of the twelfth grade – usually not much beyond the age of 18. No one considered its purview to be more than this. Surely the public school had no obligation to adults. They had already had their chance for education when they were young. The adult who thought he needed or wanted to learn something new or something more thought about college or correspondence school or trade school or business college or – most often – he just didn't think about it.

Little wonder then that when the federal government was willing to subsidize adult training programs during the depression of the thirties and again when adult education programs were demanded by skill-hungry industry during the war, the public schools were timid about the adult training responsibilities thus forced on them. Few indeed were the school administrators and especially few were the boards of education who saw in adult education anything other than a necessary evil. It was a worthwhile community service, but it was nevertheless a nuisance. "As long as it doesn't interfere with the regular program and as long as it doesn't cost anything" would be fairly typical of a school system's response to a request for adult instructional services. That attitude still existed as recently as 1964 when the NEA Research Division conducted its study entitled *Opinions of School Superintendents on Adult Education*. In this study 63.7 percent of all superintendents reported financing by tuition alone for programs in recreational skills, while 53.7 percent checked tuition alone as the source of funding for cultural programs.[1]

When adult education programs in increasing numbers began to be a sine qua non for one reason or another, superintendents began to look around for someone in the school system to do the necessary coordination. Since the offerings were often vocationally oriented, they quite naturally turned to the vocational education teacher or coordinator; and because he was oriented this way, the development of adult education programs within school systems tended to be along the lines of technical and vocational education. But, it was almost always an additional assignment, and under no conditions could it cost more. The predisposition toward vocational and technical adult education still flourished in 1964. In the same superintendents' opinion study previously mentioned, 33 percent of all superintendents reporting adult education programs in their school systems indicated that their programs were essentially vocational in nature. An additional 20.3 percent reported that their offerings were "academic, vocational, avocational, and recreational" in nature, while 14.8 percent reported that theirs were "academic, vocational, and avocational." [2]

Thus in the immediate postwar years adult education made its way into public school systems through the backdoor. Postwar school building demands continued to mandate the self-sufficiency of adult education offerings. More vocationally oriented programs were federally subsidized, and a few states began to offer supplemental financial assistance to school systems for certain quite narrowly prescribed adult offerings, but rare indeed was the school board or the school administrator who saw any value in educating the parents of the children in order to make the job of educating the children themselves easier. And rare was the school board or chief administrator who recognized at all the tremendous public relations value of offering adults rewarding and pleasant learning experiences.

Not all boards of education relegate adult education to a self-sustaining activity or a vocationally oriented program. For example, the adult education department of the Flint, Michigan, Board of Education operates under a philosophy charging that department with the responsibility "to provide educational opportunities for the adults of the community, so that each may obtain for himself the degree of education, training, and experience in which he is interested, and from which he is willing and able to profit."

At the present time the National Community School Education Association (NCSEA) is surveying its membership and is collecting samples of adult education policies from community-oriented school districts. Readers of this chapter may want to contact the NCSEA to obtain samples of community-oriented adult education policies. The address is 923 East Kearsley Street, Flint, Michigan 48503.

THE CHANGING AMERICAN COMMUNITY

The successful launching by the Soviet Union in 1957 of Sputnik did not cause the explosion of awareness of educational deficiencies in this country that followed that spectacular international coup. The launching of Sputnik I was merely the trigger. The explosion was destined to occur: The foment was there, and the explosion was inevitable. Radical changes in the way of American living had been occurring for some time, though much of the American public education establishment hardly knew what was happening.

From 1900 to 1950 America changed from an essentially rural society to a predominantly urban society. The intensification of industrialization, spurred by World War II production efforts, rapidly eliminated the demand for unskilled labor. The GI Bill made it possible for returning veterans to pursue higher education, and hundreds of thousands of young men who otherwise never would have considered it were going to college. The world was changing fast. In 1940 at least 30 percent of the jobs available to Americans demanded no particular skill. Norman C. Harris of the University of Michigan predicts that by 1970 only 6 percent of all occupations in the United States will be available to persons with less than a high school diploma.[3] There was a time when the dropout was employable on factory assembly lines, on farms, or in some form of manual labor. It was no disgrace to drop out of school after the eighth grade in depression days, but today a dropout is a tragedy.

Development of Ghettoes

The transition from a rural to an urban society has not been a simple change from rural to urban living. The transition has seen the development of ghettos, where persons are segregated not only by national origin but also along racial and religious lines, not only in the urban areas but in rural areas where the economic base of the area has changed because of technology's modifying requirements for either labor or product. These changes have not come about without strife. The recently issued report of the President's Commission on Civil Disorders discusses some of these changes and makes recommendations for alleviating the devastating results of these changes. These recommendations make the strongest possible case for further development of adult education, all forms of postsecondary education, and the nationwide establishment of community education in every American public school.[4]

Knowledge Explosion and Skill Obsolescence

Then there is the explosion of knowledge. Individuals who expect to stay in the mainstream of life know that learning can never end at any given time. Most observers agree that mankind's store of knowledge is now doubling every 10 years and has done so since 1900. It has been estimated that 90 percent of all the scientists who have ever lived are alive today. More knowledge has been discovered during the lifetime of the present adult population than existed at the time of its birth. Every minute another 2,000 pages of books, newspapers, and reports are published in the world. The continuing accumulation of knowledge at such a breathtaking pace makes it necessary to educate people today in what nobody knew yesterday and to prepare them for what no one knows yet but some people must know tomorrow. It is said that a Ph.D. in mathematics has six years of educational capital. If he then does not continue to learn he will start to decline. A Ph.D. in physics has seven years of educational capital; and a Ph.D. in engineering, nine years. So rapidly are new production techniques being developed in industry and commerce that William Haber of the University of Michigan estimates that 50 percent of all of the occupations that will exist within the economy 10 years from today are not now known.

RESULTANT OBLIGATIONS OF THE PUBLIC SCHOOLS

What role should the public school play in this scheme of things? Let us seek the answer to that question by asking and answering two questions: (a) Granted the explosion of knowledge and an accelerated obsolescence-of-learning rate, granted the intensification of industrialization and concomitant demands for relearning and retraining, what obligation for solutions accrues to public school systems? (b) Granted the change in the American mode of living from an essentially family-centered rural life to a complex, urbanized, impersonal life, what role can and should the public school play in the alleviation of human problems thus created and how can adult continuing education serve in such missions? An attempt to answer these two questions shall be the purpose of the remainder of this chapter. The following proposition directs itself to the first question.

THE SCHOOL AS A COMMUNITY EDUCATION CENTER

PUBLIC SCHOOL SYSTEMS MUST PLAY A LEADING ROLE IN PROVIDING LEARNING OPPORTUNITIES FOR ADULTS AT EVERY LEVEL POSSIBLE BECAUSE THEY ARE BEST EQUIPPED AND BEST PREPARED TO DO SO AND BECAUSE DOING SO PROVIDES EXTRA DIVIDENDS TO THE SCHOOL SYSTEM—DIVIDENDS FAR BEYOND THE REQUIRED INVESTMENT OF TIME, EFFORT, AND MONEY.

In practically every city, town, and village in the United States the largest single investment of tax funds in physical facilities is the total public school plant. Fly over any American city at a relatively low altitude sometime and look for large spaces, especially within newer housing developments. Look for the newer buildings. You will see that American communities have done well in providing public school buildings. You will note, also, that these buildings are usually located within walking distance of the residents of the neighborhoods they serve. Drive through any city, and you will generally find that the school building is one of the finer, newer facilities in the neighborhood — especially in newer housing developments and often in core-city neighborhoods. There are those who call it criminal to use such public facilities only seven hours a day, five days a week, 39 weeks a year for formal education for youngsters alone. Surely no industrialist, surely no corporation board of directors would economically permit the operation of a major plant for only six or seven hours a day, five days a week, 39 weeks a year. The average public school in the United States with a formal daytime program only operates some 1,400 hours per year. A school system operating regular hours daily, plus evening hours, six days a week instead of five, and 50 weeks instead of 39, would operate at least 3,800 hours per year — getting more than twice as much use of its plant.

Implications of Extra School Use

Now this line of thinking does not ignore the argument that the extra operation of a plant incurs extra cost. However, the fact is that in many school systems such costs are much, much lower than one would be led to believe. In Northern areas, there may be actually no extra cost at all involved in heating a school for additional hours of use. Many schools have found that little is accomplished by lowering the thermostat in the evening. Fuel subsequently consumed by the heating system to bring temperatures back up to normal in the morning is nearly equal to the amount of fuel saved during the night. The problem of the extra custodial service required can be solved by rescheduling the custodians' working hours. Rooms used by adult groups are simply cleaned at a later hour.

Lighting of school facilities for evening use surely involves some extra cost to a school system, but this may be minimal. It is common practice in many schools to keep all of the lights turned on until the custodial staff has completed its rounds. No electricity is saved by turning a light off if the light is to be turned on again within an hour.

Simple wear and tear on a school building could be thought of as an extra expense involved in extra use. Does a building wear out faster because of extra use? A moot question, surely. One seldom, if ever, sees a school building replaced because it is worn out—obsolete, perhaps—but not worn out.

Resources of the Schools

Not only do schools represent the greatest single physical asset held in common by the tax-paying public; but they are, by design, best suited to serve as educational centers. Because they are usually within walking distance of everyone in the neighborhood, they serve as natural neighborhood community centers. They house the equipment and paraphernalia necessary for the educational enterprise—classrooms, chairs, desks, blackboards, libraries, audiovisual equipment, cafeteria facilities, shop equipment, auditoriums, gymnasiums, arts and crafts rooms—facilities expensive to duplicate elsewhere.

If a community were to delegate to some omnipotent official the authority to allocate all community resources on a purely objective basis, he would surely consider the physical facilities of the school system ideally and perfectly suited to offer adult continuing education opportunities to the community because this would be making the most efficient use of tax funds.

Besides offering the best and the most suitable facilities for adult continuing education purposes, public school systems have or have access to the best teaching personnel for the purpose. Many regular teachers are happy to teach their subjects to eager adults, not to mention the incentive of extra remuneration. A public school system is accustomed to hiring professional teachers and has available to it personnel and accounting services necessary for the recruitment, hiring, and training of other personnel with specialized skills who may not be a part of the regular teaching staff.

Need for Local Adult Support

Aside from obligations dictated by suitability, efficiency, ability, and other factors previously mentioned, great benefits can accrue to the school system willing to offer extended services to adults. At this writing at least, public education in America still remains largely a matter of local control and depends on local financial support for the difference between mediocrity and excellence. The community that must depend on local public support to offer a quality public education system relies on what is in reality a minority group if it offers only the conventional K-12 program. About 50 percent of the adults in any community do not have children attending the public schools. These voters and taxpayers may not be parents, their children may have completed their public schooling, or their children may attend private schools. In effect, half of any given community has no immediate, tangible, nonaltruistic reason to support the public school system. If a school board or superintendent will realistically reduce that 50 percent to the really interested parents of enrolled youngsters, the remaining interested, potential supporters of the school system will represent a frightening minority of the voting, tax-paying public. On the other hand, the wise school system will extend the use of its facilities to services beyond the regular school day, hence serving clientele that otherwise might not have any reason to be interested in the welfare of the schools. Such a school system stands to win support and friends from an increasingly larger segment of the community.

An adult education program broadens community support for the total public education program because the beneficiaries of that program are likely to become active supporters of the school system. Likewise, a health program centered in the schools increases the potential for support of the entire school system by the beneficiaries of the health program. It is reasonable to say that to the extent a school is used by adults other than those who have youngsters attending that school, to that extent does that school enjoy the possibility of broadened community support.

An elementary principal once said that he thought the best public relations a school system could have would be to send home a well adjusted, well educated child. Surely no one can argue with this. But if one pauses to consider what it takes for the school system to send home a well adjusted, well educated child, then one has to begin calculating the cost of buildings, of facilities, of support personnel, and especially of qualified teachers—all involving financial support. And whenever one talks financial support, one must talk pluralities at local polling places for necessary funds. It is always necessary for the school system to make friends. Few ways are more readily available and more natural than for it to use its natural assets for adult education programs.

The Flint Community School Model

A case in point is that of the school system with which the author is most familiar—that in Flint, Michigan. Flint is a fairly typical Midwestern industrial community with a population of 200,000 and a public school enrollment of approximately 46,000.

From 1950 to 1968 enrollment in adult education classes grew from 30,000 annually to 80,000. In 1968 it was estimated that in an average week some 92,000 adults and youth used school facilities during non-school hours and on Saturdays. To be very specific, during the 1966-67 school year 54,588 adults participated in adult education classes while

31,377 youth were active in adult education and enrichment classes conducted by the adult education department. Using the 1960 census as a base, 27.7 percent of the adults in Flint were enrolled in adult education classes. Space limitations prevent a listing of the programs offered under the auspices of the adult education department, but 3,812 classes were offered to the populace. To give school districts operating K-12 systems an idea of the costs involved in operating an adult education program of this magnitude, it must be mentioned that 27.7 percent of the adults of Flint had an opportunity for enrichment during a year when the K-12 student enrollment was 46,322 out of a total population of 196,940. The operating budget for that adult program amounted to 3.35 percent of the K-12 budget. That same 3.35 percent of the operating budget included the costs involved for the 31,377 youth who took advantage of adult education offerings along with 64,267 people who took part in nonclass offerings of the department. And that 3.35 percent is not reduced by the nominal tuition payments which are charged by the adult education program. If tuition charges were subtracted from the gross request for funds, that percentage of the K-12 operating budget would be even less than 3.35 percent.

During this 18-year period the voters of Flint were asked on seven different occasions to increase local taxes for the support of schools. Every one of those requests was approved by an overwhelming majority. Local authorities credit the community school program, the heart of which is the adult education program, for such broad community support. A survey conducted under the auspices of Eastern Michigan University during this period revealed that 97 percent of all of the adults in Flint had attended or had had a member of their immediate family attend an adult education offering during the three-year period prior to the time of the survey. It is significant that members of several senior citizens clubs centered at neighborhood elementary schools have been among the most active campaigners in favor of local tax increases.

Further School-Community Coordination

Too often the story of a public school system's alienation from its public is the story of a school system too conservative, too timid, or too shortsighted to recognize how it may take on programing that involves very little in the way of extra expense and effort, yet yields great returns in credit and prestige. And adult education within a public school system's facilities constitutes a powerful selling and public relations device for its basic education program. Consider recreation programs that could be offered conveniently by school systems but are assumed by other agencies because school systems are unwilling to attempt them. Consider health programs — often with heavy educational overtones — which similarly are forced to operate outside the school system. Consider youth development programs — such as those conducted by Y groups, Boys' Clubs, and the like — independent agencies created to serve a need that well could be served by a school system. A school system could prove its overall worth and efficiency to its supporting public many times over if it were designed to accept programs of other agencies and to allow their operation through its facilities, extending proper credit to the other agencies and yet accruing credit itself. *A school system can no longer be a series of island fortresses isolated from the mainstream of the community and still hope to enjoy the community interest and support — it must be a series of convenient neighborhood centers for broad education and social service in order to enjoy and profit from the community support such a role engenders.*

THE SCHOOL AS A CONTINUING EDUCATION CENTER

The second major question with which this chapter deals has to do with the propriety of a school system's concerning itself with the education of adults. We have asked ourselves the question, Granted the change in the mode of American living from an essentially family-centered rural one to an urbanized impersonal one with all of its complexities, what role can and should the school play in the alleviation of the human problems thus created and how can continuing adult education serve in such missions? In answer to this question we offer the following proposition:

THE SCHOOL SYSTEM THAT WOULD EDUCATE ALL THE CHILDREN OF ALL THE PEOPLE MUST EDUCATE ALL THE PEOPLE OF ALL THE CHILDREN.

These words of Ernest O. Melby, former dean of the College of Education at New York University and Distinguished Visiting Professor at Michigan State University, are more than a catchy phrase. Practically every sociological study of the last decade or so, from Riesman's *Lonely Crowd* to the U. S. Office of Education's *Coleman Report*, makes it increasingly clear that in our technological urbanized society, the family unit — the basic unit of our society — is disintegrating. Less and less does it serve the purposes and play the roles that it once did. The youngster growing up in urban America is a product of the broad community — or lack of community, if you will — in which he lives. Surely the school cannot expect to be all of the things a family is to a child. Nor can the school overcome in the few hours allotted to it the tremendously powerful influences of peers, of the home, of parents, of the neighborhood, and of mass communications media that have so much to do with creating a youngster's values. If the objective of public education is to transmit the culture of society and the tools for critically examining that culture to the youngster, then clearly the public education institution should have a major role in transmitting the culture to all of the adults and young people of the community. The school must, in short, take the leadership in the creation of the "educative community."

THE EDUCATIVE COMMUNITY MODEL

This concept of the "educative community" was forcefully put forth by Howard Y. McClusky, professor of adult education at the University of Michigan, when he said—

Turning to the public sector, we see another resource for education. . . . Service is the term usually employed to describe governmental performance. To it should be added the idea of education. . . .

The mayor and councilmen are fashioners and interpreters of public policy. Civil servants are educators in their respective domains. For example, the fire department should be an educator in fire prevention, the health department, a school for the prevention of disease, and perhaps the most underrated potential of all is that of the apparatus of law enforcement (police, courts, etc.). In many ways the police officer should be the most carefully selected and highly trained educator in the community. This too could be spelled out in pages and volumes. . . .

And, most important, political campaigns could even more become campaigns for political education. . . . Candidates have been known to wage political campaigns for the purpose of educating the public and with little promise of victory.

An even better case can be made for the educative potential of the private sector. Even today many retail stores are literally museums of modern merchandising. Shopping tours could be as educational as trips to zoos and museums. Salesmen could be instructors in product design. Factories could be schools of the manufacturing process. Stores could be things of beauty while factory buildings could be units in an industrial park. Etc., etc. And what if realtors and mortgage bankers became educators in providing equal access to housing for all members of the community.

The same theme could be applied to the practitioners of occupations. Physicians, dentists, and nurses could become health educators. Also, lawyers, legal educators; the clergy, religious educators; bankers, business educators; architects, educators in design; social workers, social educators; waiters, restauranteurs; nutritionists; garbage collectors, sanitarians . . . etc. And they would all love it for nothing elevates the value of an occupation in the eyes of both the customer and the practitioner as the recognition of the educational role of its contribution. . . .[5]

It was one thing in past decades for the public school to accept a highly motivated youngster from an aspiring middle-class home and transmit to him from on high immutable stone tablets, fully expecting faithful recitation back. That was a reinforcement process. The school and the home reinforced one another. Such *was* and *is* a relatively easy task. It is quite another thing, however, for a basically middle-class institution to take into its little society five or six hours a day a youngster who comes from a culture that may be not only alien but antagonistic to the middle-class culture. How do you motivate a child who comes from a one-parent ghetto dwelling to learn to read when the subject matter is a visit in Daddy's car after church on a Sunday afternoon to Grandma's farm? There is no Daddy in his life, there is no car, church is in a storefront, Grandma lives with them at home, and what is a *farm*? Traditionally the school is an institution rewarding verbal skills and designed to reinforce and build on motivation toward learning supposedly inspired at home. What happens when the inspiration doesn't come from the home or from any other part of the youngster's out-of-school environment? Obviously the school must involve the entire community in the educative process.

Impossible task? The schools can't expect to be everything to everybody? — *If not the schools, who?* What other agency or institution is so perfectly equipped, located, and prepared for the task? If the public school and its sister institution — the local community college — can but recognize that they need the involvement of the community to accomplish their mission and if they will then open their hearts as well as their doors to the community, they will be the institutions that history will credit for preserving the American way of life. There are cities who had accepted the challenge of becoming "educative communities" even before the Civil Disorder Commission Report.[6] New Haven, Connecticut; Atlanta, Georgia; Dade County, Florida; and Chattanooga, Tennessee, are well along on developing the concept of the "educative community."

IMPLEMENTATION

American communities, it has been said, are not really communities at all. The word *community* has as its root the word *common* and implies a congregation of people who have something in common. The rural villages and cities of yesteryear were made up of people who had things in common, but many American city dwellers live isolated lives and are essentially independent of one another with respect to the kinds of things that gave people in yesterday's villages a common bond — national origin, similarity of employment, religious affiliation, political persuasion, etc. America's city dwellers don't even know one another. They live alone. They don't "belong." As Dr. McClusky has said, "There is too much *pluribus* and not enough *unum*." What is there or what can be done to bring to people a unity, a sense of commonality? At one time we looked to the churches; sadly, their potential for this purpose has greatly decreased. To many observers the only institution remaining with the potential for giving to people any sense of commonality is the public school. It is already a part of the neighborhood. It is commonly owned and operated by the public and offers a noncontroversial product that is highly valued. How does the school then realize its potential for becoming instrumental in developing, first of all, a feeling of community and, secondly, an instrument for the self-improvement of all members of the community?

Determining Adult Needs and Interests

One of the first things the successful adult education practitioner must recognize is that there is apt to be a tremendous difference between the wants and the needs of people. He must recognize that no one, not even the most sophisticated social psychologist or urban planner, can decide for people what it is they need. People themselves are seldom capable of recognizing their own needs. Successful work with adults must begin with wants. The child growth and development course, the lecture series, the great books discussion course may satisfy the originator's ambition to contribute something to the cultural uplifting of the community, but people often avoid such offerings. The first and critically important step is the establishment of communication with people in order to satisfy wants and—ultimately—needs. People must first be *in* your program, *in* your school before you can hope at all for them to engage in activity directed toward self-improvement. Many of the adult programs in Flint might be considered by some observers to be superfluous, but they are precisely the programs which will get people out for the first time. Offerings such as cake decorating, pedro playing, fly tying, duck calling, millinery, and so forth appeal to hobby interests or latent skills and don't pose any great threat to an adult's academic learning capacity.

Just off Robert T. Longway Boulevard in Flint is a thriving candle shop in a converted railway station. The proprietor of that shop first learned her craft as a hobby in an adult evening class. Her hobby was enjoyable, and she soon found herself making candles for friends, which led to the idea of a candle-making business – so off to adult ed classes to learn business methods. Now a thriving business is paying property taxes, is employing at least one person who is paying income taxes, the proprietor is paying income taxes on her new income, and the state is receiving sales taxes, which are returned to the city to help support adult education classes that are diploma-oriented. Yes, taxes were used to promote a hobby . . . but that little business is paying back far more in taxes than was invested in the hobby.

The Flint telephone directory lists six shops or stores involved with knitting. An informal survey of the proprietors indicated that all had learned their craft in adult education classes as had their employees. Those people got started in an effort to fulfill a want and went on to fill needs.

Every city accepting the challenge of becoming an educative community can verify similar stories utilizing very simple techniques. Community school directors who know their community – who know who opens a new shop or business – can provide meaningful information to verify the economic value of catering to the wants of people. Satisfaction of wants leads to the economic value of needs.

Taking people from gratification of wants to self-discovery, to self-improvement, and – ultimately – to community improvement of the quality of living is a subject properly dealt with elsewhere in this book. The remainder of this chapter shall be devoted to an examination of possible relationships of the adult education program to the other tasks of a school system.

Securing Public Support

Speaking practically, what do you say to the board of education member who asks, "Why should we be using valuable school space, facilities, lights, and taxpayers' funds in order to teach knitting?"

Aside, hopefully, from the practitioner's preparedness to defend the teaching of knitting on the basis of the preceding discussion, the practitioner would have been well advised long before this time to have organized his community's support in such a way that the important and essential power structure of the community has been in on the decision making.

The involvement of the formal and informal power structure of the community in decisions affecting the adult education enterprise of a public school system is often delightfully virgin territory for the adult practitioner who wishes to get support for his programs. Traditionally, public school people have been foolishly timid, carelessly aloof, or both in their relationships with the power structure of the community. Whether from fear, laziness, or whatever, most school administrators fail miserably to capitalize on the tremendous interest that industrial, business, and political leaders have in the public education process. In 15 years of asking important community leaders to advise and participate in the development of adult programs, the writer has never once been refused. Invariably, the person asked feels flattered and considers community education an enterprise important enough to be worthy of his time. Perhaps the meek shall inherit the earth, but they shall not run successful adult education programs unless they ask community leadership to share in the planning process.

The alert and effective community school director or community educator is constantly surveying his community, formally and informally, getting to know the members of his community. He knows the official power structure of the community; the elected officials; and the officers of the service clubs, churches, and social clubs, but he also knows — if he is to be effective — to whom the people of the neighborhood turn when they need help, advice, and counsel. They usually turn to their friends and neighbors, not to the official structure of the community. The effective community educator knows these informal counselors and advisers.

Administration of an Adult Continuing Education Program Within a Public School System

Thankfully, in many school systems today, adult education is no longer considered an appendage to the educational enterprise. In increasing numbers of school systems, the obligation of educating adults is seen as the duty of the entire school system. This, of course, is as it must be if the K-12 people and the adult people are to avoid stepping all over one another. Blessed indeed is the school system that decides its educational resources should be applied without exclusiveness yet with appropriate priority to all students, where adult education serves as enrichment for the day program and as a bridge between the school and community.

One conspicuous attempt to weld into one unit the leadership talent of a school system for such a purpose is represented in Figure I. This is the organization chart for adult continuing education in the Flint public school system. A *general superintendent of community education* is responsible to the board of education for the entire school system. An *associate superintendent, K-12 division,* is primarily responsible for the basic daytime program. The *associate superintendent, Mott*

FIGURE I.–
ORGANIZATION FOR ADULT CONTINUING EDUCATION
FLINT PUBLIC SCHOOLS
FLINT, MICHIGAN
1968

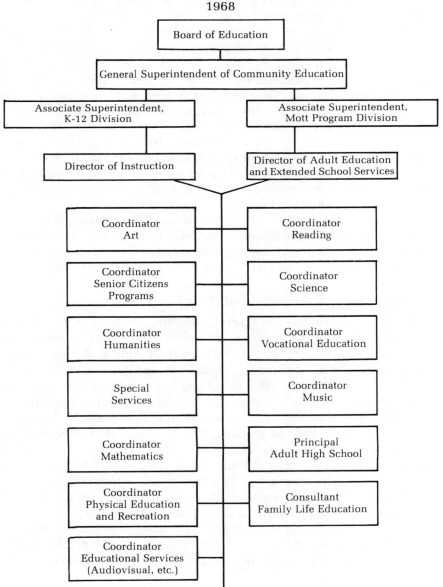

Program, is primarily responsible for the broad community services of this particular school system. The name *Mott* acknowledges the extensive support this particular program derives from the Charles Stewart Mott Foundation, a local foundation that has selected the Flint system for broad experimentation in community development. In a conventional system this position perhaps would be more appropriately entitled *associate superintendent, community services.*

Reporting directly to the *associate superintendent, K-12,* (but with definite responsibility to the Community Services Division for adult and enrichment programs) is the *director of instruction.* Reporting directly to the *associate superintendent, Mott Program,* (but with definite responsibility for coordination with K-12 programs) is the *director of adult education and extended school services.* The *director of instruction* and the *director of extended school services* then share the same staff. Each *coordinator* or *consultant* in a given field is responsible to both the *director of instruction* and to the *director of extended school services* — to the former in matters pertaining to K-12 curriculum and programing and to the latter in matters pertaining to adult and enrichment curriculum and planning.

While perhaps appearing to be two-headed, the system nevertheless works and assures coordinated, nonduplicatory, relatively frictionless operation. It certainly discourages the tendency to divide the school system's efforts and to attach undue value to one or the other part.

Administration in the Individual School

No one ever tried to use a school building for more than one adult education offering at a time without realizing early in the game that the effort needed a coordinator on duty in the building. Without such a person who directs students to the right room? Who helps the teacher set up a projector? Who takes the phone call and advises the class that the teacher will be 15 minutes late? Who has coffee and friendly conversation ready in the cafeteria during the class break? Who makes both the teacher and the students feel welcome? Who sees to it that things get locked up at the close of the night? Who sees to it that the place doesn't get torn apart? Such responsibilities may be inherited by one of the evening teachers or by a particularly interested and capable custodian or by an assistant principal or by someone hired on an hourly basis. However the problem is solved, solved it must be.

A method employed in Flint and increasing in popularity in many school districts throughout the country (a total of 165 districts at this writing) is the employment of a *community school activities director.*

A regular certified member of the school's daytime teaching staff, this person, in Flint at least, carries a one-half teaching load, begins his day at noon, and remains until the close of all school activities at nine or ten o'clock in the evening. Besides providing the important coordinative services mentioned above, this person is trained as a community development specialist. Operating in effect as an assistant principal for community involvement, the community director is charged with the responsibility for learning to know the resources and the problems of the school's community and for bringing the resources to bear on the problems in meaningful programs within the school setting. It is extremely advantageous that he be a regular member of the faculty. Programs then operating within the school under his purview are not those of outsiders, but "ours."

Much is expected of a community school activities director. Besides functioning as an adult continuing education coordinator, he is also expected to be a youth counselor, a public relations consultant, a community development specialist, a referral agent, a teacher, an administrator, a promoter, and a friend to all. Demanding as it is, it is nevertheless one of the most challenging subprofessions within the educational profession today—and surely one of the fastest growing.

SUMMARY

This chapter has deliberately avoided extensive discussion of techniques of administration and implementation of adult education programs within public school systems, as these important topics will be treated at length in the chapters to follow. Rather, the intention has been to make an observation of what appear to be trends in the increasing recognition by school systems of the tremendously significant role that adult continuing education programs can play in achieving the overall objectives of American public education. Adult education within public school systems has progressed from the role of a boarder, to that of an adopted child, to that of a regular member of the family. Perhaps it is now time to realize that it has an important leadership role to play in the educational family.

CHAPTER 3

ROLES AND INTERRELATIONSHIPS OF CONTINUING EDUCATION INSTITUTIONS

Russell J. Kleis and Donald G. Butcher

Continuing education is not confined to schools, colleges, and other "educational institutions," nor is it confined to courses and classes. Its sponsors include employers, churches, unions, military service schools, correspondence schools, community agencies, and a wide variety of professional, proprietary, and voluntary institutions. It assumes such varied forms as courses taken for credit, informal instruction on the job, intensive study without either teacher or classroom, private tutoring, correspondence study, instruction by social workers or public health nurses, and discussion groups or demonstrations in home, shop, field, or office.

A national study of the continuing education activities of adults in the United States[1] published in 1965 found 25 million adults (about one in every five in the country) actively involved in continuing education programs. About two-thirds (16,560,000) of these 25 million adults were enrolled in credit or noncredit courses. Only 40 percent of these courses were conducted by schools, colleges, or universities, public or private; 60 percent were conducted by nonschool institutions. Table 1 shows the kinds of institutions involved and the number and percentage of adults being served in the various course offerings.

A further look at these adult students reveals that about one-fourth (6,800,000) of the 25 million were earning credit toward certificates,

Russell J. Kleis is chairman, Graduate Studies in Continuing Education, Michigan State University, East Lansing, Michigan.

Donald G. Butcher is coordinator of Adult Education and Community Service Programs, Michigan Department of Education, Lansing, Michigan.

TABLE 1. – ESTIMATED NUMBERS AND PERCENTAGES OF ADULTS ENROLLED IN CONTINUING EDUCATION COURSES OF VARIOUS SPONSORING INSTITUTIONS IN THE UNITED STATES, 1962[2]

Sponsoring Institutions	Number	Percent
Churches and synagogues	3,460,000	21
Colleges and universities	3,440,000	21
Community organizations	2,450,000	15
Business and industry	2,040,000	12
Elementary and high school	1,920,000	12
Private schools	1,220,000	7
Government agencies	1,180,000	7
Armed forces	580,000	4
All other sponsors	250,000	2
Total of estimates	16,560,000	101*

*Error due to rounding.

diplomas, or degrees. This credit was to be applied toward elementary school certificates (almost none), high school diplomas (about 8 percent), a first college degree (about 23 percent), an advanced college degree (about 19 percent), or a certificate or diploma awarded outside the regular educational system (about 50 percent).

Continuing education in less structured forms is difficult to locate and count. It is clear, however, that activities other than courses comprise at least one-third of all continuing education, and it seems reasonable to assume that considerably more than half of them are being conducted by nonschool organizations and agencies.

Churches, unions, business and industry, government agencies, women's clubs, professional societies, and voluntary groups often conduct very substantial programs. Some do it in support of their other purposes; some have it as one of their primary purposes.

The intent of this chapter is to discuss some of the roles and relationships of continuing education institutions that need to be considered by administrators of public continuing education. For the purpose of this discussion, these institutions will be classified into five categories —

1. Local public schools, often identified as "K-12"
2. Educational institutions other than local public schools
3. Public agencies having auxiliary education functions
4. Work-related institutions and organizations
5. Voluntary associations.

An organizational scheme together with some general recommendations for continuing education administrators will be presented as a
form of summary.

PLURALISM IN CONTINUING EDUCATION

Pluralism in continuing education is a natural and valued feature of
American community life. It should be encouraged, and its potential
benefits should be maximized because it serves several important
purposes.

First, it acknowledges in very concrete terms that deliberate and
ordered learning is a persistently essential function in a complex
society. It acknowledges that such learning is integrally related to our
day-to-day tasks of choosing and acting and, hence, to the realizing of
human values and purposes.

Second, it permits the accommodation of a very broad spectrum of
educational goals. Many of these goals are appropriate only to private,
partisan, or sectarian groups but are desirable, or at least permissable,
within the framework of our free society. Others are appropriate to
special groups defined in terms of ethnic, educational, vocational, age,
interest, or other characteristics of members.

Third, it tends to identify and enlist educational resources not otherwise available. No single institution and no complex of public institutions can expect to identify and enlist the total reservoir of continuing
education resources available in any community. Access to these resources is greatly expanded in most communities by having a wide
variety of institutions involved in continuing education.

Fourth, it spreads the benefits of planning, organizing, interpreting,
and instructing among many individuals and groups. As every educator
knows, the learning opportunities for those who choose, plan, promote, and teach may be considerably larger than for those involved
only as students.

Fifth, it tends to produce more responsible behavior on the part of
participating groups. Unreasoned or unreasonable requests for services,
unrealistic expectation of outcome, and niggardly allocation of resources are easy practices for those who do not confront their logical
consequences. Responsibility for the education enterprise in one area
tends to produce more responsible criticism and support for it in other
areas.

Sixth, the increased number of agencies permits expansion of educational opportunities, limited only by the will, vision, and resources of
those involved.

NEED FOR PROGRAM COORDINATION

Pluralism may also have its drawbacks in that it may tend to dissipate resources; it may create or magnify divisions among institutions and groups; it may accentuate inequities and inequality of access to educational opportunity; it may result in overlooking and overlapping in education services; and it may result in gross inefficiency in the employment of educational resources.

However, in a free and complex society, pluralism's potential benefits outweigh its drawbacks, and a major task of continuing education leaders is to maximize the one and minimize the other. This can be accomplished through a systematic and voluntary effort toward communication and reconciliation among continuing education agencies. The public school director has unique responsibilities for initiating, enabling, and sustaining such a systematic effort.

The unique responsibility of the public school director is derived from the nature of his preparation, the conditions of his employment, and the institutional setting in which he works. He is publicly employed and, hence, is responsible to all sectors of the community. He has professional training and experience which equip and admit him to serve in consultant and leader roles. He has a view of the entire community from which he can note pockets of need, concentrations of resources, possibilities for conflicting or complementary efforts, and levels of success in continuing education projects. He has the advantages of continuity of service and access to such supports as instructional experts, secretarial services, communication, media, meeting facilities, and professional or community leader endorsement. In some communities he is the only professional person with this unique set of resources. In others he is one of a group of persons in position to facilitate voluntary coordination among community agencies.

A comprehensive program will be enhanced, and its benefits throughout the community will be expanded as the public school director develops close working relationships with the many other institutions involved in the continuing education enterprise. Each agency can work more specifically and more effectively toward its own goals, become more informed and responsible within the community as a whole, and serve more citizens more effectively as it communicates and cooperates within such a system.

EDUCATIONAL INSTITUTIONS OTHER THAN LOCAL SCHOOLS

Community Colleges

Community colleges and their older cousins, junior colleges, are concerned mainly with posthigh school educational programs below the level of the baccalaureate degree. Their number is expanding rapidly, and most states are currently developing community colleges as a major component of their educational systems. Community colleges already in operation are being restructured to broaden and strengthen the services they render to adults. Others are being established committed to programs of community service or continuing education.

The community college is recognized as a ready and effective instrument for serving a wide spectrum of educational objectives, among which are the following:

1. To provide posthigh school educational opportunity within the community and at moderate cost for an increasing number of youth and adults. This number is growing because (a) the population segment of college age (18-22) has been increasing, (b) an increasing percentage of these people are completing high school and want to enter higher education, and (c) an increasing number of adults now wish to continue or resume their education.

2. To reduce or eliminate the barriers of cost, distance, social status, or similar impediments to continued schooling, which now prevent many able and qualified persons from acquiring posthigh school education commensurate with their abilities.

3. To have in the American school system an educational unit at the posthigh school level which is virtually nonselective in its admissions practices and which by virtue of the scope and excellence of its curriculum, its guidance and counseling services, and its relationship to the practical problems of people is an effective instrument for human development in individuals, institutions, and the community as a whole.

4. To conduct programs that prepare people to perform semiprofessional or technician-level jobs in an economy which relies heavily on technology and advanced business and commercial methods.

5. To offer academic and preprofessional study articulated with the upper divisions and graduate levels of colleges and universities for those individuals who have aptitude, resources, and motivation for more advanced study. Only in this way, many believe, will the American university be permitted to develop its unique character and concentrate on its functions of higher learning and professional education.

6. To maintain locally available centers for continuing education and reeducation of out-of-school youth and adults.

Six major, and not entirely separable, areas of focus define the general functions of a community college —

1. *General education.* Every community college student, youth or adult, should have access to those learnings which will enable him to develop fully as a person and to function effectively as a family member and as a citizen of his local community, state, nation, and world.

2. *College education (lower division).* Two years of carefully articulated college study should be available for students who plan to transfer to colleges or universities to earn academic or professional degrees. Curriculums should offer breadth and excellence adequate to lower division requirements in the liberal arts and in various professional fields.

3. *Occupational education.* Training for occupational competence in technical, public service, paraprofessional, and similar fields should be available across a broad range of vocations. The training must be closely articulated with current and emerging manpower requirements. It should provide both entry-level competence and continuing education for maintaining currency of knowledge and skills and for career advancement.

4. *Counseling.* Assessing oneself, clarifying goals, identifying alternatives, recognizing role requirements, illuminating unrecognized assumptions, career planning, and adapting to changing conditions in life—all requirements of effective choosing and acting—may be aided at least as much by counseling as by instruction. For individuals or groups, youth or adult, student or nonstudent, counseling is a much needed and underdeveloped function in the community college.

5. *Continuing education.* In many communities those seeking post-high school education who are not full-time students exceed in number and intensity of purpose those who are full-time students. No greater justification exists for the development of excellence in all areas of community college work than to serve the continuing education needs of those daily engaged in the professions, homes, services, and governance of the community. Policies, practices, programs, and schedules should be established to serve these expanding needs through virtually every functional unit of the community college.

6. *Community development.* In an urbanizing society the realization of the human potential of individuals and groups depends at least as much on the improvement of social institutions which dominate their environment as on the more direct and familiar processes of education. Urban development authorities, welfare and rehabilitation services, religious bodies, business and

industry, unions, professions, creative and performing arts groups, communications media, manpower officials, recreation boards, and a host of other governmental and private institutions with programs of their own may be helped to improve their services by infusions of educational resources from the community college. These contributions may consist of such varied elements as loaned facilities, special training, faculty or student involvement in programs, action research, expert consultation, collaborative enterprises, or intensive development projects. Community colleges are unique in the opportunity they have for contributing to community development and improvement.

The total cause of continuing education will be better served when more community colleges expand their community service dimension by —

1. Concentrating their continuing education efforts on programs which require college resources (though not to the exclusion of all other programs).
2. Making their continuing education director or dean responsible directly to the college president.
3. Extending their services to their total service areas, utilizing public school facilities as necessary.
4. Developing a continuing technical, vocational, and paraprofessional education program, kept constantly abreast of the unique and evolving requirements of work places and of adults and out-of-school youth.
5. Providing apprentice training programs as needed.
6. Giving major emphasis to a program of general studies for adults. This should be a combination of credit and noncredit programs. For those adults who wish to earn a college certificate, the program should provide sequential offerings, at times convenient to the students, and qualifying for full academic accreditation.
7. Establishing a center for continuing education in the creative and performing arts. Such a center should (a) enlist talented persons and the resources of studio, stage, and library in a continuing education effort in its own name; (b) actively encourage and assist private and volunteer groups, amateur or professional; and (c) encourage study of the arts in local schools throughout the area.
8. Operating a center for the study of public issues. This center should be both an operating and a service center. It should operate both on and off the campus and should conduct seminars, workshops, and similar programs in such areas as the processes of

public decision making, communication and leadership in community life, objective study of current issues from local to world levels, study of persistent policy questions, the arts and ethics of partisan presentation, and the art of analysis of issues and presentations. It should also encourage and assist local schools and private and voluntary groups in the promotion of similar study.

9. Joining with the public schools in assisting voluntary, private, and public bodies in conducting their own continuing education program, a continuing professional education service, especially in such ways as training leaders, loaning or recruiting specially qualified personnel, consulting in program development, assessing needs, sharing facilities, and cosponsoring or coordinating multiple efforts.

10. Providing a professionally staffed and well equipped adult counseling center.

11. Formally undertaking to encourage orderly participation by nearby colleges and university extension services in meeting the needs for higher education resources in the area's continuing education system.

12. Participating officially and fully in a communitywide council of continuing education administrators.

Area Occupational Education Centers

Due to the many changes in technology, employment needs, and educational requirements for employment, it is nearly impossible for each school district to provide a program sufficiently varied to serve the vocational needs of all youth and adults.

To meet these needs, a centralized skill center to supplement the work of the comprehensive high school is emerging. Designed to serve several school districts by providing training in a variety of skills under the direction of qualified instructors, the area skill center's objectives include —

1. Offering training in specific skills and related instruction to both noncollege- and college-bound youth in areas of instruction not provided in the high school.

2. Equipping the noncollege-bound student with useable skills so that he becomes successfully employed.

3. Encouraging students to stay in school and graduate from high school.

4. Providing training and retraining for out-of-school youth and adults.

While the AOEC program aims to equip students with skills and attitudes adequate to obtaining entry employment, it should also encourage each student to continue his education and develop his career to the maximum of his capacity. It should provide postsecondary as well as secondary occupational curriculums. Students should have access to —

1. *Pretechnical programs* which are part of a well defined sequence articulated with the community college or other advanced technical programs.
2. *Vocational programs* which provide entry employment skills in a definable occupation for which a demand exists. These programs should be designed to serve the needs of youth who intend to enter the labor force directly after completing high school and of adults who lack this level of preparation.
3. *Opportunity programs* which are designed to provide employable skills for persons of limited ability or who have limiting handicaps.[3]

The AOEC has unique and specific contributions to make to a community continuing education program. The public school continuing education administrator must keep himself fully informed, continually striving for close coordination of program efforts between the AOEC and the public school offerings.

Intermediate School District

In most states the intermediate, county, or parish school district constitutes the consultative, coordinating, and administrative service agency whose functions extend throughout a multidistrict area. The intermediate district's relationships with local schools, community colleges, area occupational centers, and voluntary and official agencies make it, in some instances, the appropriate integrating agent for a coordinated system of continuing education. In most states, its relationships do not involve legal obligation, but its professional leadership can be effective and its coordinating service can be of great value.

If it assumes such a coordinating role, the intermediate school board should appoint a well qualified adult educator to serve as a consulting and coordinating agent. His functions would include —

1. Consulting with local superintendents, boards of education, and directors of continuing education concerning all phases of organization and operations of continuing education.
2. Enlisting the services and facilities of the intermediate district staff in service of continuing education.

3. Conducting or arranging in-service training for administrators, teachers, board members, and other personnel throughout the area continuing education system.
4. Preparing and distributing materials to inform all interested adults and out-of-school youth of continuing education opportunities available to them throughout the area.
5. Consulting with and assisting voluntary, private, and public agencies in their programs of continuing education or referring them to other sources of consultation and cooperation.
6. Maintaining close liaison with communications media, keeping them informed of significant developments, and encouraging their active participation in the continuing education program.
7. Encouraging communication and cooperation among all agencies, public and private, official and voluntary, which are concerned with continuing education in the area.

Public Library

The public library is a principal agency and living symbol of continuing education in any community. Potentially, it is to continuing education what the university library is to higher education.

The American Library Association Commission on the Library and Adult Education has identified three basic activities as the library's contribution to continuing education:

First of all, and on its own responsibility, the library owes consulting and advisory service supplemented by suitable books, to those who wish to pursue their studies alone, rather than in organized groups or classes. Such a service, which can function effectively only through a specially trained and well-educated personnel, will offer advice in the choice of books, and will assist students through the preparation of reading courses adapted to their age, education, taste, and previous experience. This is a contribution which the library is peculiarly fitted to render.

In the second place, there is the obligation to furnish complete and reliable information concerning the local opportunities for adult education available outside the library. Persons desiring class work in any particular subject, stimulus from discussion groups or lecture courses, cultural development through opportunities obtainable in the local art museum or elsewhere, should naturally turn to the public library for information, descriptive circulars, or trustworthy advice.

Thirdly, the library should recognize as a fundamental duty the supplying of books and other printed material for adult education activities maintained by other organizations. There has as yet been no definite recognition, either by the library or by the agencies offering educational classes for adults, of the need of an ample book supply for group study. Owing to the rapidly widening interests and to the complexities of present day adult life, this adequate book supply for students of a more mature age may be even more important than for younger scholars in fulltime schools. [4]

Public libraries range from exceptionally fine and vigorous participants in the continuing education enterprise to seriously underdeveloped and underused facilities. A library may simply be there available to serve such requests as come to it; or it may develop its own short-range and long-range plans and aggressively promote its own program without regard to other continuing education agencies; or it may engage in cooperative and consultative activity, aggressively developing such programs as it may be uniquely equipped to develop, offering services and facilities to other agencies to operate within the library or in close affiliation with it, and extending its enriching contribution into the work of other institutions and agencies throughout the community. In short, the public library may be a relatively impotent or an unusually potent force in a communitywide system of continuing education.

The attitude and activity of the public school director may greatly influence the level and quality of public library involvement in continuing education programs. Active cooperation between himself and the librarian and active involvement of both in the total continuing education enterprise of the community are professional responsibilities which neither can deny.

Private Schools

One expression of pluralism in American education is the wide array of schools operated under private auspices. A partial listing of such schools, in addition to private colleges and universities, would include —

Parochial elementary and secondary schools
Boarding schools
Conservatories of creative and performing arts
Theological seminaries
Trade and technical institutes
Military academies
Leadership and management centers
Business colleges
Correspondence schools
Schools of barbering, beauty, health, and so forth
Centers for advanced study in various fields.

Some of these institutions are operated for profit; some are supported by philanthropic foundations, religious institutions, or nonprofit corporations; some are cooperative ventures. Some encompass broad areas of study and serve a broad clientele; others are committed to narrowly defined areas of study, clearly limited audiences, or highly specialized purposes or interests.

Their concern for continuing education ranges from virtually zero to its being a principal raison d'être. Their attitudes toward cooperation with other agencies of continuing education appropriately range from complete withdrawal to genuine eagerness to be included. Some of them have programs, personnel, and facilities of kind and quality not available anywhere else; others might have their own services enriched by contributions of program, personnel, and facilities from other agencies.

New federal legislation explicitly concerned with schools and colleges in addition to that concerned with health, arts and humanities, poverty, professional development, urban problems, manpower and similar social concerns will almost surely contribute to major expansion of private educational ventures. Similarly, new state legislation — some of it allocating public funds to assist individuals and families as well as educational institutions — is likely to encourage their further expansion.

Public school directors are likely to find resources for enriching their own continuing education programs and opportunities for extending needed support to programs not their own by working in coordination and cooperation with the broad and growing private education sector.

Higher Adult Education

The *four-year colleges* are the oldest and most varied form of higher education in the United States, but their involvement in continuing education varies widely. Many of them conduct programs for their alumni and for the communities within which they are located. Some operate excellent programs in community development, education within industry, education for women, creative and performing arts, and similar specialized projects. Only a small proportion of four-year colleges have the resources required to provide comprehensive programs, but most of them have unique resources in one or more areas and can provide specialized programs of genuine excellence.

Professional schools and *seminaries* are becoming deeply involved in continuing education and often are concerned with lay education as well as with needs of their graduates to maintain professional currency. In many cases, they welcome the opportunity to cooperate with public schools, community colleges, and other institutions which serve a broader public than theirs. In communities remote from home campuses, they frequently conduct both professional and lay continuing education activities within the public schools and community colleges. These programs may be administered through general university extension units or, in many cases, through the administrative framework of the professional schools themselves.

Urban universities, almost without exception, have extensive programs in continuing education. Since World War II their enrollments, the variety of their continuing education offerings, and their attention to the needs of adults as individuals, in groups, and in community agencies have expanded enormously. They offer opportunities for continuing education for individuals; education inputs into business, industry, and government; studies and training in community-serving agencies, continuing professional education, counseling and consultant services, community development assistance, and cultural contributions of wide variety. Continuing education is becoming so fully accepted as a primary function by some urban universities that it is difficult to distinguish between the regular and the continuing education functions of these institutions.

The university evening college, traditionally the principal administrative unit for continuing education in the urban university, is being joined by urban studies centers, industrial relations institutes, community development centers, and a variety of other specialized units which may be appropriately included under the broad rubric of continuing education. Increasingly the principal administrative officers for these complex continuing education enterprises are being made vice-presidents.

University extension services are generally and appropriately associated in our minds with land grant institutions and state universities. In addition, however, very significant university extension programs are operated by private universities. Beginning with the personal extension activities of faculty members like Professor Benjamin Silliman of Yale in the early 1800's, with the pioneer commitments of such universities as Chicago and Wisconsin in the 1890's, with the organization of the National University Extension Association, and the establishment of the Cooperative Extension Service in the first two decades of this century, the extension of education beyond the borders of the campus and beyond the full-time youth student body has become a major function of American universities. Since World War II and more especially since 1960, universities have enormously expanded their direct involvement in social problems through continuing education.

Established and supported by the Smith-Lever Act of 1914 (with many subsequent amendments consolidated in the new act in 1962), the *Cooperative Extension Service* has become the most outstanding nationally coordinated program of adult education anywhere in the world. Its support is drawn from federal, state and local (usually county) sources and is not infrequently supplemented by foundations, corporations, and cooperating organizations. Its educational services are provided almost universally without charge to participants. Personal development; applications of technology; farm, home, and business management; home and family life; consumer education; public policy; and work with youth, both urban and rural, represent major areas of emphasis. Historically and currently the major base of operation is the rural community; however, a characteristic emphasis on social problems as well as individual learning has led quite naturally to the expansion of cooperative extension activities into suburban and even urban communities.

Cooperative planning, consultation, demonstration, local organizations, lay leadership, and direct involvement in problem solving rather sharply distinguish the cooperative extension method from the more traditional modes of extension education. These differences make it possible for an occasional public school person to be unaware of his cooperative extension colleagues and even for an occasional cooperative extension agent to be unaware that he is an adult educator.

Another branch of university extension is usually identified as *general extension* or *continuing education*. General extension is to be found in almost every state university, land grant university, and major private university. Its forms are enormously varied and its services are available over entire states, multistate regions, and even internationally. Typically, it provides both credit and noncredit extension courses, residential center programs, correspondence studies, radio and television offerings, traveling or broadcast programs in the creative and performing arts, community development, labor and industrial relations programs, continuing professional education, extensive consultation services, and a host of other continuing education services.

University extension is a major factor in the continuing education enterprise in virtually every community in the land. The 1965 Johnstone study found college and university extension programs ranked approximately equal to churches and synagogues as the most common source of continuing education for adults. Nearly twice as many adults (21 percent) were participating in university extension programs as were enrolled in public school adult education programs (12 percent).[5]

Recent federal legislation extends and intensifies the involvement of higher education of almost every form in the continuing education enterprise. The role of specialized, reliable, and current knowledge in the resolution of individual and social problems makes continuing education increasingly an essential function of normal living, and it makes higher education a major source of power for personal and social progress.

The public school director who would participate responsibly in a total community program of continuing education will find himself intimately and frequently related to his colleagues in higher adult education. He will be able to draw on their expertise and the enormous range of resources at their command. He will have the opportunity to promote, interpret, and provide supporting services for many higher adult education institutions. Surely he will be called on to collaborate with their representatives in many programs, especially those devoted to the resolution of community problems.

PUBLIC AGENCIES HAVING AUXILIARY EDUCATION FUNCTIONS

Education is a major auxiliary function of many public agencies. Departments of government concerned with health and safety, social welfare, law enforcement, employment, and rehabilitation often find that their primary functions can best be performed or supported through education programs directed at the publics they serve. These and other departments also rely heavily on in-service education for ensuring excellence in staff performance. Continuing education thus becomes a necessary complement to financial assistance, health services, law enforcement, employment, and similar forms of public service.

Health and Welfare Agencies

Generally, county and city health departments are concerned with continuing education as it relates to such topics as maternal and child health, current health issues (smoking, heart, cancer, etc.), environmental sanitation, physical fitness, mental health, gerontology, first aid, and home nursing. Family-focus agencies conduct parent and family life education. Cooperation and cross referrals between public schools and health and welfare agencies will strengthen both programs.

The local social welfare agency serves as a very good example. The agency refers to the continuing education programs many adults in need of education. Caseworkers stress the need for additional education, regular attendance, and continuing effort. They make home calls and stay abreast of the multiple problems faced by their underemployed clients. Their knowledge of individual students is useful in developing meaningful educational programs for them. Continuing education directors maintain flexibility and often alter existing programs to fulfill special needs. They may develop special classes conducted at times convenient to welfare recipients and may provide special services such as transportation or child care. They keep caseworkers informed concerning goals, problems, and progress, and cooperate in assisting client-students to new levels of life and work.

Community Action Agencies

Recently, through the Office of Economic Opportunity and its war on poverty, several new agencies, most of which serve out-of-school youth and adults, have entered the education enterprise. Community action agencies have been set up in store fronts, empty warehouses, churches, and other public buildings located within pockets of poverty. Many of these agencies have developed rapport at the grass roots level and are working to serve many needs of the poor. The Neighborhood Youth Corps, Job Corps, and Head Start parent programs represent similar continuing education functions of the "poverty war." Continuing education administrators should play a vital role in these new efforts to develop productive citizens. Doing so will call for dramatic new ways to approach the continuing education task.

Employment Security Agencies

Like the social welfare and community action agencies, the local employment security commission can be a strong component of a continuing education program. It may serve as an excellent recruitment vehicle and can help develop meaningful programs by assuring continued cognizance of employment needs and opportunities. Employment counselors regularly identify, evaluate, and refer adults who have needs for job training and placement. Continuing education administrators can greatly enhance their service to citizens by cooperating with this agency and keeping its workers informed of emerging and existing programs.

Parks and Recreation Departments

Many county and municipal parks and recreation departments organize formal programs of recreation education. These offer excellent opportunity for cooperative or parallel programs. With careful planning and coordination, duplication of effort can be avoided and potential service can be increased. Clear patterns of cooperation should be established, and new programs should involve consultation and joint planning. Instructional equipment can often be shared, as can supervision and use of facilities. Recreation programs conducted in public school buildings and education programs conducted in recreation areas can save public funds and enhance both educational and recreational outcomes.

Civil Defense Education

Civil defense education is conducted through organized channels of education for those adults who want to know more about preparedness for natural or man-made disasters. Specifically, such programs aim to —

1. Alert adults to the need for civil defense.
2. Develop among adults an understanding of the basic principles and practices of adjustment to disasters.
3. Provide adults with experience in personal and community survival planning.
4. Provide for the development of teaching techniques and instructional materials for civil defense instruction.
5. Contribute to the development and support of local and state civil defense programs.

Federal funds for civil defense education are normally channeled to university extension services or through state departments of education to public school districts for the establishment of programs. This operation through established continuing education institutions ensures adequate promotion, proper facilities, audiovisual equipment, and a ready supply of trained teachers.

It also meets three criteria of public adult education — providing services needed by people in the community, providing meaningful learning experiences to these people, and maximizing use of facilities paid for with tax dollars.

WORK-RELATED INSTITUTIONS AND ORGANIZATIONS

Labor Unions

The overwhelming majority of workers in most communities are employees, most of whom are affiliated with craft and industrial unions. Few groups in society have a greater stake in education than labor unions, and few support it more vigorously. Unions promote apprentice training; economics, liberal arts, and public affairs education; leadership training; basic and high school education; and education for leisure time, principally for their members. They are actively interested in a very broad range of educational activities.

In addition to operating programs independently, unions often cooperate with other groups in community education projects. Their facilities are available for meeting places, their officers for promotion of worthy continuing efforts, and, occasionally, their finances for necessary program support. Unions often cooperate with local school districts and offer adult basic education and high school classes in local union halls. Because labor unions represent a major source of students, facilities, experience, and support, close working relations with them should be encouraged and utilized.

Professional and Technical Societies

Practically every profession confronts the serious problem of helping its members keep up with current developments in their field. Therefore, continuing education becomes a major function of society programing and a major task of each society executive. Both profession-required topics and liberal education experiences are included in programs. The content may be highly technical and related exclusively to the professional speciality; it may be concerned with legislation or community problems; or it may be principally in liberal education.

Much of the education is directed inward to the membership; some of it is directed outward to the general public or to particular segments of it. Much of it is generated within the group itself either locally or at state or national levels; some of it is contributed by colleges, professional schools, universities, or related professions.

Many professional workers have only the minimum entry credentials for their work and desire to continue their study at higher levels for further accreditation, salary and position advances, or simply to satisfy interests of the individuals or requirements of his work.

The continuing education function of professional societies can often be improved by providing facilities, consultation, instruction, and administrative machinery for advancing it. This is especially true as professions and technical societies participate in education for laymen. Involving representatives of professions in the continuing education system can both serve and utilize the societies and their members.

Business and Industry

The business and industrial firms in any given community are major participants in the continuing education enterprise. Many of them conduct programs which range from informal induction training through apprentice or formal on-the-job training for various levels and classifications of personnel to high-level reading programs, management and technical seminars, and formal study leaves. Many employ, and some produce, sophisticated educational materials, media, and processes.

Business and industry frequently support general community education ventures; they contribute counsel, equipment, facilities, money, promotion, and special instructors to assist programs of other institutions; and they supply students in large numbers, often with maintenance of income and reimbursement of expenses. Their participation may be as individual firms or through associations. Chambers of Commerce, employers' associations, manufacturers' associations, trade associations, development councils, management clubs, and similar groups are composed entirely or predominately of members of the business and industrial community. Continuing education projects are often implemented through one or more of such groups.

The American Society for Training and Development is a national organization with many local chapters. Its membership consists principally of training directors in business and industry, and its emphasis is almost exclusively on continuing education.

VOLUNTARY ASSOCIATIONS

A large number of voluntary groups conduct programs of continuing education for adults. Churches and synagogues, faith-based associations, foreign policy associations, the League of Women Voters, parent-teacher associations, child study clubs, the Urban League, Great Books discussion groups, and others regularly conduct orderly and respected programs. Others including service clubs, women's clubs, golden age groups, veterans' groups, political organizations, and fraternal societies give varying degrees of emphasis to education. Some of their work is excellent; some of it is casual; much of it is sporadic and even accidental.

The educating power of voluntary associations is great indeed. Its results may be either positive or negative. Religious beliefs and political persuasions are shaped by it; the untiring efforts of civic leaders to realize community potential is usually a product of it; hatred and mistrust or respect and neighborliness may be built by it. There is both promise and threat in the observation that "first we build our associations; then they build us." Collaboration between professional educators of adults and leaders of voluntary associations may yield very substantial educational benefits in any community.

Voluntary Groups and Liberal Education

Continuing liberal education can be defined as education which gives enrichment and meaning to life, which is pursued voluntarily, and which is not necessarily subject to any requirement of formal education. It includes such areas of study as philosophy, religion, social and natural sciences, literature and languages, and appreciation of and participation in the creative and performing arts. It is related to the interests and concerns of mature persons and is, of all forms of education, the most uniquely adult. C. O. Houle says of it —

> In vocational education or parent education or the effort to complete formal schooling, the individual responds to certain fairly clear-cut pressures or needs, and the rewards he receives are relatively specific and definite. Liberal education, however, is a matter of perfecting the individual himself; he is engaged in enlarging his own central capacities, his personal excellence and his relationship to the successively larger groups of which he is a part. He aims not to increase his specific skills or knowledge but to gain understanding and insight. Liberal education can never, therefore, be a matter — at least in adulthood — of specific training programs leading to specific skills and with clear-cut and measurable results. It must be sustained by the feeling on the part of the student that what he learns is so rich and meaningful and varied that it is of great worth to him. His reward lies within himself. He responds not to outside pressures but to his own sense of a need for his individual advancement. In short, he directs his own education.[6]

In many communities continuing liberal education is pursued largely through voluntary associations or by schools and colleges with their active cooperation. Typical of such groups are Great Books, creative and performing arts, Great Decisions, national and world affairs, town hall, civic opera, and serious reading groups. The list could be made long, and its growth potential is great.

If, as scientists predict, large numbers of people will soon have much more leisure time, liberal education may become one of the glamour stocks of the continuing education enterprise. Whether or not that happens, it is a highest-priority item for socially concerned leaders of education for adults. Mature citizens in a complex, dynamic, hazardous, rewarding world need continuing access to study that focuses on meaning and value and that contributes toward achievement of the highest and most humane levels of personal and community life.

Liberal education is not, as is often supposed, reserved to persons of wealth and privilege. In fact the leisure and power usually associated with its pursuit are now broadly shared — even concentrated — among working-class families and the unemployed. The surge of aspiration on the part of minority and low-income people involves, among other things, a desire to understand and achieve beauty, justice, dignity, and freedom, which constitute the essential mission of liberal education.

The social significance of liberal education lies largely in its humanizing influence on those whose planning and acting give direction to social change. Thus, as social power is more broadly shared and social change more vigorously pursued, the learnings most likely to enhance and bring about human progress assume the status of social imperatives.

In the mid-1960's a new national emphasis on liberal education began to emerge. Through the Arts and Humanities Act, the federal government provided initial legislation and funding. National endowments, foundations, state councils, and local groups have formulated plans and moved forward with programs. It remains to be seen whether these developments will appear from future perspective as beginnings of a new high level of personal and community living. The potential is there. Continuing education leaders, both voluntary and professional, are among those most appropriately concerned, and on their combined effectiveness depends much of the outcome.

Churches and Faith-Based Associations

The continuing education programs of churches and faith-based associations serve more adults and out-of-school youth than do those of public schools and about the same number as do those of colleges and universities. Though this surprises many, it should not.

Churches and synagogues have always served as education centers for their members, and most of them have vigorously promoted education beyond their institutional and geographic boundaries. Lay and professional persons are hired or volunteer their efforts. Materials, staff training, and other supports are regularly provided through state and national organizations. Some programs are operated privately, emphasizing creed and doctrine, and are intended principally for members or potential members, while other programs are operated publicly, emphasizing issues of general concern, and are intended for members and nonmembers throughout the community.

Another segment of continuing education is that maintained by faith-based associations. These include Young Men's and Young Women's Christian Associations, Young Men's and Young Women's Hebrew Associations, B'nai B'rith, National Conference of Christians and Jews, Salvation Army, city rescue missions, and a wide range of similar institutions. Each is organized independently of church hierarchies, and most, though not all, are organized nationally. Often they seek and obtain broad voluntary support from individuals, corporations, and groups. In many communities the adult and young adult programs of the YMCA, YWCA, Jewish Community Centers, and similar institutions are among the oldest and most vigorous continuing education programs available.

Programs of these religious and quasi-religious institutions are widely varied. In addition to those addressed to the particulars of the Jewish, Christian, or other faith of the sponsoring body, these programs generally emphasize eight broad categories of concern —

1. Family life
2. Rehabilitation
3. Social justice
4. Human relations
5. Intercultural understanding
6. Personal and corporate ethics
7. Physical and mental health
8. Creative and performing arts.

These programs employ a variety of formats and methods and may combine education with action in ways that obscure distinctions between the two.

This can be illustrated by brief examination of two categories.

Family life programs may include marriage and premarriage counseling, family camps after the Chautauqua model, intensive instruction in child care or in psychology of adolescents, family finance workshops, homes for unwed mothers, sensitivity laboratories for parents, clubs for single parents, or family helpers for disadvantaged families. Rehabilitation education may involve intensive work with alcoholics or drug addicts; reception and relocation of ex-convicts, discharged mental patients, or refugees; or sheltered workshops and half-way houses for handicapped persons.

Churches and faith-based associations make significant and often unique contributions to a comprehensive program of continuing education. They often utilize trained leaders and resources of other educational institutions and share their resources in exchange. They and others gain strength, and the community is better served, as they are involved in the circle of mutually supportive relations among continuing education institutions.

Human Relations and Human Rights Groups

Continuing education is addressed to current concerns of mature learners, and few topics are more current or of more concern than human relations and human rights. A wide variety of groups, many of them highly responsible and greatly concerned, are organized to deal with these closely related issues.

Much of adult learning hinges on sensitivity and experience in the human relations arena. This is as true in families, work settings, and communities as it is in the broader areas of race, economics, politics, and intergroup and intercultural relations.

Accomplishing change in human relations is both important and difficult. It is likely to produce tension and anxiety at some points while yielding increased understanding and more authentic behavior and relationships at other points. Professional leaders with courage and competence are sorely needed in this important sector of continuing education. Collaboration with voluntary and official groups may lead to highly significant contributions.

In another context the issue becomes even more intense. Technological and social changes build pressure for change in interpersonal and intergroup relations. When, as often happens, educators cannot or will not intervene to facilitate learning of the required new relationships, these pressures mount. Voluntary and official efforts are undertaken to secure human rights. If education can be effectively employed at that point, needed learnings may yet result in orderly change; if it cannot, then more direct and less orderly methods of change are employed. Great and painful periods in history are marked by such direct approaches to change.

The contemporary scene presents no more significant challenge to policy and program makers in public school continuing education. Both minority and dominant group members need to learn their way to new levels of respect and relationship. Some of the learning can be done in schools; much of it must be accomplished in settings and in forms more familiar to persons who generally do not see themselves as students.

Organizations and Interest Groups

American society is characterized by a variety of associations which devote their efforts to programs of personal and civic improvement. Continuing education, whether acknowledged as such or not, is usually a significant component of their programs. A close liaison between them and professional public school leaders may yield very worthy contributions to a total community program of continuing education.

Some organizations such as the American Association for the United Nations, the League of Women Voters, parent-teachers associations, child study clubs, and foreign policy associations are highly organized. Their programs fit within a state or national pattern, and they have educational resources to share, as well as needs for local counsel and assistance.

Councils such as those on aging or safety promote educational programs in other agencies and institutions as well as those in their own name. Often they are anxious to provide materials, personnel, and other resources. Generally their interests benefit the public interest, and public schools may work freely with them with no concern about favor or bias.

Special Interest Groups and Organizations

Other groups are organized around such shared and often avocational interests as astronomy, classic automobiles, stamps, rocks, flying, gardening, investments, or crafts. Enthusiasm is usually high in these groups; they often welcome new members and encourage nonmembers to share in their activities; and they may volunteer freely to contribute materials and personnel to other groups and classes. They frequently request assistance in planning and facilities, and they may be quite willing to merge into public school programs.

Maintained in proper balance, these avocational groups merit encouragement. Their activities represent constructive use of leisure time, often contribute significantly to mental health, and add spirit and support to the entire program. They must not, however, become the entire program. If continuing education is to serve its full mission, all its aspects must be developed and put forth to the public.

Media of Communication and Instruction

Communication of ideas is the essential function of institutionalized education. Technological advances in media have enormously expanded the means for performing that function.

Face-to-face meetings of students with instructors have long been the basic medium of the school. With that as a given, buildings have been planned and built, teachers trained and employed, materials prepared and purchased, resources allocated, and programs administered.

That medium is now just one of many options.

Groups in widely separated meetings can be linked into audio and visual connection with each other and with an instructor. Learning consoles can be installed in living rooms or work centers. Messages can travel across the room, the city, or the world in roughly equal amounts of time and with roughly equal clarity and force.

Mass media can carry information to an entire population; programed instruction can pinpoint it to a particular person, time, place, or stage in the learning process. Multimedia systems, open- and closed-circuit television, computer-assisted instruction, interpersonal and intergroup telephonic link-ups, dial-access information retrieval, selective information dissemination systems, and an array of similar media are operational; others are being developed and tested.

The relevance of media to this discussion is not in their impact upon learning and teaching, though that is enormous; it is in their impact upon the interrelationships among institutions of continuing education. New industries are developing, and old ones are changing to produce and employ the new media. New educational institutions are being created. Education is a major growth industry largely as a result of opportunities posed by the new media and the social imperative for their employment.

Schools once enjoyed a virtual monopoly in the formal education enterprise. Especially as related to out-of-school youth and adults, that monopoly position has been shattered. A great variety of public, private, and voluntary institutions are entering the field. Whether the experience and expertise of professional school leaders will significantly influence this expanding continuing education enterprise will depend largely on (a) their innovativeness in employing the new media to upgrade their own programs and (b) their willingness and ability to collaborate with their colleagues in the now-possible systematizing of the enterprise.

SYSTEMATIZING COMMUNITY EFFORTS IN CONTINUING EDUCATION

In this chapter it is assumed that continuing education is a function of community life and that a wide variety of institutions — not just the public schools — are appropriately involved in it. Excellence depends on voluntary participation of citizens in mutual improvement and community betterment and on the community-serving work of both public and private institutions. Therefore, pluralism in continuing education becomes natural and necessary.

Selected institutions which share the continuing education task have been identified and their work briefly discussed. Some of these are primarily educational institutions; others engage in education in addition to, or in service of, a different function. Some are local institutions; others reach into the community from outside. Some work quite independently; others work with or through the schools. Figure I presents a summary list of typical institutions and suggests ways to assess or plan their collaborative involvement in continuing education projects.

If maximum progress is to be made, if resources are to be used efficiently, if service is to be made available to all who need it, and if institutions within the community are to work effectively with institutions at state, regional, and national levels, some scheme for systematizing these multiple continuing education relations is clearly required. Such a scheme should serve to regularize communication, build awareness of shared purposes, promote communitywide planning, facilitate cooperation, avoid needless overlapping and overlooking, and make most effective use of limited professional leadership. It should respect the

FIGURE I.—
INSTITUTIONAL INVOLVEMENT
IN CONTINUING EDUCATION [7]

CONTINUING EDUCATION PROGRAM		EDUCATIONAL INSTITUTIONS		INSTITUTIONS WITH AUXILIARY EDUCATION FUNCTIONS	
1.		Public	Local School District*		
			Community College		
			Area Voc-Tech School		
			Intermediate District		
			Co-Op Ext. Service		
			University Extension*		
			Public Libraries*		
2.		Private	Nearby Colleges*		
			Parochial Schools*		
			Proprietary Schools*		
			Voluntary Education Groups*		
		Official Community Agencies	Civil Service		
			CAAP		
			Courts*		
			Employment Security		
			Health Department*		
			Law Enforcement*		
			Social Security		
			Social Welfare		
			Other Agency*		
		Voluntary Community and Member Serving Institutions	Church*		
			Church Council		
			YM, YW, KC, etc.*		
			Human Relations Groups*		
			Professional Societies*		
			Labor Unions*		
			Labor Council		
			Business or Industry*		
			Area Devel. Council		
			Manufacturers Assoc.		
			Trade Associations*		
			Political Organizations*		
			Arts Council		
			Communication Media		
			Other Institution*		

*Specify institution you have in mind.

Instructions:

1. Enter name of program area
   e.g., Civic Education
2. List major program divisions
   e.g., Courses in Practical Politics
   Study of Local Election Issues
   World Affairs Discussion Groups
3. In appropriate cells, place letters from code at right to indicate institutional contributions

Involvement Code:

A. General Coordination and Supervision
B. Primary Program Responsibility
C. Shared Program Responsibility
D. Facilities and Facilitating Services
E. Planning and Advisory Assistance
F. Instructional or Leadership Personnel
G. Instructional Materials and Equipment
H. Counseling of Students
I. Financial Support
J. Interpretation and Promotion
K. Information and Referral
L. Professional Consultation
M. Report or Other Publication
N. Evaluation
O. -------------
P. -------------

autonomy of participating agencies and institutions; recognize differences in their purposes, commitments, and resources; and allow for differing levels of involvement and participation in the system. It should facilitate timely decision and effective action; and it should serve to relate the entire continuing education enterprise to the needs of mature persons in a changing and challenging world.

A Council of Continuing Education Administrators (CCEA) is suggested as one way of effectively organizing to serve these purposes. Such a council should be composed principally of full-time administrators with major responsibilities for continuing education. It should maintain close liaison (through designated members) with agencies engaged in voluntary and auxiliary continuing education functions.

Membership should, of course, vary from community to community, but it should generally include—

1. The director of continuing education of each school, public or private, which is seriously committed to a continuing education program.
2. The director or dean of continuing education of each community college.
3. The continuing education coordinator of the intermediate school district.
4. At least one representative of adult basic education supervisors.
5. At least one representative of adult high school principals.
6. The director of the public library system.
7. The director of the Cooperative Extension Service.
8. The dean of continuing education for each college or urban university.
9. Regional representatives for university extension services.
10. A representative of local school administrators.

The Council should meet on a regularly scheduled basis and should be provided with staff assistance. Specific activities should be developed in terms of the character and needs of the service area. In general terms, however, each CCEA would—

1. Systematically and regularly assess needs for continuing education on a communitywide basis.
2. Engage in communitywide planning, taking full account of plans of individual institutions.
3. Provide communitywide promotion and interpretation.
4. Coordinate scheduling and facilitate movement of students among institutions offering limited programs.
5. Be constantly alert to overlapping and overlooking of services,

and encourage member institutions to take such action as seems indicated.

6. Promote in-service training of continuing education workers.
7. Facilitate cooperative projects and cooperative proposals for external funding whenever such joint endeavor is feasible.
8. Communicate and coordinate requests for external funding when these are more appropriately initiated by individual institutions.
9. Maintain liaison and mutually supportive relations with —
   a. Official agencies which have auxiliary education functions, such as health, rehabilitation, recreation, employment, law enforcement, social welfare, economic opportunity.
   b. Voluntary organizations which conduct organized programs, such as professional societies, industry, unions, ASTD and similar work-related groups; churches, YMCA, YWCA, K of C, B'nai B'rith, and similar faith-based groups; NAACP, Urban League, and similar human relations groups; League of Women Voters, child study, foreign policy, creative and performing arts, Great Books, and similar special interest groups.
   c. Community organizations with auxiliary education functions, such as labor council, health and safety council, council of churches, area development council, council on aging, community services council, PTA council, and Chamber of Commerce.
   d. Mass communications media.
   e. Other educational institutions, such as proprietary schools, correspondence schools, galleries, conservatories, museums.

While the primary membership of the Council should be composed of full-time administrators, and the principal initiative and responsibility for its work should reside with them, its meetings and activities should be open to the second circle of continuing education leaders — those who carry responsibility for auxiliary continuing education functions of private, voluntary, and public institutions. Each primary member should assume, for the Council, responsibility for continuing liaison with selected members of the second circle. In this way communication can be maintained both among full-time professional colleagues and with those voluntarily or partially engaged in continuing education.

The very essence of free community life is the voluntary participation of citizens in personal improvements and community development. In these voluntary efforts, as in the community-serving tasks of official agencies, continuing education is significantly and increasingly involved. If maximum progress is to be made and maximum good accomplished, the various agencies must be aware of each other and must become mutually supportive of their common purposes and responsible in their respective educating roles. The voluntary systematizing work of a Council of Continuing Education Administrators or of some similar instrumentality would do much to unify and enhance the total continuing education effort in a community. Each director of continuing education in a public school or community college has unique responsibility for initiating, enabling, and sustaining such unity in his community.

CHAPTER 4

THE EVOLVING ROLE
OF THE ADULT EDUCATION DIRECTOR

William S. Griffith

INTRODUCTION

The role of director of public school adult education has been evolving over the past century, and this process of growth and adaptation is certain to continue at an accelerating rate. In the future both the nature of the public school adult education program and the functions and responsibilities of directors will be modified by the interactions of three forces: (a) the demands and expectations of society, (b) the perception of adult education held by decision makers in the school systems, and (c) the models of an ideal program held by directors.

The major thesis of this chapter is that because the central force in shaping the evolving role is the director himself, the model he holds of an ideal total program of public school adult education is of critical importance in determining the nature of the shaping influence he will exert. If he sees the secondary school as the model for the adult school, then his decisions and his efforts to interpret the adult program to school personnel and to residents of his community will be guided by and will convey this ideal. On the other hand, if he views the adult school as an institution which should be developed along the lines of the Cooperative Extension Service, then this is the model which will be his frame of reference in making decisions and in interpreting the adult program to his school colleagues and to the residents of his community.

A director may, however, handle his routine duties without giving a thought to the kind of institution he is building. His decisions may be

William S. Griffith is assistant professor and chairman of the Adult Education Special Field Committee, Department of Education, University of Chicago, Chicago, Illinois. Special acknowledgment is made by the author to Mrs. Ann W. Fales, staff associate in adult education, University of Chicago, for her assistance in the writing of this chapter.

arrived at on an ad hoc basis with little thought given to the precedents he is establishing and to the implications of those decisions for the future development of the adult education program. Nevertheless, thoughtful directors' activities and decisions are guided by their influence in determining the future role of public school adult education directors. The models they have are of critical importance to the development of the field.

Influence is exerted by the director both by activity which he initiates and by his response to forces impinging on his program. Such forces arise in the broader society and in the context of the secondary school system. To guide his response to these forces a professionally oriented director must have both an ideal model of public school adult education toward which he is working and an historical perspective on both societal and school influence.

DEMANDS AND EXPECTATIONS OF SOCIETY

Historical Expectations

In the United States adult education has been regarded as a corrective activity which is justified on the basis of meeting some pressing societal need. When the nation was assimilating large numbers of immigrants in the nineteenth century, cities and states established adult education programs to assist in integrating these immigrants into the developing society. When there was a great concern about foreigners in the early years of the twentieth century, emphasis was placed on adult education to "Americanize" those individuals who had come from hostile foreign lands. When there was a national concern for the production of increased quantities of food and fiber, the Congress enacted the Smith-Lever Act establishing the agricultural extension service. When it was found that many of the young men taken into the armed forces during World War I were poorly prepared academically, vocationally, and technically, federal appropriations were forthcoming to support adult education. When there was a concern for the stability of our government during the high unemployment era of the Depression, funds were made available to support adult education so that trained teachers would have jobs and so that unemployed adults would develop an understanding of the political system in the United States and so that they would become committed to the practice of productive citizenship. When the defense industries prior to and during World War II hired large numbers of adults who had been previously unemployed, federal funds were forthcoming to support vocational education for national defense. When peace came and unemployment in certain regions and for certain groups became a national concern, programs were supported to improve the employability of adults receiving public welfare payments. Other programs were expanded to increase adult literacy as employers raised their employment entrance requirements in response to an oversupply of workers, for, as has been observed repeatedly, as employers' needs for additional employees decrease, the level of education they demand of persons seeking employment rises to the highest level which will yield the required number of workers — almost without regard to the level of education held by persons hired earlier who are performing identical jobs.

Contemporary Expectations

One of the effects of the civil rights movement has been to publicize the inadequacy of the primary and secondary education obtained by the members of some minority groups. Somewhat unrealistically, adult education has been singled out as the panacea for this problem.

Despite the absence of conclusive evidence to demonstrate the effectiveness of the efficiency of adult education programs designed to alleviate these problems, a national faith in the efficacy of adult education persists. Consequently, parts of all adult education programs established at earlier times persist, although the level of funding is not at the same rate as that provided for the more popular programs currently attracting national notice.

Urban unrest and civic irresponsibility now command the attention of the Congress and of some state legislatures. Quite likely, adult education will be seen as the instrument to solve these problems also, for frequently when more immediate and direct actions to deal with the causes of problems are not acceptable to lawmakers they turn to educational programs as the least disruptive and disturbing long-term approach. Increases in the allocation of funds have been observed to follow urban riots, and school systems have not been noted for their refusals to accept funds. Accordingly, urban public school adult education directors may anticipate being handed one more societal problem to work with until a viable solution can be developed either within the schools or as a result of changes in other parts of society.

DIRECTORS' EFFORTS TO INFLUENCE LEGISLATORS' EXPECTATIONS

There was in 1968 a reaffirmation of the legislative perception of the early 1900's and the 1930's, which is that certain adults need to learn for the good of society. Such periodic expressions of national concern produce bursts of program expansion and a concomitant increase in the demand for trained personnel which outstrips the supply of trained manpower.

If the Education Professions Act is a harbinger of a new awareness of the need for trained manpower, then perhaps the jerry-built programs portrayed as panaceas may be salvaged by academically prepared directors who will state realistic objectives and devise means appropriate for the attainment of such objectives. Major questions, however, are how long will political leaders be occupied with problems for which education appears to be a solution and how effective will adult educators be in expressing the need for the encouragement of professional development within the field of adult education?

Political leaders shape educational programs and decide educational priorities. Changes are made within adult education to accommodate the expectations and demands of political leaders, and too often adult educators follow rather than lead legislative activity on education. Congressman John Brademas, at the fiftieth annual convention of the National University Extension Association, stated that if Congress waited for educators to develop support for educational legislation, none of it would be passed. He observed further that the provision of funds for special educational programs by the Congress is effective in enabling educators to "rise above principle" — to develop interest in areas where previously they had denied that any need existed.

Although adult educators as a group appear reluctant to spend the time required to develop the political sophistication requisite to enable them to gain financial support for programs they believe are needed to meet their communities' needs for adult education, effective adult education administrators will have to do more than administer financially attractive programs developed by noneducators.

Practicing adult educators face a persistent perplexing problem. Various pressure groups in society compete with one another for the favors of the adult educator. Funds are provided, according to a feast or famine philosophy, to support adult educators who agree to perform miracles. Working in an institution in which there never seems to be enough income, a director is tempted to accept financial support to develop programs which may have little chance of succeeding. Telling an eager sponsor that the program he is so ready to support is unsound and unlikely to reach its objectives is not the way for a director to bring about the most rapid expansion of his program. On a long-term basis, however, a director must be concerned not only with the rate of growth but also he must be concerned with its soundness and permanence.

Accordingly, adult educators in a variety of organizations are becoming aware that legislative activity is a major force defining their role. The need for an increasingly effective dialogue between legislators and educators is evident, and there are growing indications that the leaders of organizations of adult educators are beginning to take their political responsibilities seriously. Political leaders will continue to exert a powerful influence on the redefinition of the adult director's role. Whether that influence is in the best long-term interest of adult education will be determined largely by the wisdom of adult educators, their ability to communicate their ideas to legislators, and their ability to muster support for proposed legislation embodying these ideas.

Lobbying may be seen as a glamorous activity beyond the resources of individual directors but within the scope of activities of their national organization. Yet, focusing efforts on legislators may be self-defeating unless such activity is coupled with systematic efforts to deal with the policy-making bodies and individuals in local school districts. School superintendents are key figures in the policy formulation process at the local level for they have the responsibility to identify areas of need, to inform board members of such needs, and to recommend appropriate policies for meeting those needs.

PERCEPTIONS AND EXPECTATIONS OF SECONDARY SCHOOL ADMINISTRATORS

The Influence of School Administrators

Several factors influence the superintendent's approach to adult education and the kind of structure he encourages to support the adult program. The size of the adult program budget in comparison to the total school budget will have some effect on his willingness to devote time to the consideration of the adult program. The kind of insights he brings to bear in his analysis of the adult program may reflect the emphasis placed on adult education in his academic preparation. Perhaps of even greater importance than either the budgetary significance of the adult program or the attitudes of the professors who taught him toward adult education is the stance taken toward adult programs by his fellow administrators. His attitude toward the adult program in his district is reflected in the status which he assigns to the director's role.

Adult Education in the Total School Program

An examination of the relative importance of adult education to the total educational program of a school district may be approached in many ways. For the purposes of this chapter attention will be given to the absolute numbers of adults involved, the amount of professional effort used in directing such programs, and the budgetary importance of the adult program.

In 1962 adult education classes in the public schools reached 1,740,-000 adults.[1] Several years earlier Olds reported that although the adult program in the public schools involved more than 80,500 teachers and 1,870 local administrative personnel, the cost of the program was 1.3 percent of the total public school expenditures.[2] Historically adult education has never been a major focus of public school activity, and even today its relative importance is rather small. Because the adult program has tended to be a financially insignificant part of school district budgets and because the programs have been run primarily by part-time directors, adult education remains a minor concern of school administrators. As late as 1961, only 7.2 percent of the school systems having an adult program employed full-time directors.[3] The most recent survey of public school adult education in school systems having 12,000 or more regularly enrolled day students indicated that 41.1 percent of the 338 districts having an adult program employed a full-time director.[4] Although in the majority of districts the position of director is seen as part-time, an encouraging percentage of districts have come to realize that a full-time director is needed.

Although 61.6 percent of a national sample of school superintendents believed that the public school should assume major responsibility for community adult education programs, 54.2 percent of the sample were offering adult education programs in their school districts.[5] A superintendent's assertion that an adult program is desirable in a public school is not necessarily an indication that such a program actually exists in his district.

Kempfer, in analyzing the status of adult programs, concluded that the superintendent is the pivotal person in the establishment of programs. Kempfer assumed that if the superintendent "believes deeply in lifelong learning and looks on the school as an institution serving community needs, an adult education program can thrive. If he thinks of adult education as an appendage to the essential work of the school, it is likely to remain only that."[6]

Perhaps the perceptions of superintendents regarding adult education and their part in redefining the role of the adult education director can be understood by an examination of the insights provided by professors of educational administration and by reviewing some of the efforts of various organizations to influence the perceptions of superintendents.

ADULT EDUCATION AS SEEN BY
EDUCATION PROFESSORS

That the insights of scholars in educational administration do little to make superintendents aware of adult education can be demonstrated by an examination of *The Changing American School*, the 1966 Yearbook of the National Society for the Study of Education. Neither of the terms *adult education* nor *continuing education* is listed in the index. In one of the concluding paragraphs of the book the following statement can be found indicating the extent to which the role of the changing school in adult education is perceived:

> The schools, aroused by the civil rights movement and prompted by presidential exhortation and congressional grants are bestirring themselves uncertainly and unevenly to help *all children and young people* learn whatever is necessary for entrance to and advancement in our highly organized technological society. The uncertainty arises from the meagerness of the knowledge regarding both the differential effects of various aspects of the environment in early childhood and later and the conditions essential to the efficacy of corrective measures. The unevenness and tardiness of the response are traceable to a host of factors, including in a few cases *blindness or indifference to the need* and in others a *misperception of the schools' responsibility.*[7]

The "unevenness and tardiness" of the response of school systems to the needs for adult education are due, at least in part, to the perceptions of professors of education and to their sensitivity to adult needs. Those who direct graduate programs for school administrators convey their perceptions of the schools' responsibility to their students. If the professors have not developed an awareness of the place of the public schools in adult education, then they will not convey a sense of need to those they seek to lead.

Yet even within the same yearbook there is evidence of an awareness of the need for continuing education. After examining the challenges facing teachers, Lee concluded that there is a growing acceptance of the principle that continuing education is essential for any teacher who is to remain competent.[8] Further, he asserted that educators are coming to realize that the designation "terminal education" is a contradiction of terms.[9]

Despite the slowly dawning realization on the part of some conventional schoolmen that education must be lifelong, the prevailing attitude seems to be that the function of formal education is to equip each student to engage in self-directed learning as an adult. By stressing the "learning to learn" aspect of secondary education, some public school men believe that they eliminate the need to have structured learning experiences for adults. Even though the professional improvement of teachers is viewed as an appropriate group activity using highly qualified resource people, those who advocate such improvement seem indifferent to the needs for the continuing education of adults, be they dropouts or high school graduates. Assisting teachers to learn is regarded as an appropriate activity for a school system, but for some reason assisting adults in their learning is regarded as an activity of little or no relevance to the work of the secondary school. Even though a great deal has been said and written concerning the changing public schools in America, educational leaders continue to envision changes within the restricting boundaries of a K-12 framework.

ADULT EDUCATION AS SEEN BY ADMINISTRATORS' ASSOCIATIONS

Despite the lack of study of adult education in most of the graduate programs designed to prepare school administrators, sensitive superintendents have developed an awareness of the need for adult education programs in their school districts. Through their national organizations school administrators have cooperated with the Council of Chief State School Officers, the National Congress of Parents and Teachers, and the National Association for Public School Adult Education in developing publications encouraging local school officials to accept the responsibility for giving leadership and support to adult education programs. [10] In these joint publications a plea is made for school administrators to provide professionally trained and competent leadership so that the adult programs may be professionally organized, skillfully led, and economically administered. In addressing the 1959 convention of the American Association of School Administrators, a state superintendent of public instruction emphasized the responsibility each local superintendent has to the adult program by saying, "The effectiveness of programs for adults in terms of their fundamental purposes will inevitably be in proportion to the quality of leadership *we* select and assign to them." [11]

The need for adult education programs in the public schools has also been recognized by the National Association of Secondary School Principals in its annual conventions. [12]

Administrators are also giving some attention to supporting services for adult education programs. Hoffman, writing in the *Bulletin* of the National Association of Secondary School Principals, asserted that if education is to continue throughout life, then counseling services which enable adults to select wisely from among the alternatives can add to the effectiveness of educational programs. He states further that particularly as educational programs are designed for the purpose of aiding school dropouts, those in charge of personnel services will find it necessary to assume an energetic and active role.[13] Such statements serve to redefine the adult director's role to include the provision and supervision of a counseling service.

ADULT EDUCATION AS SEEN BY ACCREDITING ASSOCIATIONS

Guidelines provided by accrediting associations may also serve to shape a superintendent's conception of the adult program and a director's role. Efforts are being made within accrediting agencies to modify criteria and standards to guide secondary schools in better serving adults' needs. One example of such efforts can be seen in the proposal of the Secondary Commission of the North Central Association of Secondary Schools and Colleges that a unit of credit in an adult high school shall be awarded for knowledge, skill, or competency equal to that required to earn credit in an equivalent course in a regularly accredited secondary school. Under this proposal credit by examination is endorsed. Other proposed criteria which promise to modify adult programs include "adequate counseling services" and "library facilities and privileges" for adult students.[14]

UNTAPPED SOURCES OF INFLUENCE

But there are still many school board members and superintendents who seem to have been unaffected by the national statements, cooperative publications, and guidelines. This apparent lack of interest in public school adult education on the part of a sizable number of superintendents and school board members may be attributed to the lack of information they have regarding the potential benefits of operating a broadly based adult education program. The director of the adult program is responsible for keeping his own superintendent and board members informed. One of the responsibilities of directors collectively through their local, state, and national organizations is continually to convey a clear impression of the potentials of public school adult education to all superintendents and board members, particularly those in school systems lacking an adult education program. Until superintendents and board members understand the situation they cannot make wise decisions.

The Canadian Adult Education Association has sought to enhance the role of the public school adult education director by developing special programs to acquaint school board members with the potential value of such adult school programs.[15,16,17] Members of boards of education are invited to adult education meetings, and parts of some annual conferences have been devoted to matters of immediate concern to such members. Unfortunately neither the National Association for Public School Adult Education nor the Adult Education Association of the U.S.A. has fully succeeded in developing successful school board member education programs building on the Canadian experience. Perhaps this untapped line of communication could be used advantageously in persuading superintendents of the value of adult education and in convincing them of the relative value of adult education to the rest of the school programs.[18]

ASCRIBED STATUS OF ADULT EDUCATION IN THE SCHOOLS

Local perceptions of the role of the adult program director may be determined in two ways. First, superintendents' and board members' views may be surveyed. This procedure would indicate the range of opinions and provide data which might be used to predict changes. Second, the views of superintendents and board members could be inferred from the current role of director. This approach is based on the assumption that the existing situation is the product of decisions made previously by the board and the superintendent.

Data are lacking to determine what image school superintendents and board members have of public school adult education directors and programs. Without accurate data to indicate these perceptions, efforts of directors — singly and in groups — aimed at educating superintendents and board members must be intuitive. A rigorous survey of the knowledge superintendents and board members have concerning adult education would seem to be a logical step in the formulation of any program intended to influence their perceptions.

Adult education researchers have given some attention to the role of adult directors in the public schools. Clark observed that the position of director of adult programs in California is transitory and that the directorship there serves as a proving ground for those who have aspirations of becoming principals or superintendents.[19]

In such a situation the post of director is inferior to that of a principal, a situation which may encourage ambitious directors to leave the field of adult education as a condition of promotion. The existence of a number of positions in the school hierarchy between the levels of director and superintendent makes it likely that the best directors will be drawn off to administrative posts.

London asserts that adult directors are not accorded status and salary comparable to that of persons directing elementary and secondary education. Such a situation may lead directors to regard their positions as stepping stones to other higher-paying and more prestigious positions within the school system.[20] Clark concurs, stating that "the long-term problem of adult school administrators is to achieve a 'peer' position." He feels that the adult administrators badly need a parity level, clearly defined and respected by all.[21]

Despite the complexity and the demands of the post of director of public school adult education, the majority of superintendents appear to believe that the job can be handled satisfactorily on the marginal energies of a day school faculty member who may be primarily interested in some other assignment. Adult program directors have varied occupational backgrounds but generally are employees within a school system before they are asked to assume responsibility for its adult program. London noted that in California directors are usually chosen from among those persons having experience both in teaching and in some administrative capacity at the secondary level. His examination of the backgrounds of public school adult education directors led him to conclude that appointment often seems unrelated to the de facto qualifications for administering an adult program.[22]

A survey of public school adult education directors in northern Illinois led to a similar conclusion: "Prior academic preparation in adult education is either not considered to be a prerequisite for becoming a director, or . . . even though candidates with such preparation may be sought by superintendents, the lack of persons with such training makes it impossible to restrict the list of potential directors to those who have had such experience."[23]

Because untested persons are seldom given the position, it is reasonable to assume that superintendents regard the post as one requiring mature leadership and seasoned judgment. This recruitment from within the staff of the secondary school may be dysfunctional in that the directors come to their post lacking clear models of adult education institutions and hence frequently attempt to use the secondary school as a model. These data suggest that the directorship of public school adult education may be approaching but has not yet acquired professional status.[24]

Accordingly it may be concluded that within school systems the adult education function is still emerging but has yet to become a standard feature of the total program. Statements of state superintendents, local superintendents, and organizations of school administrators indicate a growing awareness of the need for professionally prepared adult program directors. As school systems place increased emphasis on the academic preparation of men being considered for directorships, it seems reasonable to assume that a growing number of persons aspiring to become directors will be encouraged to pursue graduate study for their profession.

Even though 'the actions of legislators and the opinions of school superintendents constitute major forces shaping the evolving role of the adult director, it is the director himself who may be expected to exert the strongest influence.

PERFORMANCE, CHARACTERISTICS, AND PERCEPTIONS OF THE DIRECTOR

A consideration of the evolving role of the public school adult education director entails the examination of (a) the functions of a director, (b) the characteristics of those who are directors, and (c) the model of an ideal program which can be inferred from the descriptions of functions and characteristics.

The director of a public school adult education program has many of the same responsibilities as a school system superintendent. He must set up a curriculum; he must hire a teaching staff; he must determine the competence of prospective teachers; he must evaluate the adequacy of the instruction; he must see that financial records are maintained and, in most cases, that the budget is balanced; he must see that adequate records are developed and maintained; he must see that provisions are made for supplies and equipment he must see that registration is orderly and efficient; he must see that the physical plant is properly maintained; and he must provide for the necessary in-service training of his staff.

Directors of adult education programs face the entire gamut of problems confronting other school administrators, and, like other administrators, they frequently behave as though the measure of the importance of a problem is its immediacy. From a long-term perspective, however, the problem identification process may produce a different ordering of priorities. In discussing the problems in public school adult education with secondary school principals, Luke stated that "the greatest single problem standing in the way of increased educational opportunities for adults is not the lack of materials, finances, personnel, or facilities — significant as all these are — but the difficulty of involving many students in a learning activity."[25]

The central feature which distinguishes the director's work from that of other school administrators is that in secondary education a great many of the students attend because of legal compulsion or to gain admission to a college, and in adult education they must be persuaded to participate. This single feature makes it essential that the director maintain a different relationship to his students than that customarily associated with secondary education. The existence of an important difference between two programs is not, however, a reason for assuming that the responsibilities of secondary school principals and adult education directors are totally unlike. Accordingly, just as the role of school superintendent has evolved gradually over more than a century into what Willard Spalding has dubbed "an anxious profession,"[26] the role of the public school adult education director will continue on its own anxious path of development.

Directors' Academic Qualifications

As has been pointed out, school superintendents have evidently not placed great importance on the academic backgrounds of the men they employ as public school adult education directors.

In the Illinois survey 14 of the 48 directors reported having a master's degree in educational administration, and 13 reported a general master's degree in education. No other area of graduate study was of comparable importance among those surveyed.[27]

The position of the National Association for Public School Adult Education is quite clear in its statements regarding the academic preparation of directors:

> 1. An administrator of adult education should have a master's degree or its equivalent as recognized by the state or local school system.
> 2. An administrator of adult education should meet the requirements of general administrators and/or supervisors in the state or region concerned.
> 3. An administrator of adult education should have a minimum of six (6) hours of specialized study in the field of adult education.
> 4. An adult education administrator's professional preparation should include study in the area of liberal arts, human relations, and general education administration.[28]

The emphasis placed on the master's degree by NAPSAE is both practical and realistic at the present time. Slightly more than half of the directors surveyed in Illinois reported having taken one or more courses in adult education. Nearly half reported no academic work in adult education, but this may well reflect a lack of opportunity to take such course work rather than a lack of interest. Appropriately, the Association endorses such training and encourages colleges and universities to accept the responsibility of offering course work in this area.

Directors' Academic Aspirations

Although a director's academic background is of some importance, it may be of less significance in revealing his attitude than his academic and career aspirations. Even though few of the directors in the Illinois survey had had an appreciable amount of academic training in adult education, the group as a whole apparently did not regard such study as particularly desirable. Even though one-third of the directors expressed an interest in pursuing graduate study in adult education, more than half of those indicating an interest in graduate study identified other areas of primary concern.[29] Although this study involved only directors in northern Illinois and the findings may only be applied with certainty to that group, there were no apparent reasons for considering the group studied as atypical of directors nationally.

The apparent lack of wholesale enthusiasm for pursuing academic study in adult education may be explained in several ways. First, some directors may not be aware of the existence of appropriate graduate programs. Second, some directors may feel that the courses which are taught would be irrelevant to the practical administration of a public school adult education program. Third, directors may regard their positions as stopping points on the way to a career goal in primary or secondary school administration, and in either case their academic concerns would more likely be associated with the demands of the desired position than those associated with the current position. Fourth, directors may believe (with some justification) that a typical school system rewards those who accumulate academic credits and degrees without reference to the relevance of those credits, in which case the way to better one's financial circumstances is to acquire the required number of credit hours in the easiest way. Fifth, some directors may be complacent about their adult programs and their personal performance. Sixth, a part-time director may not regard his adult education assignment as one which could develop into a full-time job, and he may therefore conclude that his personal investment in continuing education should most appropriately be made in an area offering full-time employment. This last factor may be a crucial one.

However, one indication of developing professionalism in the field of adult education is the number of students enrolled in graduate programs in adult education and a comparison of that figure with the estimated number of persons now holding a doctorate in the field. In a survey of graduate adult education programs, Ingham reported 1,077 full- or part-time students in the 1967 fall term. [30] This figure includes both those working toward the doctorate and those engaged in master's degree programs. Currently approximately 600 persons have earned doctorates in the field, a figure which indicates the relative newness of the profession because the number of persons now seeking doctorates exceeds the number of individuals already holding such degrees. Accordingly it seems reasonable to predict that the adult program director's role will become more professional as more graduate students in the field become public school adult education directors.

Directors' Career Aspirations

The directors' career interests in the Illinois survey were apparently related to the proportion of their time spent on the adult program. Those men who were spending less than 40 percent of their time in directing the adult program did not see adult education as a career possibility, whereas more than half of those spending more than 40 percent of their time in such work anticipated remaining in adult education.[31] In using financial support from the Fund for Adult Education to underwrite the salaries of full-time directors, the National Association for Public School Adult Education demonstrated the conviction of practicing adult educators that full-time personnel are essential.

So long as directors' positions are held primarily by individuals who seek to be promoted out of their adult education responsibilities, the existence of a professional role in public school adult education will be questioned. Established professionals may move from one institutional setting to another without changing the nature of their expertise. Often professionals move from one employing institution to another as a means of improving their status or working conditions while retaining their areas of specialization. School superintendents frequently move to larger school districts as a means of securing better working conditions without changing their profession. As superintendents come to accept the role of the director of the adult program as a specialized one and not merely a rung in the administrative ladder, they will increasingly hire directors who have the appropriate academic training and perhaps experience in directing an adult program in a smaller district. Also as an increasing number of directors earn their graduate degrees in adult education they will be likely to regard their work as a profession and will regard movement among institutions but within the same professional sphere as more desirable than movement within a school district requiring the abandonment of the area of specialization. Interdistrict movement of specialized professionals is certain to increase, and with it will come an increased acceptance of the profession of adult education director. In the Illinois survey, 3 directors of a total of 44 reporting had moved from a smaller to a larger program. On the other hand, at least three-fourths of those directors who expected to be in the labor force in 10 years had not considered the possibility of securing a promotion through a move to another school district having greater professional opportunities in adult education. Further, only 24.3 percent planned to continue working in adult education while 40.9 percent indicated an interest in school administration outside adult education.[32] A similar situation may exist nationally.

Therefore, on the basis of the number of trained personnel needed, the capacity of existing graduate programs, and indications of the expressed academic aspirations of those who are now directors, it is evident that in the next decade, at least, the administration of many programs of adult education in our public schools will be handled by persons who have not been trained in adult education, who do not have career expectations in the field, and who regard a move out of adult education as a promotion. The view is often expressed that the most important single step which could be taken to improve public school adult education would be to make all directorships career posts. It seems inappropriate at this time, however, to convert all directorships immediately to full-time career posts for such a change might well discourage aspiring administrators from trying their talents at administering an adult program temporarily. Until there is an adequate supply of academically prepared administrators available there will continue to be a number of desirable consequences of the movement of aspiring administrators through the post of director. The aspiring administrator who views the adult education directorship as a means of increasing his visibility and of demonstrating his administrative competence may well be highly motivated to do an outstanding job. The aspiring administrator will find ways of modifying the existing program conspicuously. A director who aspires to the superintendency is also likely to be concerned with community interests. Finally, the experience in and understanding of adult education gained by the administrator on the way up may tend to make him more sensitive to the needs and values of adult education than an administrator lacking such background.

In summary, it would be a serious mistake to conclude that directors of adult programs should never be promoted out of their area of specialization. One of the explanations for the growing acceptance of public school adult education by the professional organizations of school administration is the steady infiltration of the ranks of superintendents by former adult program directors who carried with them a professional feeling for adult education. And it is only natural for alert school board members who observe the outstanding adult program directors working effectively with all elements of their communities to offer such directors the post of superintendent.

EMERGING COMMUNITY COLLEGES FOSTER
PROFESSIONALIZATION

Emerging community colleges also favor the increasing profession-alization of the adult director's role. Because such colleges are es-tablished to provide adult education as well as career and college transfer programs, special faculty members must be hired to direct the adult program. It is only natural for presidents of community colleges to look to the ranks of successful public school adult education direc-tors in their recruiting efforts. The growing number of adult program directorships in community colleges provides an avenue of advance-ment for public school adult education directors which does not re-quire them to abandon their area of specialization. Hence, the develop-ment of community college adult education programs will favor the redefinition of the public school adult educator's role as a professional one.

APPROACHES TO DEFINING THE DIRECTOR'S ROLE

Certain problems can be identified in the growing professionalization of the role of the public school adult education director, particularly in the tendency of the adult program to be cast in the mold of the secondary program. Any search for a single "best" model equally ap-propriate for all settings can lead into a blind alley. A more viable approach appears to include a consideration of certain essential ele-ments, creative emulation of successful models, and continuing efforts to adjust the definition.

The Inappropriate Model Problem

Adult education within the public schools is evolving, and a new kind of adult education administrator is emerging in the process. His-torically, programs of adult education have been slow to reach their fullest development largely because few persons saw the administra-tion of such a program as their career goal, and few superintendents or principals believed that education for adults was anything more than a minor diversion from the school system's central task of educat-ing children and youth. But even in those school systems in which the adult program has been regarded as an essential function and in which full-time directors have been employed, the pace of develop-ment has been seriously hindered by the unfortunate tendency of directors to regard themselves as administrators of secondary school systems and to construct an adult education institution on the inappropriate model of the secondary school. It is unlikely that the programs of public school adult education will reach their fullest development unless the shaping of the enlarging and evolving role of the adult program administrator is regarded as an individual and a collective responsibility of those who see public school adult education in terms of the characteristics of adult education institutions.

Undoubtedly the most common criticism lodged against the adult director is that he fails to realize that he is not simply running an extended day program for overage secondary students. Critics have noted the inappropriate application of the K-12 pattern in the adult setting. In a recent survey of adult basic education programs in 10 states the following conclusion was reached:

> One of the pivotal problems of the ABE (Adult Basic Education) program is its failure to develop a unique professional identity outside the formal public school system. Instead, it has merely imitated that system. In its policy, its organization and administration, its instructional methods and materials, and even in its setting, the typical ABE program is curiously modeled after the child-centered public school. Like children in the public school system, adults have little to say in the educational decisions made by the program administration.[33]

If adult education in the public schools is to be designed specifically for adults, then certain special features must be built into the program together with appropriate supporting services.

Essential Considerations in Designing an Adult Program

A cardinal feature of a logical model of an adult program would be a structure which would permit the adults to express their interests, desires, and opinions regarding actual, proposed, and possible programs. An advisory committee could serve this function. The Illinois survey indicated that the use of advisory committees is rare either in programs of full-time or part-time directors.[34] Because of the lack of time which the part-time director has for running the adult program, it would be reasonable to assume that he would be reluctant to use advisory committees to the extent he believes his involvement with a committee would reduce the speed with which decisions could be made. Also, the lack of experience with advisory committees within the secondary school context would not have prepared an adult director to consider their advantages.

Yet, if he regards an advisory committee as a means of reaching better decisions that he could reach alone; if he regards an advisory committee as an efficient and effective means of securing information on community needs and interests; if he regards the work of committee members as enlarging the number of man-hours which can be devoted to program development, evaluation, and modification; if he sees the advisory committee as a means of publicly securing the support of key citizens; if he views an advisory committee as a vehicle for obtaining contributed advice from professional persons in his community; and if he perceives his work with the advisory committee as both a teaching and a learning opportunity, then he would likely be quite enthusiastic concerning the establishment and utilization of an advisory committee.

Nevertheless, operationally, the question facing the director is not, "Is an advisory committee desirable or undesirable?" Instead, his question is, "Considering my own ability and experience in working with committees, will the time I invest in establishing and working with an advisory committee be likely to produce as much desirable change in my program as would be likely to result from my investing an equal amount of time in some other aspect of the program?" Such a question takes on added importance as administrators seek to shape and mold their enlarging role. *To the extent that the program is built on adult education models the use of advisory committees may be expected to increase.*

Adults are willing to work on those projects, ideas, or causes in which they believe. Accordingly, institutions such as the YMCA have found it possible to engage sizable numbers of adults as volunteers, but within primary and secondary schools volunteers have not generally been utilized. New federally financed programs are causing some public school administrators to reconsider their notions about the use of volunteers, and there are indications that the school systems are beginning to learn to capitalize on volunteer services. *Adult programs which adhere closely to the primary and secondary school model fail to realize that adults will volunteer and that through the effective use of such services adult programs may be improved.* The role of the director as a coordinator of volunteer efforts is developing.

An increasing number of directors are taking a fresh look at their evolving role as educational leaders. Some are establishing *adequate library services* to meet adult learning needs though nearly three-fourths of the programs surveyed in Illinois revealed no provision had been made for adult library use.[35] Others are working to develop *counseling services* to enable adults to take best advantage of the learning opportunities open to them in terms of their own goals though some directors may still regard a counseling service as an unnecessary frill and would choose instead to show a net profit at the end of the fiscal year. *Still other directors have managed to free themselves from the restricting notion that adult education programs must only take place on property controlled by the board of education. And at some points serious attention is being paid to the need for market research to determine the adequacy of various methods of presenting the adult program to the community it is intended to serve.*

The Need for a Model

As directors test new approaches to conducting their own programs and to cooperating with adult program directors in other institutions, they do so in terms of some conception they have of an ideal program and the appropriate role of a director. Implicit in the planning and administrative activity of the adult education director is this notion of an ideal.

The director's ideal model, implicitly or explicitly, constitutes a plan which directs development. Although this plan is an image in the mind of the director, that model gives him a basis on which to judge the possible alternatives facing his program. And as the director strives to realize his vision, he draws on his environment—school district, state, and nation—to obtain those resources which lead toward the ideal, and he rejects those which would move his program in less desirable patterns.

Efforts To Describe an Ideal Model

The director who desires to improve himself and his program is interested in learning what characterizes a good administrator and what constitutes a good program. Numerous writers have dealt with the art and science of administration, and lists of traits of effective leaders abound in the literature. Unfortunately, the attempts at describing the effective administrator have not produced an empirically tested statement of the precise combination of knowledge, ability, and viewpoint which distinguishes successful from unsuccessful administrators.[36] Neither do the pronouncements of authorities in the field of administration provide a consistent inventory. In examining the kinds of insights which might be useful to a practicing administrator, Gordon suggested that an appropriate academic base could be drawn from several disciplines by—

> taking from psychology . . . an understanding of individual needs, motivation, learning and the like. From social psychology one may incorporate an understanding of interaction among individuals and groups, the factors that affect leadership and the psychological aspects of communications in the group setting. From sociology, one may draw an understanding of the ways in which organizations, including those not shown on the official charts, actually form and institutionalize; and the ways in which social systems

and measures of social distance develop. The insights of the anthropologist lead to the recognition that each organization actually operates in a cultural context and that some organizations more than others develop subcultures of their own. Increasingly, the analysis of organizational behavior is further enriched by concepts of political science. These apply in the study of power, interest groups, influence, representation and bureaucracy as they operate in diverse organizations. [37]

In studying the most useful kind of educational background for administrators, Gordon concluded that the insights to be gained from the social sciences are of practical value. Rather than focusing on something called administration, Gordon emphasized the kinds of understandings which administrators need to deal with the complex problems confronting them.

Sophisticated students of administration no longer ask, "What kind of administrator is best?" Instead research and study now deal with the more specific, "When a given type of administrator is placed in a given situation, on what dimensions is he likely to demonstrate what strengths and weaknesses, as judged by a given set of raters or data analyses?" [38]

The latter approach recognizes the complexities of the administrator's functions and the importance of interpersonal relationships in determining effectiveness. Acceptance of the idea that a galaxy of variables is involved in determining effectiveness in any situation is equivalent to abandonment of the notion that any exclusive constellation of qualities and competencies can be used to identify the "best" director.

Efforts to describe the successful administrator have not been limited to the trait approach. A considerable amount of effort has also been expended in making lists of the functions to be performed. Such listings are readily available for public school adult education. The 1956 edition of *Public School Adult Education, A Guide for Administrators and Teachers* and the 1963 revision each contain a 70-item checklist of practices in the administration of public school adult education covering (a) philosophy, (b) programing, (c) flexibility and policy, (d) finance and budget, (e) publicity and recruiting, (f) supervision, (g) in-service training, (h) guidance and evaluation, and (i) exchange of services. [39] A more recent listing of experience-based guidelines of public school adult education administration can be found in the 1967 NAPSAE *Almanac*. This listing, prepared by the Committee on Evaluation and Professional Standards, covers (a) educational preparation, (b) educational experience, (c) educational leadership, (d) administrative-supervisory competencies, and (e) institutional relationships. [40] Although no carefully controlled studies are cited to justify the "standards," they appear reasonable and furthermore any director who carried out all of the suggestions would likely be regarded as more effective than one who did not. A director who earnestly seeks to improve his program and his own performance would do well to consult such guidelines for, although in themselves they do not constitute a formula guaranteed to produce success, they can be useful in helping a director analyze aspects of his program which he has taken for granted.

Directors' Orientations to Role Definition

Nevertheless, there may be a way of characterizing directors which is particularly appropriate for the present stage of development of the profession. Lipham has identified two diametrically opposed orientations of men who are placed in positions of authority in organizations. One orientation is essentially administrative, that is, tending to focus on the direction of the existing structure and established procedures for attaining previously determined goals.[41] The second orientation is that of a leader and calls for the initiation of a new structure or new procedures for accomplishing an organization's objectives or for changing those objectives.[42] In this framework "the administrator is concerned primarily with maintaining, rather than changing, established structures, procedures or goals. Thus, the administrator may be viewed as a stabilizing force."[43] In contrast, "the leader is concerned with initiating changes in established structures, procedures, or goals; he is disruptive of the existing state of affairs."[44]

This leader-administrator dichotomy may be useful in emphasizing the influence of directors in redefining their roles. Insofar as the director sees himself purely as an "administrator," he will be a force for tradition and stability, and he will follow the lead of others reluctantly as they redefine his role. To the extent that a director sees himself as a "leader," he will direct his creative energies to examining and modifying the organization's objectives and to changing the structure and procedures to facilitate attainment of the new objectives. The administrator will concentrate on the efficient operation of the existing organization, and the leader will experiment with advisory committees, volunteers, community needs surveys, library facilities, counseling services, in-service training for teachers, market research, and collaborative arrangements with other organizations in his community.

If the assumption is sound that no ideal model of public school adult education can be developed to fit all situations, then the approach which is most appropriate for an adult director is that of a leader. His responsibility is to synthesize a conception of an ideal program that takes into consideration the unique aspects of his local situation.

Approaches to Model Building

A director may attempt to develop his ideal conception of a public school adult education program by borrowing heavily from the example set by an adult education program based outside of the public schools. Because of the remarkable growth of the community college movement with its emphasis on adult education, this institution provides an example of adult program development with particular relevance to adult directors in the public schools.

The Community College Example

A survey of 99 junior colleges claiming community service as a major function identified the following program objectives: (a) to make institutional facilities available as a center for community life when such use does not interfere with the institution's curricular and extracurricular programs; (b) to make faculty skills available to assist district groups in problem solving; (c) to encourage the profitable use of leisure time by promoting cultural, intellectual, and social activities; and (d) to interpret the institution to its community and to gain the interest, participation, and support of its citizens.[45]

These broadly interpreted objectives of community services have been drawn from two models—"the community school concept in the public schools, and the community development concepts in the four year institutions of higher education."[46] The central ideas undergirding the community service concept are that "citizens actually participate in the planning, maintenance, and the evaluation of the program; and the college, recognizing that it must be of the community and not just in it, participates in community life."[47] This orientation to its responsibilities and relationships leads Edmund J. Gleazer, Jr., executive director of the American Association of Junior Colleges, to predict that "the community college may well become the center for continuing education in its area."[48]

Because of their newness, the community colleges currently constitute the most likely agency for innovative program development in adult education. General extension divisions of the four-year colleges are already well established and are likely to follow the precedents set in 75 years of operation. Public school adult education has also been rendering service in a fairly consistent pattern for many years. Of these three kinds of institutions the community colleges are increasing at the most rapid rate. Partly as a consequence of their mushroom-like development these colleges are hiring adult education directors sufficiently inexperienced that they have not yet learned what "can't be done" and so may successfully attempt to develop programs which others who have tried the ideas unsuccessfully earlier would be unlikely to risk.

The director of an adult education program in a new community college may approach his task in several ways. He may ignore existing programs of other agencies and devise his own on the basis of his pre-conceptions of what would be best for the community or of what the community or state would be willing to pay for. A second approach would entail the methodical surveying of the formal adult learning opportunities in his community. Then, based on this knowledge of what is available he would plan programs to complement rather than to duplicate or to compete with existing institutional offerings. Yet a third approach calls for the director to examine not only what learning opportunities exist, but also to determine who is providing the leader-ship for each program, what programs are being developed by these leaders, and then to establish a structure for facilitating collaboration among directors.

The third approach seems to be the soundest one, particularly since categorical state or federal support programs tend to confuse rather than to facilitate interinstitutional cooperation.

Some directors may conclude that the community college approach to adult education is equally appropriate for the public schools. Cer-tainly the public school adult education director who must accommo-date his program to an emerging community college in his vicinity will find it advantageous to understand, not to adopt, the model guiding the development of the college program. Whether the intention is to com-pete or to cooperate, the adult program directors will be better prepared to pursue their objectives to the extent they are aware of each other's conceptions of an ideal program. And if it is possible to develop an ideal model for a particular institution, that condition in itself argues against the model's being appropriate for another setting and more particularly for a different kind of institution.

The Eclectic Approach

Various avenues are open to directors who are concerned about de-veloping an ideal program model toward which they may work. These avenues differ in the demands they place on the director, and possibly not all directors should be attempting every one of them. Underlying each of them, however, is a common provision for dealing with a changing environment.

The most demanding avenue is through participation in a graduate degree program in adult education. Because of the scarcity of graduate adult education programs and the large number of directors now working in the field, it seems unreasonable to assume that many of those currently working as directors will select this alternative.

A second approach to learning about alternative models of adult programs is through participation as an adult student. Labor unions, civil rights organizations, libraries, YMCA's, churches, art museums, voluntary agencies, settlement houses, residential schools, and the Cooperative Extension Service all conduct adult education programs. Although no other institution has a program ideally suited to a specific public school situation, a director who takes the time to observe one or more of these programs will undoubtedly acquire new conceptions of the nature of an ideal program.

A third way a director may gain new perspectives on the effective organization and operation of a public school adult education program is through conversations with staff members of his chief state school office. If the state staff in adult education is made up exclusively of people who are only familiar with the public schools, then directors of local programs are not likely to gain new ideas of adult education organization from them. Accordingly, it seems wise for each state to employ persons who have a broad grasp of adult education. Those state school officers who understand the organization models of a variety of adult education agencies should be able to assist local directors in developing a broader conception of aspects of organization and administration than might be expected from state officers having association with a single institution.

A fourth and perhaps the most promising avenue a director may take to gain new conceptions of an ideal program is through his association with other adult educators. Associating with other public school adult educators may stimulate the directors of the weaker programs to emulate the stronger ones. However, if professional association and discussion are restricted to those who work in the public school context, the sharing of ideas is less likely to reveal highly divergent methodologies than would conversations among adult educators from a variety of institutions. A dilemma faces the busy director who sees many organizations inviting his participation. The more restricted the area embraced by the professional specialization of the members of an association, the easier it is for the members to find common grounds for communicating, but the more homogeneous the group, the less likely the members are to formulate new approaches to problems. Consequently, for maximum professional growth, a director must maintain active relationships with other public school educators locally, regionally, and nationally; and he must also associate with adult educators from other institutional contexts as a means of gaining new insights into ways of approaching practical problems. Such affiliation, coupled with the reading of the organizations' newsletters and journals, helps keep a director informed on developments in his own institutional context and tells him about innovative approaches wherever they are being tried.

By following one or more of these four methods a director can learn about various program models and professional roles. His own professional responsibility is to select wisely from among them in building an ideal model for his role and his institutional program.

SUMMARY

The role of director of public school adult education has been evolving for more than a century, and the process will continue. Some legislative leaders will continue to see adult education as a panacea for social ills, and they will provide financial support in increasing quantities for public education programs which promise to alleviate those ills.

School superintendents and board members are showing an increasing awareness of and commitment to adult education. Recognizing a need for new programs, they are showing a growing acceptance of the necessity of employing well trained men. With this acceptance of the responsibility for providing adequate leadership there comes a concomitant realization that a whole range of supportive services is called for, each item of which makes some contribution to a redefinition of the adult program director's role.

Adult program directors, because they stand to gain or to lose more than any other group, demonstrate an active concern in the redefinition of their role. By their efforts to set academic standards for their profession; by their development of criteria to judge the adequacy of programs; by their growing commitment to adult education as a profession rather than a stepping-stone; by their willingness to try new approaches; by their acceptance of the posture of a leader rather than simply a manager; by their efforts to overcome any parochial single-institutional viewpoint; by their acceptance of responsibility for influencing the drafting, passage, and interpretation of adult education legislation; and by their eagerness to work with adult educators from a variety of institutions, they have shown that they intend to play a major part in the redefinition.

In the last third of the twentieth century the evolution of the adult director's role will accelerate. More than ever before resources are being made available to adult education leaders who have visions of new and increasingly effective institutional forms and programs. The opportunities for professional adult educators have never been brighter. Only time will tell if adult directors have been equal to the challenge.

CHAPTER 5

FINANCE AND BUDGET DEVELOPMENT

William J. Johnston

INTRODUCTION

Previous chapters have established the perspective of adult education in relation to its growth and development, to its community and to other segments of the educational hierarchy, and to its expanding future of service for individuals and for society. All these significant areas are measured and evaluated annually in terms of a budget cycle process. The annual adoption of a budget for adult and continuing education programs by a board of education clearly establishes the priority of the program within the school district and the extent of its services for the succeeding school year.

Much has been said about the advent of a population of 200 million people in the United States, the dramatic increase in technology and related needs for trained personnel, the mobility of people, the impact of the urban community, the inflation of the economy, and the need for continuing education. All of these issues and concerns call for increased emphasis on the capabilities of the educational enterprise; all of these efforts to meet individual, community, and national needs require monetary support. There is, on the one hand, a more urgent need for adult education, and, on the other, a more severe competition for tax funds.

It is increasingly apparent that special tax sources must be found for adult and continuing education alone. The enrollment growth of schools

William J. Johnston is assistant superintendent, Division of Adult Education, Los Angeles City Schools, Los Angeles, California. Special acknowledgment is made by the author to Watson Dickerman, professor of adult education (retired), UCLA, and to the staff of the Budget Division and the Division of Adult Education of the Los Angeles City Schools for their assistance in the writing of this chapter.

for youth; the importance of reducing secondary and elementary school class size; the need for special services including additional counseling time, physical and health program requirements; the importance of community relations staff for parent involvement; and the need for new classrooms have, in many instances, curtailed the funds available for adult education. Indeed, in order to establish the relative value of education programs, community tax-conscious groups, chambers of commerce, and concerned citizens are seeking ways of determining the actual measurable success of specific educational efforts in terms of the money allocated and expended. In such a financial environment, the purposes, priorities, and possibilities of adult education are often handicapped, yet it is in such an environment of concern and expectation that adult education has suggested solutions. The public will support programs which promise and deliver accountable solutions to the problem of matching men with the most imperative needs of an ever-changing society.

FINANCIAL SUPPORT FOR ADULT EDUCATION

Traditionally, public school adult education has derived its funds from local property taxes, state and federal aid, and by student fees. "Over the past decade, state-local revenues for public education have, in the aggregate, remained at about a 40-60 ratio, while the federal government's share has grown recently from 5 to 15 percent of the total public spending for education."[1]

The national funds allocated for adult and continuing education programs have remained at approximately 1 percent of the respective total district budget. It is the exception to find as much as 2 percent of a school district's budget allocated for continuing education programs.

Tax Sources

Adult education needs a dependable tax source as does every worthy public agency. The local property tax would be ideal if it were not so overcrowded with competitors who have pushed the tax rate above reasonable ceilings. Because of this, adult education must look elsewhere for at least part of its income. State and federal sources seem indicated, especially federal sources which are fortunately increasing, but it may be wise and necessary to seek other new sources. If adult education continues to grow in its capacity to provide trained workers, it is not illogical that industry should support adult education directly, perhaps through the unemployment tax or some similar device. As adult education grows, so must its income.

Local tax. The property tax has always been the avenue most generally utilized to provide for an educational program. But, because of its availability to other governmental agencies, it also provides for water, power, health, sanitation, roads and highways, public buildings, police and fire protection, and diverse other items. It has been described as "highly inequitable, regressive, distorting,"[2] but it does give the local taxing authority the necessary autonomy to provide the particular service or program desired.

With these many agencies competing for the property-tax dollar, the case for adult education must be particularly clear, concise, and meaningful if it is to obtain a fair share of available funds. In California (Education Code Section 20802.8), a 10-cent statutory tax, equal in status with elementary, secondary, and junior college programs, may be levied to provide for the expenses of classes for adults.

State aid. The availability of state support for adult and continuing education programs is critical to the encouragement and development of comprehensive programs. The stimulation of state funds has proven to be the critical component in the activation of successful efforts to provide educational opportunities for adults.

The percentage or ratio of state support for adult education should not be less than that offered for elementary and secondary levels of education.

The allocation of state funds to adult education is based on attendance records which provide "name of the school, the date and time of the class, the name of the class and teacher, the student's name and address, and the date of enrollment."[3] Generally, attendance is recorded in clock hours. Several innovations have been developed which allow use of a "census" week procedure for claiming state apportionments. This procedure is simply an acceptable formula which closely approximates results derived from previous statistical reports. "The formula is a ratio of possible attendance compared to actual attendance in a class or program."[4]

Such a formula is based on the enrollment at a given date, multiplied by the number of hours scheduled for respective students, and compared with the actual experience of previous years. It is termed a full-time equivalent (FTE) formula for computing average daily attendance for apportionment purposes.

An excellent summary of state support for adult education is found in the NAPSAE *Public School Adult Education 1968 Almanac.*[5] The report indicates that 21 of the states provide state funds through foundation programs or other general state support. In the main, these are restricted to courses which are educational rather than recreational.

Approximately 35 states, however, allow funds based on varying formulas for specific annual or biennial appropriations for nonvocational adult education. Adult basic education programs are largely funded in this manner.

Federal support. Adult education has been continuously supported by federal enactments for many decades.[6] Legislation from the Smith-Hughes Act (1917) to the George Barden Act (1946) and the important Vocational Education Act (1963) has signaled the particular emphasis of federal support for adult vocational education.

Federal support has served primarily as either "seed" money (such as the Elementary and Secondary Education Act, Title III; National Defense Education Act, Title III A and Title V grants renewable for three years) or for continuing categorical grants. The Adult Basic Education Act (1966) is an example of the latter.

The most difficult aspects of utilizing federal funds are the staff time required to develop proposals which may or may not be approved and the emergencies and delays encountered with subsequent funding approvals. Most directors of adult education support the need for such state plans as that for adult basic education, whereby federal funds are channeled through the state department of education. However, many directors have utilized state plans only to encounter direct funding by a governmental department to an unknown community group or private enterprise.

A joint study of the impact of federal funding on local programs by the California Association of School Administrators resulted in the recommendations listed below. They are general in nature and are "intended to serve as guidelines for all categorical grant programs."[7]

1. Federal funds should be allocated to state departments of education and distributed to local schools by them in accordance with state plans.
2. Federal funds should be generally predictable for year-to-year planning. This means long-term funding.
3. Federal programs should provide a fixed percentage for administrative costs and overhead.
4. All new federal programs should provide a minimum of six months' planning and development time.
5. The present practice of submitting short-term competitive project applications should be de-emphasized and a major portion of categorical grants should be placed on a long-term program basis.
6. All federal programs related to the public school should be channeled through the U. S. Office of Education.

7. All programs should continue to be subject to audit, systematically evaluated, and annually reported.

Student fees. Adult educators have taken the position that free public adult education is consistent with the principles of a democracy and with the economic facts of life. Those in the greatest need of training or retraining are obviously those who can least afford an additional tax or tuition fee. Brunner states we are "educating the educated." [8] We are creating a society which finds that those profiting from education are seeking more of it; those experiencing failure in the education process are attempting to live without its nourishment. They are listed on welfare and unemployment rolls. Kempfer states that "the effect of charging fees is seen to make it more difficult to reach adults in the lower economic and educational levels, continuing to hamper the exercise of the basic mission: to help make citizens more self-reliant." [9]

The most significant adult education effort ever conceived was the GI Bill of Rights. It is reported that 7,800,000 World War II and Korean War veterans have taken advantage of the educational provisions of that act. The Veterans Administration has stated, "As a result, they raised their income level to the point where they are expected to repay, through taxes, two and one-half times during their lifetime, the 14.5 billion dollars the program cost." [10]

All are aware of the statistics which support average lifetime incomes as correlated with education attainment. Fees and tuition charges curtail the desired participation of many citizens. Those who cannot afford such charges are not included in civic discussions favoring community development. The effect of the total adult education program in the community is minimized.

Views of School Superintendents on Financial Support

The National Education Association conducted a poll of school superintendents for their opinions on various aspects of adult education. [11] School superintendents without programs of adult education generally state a higher interest in the use of tuition fees than school superintendents of large school districts which offer sizable adult education programs. It is encouraging to note that superintendents with ongoing adult education programs realize the value of such programs for individual and community development.

Views of NAPSAE on Financial Support

The NAPSAE point of view with regard to free public adult education was fully presented in the 1963 *Guide for Administrators*[12] and notes that as adult education programs become more diversified and community-service oriented it is difficult—if not impossible—to administer a fee-charging program. According to Robert A. Luke, executive secretary of NAPSAE, "The adult educational service program of the school must be adequately supported and staffed out of public funds if it is to do all that is required of it."

BUDGET DEVELOPMENT

Climate for Adult Education

Each adult education administrator operates within a unique set of budget variables and circumstances. As he prepares his materials for the annual budgeting process, he must weigh the various factors affecting the adult education program within the total community environment it serves. It is said that "the improper conception of educational finance necessitates joint consideration of expenditures and revenues."[13] This is particularly true for the public school adult education administrator.

In order properly to effect a successful program, a process of continuous communication must exist among the school superintendent, the board of education, the local chamber of commerce, taxpayer organizations, interested community agencies and organizations such as the PTA and the League of Women Voters, the press and television media, and the adult education administrative staff. Bell asks, "How can public recognition of the value of adult education be developed within the respective constituencies sufficiently to evoke responsible action?"[14] This urgent consideration requires a communication process of respect, purpose, and responsibility. Local conditions will call for a particular program of adult education; those responsible for financing such a program will be more likely to lend their support if they are aware of all conditions, the immediate implications of these conditions on the individuals involved, and the long-range benefits to the community.

Only when a realistic understanding of what adult education is and only when specific values and case histories are documented to the community can the adult administrator expect success during the budget process.

Procedural Suggestions

Each school district has developed and continuously modifies its own characteristic budgeting process. The following suggests one way to meet the normal considerations encountered in the identification and preparation of a budget for new and continuing programs. The budget should be developed with these following considerations in mind:

1. Supportive programs of other educational divisions
2. Continuing adult education programs including a growth factor
3. Required additions to the continuing program
4. Unlimited requests in priority order
5. Other considerations.

Usually, these factors are considered, analyzed, and documented during the fall semester of the school year in order to begin formal budget discussions in January with final adoption expected in August. A successful budget is dependent on the involvement of building principals, teachers, local continuing education associations, subject area coordinators, and classified employees and respective organizations.

Other divisions. Because of time factors, the first consideration should be those requests of other educational divisions for supportive programs. Memorandums should be addressed to division heads responsible for budgeting television services, textbook needs, rent of nonpublic space, supplies and equipment, capital outlay requirements, security guards, educational aides, personnel services, public information services, and myriad other requirements necessary to support an adult education program. Obviously, early consideration is necessary in order that other divisions may include services for adult education as their budgets are prepared.

Continuing instruction. The second consideration should be the continuing adult education instructional program with adjustments for growth and policy changes. If board of education policy will allow the implementation of this budget without undue debate, the development of a continuing program of adult education is assured. The growth factor should automatically reflect the increase or decrease in student enrollment during the preceding year.

Required additions. Included in the next category should be those items absolutely necessary to meet the obligations of new legislation, board of education policy, or county council opinions. These might include recommendations for increases in fringe benefits allowed employees, matters of health and safety, urgent requests for obvious new programs, and other considerations necessary for the total program. Board of education analysis and debate on each line item is requested. On approval, the item is subsequently reflected in the continuing budget and should not normally come up again for future debate.

Priority requests. The final part of the budget preparations should include *all* of the needs of the program in a priority listing. Each item should be presented with a brief sentence or two of explanation and the cost involved to inform the superintendent and the board of education of the plans which could be implemented if funds were available. In all probability, many of the top-priority items will be funded if the need is sound and funds are available.

Other considerations. In the development of a budget for adult and continuing education programs, the director must continually interpret the problems unique to the attendance of part-time students. With the continual turnover of school staffs, members of boards of education, and community leaders interested in the fiscal problems of schools, there is an urgent need for an ongoing effort to acquaint such persons with the workings of an active program of education for adults.

Many persons are unaware of the usual large turnover or flow of people through the schools. It is normal for the enrollment of 10 part-time students to be equal in hours of (normal) attendance with the enrollment of a single full-time day school student. The adult school administrator uses current or "in-house" enrollment figures, annual or cumulative enrollment figures, and equivalent full-time average daily attendance figures. He must acquaint those interested and involved in the budget process with the meaning and impact of such considerations.

Adult and continuing education budgets should be readily visible and presented as a viable component of a district's total school budget. Such a presentation gains validity and vitality in the eyes of community representatives.

Generally, the unit operating cost of adult and continuing education programs is somewhat less than comparable cost for elementary and secondary levels. This is largely determined by the proportionate level of salaries paid for part-time (hourly) employees and full-time subject field coordinators and directors. Salaries generally constitute 75 to 85 percent of a total budget.

Other considerations include requests for subject field coordinators in evening programs; full-time and part-time counselors; funds for in-service training for newly assigned teachers; funds for weekend staff and subject field conferences; assignment of directors on annual basis; assignment of staff for preschool registration programs; assignment of community coordinators for large ethnic populations; funds for television and radio offerings; funds for rental of nonpublic space for day programs; funds for leasing portable classrooms for "instant schools"; supplemental funds for bilingual staff members; allocations for central office coordination of occupational, nursing, counseling, and other traditional programs; and special reserve allocations for school-determined needs as the school year progresses.

THE COMPUTER

"After growing wildly for years, the field of computing now appears to be approaching its infancy. . . . In the field of scholarship and education, there is hardly an area that is not now using digital computing. . . ." This is an extract from *Computers in Higher Education,* a report of the President's Science Advisory Committee. The report states that "computing is not an esoteric or specialized activity; it is a versatile tool useful in any work with a factual or intellectual content. Computing is becoming almost as much a part of our working life as doing arithmetic or driving a car."[15] Richard L. Shetler says that "the new technology of the computer and information system bids fair to be the dominant technological factor that will influence the environment of the 1980's."[16]

Certainly the impact of computers on our budget process is known or anticipated. The President's Science Advisory Committee report cites the rapid obsolescence of computers as usually three to five years. "Computing is rather a continuing expense than a capital investment. Obtaining computing is not like buying a building, it is like paying year in and year out, for light and water."[17]

The computer has many capabilities and an unlimited capacity dependent only on the complexity of the equipment and the talent of those responsible for its use. Many school districts are utilizing its services not only for budget accounting and controlling, but also for personnel requirements and student records. The payroll is one of the critical factors in any school district. The ability to expedite this function with accuracy and dispatch has often necessitated the use of computers.

Traditionally, school districts receive requests for student transcripts and information about employees, as well as controlling documentation. The advent of the computer is an answer to the amounts of clerical effort required to perform all of these tedious functions.

The advantages of the computer are both general and specific. All the above services are most helpful to the program. Some specific functions are the following:

1. Computer printout of all classes by subject indicating place, time, teacher, and school
2. Computer printout of all classes by teacher indicating subjects, time, place, and school
3. Computer printout of all classes by school, branch location, and indicating teacher hours assigned
4. Computer summaries of specific expenditures by program, spe-

cially funded programs, administrative services, and other requirements

5. Computer-organized student enrollment procedures
6. Computer-organized attendance counting as required by local and state regulations
7. Computer-organized student grades and records
8. Computer matching of jobs and students.

An important contribution of the computer is that of information retrieval. "The key to information retrieval capability is adequate planning and file development that secures and maintains all of the information that will be requested at some indefinite later date." [18] The availability of this service is particularly helpful during the budget development process. For example, immediate and exact information will be available if salaries are to be adjusted at suggested new rates.

The major objective can be the improvement of the educational program of the district. The computer needs of the Los Angeles City Schools' adult education program are described, in part, in the following memo from a large computer manufacturer:

> It would be very impractical to handle 200,000 students and 3,000 classes without the use of auxiliary storage on the computer. Direct-access storage in the form of disk packs is necessary to reduce the card volumes during the processing runs. For example, students would be registered by using a tub file approach at each school. This information would be sent to the central location and stored on disk files. The disk files would then be sorted to produce class lists, enrollment reports, attendance recording documents and other reports. This type of processing results in a much more efficient and easier data processing procedure.[19]

Obviously, the difficulties of changing from an existing budget procedure to one utilizing the computer are many. Most districts will utilize the ongoing procedure and the new computer program simultaneously for a minimum of one school year to ensure the continuance of the active program without interruption and allow for adjustments, refinements, and staff orientation and utilization for the new technique.

PROGRAM BUDGETING

The Budget Division of the Los Angeles City Schools [20] lists the following as criteria for establishing the framework of program budgeting:

1. Easily understood by public and board
2. Compatible with current accounting practices

3. Provides information leading toward improved educational programs
4. Focuses attention on fiscal impact of policy decisions
5. Flexible in development to provide for change
6. Designed so that quantitative or qualitative measures could be applied
7. Implemented in phases moving from simple to complex over a number of years.

The need for program budgeting is aptly expressed in the following statement: ". . . to break down the components of a good education into measurable units so that legislators and the voting public can compare the degree of achievement with the amount of money being spent. . . . the public is interested in how much of the educational dollar goes to basic skills, how much goes to vocational subjects, and how much goes to welfare programs." [21]

It is suggested that a program budget for a school take the form indicated in Chart I. The chart codes 15 curriculum areas, the summer school program, and the forum and lecture budget. The number of teaching positions, respective costs, and the number of students enrolled complete this program budget. Chart I illustrates the actual enrollment for the first month of the 1967-68 school year.

Chart II suggests a format for a total analysis of categorical aid programs. Codes 0625, 0655, and 0680 are exclusive responsibilities of adult education. Other adult education programs are included in 0660, 0612, and 0620.

While this information is valuable as a criterion of the dimensions of adult education, future programs will require more specific data.

"The existing balance in education programs is basically an intuitive balance. There seems to be no objective criteria for prescribing in detail exactly what should be accomplished in each program . . . By costing out each course, school administrators could shift course emphasis to obtain optimum educational output based on available financing." [22]

SUMMARY AND RECOMMENDATIONS

The future has been described in many ways. Richard L. Shetler is of the opinion that "there will be more years devoted to education, greater access to continued education throughout our lives, more time for leisure, more emphasis on cultural pursuits, and far greater technological advances in all areas, particularly in electronic information systems." [23]

CHART I.—
LOS ANGELES CITY SCHOOLS
PROGRAM BUDGET
ANALYSIS OF THE 1967-68 DETAIL BUDGET

0300	REGULAR ADULT EDUCATION PROGRAM	UNIFIED DISTRICT		
		Amount	Positions	Pupils*
0305	Elementary Subjects	$ 227,968	31.24	3,545
0310	English	459,753	63.01	7,149
0315	Foreign Language	247,104	33.87	3,842
0320	Mathematics	224,152	30.72	3,485
0325	Science	135,996	18.64	2,115
0330	Social Studies	314,189	43.06	4,886
0335	Americanization	697,289	95.57	10,844
0340	Business Education	835,275	114.48	12,988
0345	Fine Arts	358,212	49.09	5,570
0350	Homemaking	496,143	68.00	7,714
0355	Parent Education	247,104	33.87	3,842
0360	Industrial Education & Agriculture	913,753	125.24	14,209
0365	Civics and Special Fields	201,145	27.57	3,128
0370	Crafts	107,292	14.71	1.668
0375	Health and Physical Education	65,150	8.93	1,013
0380	Forum and Lecture	15,900	0	—
0385	Summer School	82,832	80.00	N.A.
	TOTALS	$5,629,257	838.00	85,998

*Enrollment—First Month 1967-68

CHART II.–
LOS ANGELES CITY SCHOOLS
PROGRAM BUDGET
ANALYSIS OF THE 1967-68 DETAIL BUDGET

0600	CATEGORICAL AID PROGRAMS	Unified District Amount	Junior College District Amount
0610	PL 88-452, Title IB, Neighborhood Youth Corps	$ 39,965	
0611	PL 88-452, Title IC, College Work Study		$ 299,115
0612	PL 88-452, Title IIA, Community Action Program	237,381	
0620	PL 89-10, Title I – Public School Projects	2,474,941	
0621	PL 89-10, Title I – Nonpublic School Projects	80,392	
0622	PL 89-10, Title II – Library Resources	739,593	
0623	PL 89-10, Title III – Planning Grant	193,321	
0624	PL 89-10, Title III – Mid-City Demonstration Project	272,181	
0625	PL 89-10, Title III – Demonstration Adult Education School	472,815	
0630	SB 28 – Elementary Class Size Reduction	1,744,512	
0631	SB 28 – Secondary – Demonstration Math Centers	96,344	
0632	SB 28 – Construction – Elementary	15,146,494	
0633	SB 28 – Construction – Secondary	832,095	
0650	PL 89-751 – Allied Health Professional Personnel Training Act		23,165
0655	PL 87-415 – MDTA	2,923,127	
0660	PL 88-210 – Vocational Education Act	46,302	645,457
0665	PL 89-329, Title I – Higher Education Act		46,618
0666	PL 89-329, Title II – Higher Education Act		76,000
0675	PL 89-750, Title III – Adult Basic Education	3,000	
0680	Community Training Program	330,000	
0685	PHS Grant PH 108-66-97 (P)	9,508	
0690	PL 88-352, Title IV – Civil Rights Act	4,915	
0695	Real Estate Education Program		11,000
	TOTALS	$25,646,886	$1,101,355

If his prediction is fully or even partially realized, the need for public school adult and continuing education will be considerable.

Summary

The basic question being asked relates the instructional program to its specific cost. Is every education program worth the price? Adult education administrators who can justify their answers to this question will be able to expand their programs with increasing community support. The ability to develop program cost-accounting, the opportunity to utilize the many diversified services of the computer, and the evaluation process required to give evidence of the success of specific programs will be the characteristics of the adult and continuing education administrators of the future.

The principal recommendations of one study illustrate these concerns —

1. Expenditure records should be maintained to clearly identify costs with programs and projects in the school system. It is important to clearly identify the adult education program and its respective costs as shown in Chart I.
2. Reports of the total cost of each school program should be made available to the state legislature and the voting public in order to provide a more meaningful basis for appropriations and bond issues.
3. School facilities (plant and equipment) should be put to use on a year-round basis.
4. Further acceleration of the public school program in order to accomplish educational objectives in a shorter time should be seriously considered.
5. Business affairs in the school systems should be handled by personnel selected on the basis of financial training and administrative ability in this capacity — teaching credentials should not be a determining factor.[24]

Adult education administrators must give a high priority to cost projections, cost reporting, and cost efficiency. The use of the computer will enable administrators and interested citizens over a period of years to develop a relationship between the number of students served, the number of teacher positions required, and the costs of the program.

Necessarily, the next step will be some identification of the degree of success of the educational attainment. Some adult educators are able to document the success of their programs by indicating the percentage of students completing a particular program; the percentage of students who secured employment on completion; and the years of grade placement advancement in relation to respective numbers of months of instruction. Such information has not yet been standardized. Community interest in knowing the degree of success of individual programs in relationship to costs is becoming a necessity. Adult and continuing education administrators must make continual experimentations in this area in order to justify current and needed programs.

Recommendations

Ideally, adult education programs should, and probably will, be supported with the following enactments and benefits:

1. Local communities and adult education programs
   a. Adult education committees on boards of education
   b. Property tax-base exclusively for adult education
   c. Use of computers for all aspects of adult education programs
   d. Emphasis on program budgeting
   e. Separate divisions or administrative sections responsible directly to superintendent designated as responsible for adult education
   f. Total involvement of business and industry leaders in planning and organizing adult education programs
   g. Greater categorical support of adult education by the federal government, particularly in large urban communities
   h. Increasing responsibility and emphasis on up-to-date vocational and occupational training and retraining
   i. Emphasis on testing and other evaluative criteria
   j. Renaissance of interest in art, drama, music, and the study of government, history, economics, and political science
2. States and adult education programs
   a. Adult education committees on state boards of education
   b. State departments of education — divisions or administrative sections responsible directly to superintendent for adult education
   c. Excess state apportionment factor for "handicapped adults" defined as an unemployed adult
   d. Use of computers for statistics, services, evaluation
   e. Liaison with business and industry.

"The imagination, ingenuity and inspirational qualities of the human being, in partnership with the vast memory and infallible calculation capability of the machine, together make up a striking *new* intellectual factor in our environment. We are only beginning to see where its possibilities can lead us." [25] Among these possibilities are the increasingly more effective financing and budgeting of funds for adult education programs. Because the purpose of any program is to attain the desired outcomes, directors in the field of adult education have both the privilege and the responsibility of utilizing all possibilities which help them realize their goals.

CHAPTER 6

THE IMPACT OF LEGISLATION ON ADULT EDUCATION

James R. Dorland

The history of adult education in this country cannot be accurately told without referring to the major legislative developments which have exerted so much influence on the adult education movement. For example, it would be difficult to find the term *adult basic education* used in many books written prior to the 1960's. Now a frequent criticism is that many adult educators pay attention to adult basic education to the exclusion of other levels of adult education. The reason for the relatively recent interest in adult basic education is the federal legislation which has pinpointed it as worthy of receiving a sizable financial subsidy.

A main thrust of adult education at the time of World War I was the agricultural extension and home economics programs made possible through the Smith-Lever Act of 1914. Following World War I, many adult educators looked to the vocational adult education made possible by the Smith-Hughes Act of 1917 and the Smith-Bankhead Act of 1920.

During the Depression of the 1930's where was the action in adult education? Much of it was in programs sponsored by the Civilian Conservation Corps, the National Youth Administration, and the Works Project Administration — all three organizations created as a result of anti-Depression legislation. What was the big educational push following World War II? Veterans' taking all kinds of courses — adult education and otherwise — made possible by the famous "G.I. Bill of Rights," the Servicemen's Readjustment Act of 1944.

This chapter will focus on education legislation enacted in the past 10 years when federal and state laws were passed which have drastically changed the focus of education at all levels — including adult education.

James R. Dorland is associate executive secretary of the National Association of Public School Adult Education and associate director of the Division of Adult Education Service, National Education Association, Washington, D. C.

RECENT FEDERAL EDUCATION LEGISLATION — 1958 TO PRESENT

The late 1950's and early 1960's marked the beginning of large-scale federal aid to education in the United States. Public school adult education programs were among the recipients of this federal subsidy. In the field of administrative leadership alone, significant growth has occurred since 1960. In 1960 there were 195 full-time directors of adult education in local school systems in this country, and by September of 1967 that number had increased to 549.[1]

For many public school adult educators, the advent of federal aid for adult education seemed to come with unexpected swiftness, yet there were straws in the wind following Russia's launching of Sputnik in 1957 which indicated that the role of the federal government in education was about to change dramatically. Interest in educational matters seemed to be transformed almost overnight from a state-local matter to a national concern. The first federal education legislation enacted following Sputnik was the National Defense Education Act (P.L. 85-864), passed in September 1958. Although its focus on mathematics, science, and guidance was not directly related to adult education, the significance of this bill as heralding the entrance of the U. S. government on the educational scene in a massive financial way cannot be underestimated.

Manpower Development and Training Act

It was four years later — with the enactment of the Manpower Development and Training Act of 1962 (P.L. 87-415) — that adult education became a more specific part of federal education legislation. This bill also marked the legislative birth of the term which has had so much use during the 1960's — *adult basic education*. Title II of the MDTA was called "Training and Skill Development Programs" and stated: "Whenever appropriate, the Secretary of Labor may also refer for the attainment of *basic education* skills those eligible persons who indicate their intention to, and will thereby be able to, pursue courses of occupational training of a type for which there appears to be reasonable expectation of employment."[2]

The use of this terminology in legislation meant that recognition was being given to the understanding that it is difficult and often impossible to train for a job a person who does not have the ability to read and write at a functional level. Other provisions of the MDTA made it possible to offer occupational training programs to persons age 16 and older. Although most of the occupational training aspects of this bill came under the jurisdiction of the Department of Labor and were administered through the local branch of the U. S. Employment Service, the educational portions of the training—specifically, adult basic education—were often carried out by adult education departments of local public school systems.

Throughout the first three years of President John F. Kennedy's administration, various professional associations—including NAPSAE—pushed hard for the enactment of federal legislation specifically for adult education. Although the attempts were unsuccessful so far as getting a bill passed was concerned, groundwork was being laid for legislation which was passed after Lyndon Johnson became president.

Vocational Education Act

The Vocational Education Act of 1963 (P.L. 88-210) was enacted in December 1963. While not passed primarily as an adult education bill, its statement of purpose made it clear that adults could be included:

> It is the purpose of this part to authorize Federal grants to states to assist them to maintain, extend, and improve existing programs of vocational education, to develop new programs of vocational education, and to provide part-time employment for youths who need the earnings from such employment to continue their vocational training on a full-time basis, so that persons of all ages in all communities of the State—those in high school, those who have already entered the labor market but need to upgrade their skills or learn new ones, and those with special educational handicaps—will have ready access to vocational training or retraining which is of high quality, which is realistic in the light of actual or anticipated opportunities for gainful employment, and which is suited to their needs, interests, and ability to benefit from such training.[3]

Economic Opportunity Act

Both the MDTA and the Vocational Education Act recognized the fact that adult basic education was a necessary prerequisite for meaningful job training, but neither bill recognized adult education to the extent that it was a central part of it or was included as a separate title in the legislation. The most significant legislative breakthrough yet for adult education came on August 20, 1964, with the passage of P.L. 88-452, the Economic Opportunity Act of 1964. This bill was the cornerstone of the war against poverty which itself was an important part of the legislative program of the Great Society as then envisioned by President Johnson. As a result of this bill, the Office of Economic Opportunity was created later that year as an autonomous federal agency to administer the various antipoverty programs.

For public school adult educators the main interest was focused on

Title II B of the Act, Adult Basic Education Programs. The Declaration of Purpose stated that —

> It is the purpose of this part to initiate programs of instruction for individuals who have attained age eighteen and whose inability to read and write the English language constitutes a substantial impairment of their ability to get or retain employment commensurate with their real ability, so as to help eliminate such inability and raise the level of education of such individuals with a view to making them less likely to become dependent on others, improving their ability to benefit productive and profitable employment, and making them better able to meet their adult responsibilities.[4]

Some of the important provisions of Title II B of the EOA follow:

- Each state had to develop and have approved a state plan specifying how the adult basic education program would be developed and the funds expended within the state.
- The programs were to be carried out by the "local educational agency," which in almost all cases was the local public school adult education program.
- The federal government assumed 90 percent of the costs, and the state and local agency were required to furnish only 10 percent.
- The funds were allocated on the basis of the relative number of individuals in each state who had attained age eighteen and who had completed not more than five grades of school as reported in the 1960 Census.

Because the Economic Opportunity Act was passed in August 1964, the OEO was created later that year, and the Rules and Regulations were not completed and sent to the states until March of 1965. The progress of the program was necessarily limited during fiscal year 1965, and less than $5 million was expended. In view of these mitigating circumstances the federal government permitted states to carry over funds from fiscal year 1965 until fiscal year 1966, the first full year of operation of the program. In a sense this was a mixed blessing in that it gave some states a false sense of how much money was available on a yearly basis because they were spending in one fiscal year the money which had been appropriated during two fiscal years.

Another problem came about because the adult basic education program was not administered directly by the Office of Economic Opportunity but instead was delegated for operation to the Office of Education. In a sense OEO controlled the purse strings, and USOE operated with the money provided by the OEO. When the state allotments for fiscal year 1966 were released in January of that year, they were approximately 25 percent lower than the states were counting on and had based their programs on as a result of the planning figures provided by USOE. The money had been appropriated and released to the OEO by the Bureau of the Budget; the problem arose when OEO sent to USOE some $6 million less than expected.

Because of this state allotment problem, public school adult educators across the country rallied their forces and mounted a successful campaign which resulted six weeks later in OEO's releasing to USOE the amount of money which the states had initially expected to receive. Although considerable frustration was experienced because of these budgetary uncertainties early in 1966, public school adult educators were able to unite behind a common concern and to experience the satisfaction of achieving their objective.

The Elementary and Secondary Education Act and the Higher Education Act

During fiscal year 1965 after the adult basic education program had been in operation for just a few months, some 37,991 adults attended classes in the 19 participating states. From a legislative standpoint, 1965 produced two of the most significant federal aid to education bills ever enacted by the Congress: the Elementary and Secondary Education Act of 1965 (P.L. 89-10) and the Higher Education Act of 1965 (P.L. 89-329). As an indication of the fiscal immensity of this legislation, Title I of ESEA received a fiscal year 1966 appropriation of $959 million and more than one billion dollars in fiscal year 1967. The titles covered in the Elementary and Secondary Education Act were these: (a) Programs for the Disadvantaged; (b) Library Resources; (c) Supplementary Centers; (d) Research; (e) Strengthening State Departments of Education; and (f) Handicapped Children. Although this bill was primarily for children, adult education programs did receive benefits — either directly or indirectly — from P.L. 89-10. For example, some supplementary centers had adult education components, and some state departments of education added adult education personnel. In Los Angeles the Adult Demonstration Center was funded for three years beginning in 1967. Under the initial administrative direction of former NAPSAE president Robert Schenz, this unique center is the only ESEA Title III project devoted exclusively to the education of adults.

As for the Higher Education Act, Title I — although not designed for public school adult education programs — was called "Community Service and Continuing Education Programs" and was specifically a higher adult education title. The definition of a community service program is quite clear as to the purpose of the program:

The term "community service program" means an education program, activity, or service, including a research program and a university extension or continuing education offering, which is designed to assist in the solution of community problems in rural, urban, or suburban areas, with particular emphasis on urban and suburban problems, where the institution offering such program, activity, or service determines —

(1) that the proposed program, activity, or service is not otherwise available, and
(2) that the conduct of the program or performance of the activity or service is consistent with the institution's over-all educational program and is of such a nature as is appropriate to the effective utilization of the institution's special resources and the competencies of its faculty.[5]

The timetables of ESEA and the Higher Education Act were similar to that of the Economic Opportunity Act to the extent that significant program operation did not get under way until the fiscal year following the initial passage of the legislation. The difficulties which public school adult educators were experiencing while adult basic education was a program delegated to USOE from OEO convinced them that their legislative strategy should be to get Title II B of the EOA repealed and included in the 1966 amendments to the Elementary and Secondary Education Act. This became one of NAPSAE's primary legislative goals during 1966, not because of any dissatisfaction with antipoverty legislation or with the Office of Economic Opportunity, but because of a firm belief that an educational program such as adult basic education should be included in education legislation and should be administered directly by the Office of Education.

Although the proposed transfer of adult basic education received opposition from the administration and from the Office of Economic Opportunity, this transfer was accomplished late in the second session of the Eighty-Ninth Congress. On November 3, 1966, Congress passed the Adult Education Act of 1966 as Title III of the Elementary and Secondary Education Amendments of 1966 (P.L. 89-750). It was truly significant legislation because —

- It was the first piece of federal legislation ever enacted specifically called an Adult Education Act.
- It became a part of the largest federal education bill ever enacted, the ESEA, and by virtue of that inclusion would be considered for renewal in the future at the same time that the Congress would consider renewing the Elementary and Secondary Education Act. In effect, it moved adult education into the mainstream of education in this country and meant that when Congress would enact

elementary and secondary education legislation it would not be just for children but for all Americans — regardless of age.
- It provided for the appointment by the President of an eight-member National Advisory Committee on Adult Basic Education.
- It provided that 10 to 20 percent of the funds available could be spent at the discretion of the U. S. Commissioner of Education for special experimental demonstration projects and teacher training.
- It authorized $40 million for fiscal year 1967 and $60 million for fiscal year 1968.

RESULTS OF THE ADULT EDUCATION ACT

Apparently, adult basic education classes partially met a national need which had existed for many years. From its 37,991 participants in fiscal year 1965, the ABE program skyrocketed to 377,660 participants in fiscal year 1966, to 406,375 enrollees in fiscal year 1967, and at least that many in fiscal year 1968. During the first year of operation only 19 states participated in the ABE program; two years later all 50 states plus the territories were conducting classes. Although fewer federal dollars were spent in fiscal year 1967 ($26.28 million) than in fiscal year 1966 ($34.13 million, because of carry-over from fiscal year 1965), the growth headed upward again in fiscal year 1968 with expenditures of approximately $40 million. Military spending resulted in the curtailment and postponed expansion of most domestic programs; yet in his fiscal year 1969 budget message, President Johnson called for adult basic education programs to be increased from $40 to $50 million, and the fiscal year 1969 HEW appropriation bill set the figure at $45 million. This was particularly significant because ABE was one of the few programs in USOE slated for an increase in a year in which the mood was one of belt-tightening and program reduction.

On the final day of the first session of the Ninetieth Congress the Adult Education Act of 1966 was amended as a part of the 1967 amendments to the Elementary and Secondary Education Act (P.L. 90-247), this time as Title VII of the Amendments. The principal provisions of the 1967 amendments —

1. Extend the present adult basic education program through June 30, 1970.
2. Authorize $70 million for fiscal year 1969 and $80 million for fiscal year 1970.
3. Grant a minimum allotment of $100,000 to each state, regardless of population, and in addition to the regular grant formula amount it had received in the past.

4. Permit private nonprofit agencies to participate in the program if included in the state plan.
5. Continue the 90 percent federal and 10 percent state-local funding ratio through fiscal year 1970 (except in the Trust Territory of the Pacific Islands where the federal share will be 100 percent).

MANPOWER AND OTHER FEDERAL EDUCATION PROGRAMS AFFECTING ADULTS

Perhaps the greatest expansion of adult education programs in recent years has not been under the strict classification "education" at all, but instead under "manpower." While previous vocational education acts were not even primarily aimed at the adult and were tightly targeted on school programs, the new acts did just the opposite.

As was previously mentioned, the first of these was the Manpower Development and Training Act of 1962 for adults and out-of-school youth and did not specify the schools exclusively, although they could be included as purveyors of the called-for training. The whole act, in fact, was placed under supervision of the Department of Labor. Labor then transferred funds to the Office of Education, which takes care of the academic part of the program while Labor takes care of the job training aspects.

For example, a job training program under MDTA ideally includes adult basic education for those in the program who need it. In its on-the-job training programs—run at the local level by unions or businesses or government agencies which plan to hire the trainees—basic education, when necessary, is also included, as it is in the Work Experience Program—for adults on welfare—run by state public welfare agencies. Other programs which put special emphasis and more money into areas of concentrated poverty also run through the cycle from ABE to job training, as in the Concentrated Employment Program or Special Impact Programs or Economic Development Programs or Operation Mainstream or New Careers or Neighborhood Youth Corps.

All of these programs are run by the Department of Labor. So are—

- Youth Opportunity Centers in or close by the inner city to refer out-of-work youngsters to specific jobs and training programs.
- Human Resources and Development Centers in poverty areas to offer testing, counseling, and referral to jobs and manpower programs.
- MA-1, MA-2, MA-3, and MA-4 operated by the Manpower Administration of the Department of Labor to help private companies find, hire, counsel, and train the unemployed.

- Apprenticeship Information Centers to interview, test, and refer youths to apprenticeship programs.

The so-called private sector is now operating in the same fields, notably through the National Alliance of Businessmen headed by Henry Ford II. Through its Job Opportunities in the Business Sector (JOBS) program, the Alliance hopes to provide summer employment for thousands of ghetto youth and more permanent jobs for hundreds of thousands of the hard-core unemployed.

COMMUNITY ACTION PROGRAMS
AND THE PUBLIC SCHOOLS

Many of these programs are locally run by the designated community action agency — whatever its local name might be — in the community. Invariably they are set up in areas of greatest need — the urban slums and the rural poverty areas from which industry has either fled or where it has laid off workers.

In some instances a combination of programs has been put together to improve the local economy. In some cases local people obtain a government loan to open a small factory to employ local people who must first be trained to perform the jobs they will eventually hold.

The public schools may play a part in virtually every one of these programs. In some of them, federal money is funneled only through the states. In other instances the government may deal directly with local training groups. Even where unions or businesses contract to do the training required, the schools may play a part.

A number of agencies (USOE, for one, provides grants for vocational school construction) are involved in the Appalachian Regional Development Act coordinated by the Appalachian Regional Commission. In addition the Act provides supplementary funds for such things as airport construction, hospitals, flood control projects, libraries, and educational television facilities, and so forth. The Department of Health, Education, and Welfare, through its Welfare Administration, provides assistance — including adult training and educational opportunities — for Cuban refugees.

By extension even the Defense Department has entered the civilian adult field with its donation of closed-down facilities to schools, colleges, and universities, among other recipients. Government Services Administration and HEW have similar programs.

The newest government department to enter the education field is the Department of Housing and Urban Development, created by Congress in 1965 to coordinate efforts to improve the community environment, particularly in poverty ghettoes. The physical environment was not its only concern.

Congress, for example, declared (in passing the Demonstration Cities and Metropolitan Development Act of 1966) that —

> Improving the quality of urban life is the most critical domestic problem facing the United States. The persistence of widespread urban slums and blight, the concentration of persons of low income in older urban areas, and the unmet needs for additional housing and community facilities arising from rapid expansion of our urban population have resulted in a marked deterioration in the quality of the environment and the lives of large numbers of our people while the Nation as a whole prospers. The Congress further finds and declares that cities, of all sizes, do not have adequate resources to deal effectively with the critical problems facing them, and that Federal assistance in addition to that now authorized by the urban renewal program and other existing federal grant-in-aid programs is essential to enable cities to plan, develop, and conduct programs to improve their physical environment, increase their supply of adequate housing for low and moderate-income people, and provide educational and social services vital to health and welfare. [6]

HUD programs which today deal most directly with adult education include —

- Neighborhood Facilities Grants, which provide financial and technical assistance for planning and developing multipurpose neighborhood or small-town centers to house health, recreation, and social services — including such services as literacy, citizenship, vocational, and job training; educational counseling; and Head Start classes.
- Model Neighborhoods in Demonstration Cities (also called simply Model Cities), which also provide funds for planning and developing a model neighborhood project

> designed to make marked progress in reducing educational disadvantage and to provide educational services necessary to serve the poor and disadvantaged in the area . . . Adults lacking in basic educational skills and adequate work skills also may need special services . . . The school board and city government should develop close working relationships so that educational efforts are linked effectively with all service delivery systems, such as health, welfare, rehabilitation, and recreation.

Adult educators also came in for Congressional attention with passage of the Education Professions Development Act of 1967 (P.L. 90-35) which, for the first time, opens graduate-level fellowships to adult education teachers as well as to preschool, elementary, secondary, and vocational teachers at both secondary and postsecondary levels. A separate bureau to administer the Act — the Bureau of Educational Personnel Development — was created within the U. S. Office of Education. Don Davies, former executive secretary of the NEA National Commission on Teacher Education and Professional Standards, was named an associate commissioner of education to head the new Bureau. Besides broadening teacher institutes and fellowships, the new legislation also authorizes programs to attract new people into education on both the professional and paraprofessional levels, absorbs the Teacher Corps, and seeks to attract retired teachers back into the field.

ADULT EDUCATION LEGISLATION AT THE STATE LEVEL

Although the principal focus of this chapter is on the impact which federal legislation has made on adult education, activities by state legislatures cannot be ignored. Detailed information on state support for adult education may be found in NAPSAE's *1968 Almanac and Membership Directory* on pages 15-23. Any examination of adult education legislation at the state level reveals extreme differences in the level of financial and statutory commitment from one state to another. This range might extend from a state having no funds and a total absence of any educational legislation specifically for adults to a state having extensive state support and comprehensive adult education legislation.

Because of the variety of laws and the uneven level of development of state legislation for adult education, no attempt will be made here to refer to specific adult education laws. Instead, it might be well to look at several trends which seem to emerge from a study of the relationship among state funds, state legislation, and program development in adult education in the various states.

- Some states first provided money for adult education after they were required to contribute 10 percent matching in state or local funds in order to get the 90 percent federal share for adult basic education programs. Some of these same states also employed adult education specialists in state departments of education for the first time when they discovered that they would need at least one adult education staff member in order to be able to participate in the federally initiated ABE program.
- Adult education programs tend to flourish in states where school districts receive state reimbursement for adult students in much the same way as they receive state funds for children. California and Florida — both of which have had extensive adult education

programs for many years at little or no direct cost to the adult participants — are cases in point. Conversely, when New York drastically lowered its subsidy for adult education students, participation in adult education programs dropped sharply.

- One alternative to a per-pupil subsidy for adult students is for the state legislature to make available money for adult education administrative leadership at the local level. New Jersey pioneered in this type of legislation in 1965. There the state department of education will provide up to two-thirds of the salary of a local director of adult education if the local school district will provide the rest of the salary and will employ the director on at least a half-time and preferably a full-time basis.

- Some of the more recent state legislative activity has been in the area of high school education for adults. Both the Eighty-Ninth and the Ninetieth Congresses considered but did not pass legislation providing a federal subsidy for high school education for adults. With many adult students completing ABE classes at the eighth-grade level and wishing to continue their education through high school, some states have enacted legislation providing state funds for this purpose. Colorado, Indiana, Michigan, Oklahoma, and South Carolina are some of the states which subsidize local programs of adult high school education. With the number of ABE graduates steadily increasing, greater pressure is expected to be applied to states asking help to fund adult high school programs.

- As educators generally and adult educators specifically become more knowledgeable of legislative strategy and power, they are likely to press for advances at all levels of adult education legislation. Most state affiliates of NAPSAE are viewing legislative programs as one of the most important action items for their association and are pooling their efforts with other groups to attain desirable legislative objectives.

ADMINISTRATIVE PROBLEMS RESULTING FROM EDUCATION LEGISLATION

Although many positive results have accrued because of the passage of this federal and state adult education legislation, certain problems have developed which are particularly frustrating to the program administrator at the local level. However, what at one time was a widespread concern that federal legislation would result in federal control of education has generally dissipated in the decade since the passage of the National Defense Education Act in 1958.

A persistent operational problem has resulted from the fact that the government fiscal year is different from the academic school year. The government fiscal year extends from July 1 until June 30 of the following year and is always referred to according to the year in which the fiscal year ends. The academic year generally runs from September until June of the following year and is referred to by hyphenating the two calendar years during which it lasts. For example, the government fiscal year from July 1, 1968, until June 30, 1969, is called fiscal year 1969, whereas the academic year would be designated as the 1968-69 school year.

Congress is in the habit of appropriating funds year by year, almost never in advance. Furthermore, several months generally elapse in the fiscal year before Congress gets around to voting money for that year's programs. Because a law may be passed authorizing a certain amount of money but a separate bill actually appropriates the money for each piece of legislation, it is often quite difficult for educators to know in advance just how much money will be available for a particular educational program. To date the idea of advance funding of educational programs is little more than a concept to which many give lip service but which has not yet been put into legislative practice to any significant degree. Therefore, making plans for a specific certain amount of money around which to plan a program when the prognosis is anything but definite represents a great problem to educators who are administering government-subsidized programs. Unfortunately, some educators have decided that the bother and the risks are too great for them to participate in the program.

Another problem is that occasionally it is necessary to tailor an educational program in order to qualify for the government financial support, and sometimes this means that nonsubsidized programs suffer. Within adult education there are those who feel that an overemphasis has been placed in recent years on adult basic education to the exclusion of the development of balanced programs of general adult education. These criticisms have been answered by the observation that federal adult basic education legislation has not only stimulated state and local matching financial support but has also attracted many people and much attention to adult education for the first time.

Perhaps the most persistent problem from a human standpoint is the added staff work which results from federal programs. In some places adult educators are asked to continue their regular duties and then to add as an extra assignment those tasks necessary for the administration of the programs made possible through new legislation. In a similar vein, much time and energy go into the preparation of program plans and project proposals. This is often in addition to regular duties, and there is never any guarantee that the program plan or the project proposal will be accepted.

LEGISLATIVE AND SOCIAL CHALLENGES FOR ADULT EDUCATORS

More fascinating than the problems are the challenges. Adult educators are being called on to learn new skills and to operate programs of increased scope and importance. They are being dared to develop approaches which will reach the educationally disinherited and which will get at some of the major social problems of our time.

It was Horace Mann who once called education "the balance wheel of the social machinery. . . . It does better than to disarm the poor of their hostility toward the rich; it prevents being poor."

Mann was talking at the time, the early half of the nineteenth century, about the common schools, which have grown up into today's public schools. But the problems of the poor and their hostility are still with us — perhaps with increased intensity during the late 1960's. The general rise in educational attainment has not been able to defeat poverty or the hostility that in recent years has accompanied poverty, particularly in the big-city poverty ghettoes. And, because the percentage of poverty among nonwhites is much greater than among whites, poverty and hostility have taken on strong racial tones. Although two out of three poor people are white, the picture of poverty that most of us carry is black because the visible concentrations are black.

But doesn't all this disprove Mann's statement? Despite more education for more people, the wheel is still out of balance, isn't it? Education really hasn't made much difference, has it? The answers you'd get from a lot of educators to these three questions are "no," "yes," and "yes, it has."

Then they'd cite the increasing population, the relative birth rates between white and black and between the poor and everyone else. They'd cite changing income and conditions of work and living. They'd argue that the disappearance of the frontier and of the necessity for muscle power and of educational attainment itself have changed the skills necessary to compete for jobs. They'd say that the wheel might be out of balance, but only because society has changed its definition of balance — even the slightest imperfection can no longer be tolerated.

Until recently the federal interest in education was totally one-dimensional, and for the most part it still is. The interest was not aimed at helping individuals fulfill their own needs but at fulfilling the needs of the nation, strengthening the nation by promoting education in agriculture (as the Morrill and Smith-Hughes Acts did), or improving the supply of brainpower needed for national defense (as the National Defense Education Act did).

And until recently federal legislation almost totally ignored out-of-school adults who did not have college degrees in areas of national brainpower needs. Those adult programs that did exist were inspired by shortages of workers in critical occupations.

But until recently, too (aside perhaps from the Depression), there has not been the interest in problems of unemployment and poverty, civil rights, slum conditions, and people obsolescence there is now.

Inner-City Strife

The problems found their focus—and their release—in the inner cities. "Of 164 disorders reported during the first nine months of 1967, 8 (five percent) were major in terms of violence and damage; 33 (twenty percent) were serious but not major; 123 (seventy-five percent) were minor and undoubtedly would not have received national attention as 'riots' had the nation not been sensitized by the more serious outbreaks." The statement is from the report of the National Advisory Commission on Civil Disorders—the Riot Commission—set up by President Lyndon Johnson to look into the rising tide of riots.

The Commission indicted white racism for fostering conditions which spawned the riots, and it went on to list those conditions, particularly of Negroes in the inner-city riot areas. The report says—

> The condition of Negroes in the central city remains in a state of crisis. Between 2 and 2.5 million Negroes—16 to 20 percent of the total Negro population of all central cities—live in squalor and deprivation in ghetto neighborhoods. Employment is a key problem. It not only controls the present for the Negro American but, in a most profound way, it is creating the future as well. Yet, despite continuing economic growth and declining national unemployment rates, the unemployment rate for Negroes in 1967 was more than double that for whites.

And the Commission went on to document the trials of the Negro big-city poor today in additional terms—housing and education among them. And, while it said "the schools have failed to provide the educational experience which should help overcome the effects of discrimination and deprivation," it did not specifically point a finger at adult and vocational education. The report did say, however, that "despite substantially increased efforts made possible by the Vocational Education Act of 1963, quality vocational education is still not available to all who need it."

Relevance of Community and Adult Education

The Riot Commission report then recommended education guidelines which included —

- Intensive literacy training in a national year-round program for the 16.3 million citizens with less than an eighth-grade education. "The principal federal literacy program — Adult Basic Education — is meeting only a small fraction of this need; as of June 1966, it had provided assistance to some 373,000 people." Literacy, the report pointed out, is "obviously indispensable to productive employment."
- Expanding training for workers, particularly the disadvantaged, in professional, semiprofessional, and technical fields.

Of course, these are only two of the recommendations of the Commission. And while the vocational training recommendations are explicit, adult training recommendations are not — possibly the Commission felt them to be implicit in the others. At any rate, the Commission, while noting that "the principal burden for funding the programs we have proposed will fall on the federal government," made no estimate of just how much that burden would be.

The report of the Riot Commission is included here in this section on legislative and social challenges for adult educators because a major test facing adult education from this time on is whether it is relevant to our times and to our people. For many decades a variety of adult education programs were developed to meet the needs largely of our middle class. These programs were not necessarily financed through federal or state legislation but were paid for at the local level, often by the adult participants themselves. Programs such as these continue to make an important contribution to our culture, but they do not represent the cutting edge of society.

The blight of poverty, the twin tragedies of undereducation and underemployment, the increasing immensity of manpower needs in an age of automation, exploding knowledge, and people obsolescence — these problems must be tackled head-on by our adult education institutions. Much legislation has already been passed; considerably more — and probably of a different kind — is needed. Recent years have taught us that adult educators can flex their legislative muscles and make a difference. However, the responsibility to support or to oppose pending legislation is not enough. If new legislation is needed, it behooves adult educators to move into the vanguard and propose it. If a massive push is needed to goad Congress into the enactment of legislation providing massive federal support of high school education programs for adults, who should better lead this movement than adult educators?

Coordinated Legislative Action for Adult Education

Professional associations like NAPSAE have at first timidly and then later rather aggressively moved into the arena of direct legislative action. The NAPSAE Legislative Committee has been organized with one committee member representing each of the nine HEW-USOE regions and with one legislative coordinator being named from each state of the union. Until 1964 Tom McLernon and then Jim Dorland were assigned from the NEA-NAPSAE headquarters staff to serve as staff liaison to the Legislative Committee and to maintain contact with and surveillance of adult education legislative activities on Capitol Hill. NAPSAE officials have testified regularly on adult education legislation.

For example, during the second session of the Ninetieth Congress, the administration introduced a Partnership for Learning and Earning Act which would have doubled from 10 to 20 percent to 20 to 40 percent the amount of the federal money set aside for special projects and teacher training in adult basic education. NAPSAE strongly opposed this move, primarily on the basis that its membership felt that not nearly enough funds were available for program operation at the local level and that any additional funds reserved for special federal grants would be at the expense of these beleaguered local programs. At the same time NAPSAE supported an administration proposal to lower the age limit from 18 to 16 for participants in ABE programs. Following NAPSAE testimony the controversial doubling of the federal set-aside was stricken in both the House and Senate versions. Ultimately, the proposed Partnership for Learning and Earning Act was replaced by the Vocational Education Amendments of 1968 — perhaps the most extensive vocational education bill ever enacted. One small part of this comprehensive bill was an amendment to the Adult Education Act which lowered the age limit from 18 to 16 for adult basic education participants.

The power of professional associations was again demonstrated late in 1968, not in the area of direct legislative action but by influencing the administration of federal legislation previously enacted. At the insistence of such groups as the National Education Association, the Council of Chief State School Officers, the National School Boards Association, and others, the U. S. Office of Education abruptly changed its direction and began shifting responsibilities from the nine regional HEW-USOE offices back to USOE in Washington. These major associations had charged that the relatively new regional concept of USOE program administration was adding yet another layer between local schools and government agencies.

It is obvious that with professional associations and other organized groups, the responsibilities for the use of power are great and the need for enlightened leadership seems to grow — particularly as we look at the legislative and social challenges all around us.

A LOOK AHEAD INTO THE SEVENTIES

The mass of federal legislation enacted from 1958 to 1968 was in some respects a mixed blessing. The peak was reached in 1965-66, and the next several years saw decreasing Congressional legislative production in educational matters. The emphasis was not so much on new legislation as it was on making laws that had already been passed work. This emphasis meant sharply revising some legislation through amendments, almost scuttling other laws by cutting down the appropriations, and in some instances not voting initial appropriations for laws which were passed with high hopes. These years encompassed the debate over the "guns or butter" issue. The year 1968 marked the end of the Lyndon Johnson administration and a new era beginning with the Ninety-First Congress. The years 1964-68 were the years of the Great Society which had as one of its cornerstones the war on poverty — a domestic war which was overshadowed and almost eclipsed by a war in Vietnam.

So, for adult educators, what about the seventies? If current trends continue, the emphases will probably be on increased adult basic education, large-scale federal involvement in high school education for adults, and job training for people at all age levels. The issues of race, school decentralization, and community participation in self-government will undoubtedly remain, but may be joined or exceeded in intensity by other issues not now so readily discernible. Poverty and ignorance mixed together in an urban setting will undoubtedly continue to give cause for deep concern. Perhaps by the 1970's the rural poor will have discovered a means to organize effectively for social action.

Admittedly, some of these challenges have their frightening aspects, but these problems are not incapable of solution. For those of us who have tried to answer the high calling of adult education — and for those who will swell our ranks in the years ahead — the seventies challenge our best instincts. If we truly believe as a society that effective change comes principally through law, what impact can adult education legislation really make on the problems which face us in the 1970's? Perhaps you will provide part of that answer.

SECTION II

PROGRAM DEVELOPMENT AND OPERATION

CHAPTER 7

IDENTIFICATION OF NEEDS
AND RESOURCES

Samuel E. Hand

INTRODUCTION

The identification of educational needs and resources in the community is a crucial first task of the adult education administrator. Until he knows the elements or the dimensions of the adult education program he should logically provide, he cannot know his own needs with respect to staff, facilities, or budget.

Experience through the years has made it increasingly clear that effective adult education programs must deal with real community problems and concerns because it is in the community that one can see firsthand the characteristics and needs of people and of the society. Also, it is in relation to or in connection with individual and community problems that educational needs exist, and the adult educator must first know what these problems and needs are before he can plan intelligently educational programs to deal effectively with them.

In earlier days the job of the adult educator in getting to know his community and planning his program was relatively simple. The migration of ever-increasing numbers of people from rural areas to urban centers during the past quarter-century has created within our cities problems, the complexity of which challenges the comprehension even of our most highly trained social scientists. Leaders in our cities are wrestling with the problem of absorbing masses of people who are untrained for the jobs required by modern technology in business and industry and who are also wholly unaccustomed to and unprepared for the way of

Samuel E. Hand is professor of adult education and director of Continuing Education, Florida State University, Tallahassee, Florida.

life they encounter in the cities. Unable to find jobs, confused and dismayed by the complexity of life around them, these masses congregate for survival in the inner city where ghetto life further reduces their hope, intensifies ethnic alienation, and spawns hostilities and despair.

Under these circumstances the adult educator today must truly be a professional if he is to be effective. If he is to understand his community, he must have an awareness of the historical factors of community development. He must also understand the nature and concept of community and the significance of the relationship between the individual and the community.

HUMAN NEEDS
AND COMMUNITY DEVELOPMENT

Communities first came into existence because of man's inherent social nature and because of the presence within him of certain basic human needs which he cannot satisfy in isolation. His physical nature and the necessities of his environment force him to unite with others to survive. This cooperation for survival ultimately leads to the establishment of certain social units in which people live under common law and common custom. The progression of societal units is from the family unit—through the tribe, the community, the state, and the nation—ultimately to the world. The community is the social unit which seems to provide the setting in which man's basic needs can best be met.

Lindeman[1] says that man is born with three instinctive traits which give direction to all his motives and acts. Self-preservation, self-perpetuation, and self-assertion—it is in these self-seeking instincts that man is forced to reveal his inherent social nature. In preserving himself, perpetuating himself, and asserting himself, man relies on relationships and cooperation with other human beings.

McClenahan explains the nature and origin of community in somewhat different terms, yet here too the basic ingredient is the social nature of man. She says—

> The community has been a continuing unit of land and people within the larger framework of human society because of its pragmatic value. It grew up many centuries ago from simple beginnings of trade and exchange, and of rest and refreshment for wayfarers at crossroads, at meeting points of caravan routes, or at other natural gathering places where people could come together for protection, for barter, for worship, or for sociability.[2]

The basic human needs which are present in every individual impel us continually toward all sorts of social contacts and relationships with our fellow man. Joseph K. Hart identifies five major needs which constitute the evolutionary source of our five major social institutions.[3] As infants and children, our need for nurture and care gives rise to the family. Our need for some broad outlook on the meanings of life and destiny gives rise to religion as a center of ideal aspirations and unsatisfied longings. Our physical needs and wants give rise to industry. Our need of opportunity for sharing and enjoying the goods of the world in some just and restraining manner gives rise to the state. Finally, our need to know and continuously to extend our capacity to know gives rise to education.

CONCEPTS OF COMMUNITY

Just as the development of the community has moved from the simple to the complex, the meaning attached to the term *community* has likewise become varied and progressively more complex. George A. Hillery, Jr., has analyzed 94 definitions of the term as found in the writings of various social scientists in an effort to establish areas of agreement.[4] In all of the definitions there was only one point of common agreement: namely, that "people" constitute an element of community.

Earlier uses of the term *community* implied a geographical area with definite legal boundaries, occupied by residents engaged in interrelated economic activities and constituting a politically self-governing unit.[5] Under this concept, hamlets, villages, towns, and cities were classed as communities, and as such were regarded as elements of larger societal units — counties, states, and nations. This early concept views community primarily in terms of structure. Its elements are definite and clearly defined. Subsequently, however, more and more attention has been given to the social and attitudinal aspects of community. The result has been that a more recent concept of community is based principally on the ideas of functional process. This change came about as a result of the doctrine of social change by which communities were seen to be in a state of continuous evolution with no clear-cut, continuously stable structure.

Lindeman makes a clear distinction between the two concepts:
In terms of structure —

> A community . . . is any consciously organized aggregation of individuals residing in a specified area or locality, endowed with limited political autonomy, supporting such primary institutions as schools and churches and among whom certain degrees of interdependency are recognized.

As process —

> A community . . . is any process of social interaction which gives rise to a more intensive or more extensive attitude and practice of interdependence. cooperation. collaboration and unification.[6]

According to Lindeman. a valid definition includes both structural and functional elements. He points out that political scientists still view the community as both structure and process and that social workers regard it as a configuration of families and as a system of institutions designed to exercise social control and assume social responsibilities.

Stroup feels that there is little reason to fragmentize our view of the community because of the divergence found in the structural and process concepts.[7] He says that here is a case of "both . . . and." rather than "either . . . or" and sets forth five prerequisites of community —

Consciousness of organization. The members of a community must be commonly conscious that they compose a community. This involves the element of loyalty.

A common territorial basis. Residents of a community are usually bound by a shared land area. This increases commonly shared interests.

Limited political autonomy. The community requires some measures of political control and expression.

Satisfaction of primary needs. While secondary groups may be present to implement the purposes and activities of the primary groups. the fundamental stress in the community is placed upon the fulfillment of the major life functions.

A social structure and a social process. These are distinctive to each community. and the social process may include conflict as well as cooperation.

Taking these five elements into account. a community may be described generally as composed of —

> a relatively large number of persons having a consciousness of their own interrelatedness. who are dependent upon a common territory. possess limited political autonomy. and seek basic satisfactions in a complex and changing social structure.[8]

Robert Ezra Park sought to give community a much deeper meaning than simply that of a combination of men and social conveniences. To him it was more than a physical mechanism and an artificial construction.

> The city is . . . a state of mind. a body of customs and traditions. and of organized attitudes and sentiments that inhere in these customs and are transmitted with this tradition. The city . . . is involved in the vital processes of the people who compose it: it is a product of nature. and particularly of human nature.[9]

Park points out that the city is an economic as well as a geographic and ecological unit. Being rooted in the habits and customs of the people who inhabit it, the city possesses a moral as well as a physical organization, and these two mutually interact in characteristic ways to mold and modify one another.

The German sociologist, Ferdinand Tönnies, evolved the classic distinction between community and society. Tönnies conceived of community as the natural, spontaneous, organic relations of people as they develop in the course of living, growing out of mutual affection, acquaintance, custom, and tradition. This he called *gemeinschaft*. On the other hand, *gesellschaft*, which he regarded as the formal organization of society by contacts, legislation, and deliberately planned agreements, grew out of and was undergirded by spontaneous *gemeinschaft*, without which it could not exist. In other words, organized society grows out of community and can thrive only so long as the spirit of community pervades and vitalizes it.[10]

Attempting a synthesis of the various definitions and concepts of community, it would seem that a community would involve enough people to enable it to function as a unit: that it would have a geographic locus and a historic past that involve the members of the community. It would have a sufficient number and variety of want-satisfying agencies to enable its members to live a large part of their routine existence within the locality if they so desire. The community itself would be an object of thought and feeling on the part of its members, and it would possess the ability to act in a corporate capacity to preserve its existence.

Thus, it would seem that a community has a life of its own, that it is in fact more than the sum total of the people who make it up. It may have needs, the same as people have needs. And adult education can be the instrumentality by which many community as well as individual needs can be served. The task is both urgent and challenging. The increasing unrest and frustration among minority groups today, growing as these have out of feelings of alienation and of being outside the mainstream of community life, lend importance and urgency to our efforts to understand and accommodate needs of the individual and the community through educational means.

THE INDIVIDUAL AND THE COMMUNITY

Relationship Theories

The relationship of the individual to the community has been analyzed in various ways. There are three basic theories which seek to explain this relationship. The first, dating back to the seventeenth century, is the social contract theory of Thomas Hobbes. Hobbes, in speaking of the "Leviathan," writes —

> And in him (the Leviathan) consisteth the Essence of the Commonwealth; which, to define it, is One Person, of whose Acts a great Multitude, by mutual covenants one with another, have made themselves every one the Author, to the end he may use the strength and the means of them all, as he shall think expedient, for their Peace and Common Defense. And he that carrieth this Person is called SOVERAIGNE, and said to have SOVERAIGNE POWER: and everyone besides, his Subject.[11]

Hobbes seems to say that society consists of a union of individuals, each with his own character independent of the society, and that the character of society is determined by the character of individuals. The individual gives all his rights to society (the contract) in return for which all his needs are taken care of by the society.

The second theory concerning the relationship between members of society and society itself is the social mold theory proposed by the French sociologist Emile Durkheim. He came close to saying that society was primary and that individuals were mere resultants of the characteristics of society. He thought of society as putting its stamp on individuals, like a mold forced over hot metal.

Durkheim made the point that whenever a number of individuals come together in a group something new emerges, the nature of which depends not just on the individuals but also on the fact of their mutual relations — the "whole formed by their union." [12] In other words, any society, any group, develops a set of rules, norms of behavior, which act as a constraining influence — a mold — on the individual.

The third theory is that of George C. Homans who says that (a) an individual brings to his group certain characteristics of mind and certain needs. These needs are at once biologically inherited and socially instilled. (b) His group has a method of cooperation for satisfying these needs, which make natural and appropriate certain forms of behavior in certain situations. (c) But while these forms of behavior may be natural and appropriate, the group has also reached the idea that they ought and must be adopted in these situations. (d) If an individual does not behave in these ways, the relations in the group are such that he will be punished. Moreover, the norms (or culture), will be taught to new members.[13]

Hobbes emphasized (a) and (b); and Durkheim, (c) and (d) of the above. Homans feels that neither is entirely right because both are incomplete. According to Homans the individual brings to his group certain needs, the group seeks a cooperative solution, the solution is influenced by or becomes tradition, and, once established, brings conformity. A practical example of this may be the individual's needs for food and clothing. These may be biologically determined, but society teaches the individual what kinds of food he should gather and eat and what kinds of clothes he should wear. When the individual fails to conform, he is punished by society through group rejection, ridicule, or otherwise.

Community-Individual Interaction

Jessie Bernard[14] provides us with some penetrating insights on the influence of community on the individual personality. She points out that popular racial and cultural stereotypes recognize the influence of community background on personality. Terms such as "hillbilly," "cracker," "okie," "tarheel," "wop," "Dago," and "kike" all reflect the way in which certain community ties are thought to determine personality. Bernard says that the influence of the community background on the individual personality need not be direct. It may, in fact, be very indirect.

The following are ways in which it operates:

1. Through its contribution to the socializing process, the community plays a role comparable to that of the family in shaping personality, including attitudes, speech patterns, prejudices, and points of view.
2. By its acceptance or rejection of individuals, it exerts a tremendous force in shaping individual personality.
3. By its selective behavior, it encourages some types of personality and discourages others.
4. By its institutional offerings, it sets limits to personality growth.[15]

The community influence on individual personality continues long after the family has done its job. It is never complete and continues for life. Community standards are so well maintained that the rules are more generally apparent in the breach than in practice.

This pervasiveness of the influence of the community on the individual is further described by Joseph K. Hart in these words—

> No child can escape his community. He may not like his parents, or his neighbors or the ways of the world. He may groan under the processes of living, and wish he were dead. But he goes on living, and he goes on living in the community. The life of the community flows about him, foul or pure; he swims in it, drinks it, goes to sleep in it, and wakes to the new day to find it still about him. He belongs to it: it nourishes him, or starves him, or poisons him: it gives him the substance of his life. And in the long run it takes its toll of him, and all he is.[16]

At another point, Hart says —

> But the community does educate! It educates all of us by its pro-
> cesses and its functions; by its structures and its institutions; by its
> repressions and its illegalities; by its sincerities and its lies; by its
> legends and its faiths; by its great spirits and its "damaged" souls;
> by its professions and its practices.[17]

Llao says that the community, which is composed of interacting individuals, each with his own peculiar biography, depends for its unity
on the common observance by its members of certain creeds or patterns
prevailing as the binding ties of their group life.[18] Every member newly
admitted to the community has to learn to conform his behavior to its
social patterns.

"The individual," says Llao, "is essentially a product of his community, and yet may by chance become a guide to it."[19] Different
individuals react on their communities in different ways, and different
communities discipline their members by different means and through
different institutions. Individual conduct becomes action regulated by
creeds and prescribed by some impelling factor, whether it be the
church, the school, the state, or the individual's conscience. The latter
is an adaptive factor, says Llao, which functions in moral situations.

Llao feels that social life is the natural means to the perfection of the
individual. Man, he says, is by nature a political animal; he naturally
realizes himself and attains true happiness through his social relationships. The state to him is simply a spontaneous development from the
family through the village community.

Under Llao's concept different communities will produce different
kinds of minds. They will devise theory according to cultural emphasis
and will shape individual growth accordingly. On the other hand, a
broad implication for education, and particularly for adult education,
appears in Llao's statement that the individual may "by chance" become a guide to his community. The job for adult education is to lessen
this element of chance by creating an atmosphere and providing the
means whereby man's growth, intellectually, civically, and otherwise,
will continue throughout life, thus enhancing the possibilities of his
giving responsible direction to his community's development.

CLASSIFICATION AND STRUCTURE OF COMMUNITIES

As is true of individuals, communities are capable of infinite variations. While there are certain elements common to them all, each community has its own peculiar characteristics growing out of its local
situation. These distinguishing characteristics serve to determine the

general nature of communities and provide a basis for their classification. While there is no universal system for community classification, the adult educator should have a basic knowledge of the factors which influence the classification and structure of communities in order to enable him better to understand his own for program planning purposes.

One system classifies communities as infantile, juvenile, adolescent, and senile, depending on their relative ages and states of development.[20] Another categorizes cities primarily in terms of their commercial interests, using such designations as manufacturing, wholesaling, and transport.[21] Most classification systems recognize the dominant influence of economic forces in determining the character of communities. Those with the same kind of economic base tend to develop similar patterns of community living.

John A. Kinneman describes eight classes of communities and gives the distinctive characteristics of each in very simple terms.[22]

Open country community, the simplest of all forms of community. The focal point of its organization may be a general store, a rural school, a cooperative elevator, or an open country church, and it exists mainly among farmers who live a considerable distance from the nearest agricultural village. The institutions of the people are closely connected with the soil.

Agricultural village, usually a village of fewer than 2,500 inhabitants. Business enterprises depend largely on farmers in the open country for the greater part of their trade, and the sole purpose of their existence lies in the services they provide for nearby farmers. Patterns of thought among editors, politicians, and business proprietors in such communities are aimed at preserving the integrity and independence of the small town.

Rurban center, a community somewhere between the agricultural village and the wholesaling center which combines elements of the agricultural village with the patterns of the small cities. It usually has rural characteristics. Many residents are farm owners. Culture is relatively harmonious and integrated. Population usually runs from 3,000 to 20,000. Schools are good; industry has some diversity. Associations are somewhat personal and intimate. The farm and the city meet in such communities.

Wholesaling center, usually a community of from 25,000 to 100,000 population. Wholesaling is a part of the behavior pattern of the people. Such a center often provides services outside its city limits for an aggregation of people three or four times as large as the population of the center itself. While jobbing is important, industry causes the wholesaling center to function and enables it to retain its population. Actually this is an agricultural-industrial center in which wholesaling constitutes an essential supplemental service.

Industrial center, a community conspicuously industrial in nature and not intimately identified with agriculture or wholesaling. Some may rely solely on one industry. The prosperity of such communities depends on operation of the industry, and the pattern of life is set by the working class. Usually a high degree of labor consciousness exists. A substantial percentage of the population may be Negro, or the center may be a focal point for foreign-born.

Metropolitan center, largest of the centers of population, usually 100,000 or above. However, the functions it performs determine for the most part its proper classification as a metropolis. The metropolitan center provides most, if not all, of the goods and services needed by the residents in the area surrounding it. It is an important marketplace; provides a wide variety of commodities both retail and wholesale; has all types of professional and personal services — specialists in various fields such as medicine, dentistry, law, and the trade services; and is usually a cultural center with colleges, special schools, conservatories, theaters, art galleries, museums, zoos, and parks. It may be characterized also by extremes of behavior patterns among the people within it.

Suburban community, a community formed from the overflow of the metropolis, whose residents, for the most part, work in the metropolis and depend heavily upon transportation facilities to commute. As places of residence they give their inhabitants prestige, and people are aware of their class and caste. They support and benefit from institutions of their choice — churches, country clubs, private schools, and colleges; loyalties are divided between city and suburb; living expenses and the standard of living are fairly high; and residents rely largely on the city for major goods and services.

Special service communities, those in which special services dominate the community life, such as educational institutions or recreation and resort areas with a large transient and seasonal tourist population.

Regardless of its classification, a community's physical structure is usually determined by a variety of physical factors associated with transportation and communication and identified with function — commercial, professional, aesthetic, and the like. It is well established that community boundaries follow such functions as retail trading, banking, newspaper circulation, and attendance at elementary and secondary schools. These "community" boundaries often transcend township and even county lines, thus demonstrating that community is a functional part of social interaction — a fact which the adult educator must continually bear in mind.

LOOKING FOR EDUCATIONAL NEEDS IN THE COMMUNITY

With an awareness of the evolving concept of community and the significant role relationship between the community and the individual, the adult educator may now address himself to the question of how best to identify the educational needs in his community. Several considerations should be kept in mind. First, educational needs exist at several levels. Individuals have personal needs which adult education can serve; community organizations have needs; and even the community at large has problems and needs, the solution for which may well depend on adult continuing education.

Second, educational needs are related to or grow out of the roles, responsibilities, and functions of individuals, groups, and communities Individual adults occupy the roles of and have responsibilities as citizens, workers, parents, consumers, and individual personalities concerned with their own self-development. Organizations and groups within the community have recognized roles and functions, either voluntary or legally prescribed, in connection with which needs exist and problems arise which can be dealt with effectively by educational means. Similarly, the community encounters problems and difficulties which can be solved through education. Recognizing these roles and functions as operational areas of potential educational needs, the adult educator can take them into account in deciding on his procedure in seeking to identify educational needs in the community.

Third, the adult educator should remember that one of the important keys to his success and to that of his program is that he know and be known favorably to as many people as possible in the community. The extent to which he and the program he represents will be called on to help solve educational problems and needs of individuals and groups will be in direct proportion to the extent to which they are known throughout the community. This would imply that the process by which the adult educator goes about studying his community should be one through which he gets out, makes many individual contacts, attends many community meetings, involves many interested people in his study, and ensures that much publicity is given to the entire effort.

A fourth important consideration for the adult educator at this point is the fact that whatever procedure chosen should be one which takes into account the basic function of adult education in our society. The adult educator should ask himself, What procedure can I employ that will offer best results in terms of real needs identified, and at the same time be consistent with and of most service to the overall purpose of adult education?

ORGANIZED COMMUNITY STUDY IS THE KEY

All things considered, systematic and continuing study of the community by the educator in cooperation with representative citizens is the best means yet devised for identifying educational needs and planning socially useful adult education programs in a community. This assertion is based on the following considerations:

1. The function of adult education in our society is the development of individuals who possess an acute sense of their responsibilities as citizens in a democracy and who have the skills and competencies necessary to enable them to fulfill their adult responsibilities effectively.
2. The development of such individuals is achieved only within the context of real experiences shared in common.
3. Such experiences occur when individuals attack the great social problems of our day.
4. These problems are identifiable and manageable as personal experiences only within the context of the community.
5. New and higher patterns of human behavior can emerge from these shared human experiences.
6. People have greater faith in an activity or program and will support it more vigorously when they have been actively involved in planning it.

To fulfill its function, adult education must be a continuous learning process conducted within the framework of the community, and it must be dedicated to the continuous reconstruction and improvement of both the human personality and the community in the light of social and technological change. It logically follows that to achieve this purpose, the adult education program must be geared intimately with the vital processes of community life. It must enhance the opportunity of every citizen to become instrumental in the development of his community. This is what Dean Ernest O. Melby was referring to when he said —

> Democracy is not an abstract philosophical concept, not merely something to talk about. It is most of all something to be lived in one's daily life in association with other men and women. Democracy means action . . . community policies should be developed as far as possible through discussion, with wide participation on the part of the citizens of the community. The present educational problems that are tearing many communities apart would become important activities for community education if there were some channel through which interested citizens could participate in the determination of educational policies.[23]

Adult education can and should become that channel. It will be only when it becomes intimately geared with the most pressing problems and concerns of the people and the community—as they view them. This means that not only must the adult educator himself study the community and identify its problems and needs, he must involve the people with him in the study if his ultimate purposes are to be achieved.

TO IDENTIFY NEEDS AND RESOURCES IS TO INVOLVE THE COMMUNITY

The adult educator approaches the study of his community with two dimensions of the task in mind. First, he personally wants to learn the community well enough to enable him to make intelligent administrative decisions in keeping with the general character of the community and also well enough to enable him to design instructional programs which will serve real needs and solve real problems in the community. Second and very important, he wants the process of community study itself to become an educational activity involving many citizens of the community so that it will increase democratic participation and facilitate community self-development.

The essentiality of the adult educator's personal knowledge of the community is obvious. Before the physician can prescribe he must diagnose the ailment, and to do this he must study the physique and history of the patient. So it is with the adult educator and the community. Also, organizing his study of the community to make it an educational activity for the community at large can serve several useful purposes for both the adult educator and the community. In the first place, it provides a ready-made program activity that can lead to the solution of community problems. As Biddle points out, the presence of problems in a community does not start the process of community improvement. That process begins only after some person or group has studied the situation, identified the problems, and awakened the hope that something can be done about them.[24] It is also an excellent means of fulfilling the basic function of adult education in developing higher levels of responsible citizenship through direct participation of adults in the study and planning processes which precede community improvement and development.

As a change agent in the community, the adult educator must recognize that cultural change does not occur overnight; that it must be introduced gradually; and that it is best assured when responsible leaders in the community recognize the need for such change and participate in the process of guiding its introduction and implementation. He should also recognize that representative citizens who participate with him in a systematic study of specific aspects of community life may have, by virtue of their familiarity with the local culture, more skillful insights into directions for program development in these areas than he does.

Another advantage of extensive citizen involvement with the adult educator in community study is the opportunity it affords the adult educator to become better known throughout the community and to get to know people who are competent to serve as teachers or leaders in his program. The next question becomes, How does he involve citizens with him in the study and identification of community problems and needs?

HOW TO INVOLVE THE COMMUNITY

To involve the community extensively may require a number of concurrent efforts on the part of the adult educator. No single approach is likely to prove wholly adequate on a continuing basis. Of the things he can do, some he will want to do continuously, some temporarily, and some perhaps not at all, depending on his particular community.

The following are some of the ways open to the adult education administrator for involving the community with him in the identification of adult education needs and program resources:

1. *Establish a personal acquaintanceship with and cultivate the friendship of key community leaders.*

These key individuals, who have extensive knowledge about the community and who are broadly recognized for their interest and influence in community improvement, can be helpful in a number of ways. Each of them is potentially a valuable source of personal advice and guidance for the adult educator, and each can serve as an individual on whom the adult educator can test his own ideas and interpretations. Also, when the adult educator has established good personal relationships with enough individuals who represent a cross-section of community interests, he may wish to arrange periodic breakfast or dinner meetings with them as a group and engage them in group discussion of specific questions relating to community problems and adult education needs. The topics discussed may be ones which the adult educator himself poses, or he may solicit from the group its assessment of community problems which imply the need for adult education activities. Such discussions may well generate ideas and project proposals which will energize these community leaders individually or collectively toward more active participation in projects designed to discover, clarify, or accommodate community needs in adult education. Moreover, such individuals, by virtue of their broad contacts, organizational involvements, and influence in the community, can increase the visibility and public awareness of the adult education program, its purposes, activities, and plans.

2. *Establish an identity with and utilize existing community organizations and groups.*

Within every community there exists a variety of formal organizations and informal groups which provide an excellent basis for the cooperative involvement of the community in the identification of educational needs. With respect to formal organizations, American community life is characterized by a great number and variety of clubs, organizations, leagues, associations, and societies into which people have formally organized themselves to pursue their common interests.

The adult educator must have an awareness of the significance of groups to community life; he must recognize that a knowledge of their leadership, basic composition, primary interest, and pattern of operation is essential to an effective working relationship with them. Their cooperation and organizational support can be of inestimable value to the development and operation of his adult education program. The question is, How does he enlist their cooperation and help?

Such organizations normally operate in areas of their own primary interest and concern, and they are not overtly seeking to help some other community organization or agency with its program unless by such cooperation and help they can help their own organization achieve its purposes. This is the opening the adult educator needs in that he can be of tremendous help to the formal organizations of the community. Virtually every organization sponsors, at some time or other, educational programs and activities for their constituents or for the community at large. By making available to them his knowledge of program planning and his skills in working with adult groups, the adult educator can enhance the effectiveness and educational value of their activities. In return for such functional services, he will be more likely to receive the support and assistance of the organization when he needs it.

Informal or "autonomous" groups are also very important. They exist in every community, but they are seldom identifiable publicly. It is generally recognized, however, that they exert a major influence on public opinion, community attitudes, and programs. Because the power structure of the community may be embodied in such groups, they often outweigh in influence the formal organizations and even the communications media of the community.[25]

Autonomous groups are characterized by spontaneous origin, lack of a formalized structure, informality of activity, and membership loyalty to the group. They are brought into being by such factors as proximity of residence, of work, or of worship of members; special circumstances within an area or proximity which furthers personal association; security found in the company of others; and personality attraction among individuals.[26] An informal group itself seldom associates openly with other groups; however, it may support other community activities along with organized groups.

No clear-cut method can be suggested which will be consistently effective in identifying or involving informal autonomous groups as such in organized community activity. Their very nature makes this difficult, yet their known influence and the communication network they maintain in the community make them potentially very helpful to the adult educator. Knowing this, the adult educator may find that his best approach to reaching and involving such groups is to identify their leaders, try to interest them, and capitalize on their influence to involve the group as a whole.

3. *Form citizen advisory committees around program content areas of potential need.*

Citizen advisory committees can be the eyes and the ears of the adult educator and his program. They represent one of the very best means of obtaining lay help in the determination of educational needs and the planning of successful programs of adult education. Such committees can render valuable service not only in identifying educational needs, but also in making the adult education program known to the community once it is in operation. They provide the people of the community a means through which they can participate actively in community affairs and help guide local educational policy.

The membership of an advisory committee is usually small, averaging six or ten members who represent a particular business, industrial, social, or economic group within the community. Members are carefully chosen on the basis of their occupational or professional competence and on the extent to which they are accepted and respected by their colleagues and fellow workers in the community.

By virtue of their specialized knowledge in the operational areas they represent, advisory committee members are in position readily to recognize and evaluate evidences of need for adult education programs in these areas. They have an enlightened self-interest in studying the needs in their areas, and they have the contacts and the capabilities to enable them to conduct surveys and studies with a minimum of effort. When properly chosen on the basis of their status as qualified and respected members of occupational and professional groups within the community, advisory committee members are able to speak for these groups in the planning and development of adult education programs.

4. *Affiliate with community organizations and groups that function in areas of personal and professional interest.*

The adult educator should become a part of his community. One way of doing this is to become a member of those reputable community organizations which relate to his personal, social, and professional interests. Through such affiliations the adult educator may extend his personal acquaintanceships in the community, gain greater acceptance and recognition for himself and his program, realize greater opportunities for continued professional growth, increase his service to the community, and achieve the personal satisfactions that come from activities and associations relating to his special interests. It is also well to remember that by his being an accepted and valued member of a group, the adult educator will probably be able to involve the group more readily and actively in his study of community problems and needs, and also secure the services of individual members of the group as professional resources for his educational program.

5. *Work with the community council or other agency designated to provide overall coordination of effort among agencies concerned with adult education or community development.*

In some of the larger, more complex communities, an adult education council exists to coordinate the efforts of numerous community organizations, agencies, and institutions engaged in adult education. Where they are able to function effectively, such councils provide a means of reducing duplication of effort and discovering untouched areas of need. They usually consist of professional representatives from the various community institutions, organizations, and agencies, both public and private, engaged in adult education. Where such a council is in operation, the public adult educator will probably find it worthwhile to affiliate and work with it. The council can be an additional means of identifying unmet needs and for interpreting his program to the community.

In some communities the coordinating function is vested in a community council, sometimes called a community development council.

This type of organization is broader in scope than the adult education council in that it is concerned with the coordination of overall community development. In many instances, the functions of adult education councils have been surrendered to overall community councils.

This type of council seeks to enrich and improve community life by strengthening the services and coordinating the efforts of existing community agencies. It also studies the changes occurring in the community which may create the need for additional services. Such councils, composed as they are of cross-sectional representation of the community, can be the means by which the adult educator becomes an active part of the total community structure and fits his adult education program to an overall program of community development. They are also organizations which, by reason of their very nature and purpose, could be easily involved in an organized study of the adult education needs in the community.

These are some of the more widely used, time-tested methods of involving the community in the processes of need identification, resource utilization, and program planning in adult education. There are other approaches, to be sure, and it remains the task of the professional adult educator to study his particular community and decide how best to involve it with him in identifying needs in adult education.

WHERE TO LOOK FOR NEEDS—WHAT TO STUDY

It has been said earlier that educational needs exist on several levels —individual, group, and community. Needs grow out of the problems encountered, the goals established, and the responsibilities assumed by individuals, organizations, and groups. Adults as individuals have educational needs relating to their personal aspirations, and they have needs associated with their roles and responsibilities as parents, citizens, workers, and consumers. The adult educator, therefore, as he proceeds with his personal study of the community and as he arranges for the involvement of others with him in an organized way, is concerned not only with *how* he studies his community, but also *what* to study and *where* to look in the community for evidence of these various levels and types of educational needs. He wants to be sure that both individual and group needs are studied and that no areas of real need are overlooked in the process.

In building his personal acquaintanceship with the community, the adult educator will be concerned with studying those aspects and characteristics of community life which carry insightful meaning for the kinds of intelligent administrative decisions he must make in planning and operating his program and in working with community groups. There are many factors operative in the dynamics of community structure and function which are important to the adult educator's understanding of his community. The following are generally regarded as perhaps the most essential:

- *Population characteristics* — age, racial and ethnic composition, population trends, and various vital statistics
- *Institutional structure* — agencies, institutions, organizations, and groups — their relationships, memberships, activities, interests, and functions
- *Value system* — the folkways, mores, historical traditions, the things the people hold dear
- *Social stratification* — the various social classes identifiable in the community
- *Economic base* — supporting industry and business, how the people make their living
- *Power structure* — the real leaders, as distinguished from apparent leaders
- *Ecological patterning* — land use, zoning, and physical planning.

Once his personal knowledge of the community has progressed substantially along these various lines, the adult educator will be in better position to design and organize a comprehensive study involving other individuals and groups in the community. A number of general guides to community study have been published and may be of considerable value to the adult educator in organizing citizen-group studies of the community.[27] These guides vary as to the relative emphasis given to specific elements of community life, and they are not wholly in agreement as to all aspects of the community that should be included in such a study. There are, however, four major elements considered by them all to be essential, and these may well serve as a beginning frame of reference for organizing a systematic study of the community for purposes of adult education program planning and community development. The four elements are the historical background and physical setting of the community; population characteristics; economic structure; and the functional operations of the community, its interactions and organizations.[28]

As he focuses on each of the segments of community life which constitute potential sources of educational need, the adult educator must decide whether an existing organization or group in the community can be utilized for studying needs in a particular area, or whether a special citizen advisory group should be formed. A comprehensive study in which maximum community involvement is achieved may well include a variety of sizes and types of groups working cooperatively and concurrently on specific aspects of each of the major elements of community study listed above. Some will be conducting formal surveys and compiling information, while others will be analyzing particular problems and potential solutions; some will be analyzing business or industrial surveys, while others will be studying the Census Report of the Community Population Characteristics; some will be studying problems of government such as crime, delinquency, health, and housing, while others will be investigating personnel needs of business or industry.

The adult educator must involve himself sufficiently with each group to maintain a proper identity with it and be reasonably informed at all times as to its status and progress, yet he must remain sufficiently detached from all groups so as to be able to coordinate the total effort and be available when needed as a consultant to any particular group. When the facts are in and analyzed, when alternative plans or solutions are considered and choices are made, recommendations should be forthcoming from each group regarding programs and projects.

GUIDING PRINCIPLES

As the adult educator goes about the job of involving the community and working with citizen groups in a self-study of educational needs, and regardless of the extent to which he forms special committees for this purpose or works with and through existing organizations and groups, certain principles of operation should be kept in mind.

1. The methodology employed in adult education activities must be consistent with the principles governing a democratically conceived adult society. Projects undertaken with citizen groups usually succeed in proportion to the extent that they are democratically planned and carried out.
2. The values which guide the development of the adult education program must be consistent with the enlightened values represented in the community.
3. The growth of the person, or persons, in the skills of democratic participation may well be more important than the activities by which they grow.
4. Programs initiated should grow out of bona fide needs; when needs are not clearly defined, they should be tested for validity before initiating programs designed to accommodate them.

5. A citizen advisory committee or study group should be formed only after the need for it is established and its task is clearly defined. Once such a committee is formed, it should be continued only so long as it is needed or the adult educator is prepared to work cooperatively with it.

In the final analysis, the adult educator's usefulness to his community will be in direct proportion to the extent that he is able to get the citizenry actively, democratically, and cooperatively involved in meaningful and socially useful programs, the need for which they have helped discover and the content of which they have helped to plan. This is a great challenge for any adult educator, but when properly done, the reward can be even greater than the challenge.

CHAPTER 8

PLANNING A BALANCED CURRICULUM

Raymond T. McCall and Robert F. Schenz

The impact of change, the new morality, the modern technology, and the social revolution have all given rise to urgent concerns for immediate attention to what we teach in the curriculum areas of public school continuing adult education. The development of a modern and dynamic curriculum offers a great challenge to the director of an adult education program. This challenge is well expressed in the following quotation:

> Tomorrow's schools will be schools without walls: a school built of doors which open to the entire community. Tomorrow's schools will reach out to the places which enrich the human spirit — to the museums, theaters, art galleries, to the parks and rivers and mountains. It will ally itself with the city, its busy streets and factories, its assembly lines and laboratories, so that the world of work will be the center of community life; for grown-ups as well as children; a shopping center of human services. It might have a community health clinic, a library, a theater and recreation facilities. It will provide formal education for all citizens — and it will not close its doors at three o'clock. It will employ its buildings round-the-clock and its teachers round-the-year. . . . We cannot afford to have an 85 billion dollar plant in this country open less than 30 percent of the time.[1]

The knowledge and skill that the director of the public school continuing adult education program can bring to bear on the challenge expressed above will determine the thrust and direction of public

Raymond T. McCall is principal of the San Jose Adult Center and assistant professor of education, San Jose State College, San Jose, California.

Robert F. Schenz is administrative coordinator of the Division of Adult Education, Los Angeles City Schools, Los Angeles, California.

adult education in the years ahead. This chapter will offer ideas and suggestions that should save the adult education director considerable frustration and time by presenting a planned approach and by the utilization of accumulated knowledge.

ESSENTIALS OF PLANNING

The experience of many directors over a long period of time indicates that curriculum development—

1. *Is a dynamic, continuous process.*
   To be viable and effective, the adult education program must have continuous evaluation and reappraisal. To meet the needs of a modern and dynamic community, a program must change to provide the educational activities and services required to meet the challenge of change.
2. *Involves those directly affected.*
   It is imperative in developing a program to begin with those most concerned—the adult students. They bring to the classroom many years of experiences that can be woven into the fabric of the class-room presentation. Opportunity should be provided for student participation in the development of the curriculum and also in assessing its effectiveness.
3. *Provides for group participation.*
   The minds and energies of many people who are in intimate contact with the interests, needs, and resources of the community will create a more effective product than the individual director could possibly provide by working alone.
4. *Requires long-term effort.*
   Enthusiasm for a proposed curriculum activity often impels proponents to push for immediate action. Every class or service that is hurriedly begun and folds quickly may hurt the long-term continuance of the total program.
5. *Is a complex of details.*
   Good program planning provides the proper instructional equipment and adequate meeting place arrangements that are most conducive to adult learning. A friendly social setting and guidance opportunities are necessary ingredients for a successful program. Adult learning is much more than a good student-teacher relationship. It involves good interpersonal relationships between members of the group and the entire program. Furthermore, a favorable attitude of individuals, groups, and organizations within the

community helps to build a needed climate for a successful continuing adult education program.

GOALS FOR CURRICULUM DEVELOPMENT

The establishment of basic goals and objectives of curriculum development provides a valuable foundation for determining educational activities and also measurement of progress at a later date. These goals should reflect the contributions that the anticipated program will make to neighborhood and community betterment as well as to the personal growth and achievement of participants. They may also suggest the desired relationships between the adult education program and the program of elementary, secondary, and higher education. Goodlad cautions that "curriculum planning has been and is still a trial-and-error business, guided at best by precepts derived from experience." [2]

Accordingly the school administrator is bewildered in his quest for structure and design in curriculum planning — not by a lack of statements on what the aims and purposes of the curriculum should be — but by a seeming lack of agreement among the many lists concerning specific aims and purposes of American education and the nature of courses which may be employed to implement these aims. "What was lacking," assert Hott and Sonstegard,[3] "was a conceptual system or theoretical structure capable of guiding curriculum research design."

Among the more notable past efforts at stating the aims and purposes underlying curriculum development in America are "Five Activities" published in 1860 by Herbert Spencer[4] in *What Knowledge Is of Most Worth?*; the seven "Cardinal Principles" of the Commission on the Reorganization of Secondary Education in 1918[5]; the four "objectives" of the Educational Policies Commission in 1938[6]; "Ten Imperative Needs of Youth," [7] Havighurst's[8] "Ten Developmental Tasks," 1948; *14 Point Statement*[9] of the White House Conference in November 1956; and the *Taxonomy of Educational Objectives*, 1956-1968, of Bloom,[10] into the cognitive, affective, and psycho-motor domains of behavioral aims.

In 1961 a joint committee of the American Association of School Administrators, the Council of Chief State School Officers, the National Association for Public School Adult Education, and the National Congress of Parents and Teachers reviewed previous lists of needs which the adult schools should serve and restated the "Seven Cardinal Principles" in terms of the needs of adult education; namely, health, command of the fundamental processes, worthy home membership, vocational training, citizenship, worthy use of leisure, and ethical character.[11] This effort yielded little that was new and did not help appreciably in simplifying and reclassifying existing lists.

Seeing a need to identify the elements of commonality and diversity in previous lists of underlying needs, principles, and purposes which form the structure and scope of the curriculum, Raymond McCall has attempted, as a possible basis for assessment of curriculum design, a reclassification of items into a five-category system under the following headings: intellectual, social, economic, aesthetic, and physical aims. While it is doubtful if it ever will be possible to identify curricular classes and areas which are completely and mutually exclusive, it is hoped that these classifications will aid the curriculum builder in establishing a more balanced curriculum and serve as a checklist for both depth and gaps in the adult school program.

Intellectual Aims

Intellectual aims are related to the attainment of information, skills, and habits required in order to think. These include communication skills, computation skills, cognitive skills, and the acquisition of facts and knowledge related to order in the universe derived from scientific methods.

Although these skills are employed to some extent in all of the curriculum areas, they are grouped together here for classification purposes. Historically, the basic level of these skills were known as the Three R's, except for problem solving by the scientific method, which is a more recent arrival on the educational scene prompted by the interest in scientific advances which have accelerated in the twentieth century.

The term *communication skills* has replaced the self-conscious "English and foreign languages" in recent nomenclature. Those skills, including the aims of "listening with understanding, speaking clearly and articulately, reading efficiently, and writing effectively," are similar in both domestic and foreign languages. A new emphasis on spoken language and on the importance of listening to correct models has begun to replace the older methods of reading and writing as the input and output systems of primary importance in communication. Experts hasten to point out that communication is not limited to verbal and auditory means, for much communication is nonverbal in nature by gesture, facial expression, inflection, emphasis, touch, feeling, and through the other senses.

Computation skills are in reality a form of symbolism to represent number relationships in quantifying reality. The use of quantitative communication is a critical factor in the space age. Even small children in the elementary school nowadays are familiar with the meaning of set theory; number systems; and communicative, distributive, and associative laws of the "new" math. Parents and teachers are increasingly turning to adult schools for retreading their math skills to keep pace with their children's schooling.

Nearly every human pursuit from family budgeting to moon travel involves mathematical knowledge. Math is used in science, engineering, and statistics to measure stresses, compute probability, study significances of differences; to predict, control, correlate; and to measure space, distance, and speed.

Cognitive skills employed in thinking, learning, and problem solving include remembering, imitating, copying, guessing, manipulating, describing, demonstrating, sensing, explaining, questioning, perceiving, analyzing, discriminating, discovering, inquiring, connecting, understanding, differentiating, systematizing, coding, classifying, serially ordering, reciting, reflecting, imagining, hypothesizing, including, excluding, eliminating, adding, subtracting, multiplying, dividing, substituting, associating, synthesizing, delimiting, exploring, verifying, predicting, doubting, reasoning, inducing, deducing, inferring, interpreting, generalizing, conceptualizing, translating, abstracting, symbolizing, applying, extending, elaborating, evaluating, modifying, reorganizing, transposing, stereotyping, creating, asserting, and judging.

The implications of using all of the thinking processes listed above are enormous. Teachers who require little more than listening, reading, and memorizing should spend some time contemplating how a greater variety of thinking activities might be employed in presenting subject matter. These suggest greater involvement of the student in the learning process as a means to more productive cognitive behavior. The importance of fuller understanding of the intellectual processes is underlined by most recent statements of education moving from "what to think" toward emphasis on "how to think."

The *facts, concepts, and systems of knowledge* related to understanding the universe which have been revealed by the scientific methods of investigation are related to intellectual aims, since these bodies of knowledge are the result of applying these intellectual skills. Adult educators wishing to keep their programs abreast of the times should experiment with offerings in the science fields. As long as education continues to honor learning what is already known as much as preparing people to solve problems not yet contemplated, the facts and structure of the sciences remain important intellectual pursuits.

Social Aims

The term *behavioral sciences* is gradually replacing "social studies" and "social sciences" as the designation of studies involved in the area of human relationships.

Social aims referred to in the literature of educational aims include studying the relation of history and geography to man, the aims of personal development and adjustment to society, the aims of fostering human dignity and human rights, and the aims of developing creative citizenship and improving social institutions and goals.

Historically, the roots of our institutions, customs, values, goals, and beliefs are in the past. Knowledge of our geographical and political expansion and democratic tradition is germane to the understanding of our present position and future prospects in the area of human relations.

The aims of *personal development and character development* are at the grass roots of social development. Maturity, wisdom, social responsibility, ethical character, and traits such as honesty, humility, trustfulness, and credibility are social goals of educational achievement. The application of ethical values to decisions and choices while striving to achieve the best that is in the person is the ultimate goal of learning.

The aims of *social adjustment* found in the literature are many and varied. Some of them are—

To find congenial companions and relate one's personality to others.
To become integrated into the cooperative brotherhood of man.
To develop rich, sincere, and varied social relationships.
To live and work cooperatively with others.
To show empathy and compassion for others.
To increase our understanding of other peoples and times.
To respect customs, traditions, and mores of other peoples.
To prefer peace, goodwill, and human understanding.
To develop acceptable behavior, manners, social graces, and courtesy.
To prefer sharing and cooperating to greed, selfishness, envy, and advantage.
To develop a balance between conformity and individualism.
To develop a balance between independence and interdependence.
To improve social solidarity and reduce factionalism.

The aims of *nurturing human dignity* are—

To develop respect and concern for those who differ from ourselves regardless of race, creed, color, wealth, or status.

To respect and try to understand honest differences in opinion.

To oppose bias, prejudice, and alienation.

To assure that reward and recognition are based on individual worth and intrinsic value as a human being.

To cultivate all kinds of abilities and capacities.

To recognize the need of all for identity, self-respect, acceptance, love, belonging, recognition, and prestige of earned image.

To accord tolerance, justice, and mercy to all persons.

The aims of *human rights and freedom* in a democratic society are —

The freedom to live, assemble, believe, worship, criticize, think, be educated, work, enjoy good health, have equal opportunity, and share in the equitable distribution of goods and services available in society.

To accept the responsibilities, duties, and consequences required as a condition of human rights and freedom.

To recognize that minorities as well as majorities have rights.

To reduce the acquisition of status, power, prestige, and privilege caused by race, class position, and maintenance of the status quo.

Citizenship aims do not refer to partisanship, narrow patriotism, or loyalty to a narrow nationalism but to the development of a sense of relevancy of citizenship to one's own life and common interests and goals based on universal rights and duties. Some of the content areas which produce civic aims are public affairs courses, leadership training, community service classes, and civic education.

The basic objective of the social and behavioral sciences is to improve the effectiveness of the individual in society, for society is as strong as its weakest link. Every incompetent, ignorant, apathetic, and hostile citizen is a menace to us all.

Economic Aims

In spite of the opposition of the proponents of intellectual goals to practical and pragmatic goals of occupational training, education is being charged increasingly with "the need to bring school more closely in contact with vocational information and needs — in order to guide the unskilled into suitable vocations." The OEO and MDTA programs of the federal government have recognized that we can no longer afford the economic waste of joblessness and have challenged the schools to accept the responsibility or face the threat of other agencies' taking over the responsibility for basic and economic education. Economic education is not limited to vocational training, however; students need to know more about the economic value of their vocational skills, more about obtaining value in the distributive system, and the consequences of not conserving our personal and natural resources.

The kinds of *vocational training* schools should offer depend on costs, employment opportunities, length of training required, and other considerations. In some areas, all industry wants is people with good general education. The rest will be provided by on-the-job training. However, as competition for employment increases, the person with some training will be preferred.

Consumer education involves a number of skills related to deriving the most value from the purchasing dollar. How to make intelligent choices; how to arrange the financing of long-term purchases; how to budget one's income; how to figure discounts, taxes, percentages, and carrying charges; how to invest and protect investments; and how to resist deceptive advertising are topics suitable for consumer education courses. Courses designed to inform the student on insurance for fire, flood, collision, property damage, illness, old age, and other conditions are also possibilities for adult education offerings.

Conservation of economic resources is one of the most neglected, but important, topics in the area of economic planning. The diseases of the city, poverty, involuntary idleness, overproduction, farm surplus, depletion of soil and mineral wealth, flood and pollution control, wildlife conservation, fire control, and military training are some of the areas of concern in conserving our physical and natural resources.

Aesthetic Aims

"Without aesthetics," according to Brumbaugh, "more complex values have no foundation." There is an effective factor in every rational decision because judgment is intellectual, but preference is aesthetic. What then are the realms of the aesthetic development? An analysis of the aesthetic aims reveals numerous cultural, aesthetic, and humanities courses which contribute to the following aims:

To develop tastes, value, and appreciations.

To promote increased aesthetic awareness, sensitivity, and receptivity.

To offer opportunities to express feelings and reflect values in creative pursuits and to express dreams and visions.

To develop interests, aptitudes, talents, capacities, and resources of the body, mind, and spirit for a fuller realization of the self and for the worthy use of leisure.

To promote happiness and satisfaction in achievement of something of importance.

To recognize merit and to honor craftsmanship and beauty.

To train the imagination.

Courses which contribute to aesthetic growth may be classified according to three sorts of activity which they promote: recreation, creativity, and contemplation of aesthetic and ethical values.

The recreational and spectator levels of aesthetic offerings provide opportunity to appreciate, enjoy, and learn about worthwhile values. These include music history and appreciation, history and appreciation of art, nature study, outdoor living, social dancing, sports and attendance at spectator activities in the theatre, art exhibits, concerts, and cinema.

The *creative, expressive, or fine arts* may include the composition or performance of music, drama, poetry, or the creation of art, crafts, literature, sculpture, architecture, and landscaping. Home arts include flower arranging, interior decorating, cooking, sewing and costume designing, gardening, and home planning. The graphic arts include printing and photography.

The *contemplative arts or humanities* deal with ethics, morals, philosophy, religion, spiritual values, mysticism, and contemplation of man's place, role, and significance in the cosmos.

Physical Aims

In the broadest sense, physical aims include areas of biological growth; medical care, health, and hygiene; mental health; physical fitness; and developmental activities.

Intelligent use of the body requires an understanding of the biological and physiological facts which contribute to human growth and functioning and to the changes in living things over time. Knowledge of the human system should include scientific facts and methods employed in studying the digestive, circulatory, excretory, glandular, heat regulatory, respiratory, reproductive, auditory, and visual systems of the body and the effect of nourishment, temperature, exercise, rest, age, and emotional strain on the organism. Elements of family life education related to gerontology, marriage, childbirth, psycho-sex roles, and child rearing should be related to scientific facts and information.

Information related to *medical care* should be available to all persons, and adult schools should offer courses related to medical findings in the prevention and cure of disease, correction of defects, and alleviation of pain. School counselors should establish relations with community health agencies where concerned students may be referred. Lecture series on disease and health in cooperation with the medical, dental, and psychiatric professions may be organized through school auspices. The time is not too distant when the right of medical aid will be as well established as the right to equal opportunity in jobs and schooling. Schools already offer *instruction in health and hygiene* which often includes first aid; lifesaving; effects of drugs, alcohol, narcotics, and nicotine on the body; sanitation; personal hygiene; diet and weight control; baby care; childbirth; and care of diseases of the aging. With time, it is hoped the list will be expanded to give protection to all of our citizens and provide them with at least a layman's understanding of the care, prevention, and treatment of disease.

Mental health societies are springing up everywhere as the public becomes aware of the social problem and extent of mental illness. Educational aims already reflect the concern over mental health, and schools are being encouraged to offer courses in the causes, identification, and cure of mental illness.

Physical fitness and development activities help to attain John Locke's ideal of "a sound mind in a sound body" as the end of education. The objective of physical fitness is even more difficult to obtain with adults than with children. These aims are —

Effective use of the body; develop better coordination, strength, endurance, stamina, and reserve energy to sustain effort, resist fatigue, and recover rapidly from strain; promote muscular fitness, efficiency, and proficiency; develop good health, posture, balance, poise, physical stability and agility, graceful and coordinated movements, alertness, control, and special skills.

The impetus which gave rise to the prominence of sports and physical education was the poor physical condition of draftees during World War I. The military services continue to require men in top physical condition to defend our country, and rigorous men are required in all walks of life to survive in this age of tension and rapid change.

A curriculum which is at all sensitive and responsive to the needs of a changing society can never be settled once and for all. The ability to change when change is needed is, and should remain, a characteristic of the best practice in adult education. This effort to evaluate aims of education in terms of current realities should be only a part of the continuing effort of adult educators to reflect the needs of the individual and the society in their curriculum offerings.

ASSESSING NEEDS AND INTERESTS

The identification of needs and resources has been treated in great detail by Samuel E. Hand in Chapter 7. He suggests looking for educational needs in the community by organized, careful community study and indicates ways of involving the community with the adult education program director in identifying these needs and resources.

A Look at the Individual Adult

In addition, the individual is a rich source of learning objectives. Havighurst [12] presents the developmental tasks of the individual and suggests these tasks as a basis on which to build the adult education curriculum. He identifies six developmental periods: infancy and early childhood (to 6 years), middle childhood (6-12 years), adolescence (12-18 years), early adulthood (18-30 years), middle age (30-55 years), and later maturity. These developmental tasks originate from the process of physical maturation, from the cultural pressure of society, and from the personal values and aspirations of the individual during the six developmental periods that each and every individual must go through.

The orientations of individuals that Houle [13] identifies are another vital area for in-depth study in identifying needs and interests of adults. He suggests (a) the "goal-oriented—those who use education as a means of accomplishing fairly clear-cut objectives," (b) the "activity-oriented—those who take part because they find in the circumstances of the learning a meaning which has no necessary connection, and often no connection at all, with the content or the announced purposes of the activity," and (c) the "learning-oriented—those who seek knowledge for its own sake." These, as Houle cautions, are not pure types, but the central emphasis of each group is clear and should provide the adult education administrator another frame of reference for assessing needs and interests.

After the identification of needs and resources, it is necessary to assess and establish priorities of needs and interests. Assessing these needs and interests can be approached from several points of view: the vocational and occupational interests of people in the community, their age distribution, creative interests, organizational affiliations, economic earning levels, number of years of schooling completed, reading interests, nationality backgrounds, and vital statistics dealing with health and welfare.

Other Sources for Determining Adult Needs

Kempfer[14] found that the content, methods, and organization of courses to meet the needs and interests of adults were determined best by the following practices, ranged in order of merit:

1. Cultivation of "coordinators" or liaison people in industry, business, labor, and community organizations who watch for opportunities for education to perform a service.
2. Receiving requests from business, industrial, labor, and community groups.
3. Study of deficiencies of adults.
4. Maintaining extensive personal acquaintanceships with community leaders and groups.
5. Examination of census and similar data.
6. Making systematic surveys of business, civic, and industrial life of the community.
7. Examination of published surveys of other communities and similar literature.
8. Examination of catalogs, schedules, publicity materials, and programs of comparable institutions.
9. Acting on hunch.
10. Being sensitive to civic, personal, and social problems of people which can be alleviated by education.
11. Checking on known interests of people.
12. Utilization of checklists and other interest finders.
13. Receiving individual requests.

Information about important population characteristics may be gained from many sources, such as the last federal census which provides pamphlets on these characteristics such as population state by state, and for communities of various sizes within each state. These statistics should be available at the local library or may be obtained from the Government Printing Office or any field office of the Department of Commerce. The use of computers in the storing and retrieving of data suggests additional sources for the director of a public school continuing adult education program.

It is much easier to get communitywide statistics and data than to try to get specific data by areas or neighborhoods. However, since the geographical location or distribution of the people by neighborhoods or districts is of vital concern in planning programs, the neighborhood picture is important. People vary greatly in many characteristics, such as educational and economic levels, not only between communities, but also in neighborhoods of the same community.

In smaller communities the job is, of course, relatively simple. Personal contacts, plus those of a program planning committee, will give considerable information. If the community is medium-sized or larger, considerable help may be secured by contacting appropriate governmental leaders at City Hall. Local Chambers of Commerce, employment bureaus, health departments, planning boards, bureaus of vital statistics, and departments of education may have background information and studies of value. By all means, consult the local library system.

As Hand suggests in Chapter 7, the process, as well as the product, of community study will be of value in community planning. The involvement of community leaders will establish a wealth of potentially valuable community leader friendships, as well as much informal but significant information about the community not available in printed form. Furthermore, the interests of the people involved in the study can promote a wide basis of public interest and support.

A few cautions might be suggested in the process of discovering program implications and the assessment of needs and interests from a community and neighborhood study —

1. Continuous effort must be maintained in keeping up-to-date with accelerated change. As conditions and situations change, people's needs and interests change.
2. Since adult education is but one factor in a complex social setting, it is very important that careful analysis be given to your findings. Many factors influence and determine people's needs and interests.
3. The need many times to quantify data should not exclude the concern for qualitative considerations. Interests and needs are influenced by the quality of the program as well as the quantitative aspects.

DETERMINING PROGRAMS

After a very careful and thorough study of the community and the assessment of the needs and interests of the people who live in it has been made, comes the difficult task of matching these interests and needs with learning opportunities. An analysis of hundreds of community adult education programs reveals the fact that courses offered tend to fall into a limited number of broad groupings. A good program that is well balanced and sufficiently diversified will include offerings in most of these groups. Moreover, the director of a public school adult program must be aware that while, in the short-run, a cafeteria-style curriculum may meet the more visible needs of the community, in the long-run, sequential, developmental, and in-depth programing must be provided to meet all the needs and interests of the total community.

A helpful listing of possible courses and activities within a balanced program and other forms of public school adult education programs commonly offered is provided in the next chapter. In addition, more specific help can be obtained from studying the programs of communities that seem to have successful adult school activities. Also, the membership directory of the National Association for Public School Adult Education lists the names and addresses of community directors who may be willing to help by sending copies of their materials and programs.

In the final analysis, however, it is the director of adult education who, after gathering and analyzing all the data available to him, makes the program decisions. Not only does the director have the responsibility for the determination of what learning activities and educational services to provide, but also he has the responsibility for putting these decisions into effect.

USE OF ADVISORY COMMITTEES

While building the curriculum and making it effective are the responsibilities of the director, he should obtain as much assistance as possible. Frequently this assistance is obtained through a general advisory committee on adult education or a number of committees advising in specific areas of concern to adult education. The efforts of many minds to identify needs and to suggest courses or activities to meet the needs are far better than the effort of one. Unlike the director of adult education, these volunteers are in the midst of community life – in business, in industry, in homes, in associations of all kinds – and collectively bring a breadth of vision denied the individual administrator.

There are numerous types of advisory committees which have proven successful in both large and small communities throughout the country. The general organization and planning of the committees does not vary greatly, but it is important for each committee's objectives to be well defined.

The general types of advisory committees concerned with public school continuing adult education are —

1. *Specific subject area advisory committee*
   This type of committee undoubtedly is the most popular in the

field of adult or vocational education. It is felt that it is of greater value than the more comprehensive general advisory committee.

2. *General advisory committee*
   This more comprehensive type of committee consists of a group of citizens who discuss the general problems of adult education.

3. *Subcommittee system*
   The subcommittee system has been used effectively in communities where the general advisory committee has used each of its members as a subcommittee chairman. These chairmen report actions of their groups to the general advisory committee.

4. *Coordinating committee*
   This committee has the status of recommending to the adult school the areas of instruction which they deem desirable. They do not participate in the recommendation of facilities, instructors, or curriculum, but merely indicate their awareness of particular needs.

5. *Temporary advisory committee*
   This committee is appointed to make recommendations concerning a specific problem of the adult school and is then discharged.

6. *Specific organization education committee*
   This type of committee is usually more characteristic of the large urban areas where clubs and organizations have specific educational committees to meet with the school administrator and assist in planning programs for the adult school.

7. *Individual lay advisers*
   This approach of gaining advice from individual citizens permits the administrator to select those persons who will represent certain aspects of the adult population. The advice is received via many personal contacts rather than a general meeting.

8. *Informal advice*
   It is important for the adult education administrator to make many contacts throughout the community. Through this informal network, he frequently receives many suggestions and ideas to strengthen the public school continuing adult education program.

The functions of the advisory committee are many and varied. Listed below are some of these functions:

1. *Instructor recommendation*
   The committee can recommend to the administrator individuals who can serve as leaders or instructors in the adult education field.

2. *Equipment selection*
   Lay persons who have had experience in the subject area are better able to recommend the purchase of proper equipment or to assist in its acquisition.
3. *Curriculum materials*
   It must be realized that the adult educator cannot fully know the exact content of materials of such varying types as are used in the adult school.
4. *Certification and achievement*
   Because certification is required in many areas of the adult program the advisory committees are invaluable in determining work-life, socio-civic life, or home-life standards.
5. *Supplementary information*
   Generally speaking, committee members have an excellent overall view of the specific area of educational endeavor. Therefore, they are able to suggest supplementary information, booklets, and other materials to be used in the instructional program.
6. *Bibliographies and surveys*
   Advisory committees have been used to make necessary community surveys or to compile bibliographies of materials on adult education.
7. *Promotion*
   There is need for promotion of cooperation between the home, business, industry, civic groups, and the school. The best promotion any program can have is from those people who act as lay advisers.
8. *New programs*
   To be most effective the advisory committee should expect to be consulted on the formation of new programs.

PROGRAM TRENDS

The trends of the times—the social revolution, the new morality, modern technology, and the impact of change—will dictate the nature and content of the adult education curriculum. Changing community, state, and world problems and crises, as well as problems that challenge the person and the family, suggest the urgency of the task that faces the director of the public school continuing adult education program.

A review of the literature of the field, a careful examination of an extensive number of programs, and a serious concern for meeting the needs and interests of adults reveal the following trends in public school continuing adult education programs:

1. *Broadening the scope of the program*
An analysis of current program announcements shows a breadth, depth, and diversity of activities and educational services heretofore unrivaled. Today, a limited, stereotyped program cannot adequately meet the varied and changing interests and needs of adults. (An exception to this trend is the intensification of effort in a few limited areas such as the federally funded Adult Basic Education, Manpower Development and Training Act, and Vocational Education programs.)

2. *Offering educational opportunities for specific groups*
The problems that people face are usually specific. The kinds of services they want through adult education must be intimately connected with their needs. Young adults, senior citizens, lower educational background groups, parents and homemakers, factory workers, professional workers, and others need learning activities tailored to fit their particular and peculiar problems.

3. *Creating partnerships with community groups*
Cosponsorship with such groups as the PTA, labor and business organizations, and other professional and civic groups not only provides sources of leadership but also assures support for the undertaking.

4. *Extending of programs into the community*
Although the program is public school sponsored and financed, more and more activities are being located in libraries, churches, homes, factories, offices, and governmental buildings, in fact, wherever the instruction can best be given psychologically and environmentally. This gives validity to the movement toward the "community school" concept.

5. *Establishing research and demonstration centers*
The Adult Education Demonstration Project, a research and development center established by the Los Angeles City Schools under Title III, ESEA, is an excellent example of the concern for experimentation and evaluation of (a) promising teaching techniques and procedures; (b) the educational hardware such as teaching machines, learning laboratories, and study skill equipment; and (c) the educational software such as books, films, workbooks, and the many other items commercially produced that support the adult education instructor in doing a more efficient job.

6. *Integrating adult education with the total educational program*
Adult education can serve and supplement educational efforts at all levels — elementary, secondary, and higher education. Courses

for the in-service training of teachers; informational activities about the school system such as "Know Your Schools," "Modern Math for Elementary School Parents," and "Teaching Reading in the Elementary School"; and opportunities for visitation to schools by adults are some of the cooperative services being provided other levels of education.

7. *Providing adult education "around-the-clock" and "around-the-year"*
   Increasing flexibility and variation in the kinds of services and the time they are offered is being provided by full-time community adult schools and occupational centers that are open from 8 a.m. to 10 p.m. all year long.

8. *Offering more creative educational services*
   Discussion groups, team teaching, field trips, educational tours, clinics, demonstrations, consultations, reading and informational services, home-study courses, workshops, forums and lectures, instruction by TV—all bring a more imaginative, innovative, and creative approach to adult education programing.

9. *Utilizing the new technology*
   The new electronic hardware now on the market is more and more being adapted to the teaching-learning process, especially in adult education.

10. *Expanding counseling and guidance services*
    More and more programs reflect the need for experienced counseling and guidance services to more efficiently guide adults into the world of work and to help them use wisely the increasing amount of leisure time.

THE FUTURE

I simply am unable to prescribe with any useful precision the school programs that will markedly alleviate the conditions that mankind faces and probably continues to face: tidal waves of knowledge and people, abject poverty, pollution, social disorganization, the sheer magnitude of grasping and shaping the culture, changing values and mores, alienation among members of all age groups, and failure to develop a feeling of personal worth. My own inadequacies in this regard would depress me less if I could see around me more plans that approximate in imagination and clarity our brilliant analyses of the conditions we face.[15]

The tidal waves of knowledge and people strongly suggest that America is likely to experience an adult education explosion during the next few decades. Johnstone [16] concludes that the typical adult education student today is young, urban, and fairly well educated, and this is exactly the type of person who will be around in greatly increased numbers in the very near future. While the population as a whole will grow by about 35 percent over the next two decades, the increase in the number of adults under 35 will be much greater than this, probably close to 70 percent. For the future, this means nearly 57 million young adults by 1982 compared to 34 million today.

Within two decades, the population will contain as many as 64 percent more adults who have been to college, 59 percent more who have attended high school, and, by contrast, some 15 percent fewer with only a grade school education. It should be abundantly clear that the potential audience for adult education is increasing at a much faster rate than the population as a whole.

The concern for the shorter workweek and the extension of automation strongly suggest many more hours available for pursuits other than work. At the same time, the trend toward even greater specialization of occupational skills in our society shows no prospect of reversal. It seems likely, therefore, that learning-for-work and learning-for-leisure will together come to dominate the adult education scene to an even greater extent than they do today.

However, the paradox is that the segment of the population which may realize the greatest increment of free time in an age of automation is, on the one hand, the least well prepared to handle it, and on the other, the least likely to turn to continuing adult education to develop and expand its spare-time interests. It is this, perhaps, that constitutes the most critical challenge to the adult educators of the future.

CURRICULUM DEVELOPMENT IN THE 1970'S

What, then, must the curriculum planners for public adult education do to meet the problems of the "tidal waves of knowledge and people, abject poverty, pollution, social disorganization, the sheer magnitude of grasping and shaping the culture, changing values and mores, alienation among members of all age groups, and failure to develop a feeling of personal worth?"

1. The curriculum of the 1970's will focus on helping adults "learn to learn"; to understand "what is going on and why"; to seek out, process, and use information and knowledge; to think, reason, and develop objectivity — and to place less emphasis on teaching specific subject matter.
2. The curriculum of the 1970's will be designed for adults in terms of both content and procedure and will be organized around

people, placing greater emphasis on the needs of the individual and his societal context than on conventional standard courses and teaching procedures.

3. The curriculum of the 1970's must create educational experiences for the entire family with more integration and overlapping in the education of children, youth, and adults. The "educational complex" will permit total family participation in a continuous learning process.

4. The curriculum of the 1970's will be directed, in large measure, to life-counseling multiformat programs involving several agencies, home video tapes, and computer-assisted instruction.

5. Curriculum development in the 1970's will be aided and assisted by large regional curriculum development centers utilizing computers and systems analysis and the broader-based resources of a region rather than the local area or district resources.

CHAPTER 9

MAJOR CURRICULUM AREAS
AND PROGRAM CONCERNS

Carl E. Minich

INTRODUCTION

There are inumerable aspects of the program about which an adult school administrator must be concerned, but there are only two basic essentials—the administrator himself and the program he devises. However you delve into the manifold problems of the administrator, their prominence becomes evident.

The administrator operates the program. Whether he does it well or not depends to a great extent on how well he organizes himself. If he fragments his energies, the program is likely to suffer. If he only looks on benignly while the teachers or students take over, the program again is likely to suffer. If he is poorly organized, if he is harried and pressured, if he cannot delegate without abdicating authority, if he cannot maintain his status and therefore the status of what he does, if he cannot inject himself into the school power structure, if he cannot carry out many other missions—the program will suffer.

He must at the same time be sensitive but show a thick skin, keep his nose to the grindstone and ear to the ground, act as troubleshooter while keeping calm, run a tight ship with a loose rein, be aggressive but know when to quit.

He must have a more than intellectual knowledge of the vital issues of the day. He must know not only what poverty is but what it means,

Carl E. Minich is coordinator of the NEA Job Corps Project Interchange, National Education Association, Washington, D. C. Special acknowledgment is made to Mrs. Evelyn W. Pickarts, supervisor, Health and Civic Education, Los Angeles City Schools, Los Angeles, California, and to Joseph Mangano, chief, Bureau of General Continuing Education, State Department of Education, Albany, New York, for their assistance in the writing of this chapter.

not only the age of "old age" but the problems the aged must face, not only recognize change but understand what change portends.

This is only to say that the adult administrator (and the adult teacher as well) must be an integral part of the life about him. He has to be a visceral thinker. He has to be personally interested in public issues. He has to be involved in causes and conditions and know other involved people.

Anybody can obtain the statistical facts about his community, but not everybody—certainly not one of the uninvolved—can know what those facts mean. Anybody can take college work in adult education, but not everybody can bring that theoretical knowledge successfully from the campus to the adult classroom.

The transition can be traumatic, yet the trauma of experience can seldom be avoided—nor should it be. Experience is the medium which tempers the metal.

And it is experience that is being widely sought now as the adult education field expands into business, industry, government—into practically every facet and institution of life. The demands for highly trained and experienced adult leaders are great. Professional studies on the campus do provide the intellectual competence, but experience to mold that intellectual competence into operating competence can be gained only on the job which tests the intellectual competencies.

This chapter, then, will identify major program areas for adult education planning and will provide practical suggestions for their successful administration.

A CONTINUOUSLY EVOLVING CURRICULUM

The basics of adult education have not changed since the movement first began in this country. While the core of public school adult education is still to provide elementary and secondary education for adults who were unable to finish their formal schooling, the field has grown in many dimensions. It has broadened its base, offering a greater variety of studies to attract the disadvantaged, undereducated, and school dropouts aiming at an elementary certificate or high school diploma, as well as other courses to attract people from every social strata. It has developed its offerings in many areas of skill and learning to include typing, shorthand, and a variety of other business subjects. At the same time, it has raised its standards, requiring an improved level of performance in even the beginning classes.

Time is a significant dimension. Adult education has expanded its classes in many parts of the country to around-the-clock operations.

At one point in adult education history, education for citizenship in some geographical areas became, perhaps, the major offering of the school. As the tide of immigrants receded, so did the importance of citizenship education, although most schools still retain a few classes on their schedules. As citizenship education receded in importance, a new study area—education for better living—took its place in order to help both new and old citizens improve themselves, their homes, and their understanding of their families.

Basic adult education in recent years has made a strong comeback in high unemployment areas where individuals frequently lacked the basic education necessary to get and hold any but the most menial jobs. Once jobs above the menial were obtained, higher goals which needed to be met were set by the people; therefore, technical education—the newest in the galaxy of adult study areas—began working alongside adult basic education in a similar capacity. There has been a steady progression of adult education in tune with the times and the needs of the people. Observable trends for the years ahead are highlighted in the sections which follow.

Adult Basic Education

The impetus given adult basic education by federal funding in 1964 under the Economic Opportunity Act has caused not only an increase in the number of classes and registrations, but has also brought the realization of the need for curriculum modifications, materials, and trained leadership. Adult basic education, if it is to meet the needs of the disadvantaged population, can no longer utilize its historical curriculum, which was developed to impart skills and knowledge to enable foreign-born adults to attain naturalization. Neither can the curriculum continue to resemble that of the elementary school.

Federal efforts to eliminate poverty and the ensuing legislation aimed at raising the economic and social levels of disadvantaged adults have brought a realization to the education world and, more specifically, to the adult educator, of the high correlation between proficiency in the basic skills of reading, writing, and arithmetic and job opportunities and job success. Many studies have shown that the child from families of low educational achievement usually repeats the pattern. These facts—the correlation between education and job success and the correlation between parental educational levels and children's success in formal education—must be the paramount criteria on which the adult basic education curriculum is being developed.

If adult education is to help in alleviating these problems, adult educators must begin to think of curriculum modifications in terms of a new definition of adult basic education which takes these factors into account.

The vast differences in the populations to be served should be considered in the development of adult basic education curriculums. No one curriculum can be designed to serve all of the segments of our disadvantaged population. For example, a program for native-born disadvantaged in urban ghettos cannot be implemented on an Indian reservation of the Southwest, nor can an English-as-a-second-language program designed for recently migrated agrarian Puerto Ricans be utilized for the native-born, French-speaking adults in some of our Northeastern states. Therefore, curriculums must be designed to meet specific objectives that will take cognizance of and have respect for the cultural differences of the population to be served. However, there are enough commonalities so that guidelines for the development of a meaningful curriculum can be stated.

Four years of intense efforts at developing literacy skills have taught that there is no such thing as "instant literacy." The time span for the development of the communication skills can and must be compressed, but aspiring to bring functional literacy levels to total illiterates in a matter of hours is, with our present-day knowledge of materials and techniques, not a realistic endeavor. Therefore, program designs must reflect an understanding of the time and the intensity of instruction which must be provided to achieve maximum results. The traditional format of one or two two-hour meetings per week is far from desirable if the program is to change the functional literacy level of the adult in order that he can achieve the economic success which, probably, has motivated his enrollment. Programs which provide a minimum of 9 to 12 hours a week should be the objective of directors.

Disadvantaged adults are often under tremendous outside pressures, i.e., economic pressures, health pressures, family pressures, etc., and may find it impossible to adjust their life schedules to predetermined adult basic education program schedules. Therefore, opportunities should be provided, through the use of programed materials, self-directed materials, and new technology, for independent study in learning laboratory situations at times of the day and evening when it is possible for them to attend. In addition, services should be provided under which child-care problems can be alleviated by providing opportunities — in consort with other agencies and programs — for child care while the parent is attending adult basic education classes.

Adults from disadvantaged groups are often reluctant to seek literacy education primarily because, in the past, there has been little relationship between their economic and social problems and the curriculum of adult basic education programs. Therefore, the curriculum must provide for opportunities not only to develop the literacy skills but also to provide supportive services which will assist the enrollee to utilize these skills. This can be accomplished by referral to community agencies and institutions which can help him meet his objectives.

To be viable, the adult basic education curriculum cannot be developed and implemented in a school situtation isolated from the rest of society. The adult basic education program should be developed in cooperation with other agencies of government such as social, welfare, labor, and employment. Continued communication with the industrial community, through the personnel men of industry, is also highly essential.

Instructors in adult basic education must be trained to diagnose reading disabilities and to interpret from this diagnosis the cure for specific inadequacies. They should also learn, through pre- or in-service training, to use wisely a variety of materials.

The curriculum should provide, as an integral part of the basic skills program, opportunities for the adult to gain knowledge and understanding in the social living skills such as health and nutrition, orientation to the world of work, family life education, and practical government. Much can be gained from discussion groups and group counseling situations. It is unrealistic to expect adults with low levels of literacy to develop more sophisticated concepts in the areas mentioned above primarily by reading. While the adult students' literacy level may be low, their degree of sophistication developed from life experiences can be appreciably enhanced, and efforts to accomplish this should be encouraged. The program must provide vehicles to develop further social living skills concepts through the use of audiovisual and group discussion opportunities. Recently developed curriculum materials for this purpose are available through NAPSAE.

Every adult basic education program should provide for intense, individual counseling services from the time the student is recruited and oriented to the program until such time as he is ready to be referred to either a higher educational opportunity, a job-training program, or a job opportunity. Throughout this time the counselor should provide open communication lines with agencies such as social welfare, health, and labor so that needed services can be provided as the student's needs arise.

It is only through the development of a relevant curriculum and a comprehensive system of services to the individual that programs of adult basic education will attract and upgrade those in our population who are educationally and economically disadvantaged and for whom such programs are designed.

Parent and Family Life Education

Adult basic education is only one of the developing frontiers open to adult educators as they plan their programs for the future. Family life education, a rapidly expanding field in which numerous agencies are becoming involved, is a natural program area for public schools and colleges because they are located wherever families are. Indeed, they have as their central purpose for existence the heart of the family — children and youth — and will in the future more and more involve parents. This involvement may take various forms, such as programs of guided observation for parents of preschool children or of children with learning and behavior problems, psychological studies of teenagers and the hazards they face in culturally deprived areas or in affluent suburbs, or studies of the nature of violence or developmental psychology. Family life education might include courses to help parents to know what their children are studying and how to work with them at home. There might be discussions of the importance of education for advancement in work and life, or the school curriculum, or how to prepare the child for college.

For a society in the process of great change, strong families and effective parents are imperative, and education for this vital role an urgent necessity. Although the need is broadly recognized and a wide variety of agencies and organizations offer programs, education for family living is neither generally understood nor universally available. Many of these educational offerings are of ancillary nature and have fragmented and disparate approaches. Frequently program goals are not as broad as education for effective family living can be. Available education for parenthood tends to be restricted by the particular emphasis of primary agency goals and characterized by limited availability.

A society which blames the family for many of its social ills without providing adequate education for child rearing and family living is not meeting its obligations. When programs of adult education do not make education for this vital life role obtainable, they are not meeting their total responsibilities to a community. In the years ahead the education of parents should be a major concern of adult education and schools. This is part of education of adults and without it that education is incomplete.

To involve people in parent education, whether in the slum or suburb, clarity of goals is an essential element both in terms of attracting the learner and subsequent involvement in the learning process. The parent-learner also needs to know something of the program's potentials and to anticipate certain successes before he experiences them. A direct message as to the parent's important role as a teacher of children—that there are ways in which he can teach his child the processes of learning, valuing, and relating—makes apparent both the needs and the usefulness. Broad programs of education for parents would do much to increase the awareness of the importance of their parental function.

When the parent sees that the educational experience can help him achieve his goals, he is stimulated to seek further knowledge. Goals should be clearly stated as a learning process wherein the parent adds to his present skills as a teacher of his child. Parent experience is looked at in terms of what he is already doing, thus giving satisfaction through the recognition of success. He learns new ways to help his child learn. He becomes involved in determining ways in which his values can be thoughtfully and individually determined. The more active the intent to learn, the greater likelihood of success.

Ideally, goals are set and the search organized by the learner, but it is done within a setting which provides a structure, stimulus material, freedom to evaluate and make personal reference. Here he can weigh the merits of numerous ideas and practices; he can see how new ideas work in practice; he can adopt or not as he sees fit. He achieves greater perception of his parent role and a deeper sense of competence.

Such education attempts to strengthen families through improved understanding. It is not a didactic fact-giving process or an imposition of external rules and values. It should provide an environment for personal decision making based on knowledge and consideration. In this way it is an effective educational medium for individual and social improvement at any socioeconomic level, with no implications of social engineering.

Recent research shows that the parent is a prime teacher of his child. He has an interest in this task and motivation toward competence. He does not always know that education might increase his personal skills and effectiveness for this parent-educator task even though he may seek education for other life roles. Most parents desire greater competence and recognize their need for more knowledge and insight. The search for competence, however, is all too often informal, haphazard, and unorganized. It is the responsibility of adult education administrators, particularly in schools, to communicate the goals and potentials of such study.

Areas of study can run the gamut of the family's experience in coming to grips with change. As indicated earlier, courses can be designed to meet the needs of families at various points in the life cycle. Interest and study opportunities can range from how the child learns to what the school teaches, from understanding the gifted to guiding the handicapped. The parent of the preschool child needs to know how he can help his child learn to learn. Home-school cooperation can be enhanced and the child's educational potential increased when parents see themselves as partners in the teaching process and learn to work with schools. Families with adolescents are faced with difficult decisions in the face of the current breakdown in traditional mores. Adult education must provide a place for individual problem solving through the presentation and analysis of knowledge about human behavior. It must continue to support and enable parents to cope more effectively with the complexities of contemporary family life.

With an appropriate institutional setting and a clearly interpreted program with well defined goals, such a program should attract a large and varied clientele. Education for family living can be the most basic of adult education. It influences both adults and children. Children's school experience can be affected. It is usable by both the advantaged and the disadvantaged. It can lead to a pattern of a lifetime of learning.

Health and Safety Education

The growing concern for health and safety is reflected in adult education programs. Courses in physical fitness and weight reduction are popular. Less frequent are the lectures and discussions on the heart and cancer. In the field of safety, courses are found in survival swimming, safe boat handling, safe handling of firearms, and, in states where such courses are possible, adult auto driving instruction. In all safety courses the primary emphasis is on the development of proper attitudes, rather than skills.

Probably the greatest threat to our collective safety is the threat of nuclear explosion and radioactive fallout. Public schools, in cooperation with civil defense officials, have added to their usual first aid and home nursing courses numerous medical civil defense courses such as the training of medical aides and care of the sick and injured. Federal aid is available to school districts through civil defense channels for such work.

High School Completion

The education level in the United States is on the rise. Two out of three adult workers will have at least a high school education in 1975, according to a recent article by Denis F. Johnston in the June 1968 *Monthly Labor Review,* a publication of the Labor Department's Bureau of Labor Statistics. Fewer than one of two workers had that much education in the 1950's, and slightly more than one of two had that much in the 1960's.

Study predicts that in 1975 among workers in 25-34 age bracket, nearly 80 percent will have high school education or better and 20 percent of these will have completed college. Workers with eight years education or less will be only one in six by 1975. This ratio was one in three in the 1950's and one in four in the 1960's.

The 1960 census revealed that 58 percent of the adults in the United States over 18 years of age had not completed high school. In 1967 there were more than 64 million of these educationally deprived adults in the United States.

The situation is not improving. Despite the impact of the Elementary and Secondary Education Act and its amendments, all too many local school systems are still largely concerned with improving the quality of education for the college-bound youth. Partly as a result of this, approximately a million boys and girls continue to drop out of school each year. These same schools then frequently feel little obligation towards dropouts once they have dropped out.

Many doors are closed to these 64 million adults without a high school education. The labor market in particular is shrinking for the unemployed worker who cannot produce a high school diploma or its equivalent. In many employment offices it is no longer sufficient for a person merely to say that he has a secondary school education. Evidence of the fact is often required in the form of the actual diploma or some other tangible piece of paper attesting to the truth of his statement. What can be done to help these undereducated adults of our nation? How can we aid these people who need a high school diploma to increase their earning power and enrich the quality of their behavior as citizens and homemakers?

One answer lies in adult high school courses which lead to a high school diploma. Such courses have been increasing rapidly in recent years in the adult education curriculum as job qualifications are raised. Most often these courses are offered for credit leading to a high school diploma, although people are admitted who want specific instruction rather than credit.

Evening high schools established in larger cities a hundred years ago offer a complete high school program to adults. This formal organization, however, does not exist in other school districts. Within the adult education program of such districts credit is offered in certain courses for which there is a demand. The students are usually high school dropouts who, after a few years, return to complete their work for the diploma. They may need a diploma to improve their employment status, or they are simply seeking a second chance after failing or forfeiting the first chance.

Another answer lies in the high school equivalency certificate program. The high school equivalency certificate is an alternate for the more mature adult. No courses are required, even though districts frequently offer a high school refresher course for candidates. The underlying thought is that a person can learn on his own from the job he holds and from all his other experiences. If he learns enough, as attested by a general achievement examination, he is granted an equivalency certificate.

Problems sometimes facing the administrator in relation to secondary education for adults are —

The problem of who gives credit. Many times the adult division cannot grant secondary credit even though it administers the program. Before embarking on a secondary program, administrators should get clarification of legal requirements and should obtain the complete cooperation of secondary school officials in the district.

The problem of certification. In most cases only a certified secondary school teacher may teach a course which bears secondary school credit. Local regulations should be checked and board policies determined.

The length of courses. In many cases courses are of approximately the same length for adults as those for children. But there is variation in this practice, and there is ample evidence that accelerated courses are desirable and practicable for adults.

Public Affairs Education

Public affairs includes such things as the encouragement of citizen participation in the civic and public affairs which affect their lives; discussions of local, state, and national issues; trends in world affairs; comparative political systems; world religions; current crises; the United Nations; the numerous problems and issues arising from poverty; local issues; and the schools.

One of the major goals set for adult education by its proponents and supporters is the development of an informed citizenry willing to make judgments about local, state, and national problems and issues. Courses and activities with subject matter ranging from small local problems to large urban renewal plans to our most complicated national and international problems — including questions about public education itself — have increasingly appeared in adult education programs throughout the country. Schools are no longer avoiding controversial issues but are accepting them as an educational challenge.

Administrators find this curriculum one of the most difficult areas. People do not stand in line demanding to be kept informed. They must be attracted to school offerings in some manner or programs taken to them in their natural group setting. As in the case of parent education, all forms of adult education must be used and the cooperation of other groups obtained. Here too the use of press, radio, and television and the exploration of new and additional ways of working with voluntary associations may hold some of the answers for the future.

In thinking about civic and public affairs it is important not to think exclusively of classes and courses. It has been amply demonstrated that, while adults will come to the schoolhouse two nights a week to learn how to do arc welding, complete a high school education, find out why Johnny can or cannot read, or study French, they will not come to school on a regular basis, except in rare instances, to learn more about their community, the structure of political parties, air pollution, the duties of a good citizen in helping solve transportation problems, problems in urban redevelopment, or many other kinds of civic questions. Rather, for whatever the reasons may be, adults go to their clubs and organizations for this kind of education. They participate in civic clubs, in luncheon clubs, in political parties, in parent-teacher associations, and in numerous other groups. The responsibility of the public schools in this area is not to seek to provide the educational experience itself (except as a specific request may be made to the school to do it), but rather to help civic leaders — through program clinics and personal consultation — perform their educational functions at the highest degree of efficiency possible.

An example of this is the service performed by a director of adult education in consulting with the mayor and his director of housing on the education implication of a community conference called on housing. Neither the mayor nor his housing expert are presumed to be experts in adult learning. But the director of adult education certainly should be presumed talented in this area. Services of this kind rendered to public agencies not only provide an important community service, but also immeasurably enhance the school system's prestige.

Occupational Education and Training

Any concept of the adult education curriculum must include adult vocational and technical education, even though in certain states and local school districts the administrator of adult education has no direct responsibility for this area. In such cases a special administrator of vocational education, an associate or assistant superintendent or a director of vocational education by title, is in charge of both child and adult vocational work. Even if not directly responsible, the administrator of adult education is still required to keep in close touch with the vocational work of the district.

In the public schools vocational and technical courses for adults make up a large part of the total curriculum. In large cities they are largely conducted in evening trade schools and evening vocational schools which compare to the evening high school. In smaller places they are taught in the vocational facilities of special buildings or of the regular high school.

Basic curriculum areas in vocational or occupational education may be described as follows. (These definitions owe much to the formulations of the American Vocational Association.)

Trade and industrial courses provide instruction for the purpose of developing basic manipulative skills, safety judgment, technical knowledge, and related occupational information. These may be pre-employment courses or courses designed to upgrade or retain workers employed in industry. Some examples are courses in machine shop, auto mechanics, blueprint reading, and power sawing. Many of these courses are now taught in an expanded curriculum under provisions of the Manpower Development and Training Act.

Apprentice training is a special program to provide manipulative skills and technical or theoretical knowledge needed for competent performance in skilled occupations. Because apprentices learn craft skills through on-the-job work experiences and related information in the classroom, the program usually involves cooperation among school, labor, and management. The minimum terms and conditions of apprenticeship are regulated by state and local statutes and agreements. Some of the apprenticeable trades are carpentry, plumbing, electrical work, and sheet-metal work.

Business education courses equip the adult with marketable skills, knowledge, and attitudes needed for initial employment and advancement in business occupations. The business curriculum includes stenographic subjects (typing and shorthand), bookkeeping, clerical practice, and office machines.

Distributive education courses offer training in the selling, marketing, and merchandizing of goods and services for the purpose of improving distribution and upgrading distributive workers, including employees, managers, and owners engaged in distributive occupations. Some typical distributive education courses are real estate, small business management, salesmanship, insurance brokerage, and merchandising.

Supervisory training assists foremen and supervisors in industry and business in various phases of their work such as the training of workers, personnel relations, and legislation. Illustrations are foremanship training, management training, industrial relations, and quality control.

Agricultural courses are designed to improve farm methods and rural living, and cover such areas as soil conservation, increased production, and marketing. A few examples are farm mechanics, dairy management, crop improvement, farm management, and pest control.

Technical courses provide technical information and understanding of the laws of science and technology to prepare adults as technicians or to give them knowledge necessary to an occupation or profession. Illustrations of these are technical mathematics and physics, electronics, refrigeration, metallurgy.

Traditional Curriculum Areas

The *cultural enrichment* area of the adult program includes oil painting, composition, understanding and appreciating music, ceramics, antiques, portraiture, photography, dance, acting, poetry, scenic design, instruction on the piano, creative writing, American literature. There are offerings in English, English as a second language, and numerous foreign languages.

In the *practical crafts and homemaking* area there are such classes as sewing, tailoring, dress design, wood and metal working, knitting, gardening, interior decoration, family finance, and numerous others.

Business courses include typing and shorthand, accounting, advertising, computers, business management, analysis of business problems, marketing, merchandising, effective listening, business psychology, world trade, economics, and the stock market.

There are also numerous *special interest* courses in such areas as swimming, judo, or driver education, and there are also special daytime classes for senior citizens.

Education About Our Schools

Today education is one of the key civic and social issues. It is front-page news much of the time in most communities. Yet, there are probably more voting citizens of a school district who do not know the tax rate that applies to education than who do. There is probably an equal number of participating citizens who are unclear as to whether a school teacher is legally an employee of the municipal government or of the state. Beyond this, it is quite clear that there are many areas of educational practice that have been well documented by research as being an improvement on present practices, but the realization of which is still in the distant future because of public undereducation about education. The ungraded primary school, narrative report cards, and free, publicly-supported adult education are examples.

In one midwestern city, the board of education held "Neighborhood Conferences on Education" in all but a few of the elementary schools of the district. The purpose was to enable citizens to communicate points of view to—and discuss them with—school officials. Following the meetings in the neighborhood schools, representatives from each of the schools went to the junior high schools, where community forums were held. Eventually the members of the board of education, the superintendent of schools, and civic leaders appeared on a television program in which they commented to the total community on the exchange of points of view that had developed through these channels.

EXPANDING OPPORTUNITIES—COMMUNITY, JUNIOR, AND TECHNICAL COLLEGES

Adult education must delve deeper and spread its net wider if it is to satisfy the manifold needs of the community of adults which it serves. A new institution of education has appeared in recent years to reinforce the efforts of public school adult education. Community junior and technical colleges have always been with us in one form or another whether they were called academies or institutes or just schools or colleges, but their numbers, until recently, were limited.

In the last decade these numbers have increased significantly. The primary purpose of these institutions is to provide low-cost, two-year college programs for commuter students. Public support for these programs grew in a period in which colleges were jammed and college costs were soaring.

Those same colleges were not long in entering the out-of-school adult field. Many of them were operated by the local school board, while others had their own community college board but were supported with public funds. So it was only natural for them to search for new ways of being useful to the local adult community by offering adult education and community service programs.

For the most part, the courses and programs were quite different from the usual courses available through the public schools. For one thing, they provided an advanced level of course difficulty, particularly in the technical areas. What was and is important about this is that coordination between adult educators on the public school and community-technical college level can provide the adult student with a continuous study series so he can strive toward ever higher and higher levels of competence in a planned sequence.

Prospects of further growth in the numbers of community-technical colleges—and therefore of increased educational service to adults—

are certain. But a major program concern of all administrators of adult or continuing education, regardless of their institutional loyalties, should be an awareness and concern for the program offerings and for the clientele of neighboring institutions and a genuine effort toward cooperative program planning.

SPECIAL INTEREST GROUPS

In attempting to meet individual needs in the various curriculum areas, administrators discovered the great diversity of adults in training, experience, and motivation. Homogenous grouping seemed to provide a partial answer. Therefore special groups were formed in the schools not around subject matter but around common interests and common needs. As early as 1926, Edward Lindeman foresaw this development when he wrote the following:

> The approach to adult education will be via the route of situations, not subjects. . . . Every adult person finds himself in specific situations with respect to his work, his recreation, his family-life, his community-life et cetera—situations which call for adjustments. Adult education begins at this point. Subject matter is brought into the situation, is put to work, when needed. *

Senior Citizens

The constantly increasing proportion of our population who may be called "senior citizens" has created numerous social problems. Government has tried to solve some of the basic problems through programs of social security and welfare. Community agencies and the public schools are making their contribution by organizing activities for the aging. Through adult education the schools have either organized and supported senior citizen groups or served with educational programs that have been organized by some other agency.

What do the schools do for the aging? What is the curriculum for the aging? Although other agencies have offered programs of a social-recreational nature, the public schools have sought to make educational contributions. In that part of the overall adult education program devoted to senior citizens there are classes and activities in at least five areas.

1. *Vocational training* for a supplementary income. Training is provided in various handcrafts on a level higher than for a nonvocational course because the product must be saleable. Also taught are production methods, pricing, and marketing. Frequently, a cooperative marketing

*Lindeman, Edward. *The Meaning of Adult Education.* New York: New Republic, 1926. p. 8.

procedure is developed. Other courses of a vocational nature are taught, such as typing and bookkeeping, which can be used for a part-time employment.

2. *Cultural activities* for enriched living. These activities include training and practice in the arts and crafts. All are active, creative pursuits. Less common is the study of philosophy, psychology, and science.

3. *Health education* to help the older person recognize what is normal in aging and what is not normal. Subjects range from accident prevention and nutrition to common degenerative diseases and emotional disturbances.

4. *Family life education* to help the aged person make a better adjustment to changed family and social relationships.

5. *Community service* to help the retired person to feel useful, have status, and consider himself part of the community.

The administrator of adult education must permit in his work with the aged a degree of informality and autonomy not present in other parts of the program. He who can afford to employ and can find a competent coordinator for this work is fortunate, for the problems are many. But the response of the aged to such special programs has been most gratifying.

Handicapped Adults

Although there are many sources of help for physically and mentally handicapped adults, the public schools through adult education are making their contribution. Courses have been developed in speech correction, lip reading, therapeutic swimming, remedial reading, and general courses for the retarded adult. Cooperation with such agencies as the Vocational Rehabilitation and Employment Service can suggest to the administrator the types of courses needed.

School Dropouts – Young Adults

The focusing of attention in recent years on the problems of poverty has clearly identified undereducation as one of the basic causes of unemployment, substandard living, and the rising number of individuals who require welfare assistance. Today, a high school diploma or its equivalent is almost a prerequisite to employment. Yet in 1960 there were 25 million adults 18 years of age and older who had not completed eight years of school.

Efforts to reach and provide educational opportunities and entry-level skills for young adults have been successfully demonstrated by several nonschool agencies such as the Job Corps. When provided with adequate counseling, individualized instruction, and materials adapted to their adult needs and interests, young men and women who have dropped out of school have been found to be highly motivated and responsive. Their capacities for learning are frequently far in excess of the standard expectancies of traditional daytime public schools and the dropout and failure labels with which they have been identified.

Techniques and materials which have been successfully demonstrated by other agencies are available and can be adapted by adult educators to specialized school programs directed particularly to this vast number of young people who desperately need to experience success and develop a positive self-image.

The NEA Division of Adult Education Service can provide information about successful programs and practices in this area.

Second Careers for Mature Women

A look about in the business, distributive, professional, and industrial worlds quickly reveals the substantial proportion of women in the nation's work force. Our society and work culture no longer place a stigma on women who work, particularly when the responsibilities of child rearing and family have been completed or adequately cared for.

Orientation programs for mature women for reentry into the world of work, followed by programs of skill training, have received enthusiastic response in numerous parts of the country when offered as part of the total curriculum of continuing education for adults. The enterprising adult educator seeking new avenues of individual and community service, with a high rate of guaranteed response and effectiveness, will be well advised not to overlook career planning for women as they approach the postfamily years.

THE PRACTICAL ADMINISTRATOR

Certainly the adult school administrator has the most direct effect on the adult education program, if not as much on the individual student as his teacher. His role is undoubtedly the most complex and the most demanding of any in the adult program. The major responsibility for the success or failure of the program rests on the way in which he handles these complexities, the way in which he manages the demand upon him, the way in which he operates.

There are a number of unique tasks he must perform which can be placed in four major categories of functional responsibility:

1. *Managing the program*
   Coordinating the budgetary sources necessary to finance a program of quality.

Providing the housing and equipment needed for meetings, classes, and community activities.

Maintaining records and making reports.

Keeping informed and observing the laws, regulations, and policies of the national, state, and local agencies concerned with adult education.

2. *Improving the educational program*

Identifying the needs of individuals, organizations, and the community for continuing education.

Planning a program and the course offerings to be made available.

Promoting the program within the community.

Registering, placing, orienting, guiding, and following up the participants.

Evaluating the program in terms of groups served, effectiveness of offerings, costs of program, and needed modifications or expansion.

3. *Selecting and developing personnel*

Securing, orienting, supervising, evaluating, and directing the teaching staff.

Providing for his in-service education of himself and that of his staff through professional meetings and organizations.

Continuing his personal professional growth.

4. *Working with the community*

Locating the community agencies and resources that can serve the educational needs of adults.

Maintaining liaison with other school officials and with community agency administrators.

Coordinating the offerings of the public school program with the work of other agencies and community groups.

Keeping community councils, advisory committees, the board of education, and the public informed on the nature and progress of programs through speeches, publications, and exhibits.

The experienced administrator of adult education who has effectively organized his work schedule will recognize that some of these functions occur almost daily, some on a regular weekly or monthly basis, while still others require extended effort, perhaps only annually, but at specific times throughout the year. Having attained a clear overview of his total job responsibilities, he will establish a routine and adopt a plan for organizing his time to ensure adequate attention to those responsibilities which are most essential at any given time. For example, there is the annual preparation and printing of the announcement of courses, the annual preparation of the budget, the annual exhibit, or the planning of periodic staff meetings — in addition to the routine duties of handling complaints, inquiries, correspondence, financial accounting, surveillance of class enrollments and attendance, and so forth. In addition, there are the unexpected emergencies which inevitably arise, which demand immediate time and attention, and which must be superimposed on, or crowded into, the most effectively organized work schedule.

THE NEED FOR FULL-TIME ADMINISTRATORS

To the inexperienced administrator of an adult education program, particularly a teacher who has suddenly been thrust into an administrative role, or one who is attempting to administer a program on a part-time basis, the above analyses of functional responsibilities may indeed appear formidable and well-nigh impossible of attainment. And indeed they are, unless it can be convincingly demonstrated by the prospective administrator that the job cannot be done effectively on an extra-time, part-time, or perhaps even half-time basis, even with careful planning and utilization of time. The effective administrator of a philosophically sound program of adult education, dedicated to meeting the needs of its contingents, will require adequate time and personnel to accomplish its manifold functional responsibilities. The aspiring administrator must constantly strive toward the attainment of this objective.

Perhaps the most effective way to demonstrate this need for adequate administrative time is the keeping of a day-to-day log or record of performance which indicates both what was planned and what was accomplished. At year's end such a record can serve several purposes. In addition to making a case for adequate administrative time, it can identify the nature and extent of daily routine duties, pinpoint the times of year when concentrated effort on special activities is required, expose duplication of effort, and suggest techniques for more efficient rescheduling and work simplification.

SUMMARY

Everybody, including adult education administrators, functions on a number of different levels at the same time. A steel worker is also a voter, a parent, a consumer, a home owner, a union member, a churchgoer, a sports enthusiast. The unemployed and undereducated are no different in that every person has several life roles, varying duties, and a range of interests.

In each of them he has educational needs. Maybe he doesn't separate himself, to himself, as a role-player. Maybe he doesn't recognize his latent educational desires or needs. And even if he does recognize these things, he may not know he can get help through the adult programs of the public schools.

It is the job—and should be the delight—of adult educators to offer programs of lifelong learning to help each individual achieve what he wants and what he needs and provide the place where he might obtain such assistance.

CHAPTER 10

COMMUNITY RELATIONS, PROMOTION, AND PUBLICITY

David B. Rauch

Adult education is something like other kinds of education, but it is also, in many ways, something different from them. Adult educators would like to believe that, while they must build certain unique features into their own program, many of the methods of administration that they have found particularly helpful would also improve other kinds of educational settings. This may be true. But successful adult education programs, whether in a public school, college, or institutional setting, do have certain things in common.

THE UNIQUE COMMUNITY FEATURES OF ADULT EDUCATION

Adult education is perhaps the only segment of our formal educational program that has not been developed, refined, and charted by educators. Of their own accord, few superintendents of schools or college presidents establish an adult education program. Adult education is rarely even mentioned in courses in educational administration. Very few schools of education have even a single course in adult education. Boards of education and boards of trustees of colleges rarely insist that their institution develop programs for adults.

Most well known adult education programs have come about at the request of the people who want them. The people themselves—the prospective participants in the program—have requested, petitioned, or even at times stormed the offices of those in control, pointing up the need and requesting that the educational institution expand its operations into the adult field. And when adult programs are threatened by budgetary considerations or lack of understanding on the part of the educational power structure, it is most often the people themselves who come to their defense.

David B. Rauch is director of Adult and Community Services, Great Neck Public Schools, Great Neck, New York.

This unique feature — no one wants adult education except the people themselves — is not only a "plus" for the professional adult educator, it is also a factor he must always consider and strive to maintain, strengthen, and build on. Channels of community participation must not only be carefully maintained, but new ideas for developing community communication must be developed and tried out. For when the chips are down, as they frequently are in our field, it is basically the community that is going to put up the fight and insist on retention and further development of continuing education for adults.

At this very moment most educational institutions, both public and private, are looking again at their relationships with their community and with their student bodies. Particularly in ghetto areas, community groups are militantly demanding a greater say in the operation of public schools. College students are organizing, striking, sitting in, publishing their own underground papers, and even rioting to dramatize their feeling that they must receive more consideration in the development of educational policy. There are even instances of community people who live around urban college campuses obstructing college development plans because they feel that they should have a say in where buildings are placed and how the college relates to the community.

The day when an educational institution could function independently of the community has obviously passed. But adult and continuing education, with its deep community ties, should have an easier time of it — if the people in charge understand the nature of what they are doing and the essential task of paying attention to, developing, and refining the two-way communication process that is inherent in good community relations.

WHAT IS "THE COMMUNITY" FOR ADULT EDUCATION?

Many features distinguish a good adult education program from a great adult education program. Some are things like creative planning, meaningful formats, and unusual faculty, but one of the most important is that the program have its roots in the community.

For a public school or community college program, the concept of "community" is easier to define than for most other institutionally sponsored adult education programs. For a public educational system, the community is a clearly defined area encompassing the legal boundaries of the educational institution. A religious community or a university community is not as easily identifiable as a governmental-school district community. This is not to say that adult education under other sponsorships cannot choose its own target groups and come up with a good rationale for being involved. But a school district is definable because we know the lines of our community. And within the district boundaries, we can become informed about the nature of the population, its problems and tensions, its interests and needs, its power structure, its channels of communication, and all of the other identifying characteristics that help us plan with and for the people, the government, the industries, and the business firms that function there. For, in the end, the basic public responsibility of adult education is to the community.

HOW TO IDENTIFY YOUR COMMUNITY

No single educational administrator or administrative staff member can possibly know and understand all that needs to be known about a given community. We each know best people in the community who are similar to ourselves—our social, economic, and educational peers. If we are administrators who have come to our positions through the regular educational ranks, we know best our colleagues within the educational system and others who have had a similar amount of education and who are earning a somewhat similar salary. For example, only very occasionally do we know anyone who has less than a high school education or anyone who is an industrial mogul.

How many "good friends" can one person have? 10? 25? 100? If you are in a community as small as 20,000, and if you really know 100 people well, there are still 19,900 people whom you don't know. And that isn't good enough for a good adult educator.

A community, then, is many different things. Even a small suburban community that is sometimes chided for being too homogeneous has many different facets when you examine it more carefully. And examine it we must, if we are to live up to the challenge of servicing the community and being alert to its needs.

Here are a few of the breakdowns I have identified in my own community—a comfortable suburban area outside of New York City. Your community has its own characteristics, and you can probably add other kinds of breakdowns.

1. *Economic groups:* those with inherited wealth; those earning high salaries; professional people and others who have good incomes but are not wealthy; middle-income people; "respectable" low-income people such as retired older people and owners of tiny businesses; low-income self-employed; those who are really poor.
2. *Religious groups:* Catholic, Protestant, Jewish; those who have no institutional affiliation but consider themselves still belonging to one of the three; nonbelievers; religiously intermarried families;

members of Negro Protestant churches who have little contact with other Protestants.

3. *Political groups*: those active in the various political parties; those who are part of the power in the political parties; the sometimes well hidden "real" power in each party; office-holders beholden to the parties; political activists in groups that cross party lines; the political expediters; judges who like to feel they are beyond party but can give you good advice on how to get political cooperation on a project.

4. *Business and industry groups*: Chamber of Commerce and Junior Chamber of Commerce; Young Presidents and Young Executive organizations; small merchant groups; service clubs; fraternal organizations; "social" organizations such as country clubs and social clubs that are, in reality, restricted to a certain business or industrial configurations; business and professional women's clubs; professional organizations such as medical, dental, and bar organizations; labor unions; employee organizations of a semi-social nature, such as the police benevolent society.

5. *Educational groups*: organizations based on educational background; parent groups such as PTA; special purpose groups such as the National Association for the Advancement of Colored People; official groups such as the board of education; groups that sponsor educational programs such as YMCA.

These five categories are not exhaustive and exist in almost any community. There are other ways to fragment a community, but this outline gives you ideas not only on how to contact people, but on evaluating your present lines of communication to make them more effective.

ORGANIZING AN ADULT EDUCATION ADVISORY COMMITTEE OR TASK FORCE

The easiest way to ensure yourself direct lines of communication with your community is to gather around you 25 people, each of whom knows different parts of the community and call them an *advisory committee*, an *adult education council*, or an *adult education task force*. To do this properly, and multiply your knowledge by 25, you formally invite 25 people (you may need to have 50 on your list to end up with 25 acceptances) each of whom is influential in some different part of the structure of the community. Don't worry about seeing that all parts of the community are represented, because that is impossible. Even a small community can be chopped up in 100 different ways. But try to get different people who know and understand different parts of the community.

Once you have the 25 together, set up regular meetings, at least once a month, and put them to work! You are not likely to overwork them, for community people are capable of doing a lot of work if it is interesting and useful. Give them specific things to do, things that you would like to do yourself if you had the time, jobs that will help them to identify with and understand adult education and that will permit them to feed back ideas, innovations, and new concepts to you.

Some of the tasks normally assigned advisory committees include—

1. Contacting employers to find out what kinds of jobs they have available, what lacks they find in applicants that adult education might supply, what kinds of in-service opportunities would help present employees upgrade themselves.
2. Talking with newspaper editors to get ideas on how the adult education story could be better told in their pages.
3. Planning coffee hours for present participants and asking them for ideas on what they would like to see in the program that may not now be there.
4. Contacting local professional groups, such as the county medical society, to explore the possibility of some kind of cooperative adult education program in a health education area.
5. Serving as liaison representatives for you on community action councils, councils of social agencies, or other coordinating groups.
6. Visiting classes that might interest them and talking with people during the break to get ideas on what other courses might interest them.
7. Evaluating the adult education budget and, if possible, attending open meetings or hearings on the public school budget to defend that part spent for adult education.
8. Discussing new course ideas and whittling them into a shape that would appeal to their acquaintances and friends.
9. Finding space in the community for daytime offerings.
10. Contacting state legislators or U. S. Representatives from your community to express support for special adult education legislation.

Community people who have served on active adult education advisory committees report great satisfactions from their work. They enjoy knowing the other members, many of whom they had not met before. They can see the results of their deliberations when new programs are started around ideas that have been mulled over by their committee. They feel closer to the educational system because they have worked on a part of the school program. And they identify strongly with adult education because it is not bound up in as much legality, red tape, and educational jargon as most other parts of education.

MAKING ADULT EDUCATION AVAILABLE TO THE "CUSTOMER"

A young man of my acquaintance came recently to the United States from Ireland. He wanted to brush up on his knowledge of American idioms and soften his Irish brogue so he would be more employable in this country. He went to a "night school" in his neighborhood and told the people at the desk that he wanted to take a course in English.

He was obligingly registered for a course in English—for the foreign born. For the first two sessions of the class the person in charge apparently did not recognize the Irish accent. At the third session she complimented him on his English and asked whether he had learned it in school or picked it up since he came to the United States. When she found that English was his native language, she told him that he did not belong in her class and suggested that he might learn what he wanted in the typing class. But he already knew how to type!

At another time I talked with a mature woman from another community who told me she had not finished high school and wondered if there were any way that she could now do so. I suggested that she call her local school system and ask for information about the high school equivalency examination and whether they had a refresher course for the examination. It took her two days of transferred telephone calls and leaving her number for people to return the call before she could get the information. And when she needed some additional information, she had no idea to whom she had talked previously or what office he was in so she could get the additional information quickly.

I mention these two incidents because sometimes we unknowingly set up barriers for the person who wants adult education, barriers that make it very difficult for people to find us or to get the information they want.

You may want to test out some of these things about your office to see if you are providing a hospitable atmosphere:

1. A "covered" telephone. Is there someone to either answer the phone from your office or to take messages if your office doesn't function during the regular business hours? If you are on the school switchboard but your office doesn't open until 1:00 p.m., what happens to calls that come in before you open? Is there any office that can take messages for you? If you have a separate telephone number but are not open during regular business hours, have you

investigated the cost of an answering service or an answering device that can take messages and tell callers when you open?

2. When your phone is answered, do people identify themselves? The telephone company says that the correct way to answer a phone is "Adult Education, Mrs. Davis." And the correct way to pick up a phone that has already been answered once is with your name, "This is Mr. Bradshaw."

3. If your office is in a school or in a central administrative office, can people find you easily? A sign with directions for finding the adult education office should be at every entrance to the building.

4. How easy is it for people to see the person in charge? Even if you are top man in adult education, it is wise to make yourself easily available to anyone who feels he wants to see the top man. During registration and other busy times, you can learn a good deal just by lingering around the desk to see what questions people are asking or picking up the telephone when it rings to get an idea of what's on people's minds.

5. If you have extra help during busy times, how well do they know the program? It's worth it to take one hour to orient them quietly. Be sure to tell them to ask someone else if they don't know the answer, not to make up an answer.

6. Have you alerted those in your office who have contact with people not to use educational terminology or abbreviations? Adult education participants are not like students on a college campus. When staff people say "adult ed" or "driver's ed" or "econ," potential participants feel like outsiders. Abbreviations or initials may be common around the school system, but they should not be used with the general public.

7. If you have a large personal registration, how about asking those who handle it to wear nametags? It would be helpful for the registrant to know the name of the person on the other side of the desk.

An important part of public relations is to personalize your program as much as possible. These seven points are general suggestions, and you can think of others. It takes a little effort to be personal, but it helps — everyone likes to be treated well.

HOW TO LET PEOPLE KNOW WHAT YOUR PROGRAM HAS TO OFFER

Every public adult education program puts out some kind of catalog, course listing, or brochure. The most common faults of these important publications are that they are hard to read, don't give enough information, and are either unattractive or just dull.

Everyone has budget limitations, but it is a waste of money to prepare a catalog that doesn't get read and doesn't invite people to participate.

Even a mimeographed bulletin can be good-looking, but it is hard for a mimeographed job to compare with something that has been printed. The following are good rules of thumb about producing something in quantity:

1. For 25 copies or less, it is quicker and more efficient to use a Xerox or photocopy machine.
2. For 25 to 150 copies, use a spirit duplicator, "Ditto" or "Azograph."
3. For 150 to 3,000 copies, use a mimeograph, if the publication has only one or two pages.
4. For more than 3,000 copies of any publication longer than two pages, take it to a local print shop. Photo offset printing is usually the least expensive and most flexible method of printing.

If you have decided to take your material to a print shop, there are a wide variety of methods available to you.

1. Your own secretary can type up the material on her typewriter. The printer will then "shoot" the page photographically. It can also be "blown up" to a slightly larger size or "reduced" to a slightly smaller size. You can paste pictures on the typed sheets, underline, draw boxes around items, etc. to liven them up. The problem with typed material is that the right-hand margin is uneven, and there is little design flexibility.
2. With an Executive typewriter any trained typist can adjust the right hand margin, but she has to count the number of characters on each line and then type everything a second time. This is time-consuming but results in a nicer looking page and closely resembles regular printing. There are also various commercial paste-on or transfer letters that can be bought reasonably to set headlines or course titles.
3. VariTyper looks like printing but is done on a typewriter-like keyboard and offers a variety of type faces and sizes. Most offset print shops have a VariTyper. It looks almost exactly like regular printing but does not offer as much variety in type faces or as much flexibility as Linotype.
4. Linotype is regular printing and is the most expensive method of setting type, but it offers the widest possibilities. Because of the wide variety of type sizes and faces available, it may permit you to save a little on the number of pages of your publication.

With this much information you may go to a few printers with some idea of what you want done and ask their advice. Most will go into detail on the variety of services they can offer, and a good printer will be able to offer advice on different ways to make your catalog or brochure more attractive and to reduce costs. It is wise to get formal or informal bids from at least three printers. Printing costs depend on the size of the shop, the kind of presses and equipment the firm owns, and how many additional jobs the printer feels he might get from you.

Some adult education programs print a limited number of brochures and make them available only on request. This practice is very limiting because it means that you are making your program known only to those who already know about it. The more catalogs you can afford to print and the wider the distribution you can give them, the more registrants you will have. Many adult education programs set up boxes for catalog distribution in banks, supermarkets, libraries — anyplace where people gather. The ideal method practiced in many smaller communities is to direct mail one to every household in the community, but this may be out of the question for large urban centers.

Your catalog should be your primary "selling" piece. Remember that it has to compete with all of the other well designed and attractive junk mail that everyone gets, so it is worthwhile to take some pains to assure that it is read by the consumer. The cover of the catalog is important because it not only determines whether the receiver will pick it up at all, but whether someone will open it up and start reading it. Adding one extra color is generally considered to be worth the extra cost. However, if cost is prohibitive, colored ink is no more expensive than black ink, and colored paper is only slightly more expensive than white paper.

As you look through your latest catalog, think of the person who has never heard of your program and see if he is likely to pick it up, open it, and if it really gives him the information he needs. Adults who participate in adult education are usually as interested in the faculty as they are in the course itself. Too many people have been stuck in a course with a teacher who cannot communicate. It is wise not only to list faculty names, but also to include a line or two about them — what qualifies them to handle the course or activity. Be sure to include practical experience that will help the reader realize that your professional leaders know their subject.

WHAT ABOUT THOSE WHO DON'T — OR CAN'T — READ CATALOGS?

The catalog or brochure is an important device for communicating with an educated adult population, but more and more we are obligated to communicate with and plan with and for the less well educated or "disadvantaged" section of our population. People who don't read English cannot possibly read about a course you have for them in your catalog, and adult illiterates cannot be recruited through a printed piece. Generally, adults who have less than a high school education, people sometimes identified as "blue collar" or the "educationally disadvantaged," frequently do only a limited amount of reading and are not apt to react to a catalog or complicated printed piece.

The nonreader or less sophisticated reader requires, then, another method of contact. Reaching him is not easy. It not only means finding a way to let him know you exist, but also making sure that when he does arrive he can find his way easily to the program he wants and that he will receive a hospitable welcome.

To reach any target group you have to think a little about where these people are, the places they meet, the things they do, and the newspapers, radio stations, or television programs that might interest them.

In larger communities there are "ethnic" newspapers and radio stations, and sometimes "ethnic" TV stations or TV programs. "Ethnic" refers to the fact that they cater to a particular group — Negroes, Mexican-Americans, Puerto Ricans, German-Americans, Italo-Americans, or what have you. Some of the "ethnic" newspapers cover a broad geographical area but have columns devoted to news of specific localities.

Most radio stations have time devoted to public service announcements, and your adult education activities certainly qualify. If you send to local radio stations very short announcements about a particular course or curriculum, be sure to include the "who, what, when, where, and how." If you are trying to reach a foreign language ethnic group, be sure to have your spot announcement translated into the proper language by one of your language teachers.

Television is less likely to use spot announcements, unless they are filmed. This is expensive to do, but maybe a group of public educational systems within the television listening area can get together and share the expense for a film for television spots. Sometimes television will use a slide made up like a poster which has an accompanying taped announcement.

What television does use — and local radio, too — are guests for interview shows. Unusual faculty members, participants, or even members of your advisory committee may make good guests to tell the adult education story. Remember that a "soft sell" is often the best approach. A young lady who took a cooking course in adult education and is now self-employed as a caterer may make an interesting guest, even if she tells little about adult education except that it's how she made her start. A faculty member who has recently had a book published may spend most of the time talking about the book, but urge him to repeat a few times that he is teaching a course in adult education. An advisory council member who has completed a study for you from the census tracts on how many people in your community are undereducated need only tell why she did it and what the council is planning to do about it to be a good ambassador for adult education.

As you, or members of your advisory council, go out to talk with "target groups" wherever they naturally meet, be prepared for some rebuffs and some less than enthusiastic greetings. Many of these groups are antagonistic to the schools or afraid of them. They may thank you and never contact you again. But persistence frequently pays off. Don't go to sell them on something you already have. Ask them about kinds of programs that might interest them and see if you can get them to accept some responsibility for recruiting or sounding out people. If you leave with some agreement on what you will do and what they will do before you meet again, you at least have an excuse to meet again for a report. It may take a number of meetings before a workable program can be developed.

It is wise, when you are meeting with a new target group, to do everything you can to give them the feeling that they are planning for themselves. If they suggest something you already have in your program, don't reveal this immediately. Ask them more questions about it and tell them that you think you can work out a program to suit their needs if they will see to it that enough people attend.

REACHING THE MASSES THROUGH THE MASS MEDIA

We have already talked about the specialized press, radio, and television. These, plus magazines, are collectively known as the "mass media." In working with representatives of the mass media, remember that as specialists in their own field they don't react well to someone from the outside telling them what to do. They decide what is and is not news from their own point of view. And radio and television people decide what they can program and what they don't want to program.

If they don't use your material, don't get exasperated. Instead, try to find out from them what you are doing that might be of interest to them, and how to prepare the material in a manner most useful to them. It has become a cliché to say that the news media is more interested in a scandal than in an honest success story. This is true because readers and listeners always react to a scandal. A narcotics raid on a college campus makes the headlines, but a student scientist who conducts an unusual or outstanding scientific experiment rarely gets mentioned or attracts public notice.

It is therefore up to you to find out from your local mass media people what you can feed in to them that is likely to be used. A very unusual project will probably merit some space, but you may not always be the best judge of what is unusual. At the start of a new semester they are more apt to mention one very interesting course than to run a long list of every course being given.

Kinds of stories most likely to receive news coverage include—

1. A story that is tied in to a more important news happening. A group that is studying space science at the same time as some national event is taking place; the visit of a candidate for mayor to a group that is studying consumer economics; a current affairs group that invites a spokesman from a ghetto area to discuss living problems with them. Anything you can tie in to what is generally in the news anyway can be an interesting and newsworthy story.

2. A feature on an individual in your program who has met with success partially as a result of participation in a course. Anyone in a writing class who gets published; a craftswoman who sells bead flowers that she learned to make in school to a local department store; an artist who wins an award in an art show; a senior citizen who is a leader in a charity drive; a well known local citizen who, in addition to other activities, passes on his knowledge by conducting an adult education class. Generally an individual is more interesting than a group.

3. A one-session event or meeting is easier to publicize than a 10-week class because it is simpler to explain and it has somewhat the same appeal as a film showing or a play. If you set aside one evening when people with income tax problems can get help, or a one-session lecture on the state of the stock market, or if a class is having a guest speaker and the public is invited, you can usually get mention of this on the air as well as in the local press. Radio and television stations that have Community Bulletin Boards for public service announcements will almost always carry an announcement of a one-time event or meeting.

It is not hard to get mass media news coverage. The most difficult task is getting the material written up in a suitable form. If the news media have to rewrite the material from a letter you send them, the chances are slim that they will bother.

Personalizing Your Media Contacts

If you have one or more daily papers in your community, try to get a list of the names of the various editors—the women's page editor, the education editor, the science editor, and so forth. Then when you have an item that might interest a specific person, send it directly to him by name, or if you think something is worth coverage by the paper's staff, call them and give them the information. If you have given them a few ideas that they have not used, call and ask for suggestions as to the types of items they are interested in. At least once a year it is a good idea to try to meet with the mass media people personally, if only to say hello. Press and television people are more apt to do something for you if they know what you look like – if you become more than a signature or a telephone voice.

If you have a local citizen council or advisory committee, try to get someone from the mass media on the committee – not just so you can get coverage for your events, but also to help you plan from their knowledge of the community and its needs. Mass media people are not only useful contacts because of their power, they also frequently have a very sharp picture of the community because of their jobs. They usually have a good idea of the pulse of the community, what areas are of interest to the people, and what areas are of little community interest.

Both the schools and the mass media have specific community responsibilities. Press, radio, and television consider themselves to be educational forces in the community. Community improvement is as much an interest of theirs as it is yours.

Most of the interesting things that are happening in your program are happening inside classrooms, and the people who know what's happening are often your faculty members. Ask members of your faculty to let you know of newsworthy happenings. Or better yet, keep them supplied with some sort of form to fill in when they feel they have a news item.

Supplements to Mass Media

Don't depend on the mass media to do your sales job for you. If you do, you will have frequent disappointments when your story is not used or its essential components deleted. The most to ask of the mass media is that they keep your program in the public eye and let people know that you exist, so that when you are needed you have a ready identification. People rarely rush out in great numbers to register for a program they have read about in the paper. You are more likely to find that someone will ask you a year later how some course or event they had read about worked out. Or they will come in a year later and ask if the course is still being offered because they now need it. But constantly seeing to it that your program is before the public builds your reputation as a meaningful community-centered institution. Further visibility can be achieved through the use of flyers, handbills, news-letters, posters, window displays, and telephone appeals by interested volunteers. In addition, the regular use of information booths in public places, speeches before civic and service groups, open-house programs, and participation in community special events such as local fairs, homecomings, and centennial celebrations serve as a continuing progress report to present and future adult supporters.

COMMUNITY RELATIONS WITHIN YOUR OWN INSTITUTION

One of the odd things about adult education is that it is considered an appendage to an educational institution and is frequently unknown or misunderstood among regular staff and employees. It is hard to present a more positive image because your program, in many ways, interferes with other programs of your school—you share facilities and equipment, you meet at odd hours, the courses you offer are somewhat "crazy" in their eyes. And if you are running a program that has good community support, you may be getting more publicity and have more community support than the rest of the school program.

Be sure that all school employees—professional and supporting—receive copies of all of your announcements. Some of them may want to participate in the programs you have planned. In a public school, where teachers have the feeling that they "own" their classrooms, see if you can arrange for the adult teacher to meet the day teacher. Simply saying hello and letting the day teacher know the exciting things that are going on in her classroom at another time will improve morale and promote mutual understanding.

If your institution has a staff publication, get news into it about adult education and play up members of the full-time staff who are also doing something in adult education. Unusual people with unusual backgrounds from the full-time staff may be willing to come in as guests to some of your activities to tell about their experience in the Peace Corps or as a VISTA Volunteer. The head of the language department of the full-time staff may be willing to meet with the adult foreign language staff and advise on texts or methodology. Building custodians who have entree into the lower-income part of the community may be willing to serve as recruiters for a basic education program. Using programed literacy material, we trained a duplicating machine operator as a teacher aide and are using him after his regular working hours. He is not only an outstanding teacher aide but has also become an important public relations man for adult education among his colleagues on the full-time staff. There is no need to give preference on part-time employment to full-time employees of your institution, but, all other things being equal, you may find that employing them when possible is an added "plus" because they serve as goodwill ambassadors with the full-time school staff.

COMMUNITY RELATIONS IS EASY—OR VERY HARD

The specific techniques of working with the mass media and developing good community relations within your own administrative structure take time and skill. There are many guidebooks on dealing with the press, layout and graphic design, establishing good human relations, and other technical topics that will help you with the specifics. It's a challenge to develop creativity in your printed material and in your press, radio, and TV contacts. *If you remember yourself, and impress on your superiors, that adult education is something different for people different from those the institution is used to dealing with, you will find that there is no reason to follow some line or philosophy just because it is the way your institution has always functioned.*

The essence of good community relations is in the point of view of the person in charge—you. Office efficiency is not your prime motive. Never permit your office staff to balk at a new way of doing things because it is too much work. Your management techniques must reflect the needs of your constituency. "If no one registers for our program, we will all be out of jobs," I reiterate to the people who work for me, "so let's find the methods that yield the greatest comfort for the people who are using the program."

"If they read the directions we wouldn't have this problem," an office staff person frequently cries out. But if they aren't reading the directions, one must just accept this fact and either redo the directions or set up a less complicated system.

"How does he expect me to know?" an office person may ask when a potential participant calls on the telephone to ask whether he should register for Beginning French or Intermediate French since he hasn't studied French for 15 years. "But he is doing just what he should do," I reply. "He has a question and he's calling the central office to get an answer. Where else would you expect him to call for an answer to his question? We have to find some answer for him."

I tell my colleagues that the joy of being in adult education is that when a program succeeds, I take all the credit. But when a program fails, I refuse to take the blame—except to consider what procedure went wrong and how to reorganize the project to more nearly ensure success.

An adult educator must find a way to establish methods and procedures so the program can function. But he must also keep his eye on the registrant or the participant to see how it all seems from the other side of the desk or the other end of the telephone. All the good adult education teachers are prima donnas. This is important if they are to project well and excite those with whom they are working. Our job is to set up a system of handling a stable of prima donna faculty members.

And all present and potential adult education participants are individuals. We must find ways of arousing their curiosity and interest, of having them look to us when they feel there is something more they want to learn, and of preventing them from getting lost when they make that first, if only tentative, step to seek us out as a possible place where they can get help. If they don't naturally seek us out, we must seek them out, wherever they are, to let them know what we represent and how we might be able to work together to satisfy a personal need, a need of their group or associates, or a need of the community.

SECTION III

THE
ADULT
PARTICIPANT

CHAPTER 11

ADULT MOTIVATION
AND RECRUITMENT

D. Ray Ferrier

The process of adult development and normal changes in expectations, roles, life patterns, aspirations, and crises has still to be adequately researched; especially needed is work on the preretirement years from 20 to 60 which include the crucial adjustments and role changes of employment, marriage, family responsibility, "middlescence," [1] middle age, family separation, and preretirement. This is unfortunate because with each of these phases of development come new and varied motives as the individual attempts to fulfill his basic social and status needs.

No longer can "adults" be thought of as a somewhat homogenous group sandwiched between adolescents and senior citizens with rather uniform but generalized motives. Instead, their inner drives and impulses must be analyzed as a sequence of motives and stresses which gradually but radically change as they mature and move through their life cycle.

Accordingly, it is essential that adult educators focus on motivation in their strategies for recruitment, since continuing education can only succeed in fulfilling its obligations to society if it successfully identifies the motives which bring adults to and hold them in classes.

For purposes of simplification, the discussion of motives has been divided into two sections. The first includes a review of those common factors which motivate most adults throughout their lives, and the second involves an appeal for movement beyond these commonalities to an analysis by adult educators of the more specific and impelling motives which become very urgent at the different chronological stages and social role shifts in every adult's development.

D. Ray Ferrier is director of Adult Education, Continuing Education Department, Detroit Public Schools, Detroit, Michigan.

"Motivation is certainly not something the educator turns on and off at will, nor can it be thought of solely as an internal push which 'will out' regardless of circumstances. Rather it is a process in which the learner's internal energies are directed towards various goal objects in his environment." [2] It should be noted that one of the key words is *directed*. Because of his strategic position, the adult educator is able to provide satisfactions and manage situations which will fulfill student objectives. The educator may also help by stimulating the student to focus on, analyze, and internalize new goal objects, the need for which he was previously unaware. The greater the number of personal goals which the student accepts, the more ways his basic need, e.g., possibly to gain peer approval, has of being satisfied. This greater number of personal goals also enables the teacher to more frequently and easily relate the lesson to individual student objectives.

COMMON MOTIVATIONS OF ADULTS

Throughout the entire adult life span there are certain basic needs which influence or motivate behavior. Good teachers are aware of them and seek to satisfy them in a general way by establishing a supportive classroom atmosphere and providing generous measures of "love and attention." Excellent teachers go one step further: They look for the specific interests and motives of their individual students, the "real" reasons the adult is attending the learning group, and attempt to modify standard course work and thematic content accordingly.

Among the most common motivations of adults may be the desire—

1. For a feeling of importance.
2. For social approval.
3. To improve their self-esteem.
4. To avoid pain, either mental or physical.
5. To enjoy all things which are tension-reducing.
6. For a friendly social atmosphere.
7. To discover and learn something new.
8. For heterosexual adjustment.
9. For independence.

If we examine the basis for adult participation in most adult education classes, one or more of the above motives will probably be involved. Unfortunately, in the teacher's desire to have the student learn the subject matter, the basic reason or motive for his enrollment may not be analyzed and selected and adequate efforts made to provide gratification. Therefore, the teacher must always create an atmosphere in which student motives can be (a) assessed, (b) fixed on educational goals, and (c) satisfied as success is achieved.

Simplified, it might appear as follows:

A. *STUDENT:*
1. *Basic need* (example)
To be independent
2. *Activating motive* (one of several "independence" motives)
"I want to be *financially* independent."
3. *Resulting behavior* (one of several behavior patterns exhibited in an effort to achieve financial independence.)
Attendance at an evening vocational school
4. *Accepted short-range goal* (one of several short-range goals)
To learn to read blueprints
B. *ADULT EDUCATOR'S ROLE:*
1. Channel motivation and resulting behavior toward educational objectives which are likely to be attainable.
2. Sequence steps to achieve success.
3. Teach.
4. Support by ensuring that other needs (status and social) are satisfied during the learning period.
5. Assist with job placement, to the degree adult education can assist, so as to help ensure that the student's original need is satisfied.

ANALYZING INDIVIDUAL STUDENT MOTIVES

While an understanding of common adult motives forms a preliminary basis for satisfactory instruction, teachers seriously interested in adult motivation must review the specific motives of each individual in the class if the exhortation "ensure that the new adult student meet with immediate success" is to be achieved for each particular student and *his* objectives.

This can only be achieved after interaction and discussion with students enable the teacher to modify "standard" lessons where necessary. Such interaction also helps ensure that each student understands the pertinent relationships between the lesson and his own life, as well as the educator's special interest in him. Thus, the teacher should always be able to answer the question "What difference does my lesson make to these students?" in terms of what their specific motives are for attending class. The successful instructor is able to perform this difficult role and is admired and loved and his classes are well attended as a result.

Basic Life Groupings

Kuhlen[3] states that the course of human life tends to be dominated during the first half by "growth-expansion" motives, with needs stemming from "insecurity and threat" becoming more important in the later years. In general, adult "growth-expansion" motives are related to employment, career development, marriage, and the rearing of a family. "Insecurity and threat" motives tend to dominate in later years because of (a) the higher status accorded youth in our society, (b) the limitations and pressures of time and money, (c) physical change and decline, (d) skill deficits generated by rapid technological advances which have left the older adult outdated, and (e) the tendency to get "locked in" a particular environment of marriage, family, investments, skills, employment, and seniority.

Successful adult educators see adults in a variety of basic life groupings, each with somewhat predictable interests and motives. In general, these have a dimension of commonality such as age; family responsibility; or social, cultural, or employment backgrounds, interests, or aspirations. Even common deprivations may form a life grouping situation in the case of economically poor adults who meet for the purpose of forming food-buying clubs and credit unions or to learn about their rights and responsibilities as "renters."

The reasons for the very small enrollment of adult education students who live in disadvantaged areas of the community vary; however, the majority of them apparently see little relevance between the broad objectives of most adult education programs and their own specific short-range goals and requirements. Consequently, to gain credibility with these adults (or any adults for that matter), programs must be further refined, developed, and coordinated to cater to those motives which are most real and unmet in their lives.

Through this approach, adult educators are able to establish programs whose purposes are limited and specific enough to (a) be understood by potential students, (b) ensure that observable progress will be made, and (c) enable additional courses to be sequenced. At present, such life groupings have usually been overlooked. Even the simplest of offerings which might appeal to various "age" groupings have not been explored in terms of their resultant variety of motives. The whole middle-aged "crisis of generativity" is ignored unless by coincidence classes with some special relevance happen to be organized, not as is usual to ready middle-agers for retirement, but better to prepare adults who have nearly completed their basic family rearing responsibilities for the important societal roles they should assume during "middle age."

Middle-Age Crisis of Generativity

In discussing the eight stages of man having to do with the formation of basic trust, autonomy, initiative, industry, identity, intimacy, and ego integrity, Erikson[4] discusses generativity, the important preoccupation of middle age concerned with establishing and guiding the next generation. This concern generally relates primarily but not exclusively to the investment in one's own children. The crisis occurs as a man balances what he has generated or helped to generate and finds it good or wanting.

Traumatic periods continually occur throughout adult life—when parents see their children leave home and become aware of the implications of switching into "childless roles"; when strong laborers or athletes realize that their strength no longer sustains them; when breadwinners realize that they have received their last promotion and their life goals are not yet achieved, that what they have "generated" is not enough.

These and many other situations are very common and critical periods for most adults and certainly provide an array of opportunities for continuing education to assist. Thus, middle-aged adults could be better prepared to accept power and assume social and personal responsibility within their churches, cultural centers, and all organizations which make a community out of an aggregate of houses. "No other group is as well fitted for this task as they who are wiser than the young, stronger than the old, and freer than either...." [5]

Unfortunately, without an organized assist, many middle-aged individuals, especially in lower-class society, fail to appreciate their "moment" and in doing so fail to make their essential contribution to the community. This loss to the community of the efforts of thousands of individuals can be very detrimental over a long period of time and is equally so to the middle-ager who, according to Erikson,[6] may stagnate for the rest of his life.

Influence of Age on Motives

When the adult educator is able to see students in more common or homogenous groupings, he is in a better position to summarize their basic motives into a profile of factors around which courses can be developed or modified in order immediately and in a continuing fashion to fulfill the needs and expectations of enrollees. For example, whether men are 20, 40, or 60 will alter the intensity of their motives for seeking additional education as well as their confidence, goal selection objectivity, and possibly some of the motives themselves. A 20-

year-old in good health, looking for date and entertainment money, willing to accept some type of entry employment, and optimistically feeling that life will tend to get better as he gets older, will have different intensities of motives than a 40-year-old whose family expenses have peaked, whose dreams of youth have not materialized, and who is having serious reservations about his employment future. The latter will also have different motives, (e.g., at his age job changes become more difficult because of employer reluctance to hire older men; therefore, permanence of employment becomes a significant motive in seeking additional adult education). A 60-year-old, if his physical assets still allow him to consider employment, is looking for a modest role to see him through his waning years and will be driven by still other motives of varying intensity.

ROLE OF THE ADULT EDUCATOR IN SATISFYING INDIVIDUAL NEEDS

As the adult educator strives to understand individual student motives he is able to —

1. Help the student relate a variety of nebulous motives or goals to a specific basic need which the student is attempting to satisfy through adult education activities.
2. Help the student focus his motives on a variety of attainable short-range goals.
3. Modify the standard course so that it is directly related to the short-range goals whenever and wherever feasible.
4. Continue to expand the variety and depth of goals until both teacher and student are confident a basic need can be satisfied (i.e., to the degree that adult education can assist in the fulfillment of this basic need).

In his effort to demonstrate that continuing education can be a satisfier of basic needs and motives, the adult educator must concentrate on those goals his program can reasonably expect to satisfy, while referring potential students with unobtainable goals (e.g., an immediate employment goal for a student enrolled in a high school completion program) to other agencies. Specifically, this might involve referring students interested in dental technology or computer key punching to a community college specializing in these areas; those interested in body bumping, diesel engine repair, or custodial training to the local Manpower Development and Training Act Center, etc., if these training facilities were not available within his program. Urban areas with large Negro populations are providing various self-help agencies such as the Opportunities Industrial Center or the Career Development Center which may be able to assist.

Unfortunately, most psychologists and sociologists prefer to study adolescents and children rather than grown-ups because the early period of life is so important and school systems are able to supply them with subjects. Thus, although it is needed, the mass of data on adults is not equivalent to that available on youth. The accumulation of hard data is made more difficult by the fact that longitudinal studies of adults require much longer periods to collect. In the life of a child there are many changes during a year, but many months and even years of an adult's life can elapse without leaving any observable change. However, at all times important changes are occurring both physiologically and psychologically, each modifying the type and intensity of the adult's motives and motivation and each of significance to the adult educator. Readers interested in studies of this area are referred to authors Verner, Fried, Neugarten, Erikson, and Kuhlen mentioned in this chapter's Selected Readings.

STUDENT SUPPORT

While the student strives to satisfy his basic need for "independence" and is motivated to try to achieve a degree of financial independence by accepting a vocational goal, the teacher should try to satisfy all facets of his other basic needs (e.g., for social approval and status) by being extremely supportive.

In more matriarchal situations where husbands have been unemployed for long periods of time and may have assumed various domestic responsibilities, it may be necessary to counsel wives to give their husbands their blessings (support) as each enters an occupational training or retraining program.

Directors of continuing education programs can supplement the supportive atmosphere by enlisting organizations such as block clubs, unions, churches, and business and fraternal groups whose members can be encouraged to meet for some common educational purpose. Efforts by adult educators to create and maintain this positive group influence on students do much to ensure initial and continued participation as the enrollees strive for realization of their personal goals. Such cooperative efforts have continued for several years between the Detroit Public Schools and the United Auto Workers (UAW) as well as between the Utica, Michigan, Public Schools and the Ford Motor Company, Sterling Division.

GOAL MODIFICATION

As the number of federal retraining programs centered on the public schools increases and as the implications and positive correlation of adult education to increased earning power and employee effectiveness are better understood, there will probably be an increase in the number of unemployed and underemployed adults seeking public school adult education assistance. Unfortunately, less privileged adults are often unrealistic in their vocational aspirations and objectives because they have had little previous experience in their "selected" vocational areas. In this situation, the teacher has a serious and incumbent responsibility to help them modify their goals and "wants" to a realistic level, thereby increasing chances of success.

GOAL FORMATION

It is also important for adult educators to assist the student in the formation of new goals. Provincialism and lack of experience limit most persons in their understanding of the range of possibilities open to them. Such a situation might occur when a mother whose children have left home returns to school to sharpen her clerical skills and is "awakened" to consider continuing on to specialize as a medical or legal stenographer, become a dental assistant, or enter college and receive a teaching certificate.

Through field trips, special speakers, audiovisual presentations, and formal and informal discussions, the student's original goal may be entirely replaced as he sees a much larger role for himself than that possible had he only his own or his community's experience as a decision-making base. Such assistance in goal formation will be a key responsibility of adult educators as the "new careers for the poor"[7] concept is implemented and continuing education becomes an important way of upgrading the employment levels of underemployed adults.

The areas of goal modification and goal formation are very delicate, and any extensive counseling should probably be referred to an experienced counselor.

For continuing education to fulfill its vital role in this area, increased coordination with other agencies such as the U. S. Employment Service will have to occur and be coupled with various follow-up services. In addition, better trained and full-time teachers operating with classes small enough so that they can move beyond subject matter to a more intense analysis of individual student limitations and objectives must always be a program objective.

ADULT EDUCATION FOR ALL ADULTS

Although there is presently much emphasis on education for disadvantaged adults (and in terms of society's most pressing needs this is proper), it must also be remembered that adult education is for all adults. Consequently, educators must be alert to the specific needs, motives, and goals of more advantaged segments of the population such as mothers returning to the working world as a time- or interest-structuring strategy.

Civic, religious, and political leaders of every community need the assistance of continuing education programs in their efforts to focus adult attention and energy on serious community changes such as industrialization, pollution, urbanization, water scarcity, "open housing," and the white society's implication in and relationship to the ghetto.[8]

Community schools and colleges must increasingly direct a larger percentage of their resources toward technical programs to develop adults for the "middle manpower jobs" ranging from the semiprofessional and technical to clerical and sales positions, which will soon compose 50 percent of the employment opportunities according to University of Michigan technical education expert, Norman C. Harris.

In addition, the areas of political adult education, recreation adult education, physical therapy, and so forth must be remembered as well as those other facets which are merely pleasurable and revitalizing.

SUMMARY ON ADULT MOTIVATION

Since public school adult education is a voluntary involvement by adults in procuring additional education for themselves, an understanding of the various factors which either discourage or encourage their enrollment as well as the factors which underlie their continued attendance is absolutely essential for any administrator, teacher, or supportive person who wishes to be consistently effective. All facets related to motivation must be considered whenever classes are established, curriculums developed, and recruitment programs initiated. Since enrollees have elected to invest a portion of their spare time in education rather than in dozens of other activities, their reasons for doing so must be immediately discovered and at least partially gratified if they are to gain the initial satisfaction necessary to ensure continued participation in the program.

Contrary to the popular use of the term, "motivation" is not a bag of tricks which the teacher uses to produce learning; rather, it is a process which belongs to the pupil.[9]

The motivations of adult students are to be found in the basic status and social needs common to each of us and are manifested through various inner drives. The teacher, working in concert with the student, must modify the "standard" program so that it becomes the vehicle through which motives can be maintained until goals are achieved.

Most adults who elect to attend adult education classes enter at a high motivational level and continue to attend primarily because the teacher has —

1. Diagnosed the individual student's motives or interest in attending class (through counseling or agency reports, informal conversation, comments of fellow students, or formal evaluation) and has planned class activities accordingly.
2. Helped the student modify and relate his motives to clear-cut short-range goals which can be achieved in class (through individual or class discussion, written handouts, etc.)
3. Demonstrated to the student's satisfaction that at least some of the other standard objectives of the class will be able to satisfy his motives for enrolling.
4. Attempted to immediately relate class proceedings to the student's accepted goals.
5. Continued to directly relate class discussions and lessons to the student's goals whenever possible and provide clear-cut knowledge of progress.
6. Satisfied the original short-range goals and helped the student formulate new or longer-range related goals.

A lack of understanding by an adult educator of the relationship between basic needs, motives, goal selection, and achievement will result in boredom, inefficient learning, increased inattention, and a feeling that the activity has no personal relevance, all of which will quickly lead to withdrawal by the student. An understanding of these factors and appropriate program modification brings to any classroom interest, vitality, good morale, and continued participation.

ADULT RECRUITMENT STRATEGIES

At present, public continuing education has been providing a relatively satisfactory service to society in terms of quality; however, its effort to provide extensive additional educational assistance to the vast number of adults in serious need has been extremely poor. One has only to review the 1960 federal census[10] to be appalled at the wide discrepancy between adult education enrollments in each community and the number of adults who have not completed elementary or high school. The influence of public continuing education for social action and improvement in the important areas of parenthood and citizenship has also been extremely limited. From the statistics of the U. S. Employment Service one can see the vast number of people unemployed or underemployed and realize that adult education must embark on a greatly expanded role in many areas if it is to be a truly viable and effective force in our society.

With the publication of books such as Michael Harrington's *The Other America*,[11] the Moynihan report,[12] Edgar May's *The Wasted Americans*,[13] the Kerner Report,[14] and the recent increased sensitivity on the part of American society asking whether, in good conscience, it has really tried to assist millions of less fortunate Americans, public school adult education programs have been increasingly delegated increased responsibilities for the improvement of the commonweal. In order to fulfill this responsibility, all adult education staff members must review programs within their jurisdiction to increase their effectiveness as agents for social improvement. This, in turn, involves focusing attention with renewed vigor and insight toward the large segments of the population which are mired in self-perpetuating ignorance, social alienation, and powerlessness. It means broadening the spectrum of adult education services and skewing them toward persons who do not consider this a land of opportunity which has given its citizens unique advantages and liberties.

Although the broad appeals via the mass media discussed in Chapter 10 are important as a method of informing the general public of the emerging role of public school adult education and are also a fine morale booster for adult education staff members, effective recruitment requires some selectivity of target groups which are to be helped, an analysis of their life styles and goals, and an organized effort to establish individual contact.

For more literate and motivated persons recruitment efforts may be limited to general announcements and individual mailings. In addition, the aid of community leaders and groups interested in adult education can usually be enlisted to aid in publicizing local programs. In these situations, the measures discussed in the previous chapter will usually be adequate, providing the program fulfills the short-range goals and objectives of enrollees.

With less literate or more disadvantaged populations an active program of direct person-to-person contact must be instituted. *Basically this involves working through intermediaries who have regular and close contact with potential adult students in religious, cultural, business, fraternal, or employee organizations.* This is especially important among poorly educated low-income Negroes where participation in organizations is considerably greater than among comparable white levels.[15]

The disadvantaged portion of the population constituting "about 25 percent of the total population — between 40,000,000 and 50,000,000, depending on the criterion of low income that is adopted"[16] should always be defined —

> In terms of those who are denied minimal levels of health, housing, food, and education that our present stage of scientific knowledge specifies as necessary for life as it is now lived in the United States;
> Psychologically in terms of those whose place in society is such that they are internal exiles who, almost inevitably, develop attitudes of defeat and pessimism and who are therefore excluded from taking advantage of new opportunities;
> Absolutely in terms of what man and society could be.[17]

The problem, plight, and frustration of adult educators at the lack of progress in recruiting these individuals is summarized by the Kerner Report's[18] statement that "segregation and poverty have created in the racial ghetto a destructive environment totally unknown to most white Americans." It is the implications of the words *totally unknown* which must be grappled with if more effective recruitment strategies are to be developed for these citizens.

Organization Approach

The organization approach is an important recruiting device. It is effective because of the allegiance of members to their leaders which ensures them an acceptability and credibility the less well known adult educator lacks. Consequently, the leader's remarks about the advantages of adult education participation are much more likely to receive adequate and serious consideration. In addition, the organizations' officer and committee structure can ensure rapid dissemination of information, creation of support, and active participation. If, on the other hand, a group's own members are not the adult education program's specific targets, they are much more likely, after an exhortation by their own leader, to assist in recruiting by acting as intermediaries themselves.

Organization Selection

The selection of a contact with such organizations should be made only after the completion of an inventory and analysis to determine which ones could provide the greatest support for such recruitment activities if properly approached because —

1. Their goals are similar to those of the particular adult education program being publicized, or
2. With negotiation their objectives could be broadened to include those of the program.

In general, contact should be established with those who have had a history of adult education cooperation, those whose leaders are especially interested and effective, and those who have direct access to the target population.

Organization Recruitment Participation

Steps should be immediately initiated to show the leaders and their key assistants the implications and possibilities of the new adult education program as an aid in helping them reach their own goals. Such cosponsorship should be followed up by—

1. Outlining coordinating strategies.
2. Establishing a clearinghouse to expedite recruits into class.
3. Ensuring that liaison is continued so that future group or agency support is assured.

Recruiting Less Advantaged Adults

While there is no simple or easy strategy when working with less advantaged adults, the "organizational" approach is relatively effective. In the Detroit Public Schools' Project R.E.A.D. program, this approach has often been successful with union, church, community center, and fraternal organization leaders and their followers.

Program directors must also be alert to the emerging grass roots and self-help leaders who are reestablishing contact with vast numbers of alienated and unorganized adults. Needless to say, approaches to these more militant and initially distrustful leaders must be made on an "Is there any way in which this adult education program can help you help your members?" basis. Such an approach is often more acceptable through the previously mentioned "intermediary." Its use presupposes an abiding faith that additional education will lead most individuals toward responsible leadership in a democratic society.

When considering adult education recruitment, it is important to remember that serious difficulty is not encountered so much with those who have had many satisfying and successful experiences in school, but with the millions who, either as children or youth, were failed or disappointed previously. Most of these individuals have been relegated to the lower or "underclass" [19] of our society, and their poverty and powerlessness will tend to be repeated in their offspring unless the cycle can be altered. These millions of underclass adults represent the most difficult segment of our population to involve in adult education as well as the group most in need of its advantages. Their basic status and social needs remain the same, but for a variety of reasons (i.e., feelings of powerlessness, alienation, rejection, and isolation) they are often reduced to accepting very marginal goal selections which they feel are obtainable but which are quite different from those of the middle-class population segment (e.g., adjusting to permanent public aid versus temporary aid or an earned livelihood). To achieve these goals which are less acceptable to the majority of society, they tend to employ strategies which probably do not require formal adult education as it is normally constituted and taught.

In this situation, the rationale employed by those who see education as a vehicle for upward social and status mobility, for securing material satisfactions, and for controlling one's destiny is probably not considered practical or even relevant. For this group, curriculums composed of basic coping strategies applicable to improving a limited existence may be acceptable if they are really relevant to the potential student's daily life, if they can be taught by a teacher who can relate easily, and if the student does not have to surmount too many distance, transportation, form, and fee problems.

The problem is further compounded by the fact that to a believer in continuing education understanding that millions of adults have been reduced to operating at this level is almost incomprehensible. Unfortunately, this ethnocentrism on the part of both groups tends to preclude (a) any serious communication which might lead to a redirection of some adult education programs through the incorporation of material of greater significance in the lives of these individuals and (b) their better understanding of how adult education might drastically improve various aspects of their lives were they to participate for a sufficient period of time.

Unfortunately, this confusion and the resulting frustration on the part of continuing education staff members is likely to continue, where Negroes and certain other minorities are concerned, until educators appreciate the importance of assisting such disadvantaged and disillusioned groups attain greater pride and economic and political power.

These are difficult matters to discuss and develop within the confines of a single chapter. Consequently, those readers interested in the sociological difficulties of recruiting seriously disadvantaged adults may wish to read and consider the implications of The Other America and the Kerner Report before proceeding.

INDIRECT FACTORS INFLUENCING ADULT RECRUITMENT

Any serious discussion of adult recruitment would be incomplete if the factors which indirectly influence adult recruitment were omitted. It is these factors which provide an important portion of the base on which recruiting takes place and is either facilitated or limited. Examples might be—

1. Availability of public transportation facilities. Adult education centers located at an intersection of two perpendicular public transportation lines are preferred. Contact should be made with local companies to alter bus schedules to coincide with the beginning and, even more important, dismissal of evening programs.
2. Adequately lighted parking areas. If at all possible, adequately lighted and supervised parking areas must be secured. The physical safety of students is a seldom discussed but crucial element in any program continuing after dark.
3. Classes scheduled throughout the day, i.e., morning, afternoon, and evening as well as Saturday morning. Because workers on late shifts have great difficulty in constructively structuring their daytime activities, adult education classes offered during this period are especially appreciated. This period is equally important to the unemployed who may welcome adult education activities for a variety of reasons.
4. Planned "share the ride" arrangements. Getting together is always fun and the knowledge that someone will be tooting the horn for you in a few minutes is an added inducement to get ready mentally and physically for an adult education class.
5. Location of some classes in nonpublic school facilities, e.g., union halls, churches, community centers, and factories, as part of an outreach program. Although increasing the administrative complexities of any program, contact with many adults can only be made in the institution or organization in which they feel comfortable. Hopefully, after a degree of success, they will be ready to move toward the larger, more efficient learning centers.
6. Deliberately planned heterosexual programs such as ballroom or square dancing, improving family management and living, changing parental roles and responsibilities, etc.

RECRUITERS

Because adult educators increasingly appreciate the personal, program, and communication limitations when recruiting under- or lower-class citizens, many have employed "community contact agents" to perform the necessary but difficult liaison role between themselves and these target groups.

These recruiters may be paid staff members or may be volunteers. Volunteers usually come from groups or organizations (e.g., Girl Scouts, Campfire Girls, union stewards, women's groups, and religious organizations) that are convinced that the objectives and results of the adult education program warrant the time they are investing. Paid recruiting agents include (a) members of the adult education staff or (b) local part-time aides who are paid a lesser amount depending on their responsibilities and effectiveness. Such agents and aides are especially necessary when the adult education program is directed at a particular segment of society which has proved less approachable through the broader mass appeals and when the needs of society to upgrade that segment of the population are particularly urgent.

Qualifications of Recruiters

One of the primary considerations in the selection of such intermediaries is the ease with which persons in the target group can relate to them. Thus, an agent would do well to have all or most of the following qualifications:

1. Live in the area for which he is responsible.
2. Be a regular participant in a variety of social, fraternal, political, recreational, and religious groups.
3. Be of the same ethnic or racial background as those he is attempting to recruit.
4. Be a persuasive individual, a real salesman, a person willing to discuss details with all individuals and groups, anytime, anywhere.
5. Have a deep understanding of adult education and its role in helping upgrade the target population socially, culturally, politically, and economically.
6. Be mobile, energetic, concerned, empathetic, and sensitive.

Because of their personal attributes, working knowledge, and experience, such contact agents will be much more likely to identify and communicate with their target group and, as a result, increase drastically the percentage who enroll. Continued attendance of these new enrollees, however, depends on the ability of the teacher to immediately alter the standard program so as to work with, and possibly modify, the unique motives, interests, requirements, and goals of this increasingly important segment of the population.

Recruiter Accountability

Since the liaison agent is largely self-directed, the integrity of the program can be maintained only if all parties agree that during "working hours" he—

1. Will recruit for and discuss only those details related to the adult education program. This point must be well understood since a good agent is, of necessity, seriously involved in the political, social, and religious activities of the community, and his actions and comments may be easily misinterpreted as a misuse of government funds to support the purposes of a particular group or organization.
2. Will maintain an accurate log which includes the names of all contacted persons with appropriate dates, addresses, phone numbers, results of discussions, and the amount of time spent. Such information is valuable to the administrator because it—
   a. Improves the agent's efficiency of operation.
   b. Provides information on previous contacts for new agents.
   c. Provides supportive pay data for auditors.

Feedback Implications

It should be noted that an important side effect of a properly organized community contact system is the information feedback from potential students regarding what they consider to be their special needs and their views of the adult education program. This information should be carefully considered for altering the program offerings, curriculum content, and teaching styles better to reflect the expectations of potential students.

SUMMARY ON RECRUITMENT

Strategies of adult recruitment will be determined primarily by the funds available for this activity, the type of population the adult education program is attempting to service, the speed with which society has decided to upgrade that population, and the understanding of the adult education administrator about how to proceed. While middle-class adults have usually had a relatively satisfactory educational experience as children and may be expected to enroll in adult education programs if they are interested and are notified by mass appeals, individual mailings, etc. (see Chapter 10), the less advantaged portion of the population quite often has not been able to overcome the "don't go" beliefs of their lives such as—

1. Nothing can really make a significant difference or improvement.
2. Formal adult education has little personal relevance.
3. The doubt that they can learn or succeed.

Such attitudes require that the adult educator analyze his population in terms of their needs, interests, and motives, but not, as in the first portion of this chapter, to modify the program and quickly satisfy them, but in order to identify them so they can be referred to and used as stimulators and teasers in a recruitment campaign. Operating on the theory that "you can't interest or stimulate them if you don't know what they want," the adult education recruiter must use every available feedback device. However, to think of adult education recruitment only in terms of satisfying people's wants is to oversimplify an extremely grave, difficult, and important problem, especially when recruitment involves seriously disadvantaged adults in the lower- and under-classes who have concluded that society as it is presently organized has no means by which their basic status and social needs can even be partially satisfied.

To recruit adults in this type of situation is a difficult but not impossible task if adult education leaders can accept their own serious personal and communication limitations and rely more on liaison or community contact agents whose personal backgrounds have made them especially knowledgeable concerning the characteristics of the target population and whose personal attributes enable them to establish quick and firm rapport with its members. Such agents working through the leadership of religious, fraternal, recreational, and similar organizations can reach most members either as enrollees or volunteer recruiters, each of whom will continue to support the adult education program if it is modified to reflect the particular requirements and goals of the population it is attempting to serve.

This situation, of course, is no different than the role that adult education should fulfill for all segments of the community; however, the negative or seriously limited previous educational experiences of the disadvantaged, the ethnocentrism of adult education staffs, and the traditions and precedents of adult education offerings all tend to increase the difficulty of making a prompt, comprehensive, and adequate response with this group.

Adult recruitment using the approaches outlined in this and the previous chapter will prove successful provided the crucial related factors of a relevant curriculum, supportive staff, adequate public transportation, lighted parking areas, spread of scheduled times and locations, etc., are also available.

CHAPTER 12

COUNSELING AND GUIDANCE SERVICES

Golden I. Langdon

The enduring characteristic of modern society is change. Change will inevitably occur and, as it does, people must make adaptations. Guidance services are designed to make the transitions easier and more beneficial for all concerned. Through a basic program of guidance services the adult learner is helped to know himself and how he has come to be. He is apprised of environmental components and opportunities, and he receives the personal assistance of a professional counselor in his quest for selfhood in relation to the world of experience. In essence, he is afforded maximal opportunity to become whatever heredity and environment allow.

At the time of this writing, guidance personnel are in short supply and large demand. Elementary and secondary schools, as well as institutions of higher education, cannot hire adequate numbers because they are not available. The shortage is further magnified by the fact that government, industry, and business are employing many guidance workers. The law of supply and demand has dictated a situation in which guidance specialists in adult education are, in many instances, regularly employed as counselors in other school situations and part-time in programs for the adult. Obviously, counselors should be employed full-time for the adult program, but reality often necessitates compromise. Therefore, it is important for everyone concerned with adult education to become well versed in the area of guidance services.

Accordingly, this chapter is designed to (a) inform the administrator of the role and scope of the professional guidance worker, (b) assist the teacher in developing a guidance point of view, and (c) inform

Golden I. Langdon is dean of students at Augusta College, Augusta, Georgia.

the professional guidance worker of specific techniques for providing counseling and other guidance services.

THE COUNSELOR'S PROFESSIONAL PREPARATION

The professional counselor employed in the adult education program should have a master's degree in counseling and guidance from an accredited institution of higher education. His academic background should include work in the following areas:

1. *Individual inventory techniques.* Course requirements should be designed to familiarize the counselor with tests, inventories, and sociometrics which yield information about interests, personality, aptitudes, achievement, intellectual growth, self-concept, and interpersonal relationships. Further, the course should enable the counselor to be competent in the selection of techniques and in the interpretation of results.
2. *Information services.* The course work for this requirement should include occupational, educational, and personal-social information services. Methods of gathering, evaluating, and presenting all manner of information should be included.
3. *Counseling theory.* This course should afford extensive exposure to major counseling theories so that each counselor can finally select what will work for him.
4. *Practicum in counseling.* The practicum course should place the counselor in actual counseling situations under the supervision and observation of a mentor who can further his development.
5. *Research and experimental design.* The counselor should be familiar with research methodology and the statistical tools which facilitate such research. The course further serves to provide the counselor with requisites for interpreting and evaluating the research of others.
6. *Personality.* The components of personality and the multifarious influences which affect personality development should be studied by the counselor. He must be able to assess the individual as he is and as he has come to be.
7. *Group guidance.* The counselor is often involved in group activities. Consequently, he should understand the nature of groups, the relationships of individuals within groups, and optimal methods of promoting positive group behavior.
8. *Sociology.* A course in sociology should be included to make the counselor aware of the ramifications of social class structure and

interaction. Sociological characteristics of the populace must be attended to so that the counselor can communicate effectively with persons from every social sphere.

9. *Survey course in adult education.* The survey course in adult education should familiarize the counselor with developments and trends in the area. Organization, administration, material, and methodology should be presented in overview form.

10. *Seminar.* A seminar course during the later stages of the master's degree program should unify experiences and put the relationship between guidance services and adult education in perspective.

The areas cited above represent minimum requirements for the individual in a master's degree program who plans to engage in counseling and guidance with adults. To date, few programs prepare counselors specifically for guidance work in adult education programs. Consequently, the recommendations must be modified in line with reality. The time is fast approaching, however, when many such programs will be offered. Until then counselors will have to assume much of the burden of professional preparation through their own efforts.

Counselors for programs of adult education will be recruited primarily from the ranks of those engaged in public school work, but the administrator should note that many qualified counselors work with social, business, and industrial agencies and firms as well as colleges, universities, and technical schools. These sources should be considered when staffing needs are in evidence.

In addition to academic requirements, the counselor should participate in preservice and in-service training programs. The counseling is essentially the same despite student background and experience, but the adult education program and the aims, goals, and experiences of the participants vary from public school situations to an extent which makes further professional preparation quite necessary.

Prior to assuming the position of counselor in the adult education program the counselor should examine the facets of student and program which diverge from the customary climate of public school education, and he should be exposed to periodic in-service seminars with highly skilled professionals who can help him to develop and maintain a perspective consistent with his role.

THE COUNSELOR'S PROFESSIONAL RELATIONSHIPS

In the area of autonomy and staff position the counselor is unique. He reports to the administrator in charge, but he is allowed to maintain professional silence in many areas. He is not administratively responsible to teachers, supervisors, or curricular personnel, but he is directly involved with all program personnel as an integral part of the total system. He serves as a member of various committees which work toward the optimal program, and he works closely with situations which involve particular students. As a highly skilled professional with advanced training his value is generally reflected in his salary. The common public school practice of paying the counselor somewhat less than administrators but somewhat more than teachers has carried over to adult education.

These and a host of other characteristics which inhere with the role of counselor in adult education sometimes lead to misunderstandings detrimental to the program and its students. Obviously, a sound program for developing good professional relationships is a high priority item on the counselor's agenda. Since personnel relations are positively influenced through information, involvement, cooperation, and observation, it follows that the methods of achieving an informed and involved faculty and administration outlined below should be followed fully.

Information About the Guidance Program

The conscientious counselor realizes that other personnel involved in programs for adults have a right to information concerning the nature and anticipated outcomes of guidance services and that such information is directly beneficial to program personnel and indirectly to students. As program personnel become familiar with guidance, they are more disposed to lend support, and students reap the rewards. An uninformed faculty or administration is not likely to support the initiation and implementation of guidance services.

The counselor should be afforded adequate opportunity through regularly scheduled faculty meetings or in-service activities to present information pertaining to guidance services. The actual approach to presenting information to program personnel varies with unique aspects of the total educational program and according to the backgrounds of all involved. From a practical point of view, however, one would proceed in logical sequence through the guidance services offered and anticipated. Consequently, the testing service would receive attention according to its implications for faculty and students. The same principles would apply to other services.

Because of its nebulous and confidential character, the counseling service deserves special attention. The theories and techniques of counseling are, in many instances, foreign to the orientation of teachers.

The basic philosophy of teaching and counseling is defined in terms of assisting students in the search for untroubled adequacy, but the approach is somewhat different. Teachers are in the business of informing, telling, imparting information, explaining, etc. The counselor is in the business of assisting the individual to achieve personal adequacy through a process of self-actualization. In the counseling relationship, the counselor does not tell or prescribe, but rather fills a supportive function. It is sometimes difficult for a teacher to accept the theories and techniques of counseling because of the methodological differences. The barrier, however, is not insurmountable. Through various presentations utilizing lectures, discussions, and demonstrations, understanding and cooperation can be attained.

Information About Students and Groups

Throughout this chapter, the matter of confidentiality is emphasized as it relates to information gained in the counseling interview. However, this does not preclude either the professional sharing of information with the expressed permission of the counselee or the professional sharing of objective information which is clearly necessary for a cooperative effort to provide assistance. The counselor should be available for case conferences which relate to specific students. At such a conference, the counselor should make available and interpret whatever information is necessary and within his ethical freedom to divulge.

On a less personal basis, the counselor should provide his professional associates with statistical analyses of objective data such as achievement test results and social and sociometric observations and analyses. The counselor is a constant and vital source of information concerning individuals and groups.

Involvement

Involvement of faculty and administrative personnel increases understanding and personal concern. Insofar as possible, program personnel should be directly involved in guidance services. The involvement can range from committee work and evaluation to direct responsibility for initiating and implementing guidance services.

Such participation gives personnel direct insights into the planning, methodology, and outcomes of guidance, and consequently allows identification with the service. Not only does such involvement allow direct experiencing of positive outcomes, but it also makes for situations where the person works diligently for the activity's success.

As to involvement in the actual counseling relationship, program personnel must simply be aware of personal-professional competency.

Any time one helps another with a problem by listening, he enters a modified counseling relationship. Persons other than professional counselors often give significant assistance to the troubled. Thus, the differences between such situations and counseling are largely matters of degree. The counselor should help teachers and administrators to acquire basic interviewing skills, but he should also help them realize the point at which lay counseling must be replaced with professional counseling.

Observation

Personnel relations are often strengthened through observation of guidance activities. While the counselor is not at liberty to allow observation of counseling interviews, he is able to let his functions be known through various group activities. Consequently, the counselor should plan strategically timed programs which allow for observation by other personnel. It is often easier to show people the value of guidance than to tell about it.

The counselor must have the support and professional sympathy of the faculty and administration if his work is to be optimally beneficial to the adult student. Lack of support can nullify even the best organized program of guidance services.

COUNSELING

The nomenclature of many fields is so ambiguous that definitions must be exact to ensure effective communications. Counseling is no exception. The definition presented here is generally acceptable, and it relates specifically to the matter of counseling with adults. Counseling is a personal, one-to-one, confidential relationship in which a counselor, by virtue of his experiential background, assists a counselee, the product of an infinitely different experiential background, to achieve personally and societally acceptable reconciliations of self and universe of experience, and finally to achieve a state of untroubled adequacy.

Certain of the definitional components deserve individual attention because of their intrinsic importance.

Personal

Counseling is personal in the sense that two individuals are interacting freely; the counselee is giving unabashedly of himself, and the counselor is, to the extent of his ability, experiencing the reality presented by the counselee.

One-to-One

Counseling is not a group relationship but a face-to-face relationship between two persons. When more than two individuals are involved, the relationship is known as group guidance.

Confidential

The counseling relationship is not designed to ferret out information for use by teaching or administrative officials. Except in extreme situations discussed later, information revealed in the counseling relationship is privileged as are lawyer-client relationships.

Assisting

The counselor is not an adviser, and he does not make decisions for the counselee. In the final analysis, the counselee is allowed to make his own decisions, and he must assume personal responsibility for the outcome of resultant behaviors.

Personally Acceptable

Decisions growing out of the counseling relationship must be acceptable to the counselee. Because of the difference between making a decision and accepting or internalizing that decision, one does not necessarily imply the other. Consequently, the counselor must provide assistance which ensures the possibility of personally acceptable and fully functional decisions.

Societally Acceptable

Since counseling is concerned with the process of self-actualization, it has been argued that solipsism is a danger. However, the argument is invalidated by the fact that the goal of self-actualization is to be an acceptable and contributing member of society.

Untroubled Adequacy

The end result of counseling is a state of being in which one is comfortable with his self and with the society of which he is a part.

Counseling can be defined in generally acceptable terms, but the practice of counseling is subject to individual interpretation based on theory and experience. However, there is a common factor which lends coherence and stability to the field: the relationship which exists between the counselee and the counselor.

The counseling relationship offers the person unique opportunities to effect a reconciliation of self and the universe of experience. He is warmly accepted in a permissive atmosphere where he is free to be what he is without fear of judgment or betrayal. He is valued as a person of worth and dignity who is capable of making his own decisions and accepting the consequences of behavior based on the decisions. With the assistance of a competent counselor his disorientation and confusion diminish as he is able to pull together the elements of his world and construct an orderly and coherent world within which he can exist in a state of more untroubled adequacy.

COMPONENTS OF THE RELATIONSHIP

The counseling relationship per se is comprised of and affected by a multitude of operants which can be defined or implied. The counselor can seldom identify the exact operants which contribute most effectively to a genuinely helpful relationship, but he can proceed safely on the assumption that the operants discussed in this section are likely to enhance optimal relationships.

Counseling Is Not Advising

The counselee who is confronted with a "telling" counselor becomes insecure and is caused to feel inferior, threatened, and rejected. The counselor is perhaps gratified through an assertion of his superiority, but he has done nothing to assist the counselee—in fact, he may have exerted an infinitely hurtful influence. The effective counselor creates a situation within which the counselee is able to develop understandings and insights based on his own cognitions.

When the counselee makes a direct request for information concerning employment, education, public assistance, and the like, the counselor rightly assumes responsibility for providing the required information. Such situations, however, cannot be construed as advising. The use of information and the ultimate solution of personal-social problems are correctly the responsibility of the counselee. The counselor has no right to make decisions for a counselee because such decisions are drawn from an inappropriate point of reference. The correct reference point is the self which must abide by the decision.

The Effective Counselor Is a Good Listener

In theory the counseling relationship represents a conversational situation, but it is unique in that one person dominates the conversation while the other is content to lend an attentive ear. The counselor understands that if he is to be of assistance he must listen to the verbalizations of the counselee. A major shortcoming of many counselors, particularly those less experienced, is the inability to refrain from talking. When one is talking he cannot listen, and when he is not listening he cannot hear the verbal clues which serve as bases on which to provide assistance.

The Counselor Reflects Verbalizations

The counselor often reformulates significant statements made by a counselee and reiterates them in modified form so that the counselee is placed in the position of reexamining his original statement and its significance. The process of reexamination often produces insights which lead to new interpretations of significance.

Counselor Verbalizations Must Be on the Counselee's Level of Understanding

Most people in our society speak the English language with varying degrees of proficiency, and the counselor by virtue of his experiential background, particularly his educational training, is among the more proficient practitioners. As it is difficult to conceptualize the world from the point of view of someone else, it follows that communications and particularly the nomenclature, semantics, and connotations of communications are often ill understood from the point of view of another person. The counselor must attempt to put himself into the "verbal shoes" of the counselee so that they will both be speaking the same language and also understanding the same language in an identical manner. It is through effective verbal and physical communication that positive outcomes can result from the counseling relationship.

Information Revealed by the Counselee Must Be Held in Confidence

With the possible exceptions stated below, matters discussed in a counseling interview must be treated with strict and absolute confidence. Exceptions are permissible (a) if expressed permission is granted by the counselee and (b) if withholding the information constitutes a clear and definite threat to society. In all other instances information revealed in a counseling relationship is as privileged as that of the lawyer-client or physician-patient relationship.

The Counselor Recognizes That Behavior Is Not a Simple Matter

Behaviors are generally the result of diverse and complex motivations which may or may not be known to the counselee himself. Consequently, there is no easy way to assess behavior. The primary rule of thumb is to relate behaviors to the total context from which they are derived. The counselor must strive to perceive the counselee's phenomenal field, life style, and self-concept. It is only through such firmly based perceptions that behavioral characteristics can be expected to assume real meaning.

The Counselor Distinguishes Between Symptom and Cause

Just as the word *desk* serves to identify the object but is not the object, the symptom manifested by a counselee serves as a clue to the identity of the underlying cause, but the symptom is not the cause. The basic distinction is too often overlooked.

The Counselor Recognizes the Limits of His Competency

It is difficult at best for the counselor to accept the recognition that he is inadequate in a counseling relationship. However, it is obvious that occasional cases will require more experienced or professional assistance than the particular counselor can provide. Such a situation should not threaten the counselor's ego because it is to be expected. The counselor who holds on even when he feels that he can no longer be of service is hurtful to the counselee, to the profession, and to himself.

THE TESTING SERVICE

Testing is an integral component of the adult education program. The results of properly selected, administered, and interpreted tests can contribute significantly to the program, but testing is not an end in itself. The test is one tool which assumes meaning only as it is related to the total phenomenal field of the individual who has taken it. In the final analysis, only the individual can be fully aware of himself, but the test can help him to become more fully aware of his characteristics through an external interpretation, and it can assist the educational personnel in their efforts to provide a full range of necessary services. Tests, then, are used to complement and supplement other informations. They are not designed to serve alone. Testing can be justified only in this context.

Tests and Inventories

A wide variety of tests and inventories is available for the adult education program. The test is distinguished from the inventory by its objectivity. That is, whereas the test can be answered with a definite response, the inventory is essentially a subjective instrument which is answered according to the personal perceptions of the testee. Generally speaking, the following types of tests and inventories are most applicable to the adult education program: (a) intelligence tests, (b) personality inventories, (c) interest inventories, (d) achievement tests, and (e) aptitude tests.

The intelligence test. Intelligence, a product of the infinitely complex interaction of heredity and environment, is demonstrated in the ability of an individual to make personally and societally acceptable adaptations to the elements in his environment.

The IQ or intelligence quotient is a theoretical concept based on a bell-shaped curve of frequency distribution, which purports to measure the individual's *rate of intellectual growth*. If an individual achieves an IQ test result of 100, he is growing one year intellectually for every year of physical growth. If he scores 121, he is growing one year intellectually for every year of physical growth plus 21. However, the IQ result must be interpreted in terms of the test which yielded the results, because standard deviation and standard error of measurement vary from test to test. An IQ of 121 on a particular test does not necessarily have the same meaning as an IQ of 121 on another test.

Two additional points require clarification. First, the IQ is not a stable entity. It tends to remain relatively constant because the individual tends to become more and more like himself by keeping a constancy of environment and response. But it has been shown that environmental and experiential changes can cause upward or downward fluctuations of the IQ. Second, the IQ is not indicative of potential, interest, or motivation. Therefore, one cannot predict what an individual can do or what he will do. We can infer that he will continue to grow at a relatively constant rate and that others who have similar IQ's perform certain tasks, but we cannot infer his potential for growth, nor can we infer his will to perform.

The personality inventory. One's personality is constantly being assessed on a subjective basis by one's associates. An individual may be described as melancholy by his friend who is happy. Another may be described as witty by a peer who is dull. Such descriptions, generally based on behavioral observations, represent subjective attempts on the part of the observer to categorize the dominant personality characteristics of the person to whom the adjectives apply.

Such descriptions, however, are misleading. Personality is not a single entity but a multifaceted total with many components. While an individual may exhibit overriding tendencies toward melancholy, he is at times happy or ambivalent. The personality inventory represents an objective attempt to classify personality characteristics common to a population and to establish norms by which the gradients and valences of the characteristics of a given individual can be appraised.

The properly utilized personality inventory can provide information which (a) assists the testee in making personal-social, vocational, and educational choices; (b) assists the educationist with program development; and (c) assists the counselor in establishing a helping relationship. When related to the totality of the individual in question, the personality inventory can serve to supplement and complement other informations and can partially complete his picture of himself and the picture of him perceived by others.

The interest inventory. Interests may be defined as those things and activities an individual enjoys. As an individual interacts with his environment, he develops likes and dislikes which are expressed in his behavior. Acting on the assumptions that (a) interests are identifiable, (b) interests can be measured, and (c) persons engaged in similiar vocations have similar interests, scientists have developed interest inventories. Thus, the interest inventory is an instrument designed to compare the interests of a testee to the interests of individuals who are successful or unsuccessful in various fields of work or specific vocations. If an individual scores at the ninety-sixth percentile point in the mechanical area of an interest inventory, he is assumed to have interests which correlate highly with interests of individuals who are successful mechanics. If he scores high in the social service area, he is assumed to have interests which correlate highly with interests of people who are engaged in occupations which require an interpersonal helping relationship. Obviously, the basic assumption underlying interest inventories is that people with similar interests enjoy similar work experiences.

The interest inventory can be best used with the adult in terms of vocational choice. In many instances the results of such an inventory will serve to confirm previous conclusions, and at other times they may reveal previously unidentified interests. A particularly important aspect of the interest inventory lies in the area of related work activities. The testee who indicates a high interest in the mechanical area, for instance, might also be interested in a variety of mechanical activities in addition to machanics as related to automobiles per se. He might also be interested in tool and die making or machine shop work or any number of related activities. The interpretation of inventory results could serve to bring such related activities into focus.

Caution must be used when interpreting the results of an interest inventory because interests depend directly on the experiential background of a testee. Since interests follow a developmental pattern in line with environmental elements to which one is exposed, the results of an interest inventory reflect the background of the person. If he has lived a life of occupational, educational, and social deprivation, his scores will reflect the deprivation. If he has been an advantaged person, his scores will likewise reflect the advantage.

The achievement test. The achievement test is an instrument which measures the level of academic attainment in one or more areas. It is particularly important in programs for the adult because it provides a partial basis for (a) educational placement, (b) measurement of progress, (c) planning curricular programs, and (d) pinpointing academic strengths and weaknesses.

Achievement tests are available in profusion for many populations, but there is a sparsity in the area of adult basic education. However, the gap is fast being closed. The primary difficulty encountered by those who administer an achievement test is that of selecting an appropriately normed instrument. The majority of instruments are currently based on school populations which may or may not serve as an acceptable basis for comparison with adults. It behooves those in adult education to exercise care and selectivity when planning a program of achievement testing.

One other point merits attention. The adult may not score highly on achievement tests, but he has nevertheless achieved a wealth of experience in living. The academic program and the testing program must be designed in light of his experience.

The aptitude test. The aptitude test is designed to predict success in the acquisition of skills. Although the term *aptitude* is ill defined, test makers have discovered that certain measurable characteristics consistently accompany certain types of learning. Thus, they have been able to isolate and measure a variety of aptitudes which are identifiable with the ability to acquire the skills necessary for a variety of educational and vocational competencies.

Aptitude tests can be categorized in the following manner:

1. Scholastic aptitude tests used to predict academic success
2. Special aptitude tests used to measure specific aptitudes, i.e., musical, clerical, etc.
3. Multi-aptitude test batteries used to measure a variety of aptitudes.

Obviously the primary advantage of an aptitude test or battery lies in its predictive value. The results of such a test, combined with other pertinent information, can be of great value in educational and career planning. Government, industry, and education make extensive use of such tests, and the adult education program can enrich student experiences by offering aptitude testing in conjunction with other available services.

Test and Inventory Resources

The most comprehensive and reliable source of information concerning tests and inventories is contained in the following reference:
Buros, Oscar Krisen, editor. *The Sixth Mental Measurements Yearbook.* Highland Park, N.J.: Gryphon Press, 1965.

The tests and inventories cited below are representative of instruments which might prove valuable in assisting the adult student. Obviously, the list is not exhaustive, but it serves as a ready reference.

Adult Basic Education Tests
> *Adult Basic Learning Examination.* Harcourt, Brace and World. New York, N.Y. 10017. 1967
> *Adult Basic Education Student Survey.* Follett Publishing Co. Chicago, Ill. 60607. 1967
> *Tests of Adult Basic Education.* California Test Bureau. Monterey, Calif. 93940. 1967

Intelligence Tests
> *California Test of Mental Maturity* (Short Form and Long Form). California Test Bureau. Monterey, Calif. 93940. 1963
> *Culture Fair Intelligence Test.* Institute for Personality and Ability Testing. Champaign, Ill. 61822. 1963
> *Otis Quick Scoring Mental Ability Tests.* Harcourt, Brace and World. New York, N.Y. 10017. 1962

Personality Inventories
> *Sixteen Personality Factor Questionnaire.* Institute for Personality and Ability Testing. Champaign, Ill. 61822. 1963
> *Edwards Personal Preference Schedule.* The Psychological Corporation. New York, N.Y. 10017. 1959
> *Myers-Briggs Type Indicator.* Educational Testing Service. Princeton, N.J. 08540. 1962

Interest Inventories
> *Strong Vocational Interest Blanks.* The Psychological Corporation. New York, N.Y. 10017. 1966 (men), 1946 (women)
> *Kuder Preference Record-Vocational.* Science Research Associates. Chicago, Ill. 60611. 1962
> *Guilford-Zimmerman Interests Inventory.* Sheridan Supply Co. Beverly Hills, Calif. 90213. 1963

Achievement Tests
> *Wide Range Achievement Test.* The Psychological Corporation. New York, N.Y. 10017. 1946

Sequential Tests of Educational Progress. Educational Testing Service. Princeton, N.J. 08540. 1963

California Achievement Tests. California Test Bureau. Monterey, Calif. 93940. 1957 (1963 norms)

Aptitude Tests

Differential Aptitude Tests. The Psychological Corporation. New York, N.Y. 10017. 1963

General Aptitude Test Battery (GATB). Available through departments of employment security

Flanagan Aptitude Classification Tests. Science Research Associates. Chicago, Ill. 60611. 1962

For those individuals who have attained the necessary academic proficiencies, but who have not received a high school diploma, the General Educational Development (GED) testing program may be of interest. Successful completion of the GED entitles one to a high school equivalency diploma which is generally accepted in lieu of the regular high school diploma. The test, released through the American Council on Education, 1785 Massachusetts Avenue, N.W., Washington, D. C. 20036, is generally administered through local school systems, colleges, and universities under the auspices of state boards of education.

Adults who plan to attend college will probably be expected to complete one of the following entrance examinations:

College Entrance Examination Board (CEEB)
Published by: Educational Testing Service
Princeton, New Jersey 08540

American College Testing Program (ACT)
Published by: American College Testing Program
330 East Washington Street
Iowa City, Iowa 52240

Both tests are administered nationally on dates prescribed by the publishers and on other dates at the convenience of local authorities. Information can be obtained from the publishers or, in many instances, from local colleges and boards of education.

Testing Prerequisites

The process of developing and implementing an adequate program of testing in adult education is difficult at best, and problems are often compounded through failure to observe some very basic rules. The prospective tester should be particularly cognizant of the following prerequisites:

1. *Establish the goals of testing.* The testing program initiated without proper consideration of the sought-after goals is doomed to become a helter-skelter affair whose end results will be of little value to anyone concerned.

2. *Be certain that materials selected will fulfill the goals of testing.* Tests and inventories are available in abundant supply, and the test-making industry is rapidly expanding. Thus, the tester encounters the problem of test selection in a rapidly expanding field. He must be both knowledgeable and up-to-date if he is to achieve the prescribed goals.

3. *Adhere strictly to the publisher's instructions.* Tests are normed in terms of specific rules of administration, and when the rules are violated the test results are invalidated. It is just as easy to follow directions as to make them up as one goes along and infinitely more beneficial to the testee.

4. *Prepare the individuals to be tested in advance.* The human organism is more comfortable in familiar situations. Considering this basic psychological premise, it follows that a foreign situation is likely to cause anxiety resulting in inefficient and/or inappropriate behavior. It is highly upsetting to be unexpectedly confronted with a test when one knows neither the tester's motive nor the nature of the test.

5. *Testee-tester rapport is of the essence in a testing situation.* During the period of time immediately preceding the test, the tester should converse with the individual and/or group in an effort to allay possible tensions and misgivings.

6. *The physical setting should be as comfortable and as free from extraneous influences as possible.* Comfort and quiet are essential to the optimal testing situation. The absence of either can affect performance and invalidate results.

7. *Be prepared with an adequate supply of materials.* The tester should assume responsibility for providing those materials which are necessary in order to complete the test. He should not rely on the student to bring materials with him. Test booklets, pencils, scratch pads, and other material should be in abundant supply at the time of testing.

8. *Always conduct a follow-up.* The adult is particularly concerned with the results of his performance in a testing situation. Consequently, the results of testing should be made available for his inspection at a time which is mutually convenient to tester and testee.

THE INFORMATION SERVICE

The society in which we exist is currently in a state of flux characterized by rapid changes in personal-social relationships, the world of work, and the nature of education. As a consequence, the individual is constantly under pressure to make adaptations, and he needs valid and reliable information for decision making. The adult education program is uniquely privileged to afford the student opportunities to acquire meaningful information.

The counselor in such a program is responsible for assimilating and disseminating information to individuals and groups. In order to provide the greatest benefit to the greatest number of people, the counselor will utilize the group methods described here.

Orientation and Advisement Programs

The adult enrollee can legitimately be expected to be apprehensive with regard to his new educational situation. The orientation and advisement functions are designed to assist the student in making a satisfactory adaptation to the program. Basic components are outlined below.

Academic components. The academic component of orientation provides the adult learner with an overview of the nature and goals of the total program. Administrative policies, content of instruction, program goals, and values are discussed with the students. It is particularly important here to impress the student favorably so that initial rapport is established. The enrollee is an adult with adult experiences, and he must be treated accordingly. He must never be talked down to or regarded with a condescending attitude, for attendance is at his option. If he is treated as a child, he may not wish to remain in the program.

Personal-social components. The class for adults is largely a social situation, and the success of the program will depend on the manner in which the student perceives his social sphere. The orientation provides an excellent opportunity to establish a comfortable social atmosphere. The human organism fears those situations which it does not understand and which are unfamiliar. In this situation fears and misunderstandings must be avoided in the introductory stage so that the student will have positive attitudes and truly benefit from the program.

Continuous components. Orientation and advisement comprise an ongoing process of interlocking steps beginning when the learner approaches the program and continuing throughout his involvement. The counselor is the primary agent who assists the learner with registration, evaluates his records, and provides all manner of pertinent information.

He is at once an adviser who helps the learner to take the next step and the detective who finds the information which enables the learner to enroll and pursue his most optimal course.

Community Resources Programs

Industrial plant tours. These offer the adult a firsthand opportunity to be apprised of (a) industrial function, (b) possibilities for employment, and (c) worker requirements and responsibilities. This technique is particularly appropriate for adult basic education classes. Students in such classes are characteristically limited in direct exposure to work which requires a higher level of educational background.

Business tours. The adult student is well acquainted with the world of business from the purchaser's side of the counter, but he is not always knowledgeable with regard to the operation and management of, for instance, a major department store. Nor is he always aware of the many and diverse opportunities for employment. The business tour offers an opportunity to see the inner workings of enterprises with which the adult is in constant contact.

Tours of public and government facilities. Tours of many state, local, and federal facilities offer positive learning experiences for the adult. Of the many possibilities, several are listed below. The reader can readily think of others and modify the list in accordance with the availability of facilities in his area. Tours are generally accepted as routine, and visitors are welcomed.

Military installations
Courts
Mental institutions
Penal institutions
Clinics
Department of public assistance
Department of employment security
Veterans administration
Libraries.

The list could go on to include fire departments, family counseling agencies, museums, educational institutions, and a host of others. The extent to which the tour is utilized as an informational tool is limited only by location, student need, counselor initiative, and administrative policy.

Guest speakers. Through the utilization of guest speakers, the adult is offered personal-social, educational, and occupational information straight from the proverbial "horse's mouth." The counselor is generally a well informed individual who has gathered a wealth of information for the adult student and who can present it in a meaningful manner. However, the use of printed information presents, at best, vicarious experiences, and even the best informed counselor is unable to discuss every possible topic in depth. The guest speaker, on the other hand, is able to present pertinent information in depth because he functions with it in daily life.

Speakers are in abundant supply, and the choice of possible topics is virtually unlimited. Topics relating to family relations, child rearing, vocational choice, job interviewing, vocational training, public welfare, physical health, mental health, nutrition, and personal hygiene are only a few of the many topics which might be of interest and value to the adult student. A representative few of the many possible speaker sources are listed below.

Business firms
Civic service clubs
Colleges and universities
Counselors
Department of employment security
Department of public assistance
Employment agencies
Fire departments
Health clinics
  Mental
  Physical
Industrial firms
Labor unions
Libraries
Physicians
Police departments
  State
  Local
Psychiatrists
Psychologists
Social security
Veterans administration
Vocational schools.

GROUP DISCUSSION

The counselor will often serve continuing discussion groups whose members have problems of a similar nature. When a person becomes disturbed, he often feels alone in the world and that he is peculiar because no one else has problems like his own. The group process gives him an opportunity to identify with other individuals in a permissive atmosphere within which he can freely bring out the disturbing elements of self. Through a free interchange of information, thought, and ideas, he comes finally to a point which allows him to objectively analyze his situation and, consequently, make successful adaptations.

The counselor assumes a role which is largely anonymous and helps to keep the discussions in perspective. He adds information and clarification without assuming direct leadership and provides for group involvement without being dictatorial.

Group discussion of this nature is no place for the amateur, because an inept person can become threatened or cause group members to become threatened when emotionally toned discussions arise. This group technique requires the professional competencies of a skilled counselor.

SOCIAL FUNCTIONS

The fact that the classroom presents a situation which is largely social in nature presents wide-ranging implications for those who administer the adult education program. The holding power of such programs is greatly affected by the prevailing social atmosphere. Studies conducted by industry have shown conclusively that attrition rates among workers are highly dependent on the prevailing social atmosphere, and the same findings are applicable to the adult class. When the student can identify with his peers and function effectively on an interpersonal basis, attrition rates decrease. If, on the other hand, there is little cohesiveness as indicated by poor interpersonal relations, the attrition rate can be expected to rise. When one is an accepted member of the group he is generally satisfied, but when he is not accepted he will often drop out. Social functions offer effective avenues through which to create positive social relationships among members of adult classes.

The class-time "coffee break" is heartily recommended. Students use such time to socialize and get to know one another better. One teacher used an interesting variation. He asked each class member to take a turn at furnishing coffee, cake, and cookies for the break on a rotating schedule. The variety of refreshments was remarkable, and class members appeared to enjoy the activity. Class luncheons, dinners, breakfasts, picnics, and group visitations comprise only a few of the possible activities. Teachers, counselors, and students will think of many other possibilities.

THE COUNSELOR'S INFORMATION FILE

The information needs of individuals and groups necessitate a comprehensive and ever-expanding file of valid and reliable material which the counselor should have readily available. In developing the information file, the counselor should concentrate first on the many items which can be obtained at little or no expense through the community and regional survey. A wealth of pertinent information about opportunities in business, industry, and education can be gathered through telephoning, writing, and visitations. Add to these pieces of information the material which is available through agencies of the federal government, and the file has a firm foundation.

If finances are available, and if the counselor is patient enough to examine a vast amount of material in order to select that which is particularly appropriate for the adult learner, the following publishers of guidance materials should be contacted. Each publisher will furnish brochures and catalogs on request.

1. Science Research Associates
   259 East Erie St.
   Chicago, Ill. 60611
2. Careers
   P.O. Box 135
   Largo, Fla. 33540
3. B'nai B'rith Vocational Service
   1640 Rhode Island Avenue, N.W.
   Washington, D. C. 20036
4. Chronicle Guidance Publications
   Moravia, N.Y. 13118
5. Guidance Exchange
   P.O. Box 1464
   Grand Central P.O.
   New York, N.Y. 10017

The most comprehensive and accurate source of occupational information currently available is published by the U. S. Government Printing Office in the volumes listed below. Their use is much increased by the inclusion of a variety of information on worker traits, job outlook, earning potential, etc. The DOT filing system (which is fully outlined and utilized in each of the publications) is of particular value to the counselor who seeks to establish a comprehensive file. The DOT filing system is probably the most efficient and widely utilized system available today.

1. U. S. Department of Labor, U. S. Employment Service.
   Dictionary of Occupational Titles, Volume I,
   Definitions of Titles. Washington, D. C.:
   U. S. Government Printing Office, Latest Edition.
2. U. S. Department of Labor, U. S. Employment Service.
   Dictionary of Occupational Titles, Volume II,
   Occupational Classification. Washington, D. C.:
   U. S. Government Printing Office, Latest Edition.
3. U. S. Department of Labor, Bureau of Labor Statistics.
   Occupational Outlook Handbook. Washington, D. C.:
   U. S. Government Printing Office, Latest Edition.

For a ready source of accurate information about the characteristics of the society every counselor should have a copy of a U. S. census abstract:

U. S. Department of Commerce, Bureau of the Census.
Statistical Abstract of the United States.
Washington, D. C.: U. S. Government Printing Office,
Latest Edition.

Personal-social information is largely a matter of counselor experience. His training and background should enable him to establish adequate resources. Educational information can be obtained quite readily through any of a number of standard guides to junior and senior colleges, vocational schools, and home study courses.

THE PLACEMENT SERVICE

The program of guidance services in adult education should include a placement service designed to assist the student in taking the next educational or vocational step. The completion of an educational program is often a point at which the graduate needs further assistance in planning and initiating advanced education or employment.

Advanced Education

The educational placement service will vary according to needs of the graduates and characteristics of the program. In the case of a program designed to prepare students for eighth-grade equivalency, emphasis on educational placement might differ from the emphasis of a program designed to prepare for the General Educational Development examination.

At any rate, the counselor must be aware of possibilities for academic and vocational education consistent with the qualifications and needs of graduates. With minimal effort, the counselor can gather information about educational opportunities and establish working relationships with officials of educating institutions. Further, such officials are generally quite willing to communicate information in person.

The matter of financial assistance is directly related to the educational placement service. The adult student often faces a difficult financial situation when preparing for further education. A recent increase of legislation has alleviated this problem in large degree. Loans, grants, and workshop opportunities are available in such proliferation that few persons are deprived of education because of finances. However, the matter of obtaining such assistance often requires the help of well informed individuals. The counselor is obliged to become fully cognizant of the availability of financial assistance and the intricacies of obtaining the assistance.

Vocational Placement

The vocational placement service is one of the most significant components of guidance for it helps the adult education program graduate to acquire a position consistent with his newly gained academic proficiencies. The service is best implemented in cooperation with the department of employment security. In addition to testing and counseling services offered through such departments, the prospective employee benefits from comprehensive listings of employment opportunities.

The details of such an arrangement between the educational program and the department of employment security are dictated by individual situations. Generally speaking, the arrangement should provide for a free interchange of information about prospective employees and employment opportunities. The counselor is required to compile a folder descriptive of the student and make it available to officials of the department. The department is required to add supplementary test and interview data. In some situations the educational facilities offer adequate conditions for employment interviewing. However, the department of economic security usually has better facilities for such purposes, and the staff is professionally trained in the intricacies of employment.

Obviously, there is no perfect formula for the organization and operation of the educational and vocational placement service. While basic needs of graduates are generally consistent from program to program, specific components of the service are dictated by individual situations.

THE REFERRAL SERVICE

Referral is a highly important guidance function which can serve to supplement and complement the work of the counselor and, in turn, provide extensive assistance to the counselee. A multitude of referral sources is generally available for the asking in any given community. However, the counselor must assume responsibility for establishing working relationships with them. The counselor should have ready access to a wide range of state and local agencies as well as private individuals who can provide physical, social, educational, and psychological services necessary to enable the individual to achieve his goals.

The method of referral must be an individual matter. The prime requisite is that referral be construed by the counselee as an effort to assist and not as a rejection. A referral for an employment interview might be quite simple, whereas a referral involving mental health might not be so simple. Professional counseling skills may be much needed in certain situations.

In addition to the implications of the statements above, there are guidelines for referral.

1. Refer to a specific person. This technique enhances motivation by allaying some of the misgivings associated with meeting "strangers."
2. Make the appointment for the person being referred. The counselor is usually familiar with the referral source, and this added effort helps to ensure the appointment's being kept.
3. Sometimes accompany the person to the appointment. The counselee may not be able to carry through without continued support. Should his attempt fail, he will often be ashamed to return to the educational program.
4. Do not inquire too deeply about the results of referral. The counselee will reveal what he wants to be known. Genuine interest, if it is not tactfully presented, may be misinterpreted.
5. Do not expect miracles. The counselee has learned through years of experience. He will not change overnight.

THE FOLLOW-UP SERVICE

The follow-up is an essential guidance service designed to ascertain the current status of adult basic education students, graduates, and others. Although it is not primarily used for evaluation purposes, it can serve such ends in that it allows comparison of what was with what is.

Program Graduates

To be most effective, the follow-up of graduates should be conducted at the end of six months and one year. Long-range follow-up could be conducted at three- and five-year intervals. In the case of the adult basic education student, follow-up procedures should be initially implemented at six-month and one-year intervals because of the mobility of graduates and because increased educational experience may contribute to rather immediate changes in environmental opportunity.

Generally, the follow-up is most expeditiously conducted through mailed questionnaires. Questions should be stated briefly, and the answers required should not prove burdensome to the respondent. A further consideration is important here. The questionnaire should be in keeping with the known abilities of the respondent. The follow-up questionnaire mailed to a graduate who completed academic requirements at an eighth-grade level might differ considerably from the questionnaire mailed to the graduate of a twelfth-grade or community college program.

As to the information sought, no specific criteria can be cited which are equally applicable to all programs. Information sought varies from program to program. However, questions are often asked in the following areas:

1. Occupational status
2. Educational status
3. Occupational aspirations
4. Educational aspirations
5. Community activities
6. Marital status
7. Place(s) of residence
8. Evaluation of the adult education program.

Enrolled Students

The follow-up of students currently enrolled becomes largely a matter of extended personal contact, observation, and conferences with other program personnel. This points up the very important function of "outreach" by the counselor. The counselor cannot sit behind his desk and be actively involved with the program. He must visit with students and other pertinent individuals so that he can know them and become known.

As a point of clarification it should be noted that "outreach" activities do not imply forced referral. To be truly effective, guidance services should pose no threat to the individual. However, force is quite unnecessary if the counselor will utilize the advantages that inhere with his position. He offers valuable services, and he must communicate this concept to the adult learner and to other interested professionals.

The counselor should seize on every opportunity to meet with individuals and groups who may utilize his services or encourage referrals. In addition to opportunities within the school setting, the counselor serves as a communications link with individuals and groups in the society at large. Obviously, the nature of his work will put him in contact with various and sundry civic, social, business, welfare, and governmental agencies and groups which are vitally interested in programs for the adult learner.

Program Dropouts

A further extension of the "outreach" activity should be noted in terms of the school leaver—the dropout. Certainly such persons should be contacted by program personnel. The classroom teacher is probably closest to the situation, the administrator represents the program, and the counselor occupies a specialized slot. The choice of the contact person will depend upon the circumstances of the particular case and will be most expeditiously determined through a case conference. However, the counselor presents many attributes which qualify him to follow up, and he should always be available for such assignments.

The counselor who fully utilizes his "outreach" potential will be a key factor in program growth and development. By following up and reaching out, his services will be felt and appreciated by everyone connected with the educational program.

RECORDS AND RECORD KEEPING

Records are an essential component of the educational process, but no unnecessary record should be made or kept, and in all cases the learner's right to privacy must be respected. Therefore, the counselor will keep two sets of records. One will consist of information concerning certain nonacademic aspects of the learner such as records of personal counseling interviews and will not be available to others except under court order or with the express permission of the person to whom the information pertains.

The second set of records is largely comprised of academic data and personal data of an objective nature, the release of which could only be helpful to interested professional personnel. Information on background, academic achievements, health, test scores, rating scales, and so forth should be compiled in a cumulative folder to provide an ongoing source for assessment of the learner and his progress.

Records of counseling interviews will be kept in a four-part form:

1. Precise excerpts from the counselee's statements
2. Counselor's interpretation of the counselee's statements
3. Counselor's prognosis of the case
4. Summary (optional).

Cumulative records may be accumulated in a variety of forms. The counselor may adopt one form of record keeping from the many standard forms available on the commercial market or he may develop something unique. The particular forms and processes should ultimately be selected in light of specific needs of learners and program personnel.

SUMMARY

The counselor in adult education is a highly skilled professional who utilizes his competencies in an effort to assist the adult student in his quest for untroubled adequacy. He provides a relationship in which the individual can achieve reconciliations of self and universe of experience through counseling, and he is a source of personal-social, educational, and occupational information for program personnel as well as the student population. Through a well organized testing program the individual is afforded opportunities for self-appraisal, and educators are assisted in their efforts to provide appropriate learning experiences. Thus, the work of the counselor is consistent with the basic tenets of adult education.

CHAPTER 13

EXPANDING FACILITIES
FOR ADULT LEARNERS

Floyd N. Peters

The controlling purpose of adult education is to provide adults in a growing, changing democratic society with the opportunity to continue learning and may be described as including all the activities with educational purpose that are carried on by people engaged in the ordinary business of life.

Accessibility to adult education classes is a problem that faces any community providing such a program. While the individual student must remain a prime consideration, the overall population and geography of the city or locality will often dictate the location of classes. Generally, classes that are more than three blocks from a stop of public transportation will operate at a disadvantage. Good highway and street approaches and parking facilities add greatly to the success of a center.

A decision that every school board must make is whether to establish a central or a district center system of adult education.

THE CASE FOR THE CENTRALIZED PLAN

An outstanding adult educator states that in cities of less than 200,000 population all adult education programs should be located in one center. The central system has many advantages, such as economy in building facilities; no duplication of teaching equipment is required,

Floyd N. Peters is director of General Adult Education at the Lindsey Hopkins Education Center, Dade County Public Schools, Miami, Florida. Special acknowledgment is made to John Doughman, supervisor of Vocational Teacher Education, Dade County Public Schools, for his assistance in the writing of this chapter.

overhead operating costs are lower, fewer administrative and super-visory personnel are required, and travel expenses are lowered. A result of the advantages listed is, of course, a decrease in cost per student hour in as much as the capital outlay expenditures are for one building only. In addition, the morale of the administrative-teaching staff is less often a serious problem because communications are less likely to break down and the opportunity is greater for good teacher-teacher relationships as well as improved teacher-administrator relationships.

However, in localities where the population is large and travel distances are great, enrollment is usually curtailed. Other problems which are evident in centralized centers are the problems of providing adequate parking and the availability of public transportation facilities. The establishment of more than one adult center with duplicate facil-ities is expensive and increases the cost of administrative and super-visory personnel. With a second center cracks begin to form in the communication system, and the teacher-teacher relationship is not so close and neither is the teacher-administrator relationship.

THE CASE FOR THE DISTRICT PLAN

However, there are advantages in placing classes in various locations throughout the city. First and probably the most important is the accessibility of the classes to the public. Students' having classes in their "backyard" tends to build community interest and support as well as increase the enrollment. With outlying centers it is possible to serve more adults, and that is one of the major objectives of adult education. Offerings can be diversified and tailored to meet the needs of a community, and this is also an objective of adult education. A final advantage of the district plan is that of employing instructors from the local community. The Office of Economic Opportunity sug-gests that classes for the disadvantaged be established in the areas where the students live. In short, take education to the student. Ex-perience shows that this procedure will work. The Mott Program follows such a plan and establishes "Community Schools" in the neighborhood. These daytime facilities for children and youth are then used for adults and families at night.

There are disadvantages, however, in the use of the district plan. The cost of duplicating equipment and personnel is a major item of expense. The cost of time for an administrator or a supervisor to travel from one center to another is additional but necessary in a district plan. While further instructional personnel sends a budget up at a fast rate. Still experience indicates that in cities of over 200,000 population a district plan for an adult education program should be considered.

Adult basic education is an area that lends itself well to the district plan. The adults who enter these classes are those who have had no or little education and are reluctant to show this to persons outside their neighborhood. They are more at ease with their neighbors.

For the development of neighborhood and action groups the district plan has been found to be very effective. The public schools' facilities are in use from early morning to late evening. This extended use of school buildings and facilities is much appreciated by the taxpayer.

Many parts of the plant such as the gymnasium, the music rooms, the auditorium, and the outdoor physical education areas can be put to excellent use by the community school plan. As an example, the city basketball leagues can be invited to use the gymnasium, and those other activities that lend themselves to the use of large indoor areas can also be scheduled in the gym.

Community sings and guitar groups, for example, also can be urged to use the school facilities, thus creating and establishing a good community atmosphere. Such activities serve the needs of the public.

PHYSICAL FACILITIES

Architectural plans for new school buildings must include planned space for the adult school personnel from the principal to the secretarial clerk. School planners must show foresight and provide offices for the administrators of the adult program and his staff because of the overlapping time between the day and evening programs. Not only does office space need to be supplied but also storage space for laboratories, classrooms, and vocational shops needs to be planned from the beginning.

In addition, location of the adult administration offices must be considered. They should be near the main entrance of the school plant, and directional signs should be provided.

The title *director* has many meanings to many people. For the record, the director of adult education is responsible for the adult program operating at the local level. The office of the director should be located in the central school administration building. He should be a member of the superintendent's staff and should be consulted on all matters pertaining to adult education and on matters of the day school that continue on adult program time.

When the facilities of a building are shared by both the youth and adult programs, the principal of the adult high school should have an office similar to that of the day school principal. Likewise, he should be included in day school faculty meetings and extend the same courtesy to the day principal by inviting him to attend the faculty meetings of the adult teachers.

COUNSELING

Counseling is basically a matter of personal contact, observation, and conferences with students. In view of this fact, offices for the counselors should be readily accessible to the student from the registration area.

An experienced counselor in both the academic and vocational areas should be available to the adult students. Counselors should be well versed in the offerings of the school and should also be knowledgeable in the personal needs of the adult student.

Likewise, a counselor familiar with the world of work and vocationally oriented should be available to those adult students who wish to enter trade programs.

Adults enroll in two kinds of courses — namely, those that meet their interests and their needs. Their interests are not necessarily their needs; therefore, counseling is needed. Privacy during the interview is necessary if the counselor is going to be able to communicate freely with those being counseled.

THE COUNSELING SUITE

Professional counselors should be employed in the adult education program, and they must be provided with adequate physical facilities. The basic guidance suite consists of the following elements:

1. *Large multipurpose area.* This area houses academic and vocational information and provides for reading and for waiting to be counseled.
2. *Secretary-receptionist area.* This area should be contiguous to the multipurpose area. It should be so situated that visitors are easily greeted and assisted.
3. *Counselor's office.* Each counselor should have an office which is private in every respect. The counselor-counselee relationship must not be affected by extraneous distractions which prevent complete communication from taking place.
4. *Testing area.* A testing area which is quiet and private should be provided for individual or group testing sessions.

The counselor's office need not be lavishly furnished, but it should ensure comfort and a peaceful atmosphere. The lighting should not produce excessive glare and reflection. For this reason the office should be equipped with floor and table lamps rather than with the customary overhead fluorescent lights. The color scheme should feature soft pastels. Bright reds, yellows, etc. should be avoided because such colors increase emotional tone. The office should be neat and tidy at all times.

The counselor's chair and the counselee's side chair should be comfortable. Straight-backed wooden chairs add to the discomfort of both parties. The counselor should be provided with space in his office for confidential folders. A desk or filing cabinet which can be locked serves this purpose.

Tape recorders and other communications devices will be used at the discretion of the counselor; and the duplicating, printing, storage, and filing facilities will vary according to the needs of the particular program.

PLACEMENT OF CLERICAL PERSONNEL

Seating of the clerical help in the front office depends on the number of persons involved and the duties that each performs. When floor plans are being formulated two or three plans should be drawn up for study in order to determine economy of space, the availability of materials, and the maximum use of personnel. With the increasing numbers of adult programs, it is good planning to project future space needed.

TEACHERS' REPORT AREA

It is absolutely necessary that adult administrators plan facilities comparable to those found in day programs. The welfare of the adult faculty is always as important as that of the day faculty.

Plans for the teacher "reporting area" should include mail boxes for the roll books and personal mail and messages and teacher check-in sheets or a time clock for the hourly teachers.

Perhaps two bulletin boards should be mounted, one for the official school notices and the other for general information. In conjunction with the "reporting area" should be a teacher lounge provided with comfortable furniture. As many types of vending machines as possible should be provided for convenience. All these accessories add to teacher morale.

DUPLICATING AND AV FACILITIES

There should be an instructional aids production department in every adult center for the preparation of course outlines, job sheets, assignment sheets, tests, general information, and any other printed material requested or used by teachers. If a production department cannot be provided, a mimeograph or a spirit duplicating machine should be supplied. The responsibility for the care and operation of the equipment can be assigned to one of the clerical personnel. Some type of duplicating services must be made available to the teachers if quality instruction is to be expected. Increased availability of films, filmstrips, records, tapes, and other audiovisual aids for adults likewise requires convenient check-out and preview stations for the use of the busy teachers.

REGISTRATION FACILITIES

Registration procedures should be planned so that the public is served in the easiest and quickest way possible. The ease of securing registration information by the student should be considered from the standpoint of the clerical help and the adult student being served. If registration is by IBM machine operation, working bins with prenumbered cards should be arranged in advance and placed in an organized plan for distribution. All information for the registration clerks should be placed in loose-leaf notebooks, and each clerk should have one in his possession and should become familiar with its contents. A course outline for each of the courses offered should be a part of the notebook.

Several methods of registration are used in adult programs. In order to facilitate registration some adult programs use a plan where the student can register by mail. One advantage of this system is the establishment of classes before the opening date.

In a program where the enrollment is large and the next scheduled term starts immediately after the present session is completed, re-registration becomes a concern. One way of handling this situation is somehow to divide the student body and schedule the students into the registration office at different times.

Another way to handle this kind of reregistration problem is to assign a registration clerk a number of rooms to visit and to have him reregister the students there for the next term.

Another problem of registration is to keep prospective students informed of the starting dates for classes in which they may be interested.

Many programs use a preregistration card on which the applicant supplies, in the spaces provided, the name of the course desired, current date, phone, name, and address. This information is on the stub end of the card. On the reverse side of the stub the mailing date is recorded.

The large section of the card carries on one side space for the name and address of the student. The reverse side of the card carries all data necessary to inform the enrollee when to appear for the class of his choice.

OFF-CAMPUS FACILITIES

Adult education is on the go. Figures for one program show a constant increase in adult students. In 1965, 41,067 students enrolled in adult education classes; in 1966, 42,453 students enrolled in classes; in 1967, 48,270 students enrolled in classes.

With the constant increase of students and the aim of the adult educator to offer the opportunity of attending classes to all who desire to improve themselves, facilities must be expanded to off-campus locations.

Usually adult education programs are operated during the evening hours and utilize the existing facilities of the day youth program. However, an adult daytime program is handicapped because youth facilities are not available, and it is necessary to find separate housing for the adults. In searching for such facilities the adult educator must not overlook any possibility. In one county in Florida, such places as empty apartments in housing developments are used for classrooms; recreation rooms of the senior citizen complexes are used for classes: the recreation center classrooms of various municipalities are pressed into service; financial institutions usually have available classrooms, especially during daylight hours; churches have Sunday school rooms available to the adults; empty business rooms can be rented; some students will permit the use of their homes for classes; and if at all feasible, some classes even lend themselves to the great outdoors. On the other hand, the numbers of full-time adult schools are increasing throughout the country and can now be found in most large cities.

HOME STUDY COURSES

Television

For some time far-sighted and imaginative adult educators have indicated that there are many areas in adult education that could be taught through the medium of television and that adult program administrators should be exploring the possibility of using this mass medium.

In some instances the administrator has the opportunity to use an existing educational channel; others may have to seek the cooperation of the local commercial stations to air their programs.

Classes that are popular with the adults and show large enrollments at the adult centers can be used as a nucleus around which a television series can be built. Basic education, typing, psychology, home economics, and some methods of shorthand are examples of good television classes for adults.

The adult home economics department of Dade County, Florida, uses the local educational channel to provide adults with lessons in preparing food. Each week a different recipe is presented with the teacher demonstrating to the viewers the proper procedure in preparing the food.

Even though the presentation of education through television sounds glamorous, there are some obstacles such as financing, obtaining time, production, listening posts, and time for planning. Even in the face of these obstacles television has an increasing place in adult education.

Correspondence Study

Correspondence study is a situation in which an adult student can work alone and at his own pace without a regularly scheduled meeting with an instructor.

Learning by correspondence is a big business and involves a great number of adults who study many programs. A recent survey shows that several million people study correspondence courses yearly.

There are many reasons for the popularity of these courses. One reason is that people of the United States move about and cannot subscribe to an educational program that requires a long attendance period. With correspondence study highly specialized material is available, and the student can procede at his own pace.

Opportunities in correspondence work are available from private schools as well as armed forces, industrial, and business programs. In addition, the universities and colleges are expanding their offerings in the area.

PHYSICAL DIFFERENCES OF YOUTH AND ADULTS

Adults are not to be considered oversized children by the adult education teacher. The adult student differs in many ways from the youth. Body characteristics, different motivations, values, interests, reaction speed, and personality are a few of the differences between youth and adults. However, two main differences lie in the senses of sight and sound.

"Old sightedness" – presbyopia, the decline in visual acuity – sets in during the late twenties. The next stage is referred to as bifocal vision and occurs during the forties. Such facts about adults should prompt us to think about providing better illumination in the classroom as well as the use of larger letters in the printed material used.

We know, too, that auditory acuity declines throughout life. Hearing acuteness is at its sharpest between the ages of 10 to 14. After age 15 the percent of hard of hearing problems increases. The older a person is, the longer it takes him to hear a message. This known medical fact should cause the adult administrator to consider the acoustics of an adult classroom or the possibility of using a sound system. Such a situation is serious because difficulty in hearing can cause an individual to have a distorted picture of himself which could easily cause a change in personality.

The aging process leads to the deterioration of all body processes. Restroom availability should be considered when locating a class of older adults. For the same group of students more frequent breaks should be planned.

In buildings where elevator service is used, schedules need to be established so that dismissals and evacuations, in emergencies, can be carried out in an orderly manner.

In coordinating class dismissal and elevator service, the older adults should be released first if at all possible.

PHYSICAL FACILITIES FOR CLASSROOMS

Occupational Training

With the passing of the Vocational Act of 1963, a new meaning has been given to vocational education. A program that once was just another facet of education has taken a place among the leading programs in many school systems. A new challenge faces adult education and it must be met with practical and workable solutions. In providing successful occupational training, the shops must be equipped with tools and equipment found in the industry for which training is being given. Not only should equipment types be considered, but also the placing of the machines with relation to safety, availability, and health requirements as found and recommended by industry.

Dual Toolrooms

One method of tool control in shop courses is the use of dual tool-rooms when both the day and evening programs share the same shop facilities and equipment. Through this arrangement many petty bickerings centered around "who lost the tools" and "who committed a violation of rules and regulations" can be prevented.

When two classes of adults use the same shop facilities, tool control becomes a problem with another solution. A probable answer to this situation is individual tool boxes.

Project Storage Space

For those classes such as upholstering, woodworking, and others, storage space must be made available to students because the projects cannot be carried home each night and back to the next class.

Avocational Training

Training on an avocational basis is becoming more important to the adult. One reason is the shorter work week and another is early retirement. Practical arts courses using equipment found in junior and senior high schools' shops and studios supply learning experiences of an avocational nature. Opportunities for the display of adult work should be requested on an alternating or continuing basis.

Laboratories

Business. Regardless of the type of adult center, central or district, the adult instruction must be geared to the practices and techniques used in the outside business world. Business laboratory courses must be established to meet new trends. A business laboratory could be patterned after one successfully operated in Dade County, Florida. A console with three tape recorders provides dictation at three speeds. Each recorder is wired into each student desk. Using a set of ear phones with a jack, the student plugs into the speed at which he can operate.

Language laboratories. Laboratories for the teaching of a foreign language have become rather commonplace throughout the nation. Language laboratories provide an excellent opportunity to carry out the philosophy of adult education, which is one of individual instruction. Language laboratories are also useful in teaching English to foreign-born students as well as a foreign language to English-speaking people.

Programed learning. Programed learning courses and teaching machines are great assets in meeting individual needs through remedial instruction and enriching course content. Another advantage of programed instruction is the opportunity for absentees to make up work without interrupting the daily routine of the whole class through the use of a tape recorder, record player, and other equipment.

NEEDED STUDENT FACILITIES

Cafeteria

If an adult student can save time by going to school directly from his employment and can be assured of a good meal, he will continue to attend class. Students who start classes in the afternoon and need to continue into the evening must also be considered in the planning and operation of an adult center cafeteria.

Snacks and Coffee

If students are in a class that meets for three hours, there should be a break period, at which time it is necessary to make snacks available; if the day cafeteria manager is cooperative, there is no problem. However, if service from the day cafeteria personnel is not available, the administrator can contact operators of lunch wagons to supply students with snacks. In some instances, arrangements can be made with a school-sponsored club or organization to assume the responsibility of providing snacks for the adult students.

The coffee break period is a fine time for teachers and students to mingle with teachers and students from other classes. This socializing is as much a part of adult education as classroom work. Casual acquaintances made over coffee and donuts can turn into lasting friendships.

Library Services

The adult student has need for current literature of all types. Where the adult center is in the same facility as the day school, an arrangement should be worked out so that the work hours of at least one librarian cover the operation of the adult center. If a full-time librarian cannot be provided, services should be made available on a part-time basis.

Teachers should be advised early and often that a library is available. Part of a good education is the knowledge and ability to locate information when needed.

The library facility can be used in many ways, some of which are routine check-out of books, periodicals, and papers; classroom for a library science course; reference books for research papers; indoctrination of students into the hidden literary treasures to be found in the stacks; and small group use of the conference and study rooms generally available.

All adult administrators must provide the funds with which to operate the library for their program.

Student Store

Students need supplies of all kinds such as pencils, paper, erasers, and other classroom materials. The administrator should make a well organized and well stocked student store available to the students.

Ground Lights

Ground lights should be placed so that parking lots are lighted and that all approaches and walks around the building are lighted. This serves as a safety measure for the student as well as administrative personnel.

Public Telephones

Telephone service should be made available to the students both for emergency and social calls. This is the only contact some students have with their family from early morning until they return home from school in the evening.

The adult administrator needs to plan with the telephone company concerning the type of booth installation to be made. The student should have to stand to make his call as this encourages rapid completion of calls and lessens the accumulation of dirt and litter.

Parking Facilities with Security

With the increasing numbers of students attending adult centers the parking problem is becoming acute. School boards need both to supply adequate parking for the students and also to provide security for the parking areas. Protection for parked automobiles must be provided if class attendance and school enrollement are to be maintained.

Auxiliary Lighting

To lessen the threat of panic in an emergency, the administrator must consider the time when the lights in the building are off because of power failure. Many students are older, and movement on stairs and in dark hallways is dangerous. A simple auxiliary system can be installed at a nominal cost which provides light if the main power flow is interrupted. With this type of lighting installed the school building becomes a place of shelter during a natural or man-made disaster.

In order to meet county or city fire regulations, every adult administrator must have a plan for evacuating the building in case of fire, bomb scare, or other causes. Likewise, in some cities, school authorities are required to hold fire drills at certain intervals. Also the regulations for the proper operation of fire extinguishers, hoses, and alarms found in their buildings must be met.

SUMMARY

The public schools and community colleges are of, by, and for the people. Their public buildings cover the nation and should be the main facility resource for the educational activities of the adult population. The more the people of the community share in the belief that the community adult school is the center or hub of purposeful activities that are not unique to other institutions, the more will the public school and community college share in the overall development of the community.

Truly, in the forefront of adult education is the teacher in the classroom, and the prime aim of each adult administrator is to assist the teacher in achieving optimum classroom success through ever-expanding facilities appropriate for adult learners.

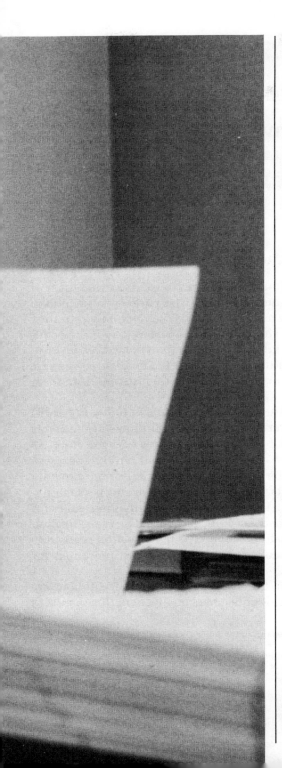

SECTION *IV*

IMPROVEMENT
OF
INSTRUCTION

CHAPTER 14

SELECTION OF TEACHERS, LEADERS, AND OTHER SUPPORTIVE STAFF

James A. Sheldon and Gordon B. Wasinger

INTRODUCTION

The key to successful continuing education is good instruction, and good instructors are where you find them. The participant in public continuing education engages in an educational activity on a volunteer basis to fulfill self-felt needs. The instructional role for continuing education, however, involves a great deal more than a median level of performance. Professor Hew Roberts indicated the challenge when he said, "In adult education we take people where they are and lead them to where neither we nor they know where they want to be." [1]

In addition, public continuing education programs today represent an increasing diversity and variety of educational opportunities. It is quite evident that expansion of educational services will continue. As a result, the continuing education instructional staff will be representative of this diversity not only in content specialty and program uniqueness, but also in talents, training, experience, and personality. Each instructor should possess the set of unique qualities necessary for the educational service provided for adult learners. The identification of some of the qualities, indication of sources, and selection of instructor and supportive staff for continuing education are presented for consideration in this chapter.

Instructional personnel, for the purposes of this presentation, are separated into the two categories of teachers and leaders. *Teachers* will

James A. Sheldon is director of the Department of Adult Education of the Des Moines Public Schools, Des Moines, Iowa.

Gordon B. Wasinger is assistant professor in the College of Education and assistant director of the Bureau of Instructional Services, Division of Extension and University Services, University of Iowa, Iowa City, Iowa.

be used for those educational activities that are more formal or more related to classroom programing, while *leaders* will be used for the less formal or nonclassroom type of offerings. This is not intended to imply that those identified as teachers do not perform a leadership role or that those called leaders do not provide teaching services.

SELECTION OF PERSONNEL FOR THE INSTRUCTIONAL PROGRAM — TEACHERS

Even though the teaching staff represents uniqueness, diversity, and variety, there are basic characteristics of good teachers that transcend these differences.

Harry and Bonaro Overstreet [2] present a chapter in their book on each of the following five qualities:

1. *The learning mind.* The fact that teachers must be the learners is the important thing. Any teacher who stops getting better and better is no good. And part of the process of getting better is that of continuing to grow, not only as a technician of the teaching trade, but also as an individual interested in our many-sided world.
2. *The importance of the specialist.* The adult educator cannot be simply a person of goodwill and generous impulses — and large ignorance. He must know something well. Neither can he be simply a person who knows something well but who is profoundly ignorant about the mental and emotional makeup of the adult human being and of the society in which he resides.
3. *The importance of the generalist.* It is because the adult education leader must have in mind the whole experience range necessary to balanced living that he must be both specialist and generalist. He must have tapped the sources of power that reside in a mastery. But he must also be able to encourage one type of experience here, another type there, and yet another type there. He must see in people not only what they are at any given moment, but what they would be if they were living on a properly balanced diet of experience.
4. *The sense of community.* A power to think and act in terms of the real problems and resources of real places where real people live is an absolute necessity for a really good teacher.
5. *A person among people.* This involves the peculiar status of adult educators; a functioning respect for other people as possessors of ideas, feelings and experiences; a subtle sense of drama; a certain nonroutinized interest in life that exists side by side with necessary routinized interests; a certain buoyant confidence that

makes it seem reasonable to undertake ventures that would make a narrowly prudent person feel foolish and conspicuous; and the importance of background and experience.

The California Department of Education presents another meaningful set of five characteristics applicable to all continuing education teachers.[3]

1. An understanding attitude toward their students. Leadership, tact, and patience are of great importance.
2. Mastery of their subjects. To this should be added breadth of knowledge and experience in related fields. Practical application is an important factor when working with adults.
3. Ability to interest a group of students with a wide range in age, capacity, education, and experience. Teachers of adults must continually adjust subject matter and instruction to meet these differences in their classes.
4. Physical stamina to stand the strain of teaching one or two evenings a week in addition to a daily program and of making necessary preparation for teaching. Most instructors have already completed a day's work before beginning the evening school assignment.
5. A broad concept of the whole community adult education program and its relation to the community.

The following qualities are taken from *Techniques for Teachers of Adults:*[4]

1. Teaching skill
2. Personality to put across the course
3. Sense of humor
4. Ability to get along with students
5. Broadmindedness
6. Knowledge of the subject
7. Patience and helpfulness
8. Consideration for people
9. Appearance
10. Good speaking voice
11. Fairness and impartiality
12. Consideration of students' time
13. Interest in subject matter
14. High ideals
15. Sincerity and honesty
16. Initiative

17. Youthfulness in thinking
18. Ability to pronounce names correctly.

These listings of general characteristics applicable to all engaged in continuing education may be very useful as a base line for selecting potential teachers; however, the selection should also be based upon unique criteria.

Adult Basic Education

National workshop activity on adult basic education developed the following characteristics desirable in an ABE teacher: [5]

1. *Patient.* The student always takes twice as long to do a job as you think he will. The ones who finish earlier need to have things which they can do on their way to help themselves.
2. *Versatile.* Students have a short attention span and need four short things to do per hour. Lots of drill is needed, but it needs to be disguised a bit each time. They don't like what "we did before."
3. *Quickly analytical.* The teacher needs to be able to size up the lacks, weaknesses, and strengths of the students in one class period, if possible, without seeming to be doing this.
4. *Humorous.* The ability to see the funny side of even pathetic problems and never to "get down."
5. *Optimistic.* The teacher needs always to believe in miracles and never give anyone up, and never think of any problem as impossible. He needs to send out rays of this feeling to the students because they are easily discouraged. He needs to feel that with time the students will pick up what is going on.
6. *Understanding.* The teacher needs to know their fear, sense when things are too much for the students, and ease up on them. At the same time, he constantly needs to expect more of them and to push them GENTLY on to doing more . . . using the things they have learned. *Expect* them to do this.
7. *Philosophical.* He needs to be trying to get the students to assume responsibility for their own learning, to help them face fears and get around them. He needs to explain the reason for each lesson, *why* it is so designed, *what* it is to teach, *how* to do the lesson to learn the most. These students are often pigheaded about finding shortcuts or devising their own method of doing, or doing the thing backward . . . defeating the learning process, but "getting it done."
8. *Creative.* He needs to be able to think of new approaches — go at the same lesson a bit differently.

9. *Perceptive.* He needs to be able to *see* practical application, short-range tricks, so the students can learn *something* quickly and see their success, along with long-range work, so that *something* is always growing and building up.

10. *Tomorrow-looking.* He should be able to instill in the students AWARENESS of the world around them . . . all the interesting things they don't know but could learn about, and he should recognize that he will not teach them all they need. Students need to learn to teach and graduate from the teacher's loving care into responsibility for their own learning.

11. *Flexible.* He should be free to have a "hot spur of the moment" inspiration and time to try it. If what is planned is not quite right, drop it, adapt it, or forget it.

Americanization Program

The preparation of foreign born for American citizenship separates into the subject areas of communications skills and civic understanding.

Special characteristics of the teacher for the communications skills would parallel those for adult basic education. Bilingual ability of the teacher may provide unique advantages in getting classes started and in understanding the problems of a learner who is developing a second language.

The second area of civic education is most important for the foreign born. Civic education does not simply imply knowledge and understanding of the responsibilities of American citizenship: It also requires acceptance of those responsibilities along with meaningful experiences. A good adult teacher in civic education will be well trained and involved as a citizen, but more importantly the teacher will provide actual experiences and the opportunity for involvement of the learners during the educational process.

Vocational Programs

A major portion of public school continuing education involves fulfilling the need for occupational improvement. Vocational programs are, however, usually identified as those eligible for reimbursement through the "vocational education" laws. Such fields as trades and industry, home economics, parent and family life, agriculture, and distributive education are included. There are other "craft" programs fitting this category which were not included before that are now offered at community colleges or area technical schools under recent legislation.

The major characteristic of a teacher for a vocational program would be recognized skill and knowledge of the trade, craft, or paraprofessional group represented. Along with this outstanding knowledge and skill would be a commitment and a desire to share this skill and knowledge to develop additional craftsmen in the field. Vocational education teachers will require certification by the state educational agency to teach.

Adult High School

The adult high school programs have been stimulated by the growing numbers of people completing the eighth grade under the adult basic education programs.

Adult high school programs usually require certified teachers because of state regulations and standards of accrediting associations. The typical secondary school teacher must provide for flexibility and individualized rate of development when providing courses at the adult level.

Humanities and the Arts

There is a strong drive in people for understanding, truth, and beauty. This drive produces the need for programing in public school continuing education for the "liberalizing" fields of study. Robert Redfield stated [6] that —

> Education is of course learning something. More importantly, it is becoming something. Although knowledge is needed for education, an educated person is not the same as a man who has knowledge. An educated person is one who is at work on his enlargement. If we learn things that become parts of us, if we make efforts to develop our own particular understanding of life and the order of life's goods, it is education we are doing. A person is something that it takes time to make; there is on everyone an invisible sign, "Work in Progress"; and the considered effort to get along with the work is education.

A teacher in the humanities and arts must be a specialist in the subject area, but he must also have that unique quality of seeking an education.

Teaching Aides

The development of teacher aides or classroom aides at many levels of the education structure is the result of the great number of activities attending the instructional process. The use of instructional assistants would seem worthy of consideration for some continuing education activities. Teacher aides may be paraprofessionals where a team teaching approach is appropriate or subprofessionals that have some college work and take care of clerical details as well as assist in the instruction process. Classroom aides are people who serve as liaison between the teacher and the class in a social sense. The classroom aide may be responsible for clerical details and as an aide to students on a one-to-one basis. Teacher aides and classroom aides may be paid members of the staff or may be volunteers. In many instances classroom aides are obtained from the source group that the educational activity is attempting to serve. Teacher aides are used primarily for the improvement of instruction by relieving the teacher of some of the necessary "chore" activities; however, serving as an assistant may be valuable experience for the prospective adult teacher.

SELECTION OF LEADERS FOR NONCLASSROOM ACTIVITIES

A well balanced continuing education program, of course, is not limited to the classroom. Directors are fully aware of the need to expand the services to other areas — public affairs, discussion groups, international understanding, community development, and educational television — to name a few. Personnel for leadership roles is again the key factor in the success of such programing. Criteria for leaders vary somewhat from that for teachers, and, of course, the source in many cases is different. Effective personnel is so vital for such programing that it is suggested that before a director introduces a program of new activities, such as those listed above, he should be reasonably certain that he has competent leaders to assume responsibility for the programs. Such leaders can usually be found in any community. We shall explore these areas of service and examine some of the requirements for personnel.

Public Affairs Programing

Many directors feel quite strongly that they have a responsibility to provide their communities with opportunities that will result in a citizenry better informed on local, state, national, and international affairs. As a matter of fact, they would go a step further and explore every possibility that would motivate citizens to take a more active role in civic affairs. Certainly some agency within a given community should be responsible for an effective public affairs program. Why not public school continuing education departments? What then are the personnel needs in the area of public affairs programing? It depends, of course, on the nature of the programs, but let us assume that in most cases they are in the form of public meetings or forums. The success of a public meeting or forum depends very much upon the type of moderator selected. Let us consider the qualifications.

1. Cheerful and pleasant, "unflappable"
2. Interested in people and able to draw them into the discussion
3. Some knowledge of the subject, prepared to throw in questions to enliven dead spots
4. Not too large an ego—keep himself out of the limelight—act as a catalyst only
5. Firm—able to control any dissension
6. Good voice
7. Sense of timing and organization—keep to the subject and not too long on one point if audience grows restless
8. Alert, able to analyze, and perhaps summarize
9. Able really to listen to what is going on—can detect new trends, can bring out a shy one, etc.
10. Able to establish good relationship with the group.

After having selected a moderator who meets all necessary criteria it is essential that there be planning meetings: Nothing should be taken for granted. This is one way to have successful programing. Some directors find it advisable to conduct leadership training workshops for moderators. This would, among other things, provide a degree of consistency in procedures as well as a pool of talent for all meetings.

Discussion Leaders

Many continuing education departments throughout the country organize discussion groups that enable people to share their convictions relative to subjects of interest. Once again the success of this type of programing depends upon the effectiveness of the leader. The following criteria are suggested:

1. Enthusiasm!
2. Must be knowledgeable in the field to be discussed, but not someone who feels compelled to demonstrate his knowledge. The purpose of this is to know when wrong directions are taken. Strong but neither dominating nor shy.
3. Someone who knows how to ask provocative questions to get everyone in the group to participate and who is willing to conduct discussion. He should not express personal convictions himself so that group participants get their learning from a method of discovery (the opposite of a lecture).
4. Must relate to people and be able "to read their faces." Needs to encourage shy ones and restrain those too talkative. Participants feel more satisfaction if they take part, and, therefore, the leader should see that all people have their say.

5. The leader should be objective. It is desirable that the group should not know how the leader feels in order to encourage thought.

Educational Television

Considering the country as a whole, continuing education programs are utilizing educational television on a limited basis. However, the time is not far distant when most communities will have this opportunity. Directors will want to be prepared to make the best use of ETV because those who have had experience with the medium consider it a most effective tool for certain types of adult learning whether it be via telecourses, public affairs programing, creative arts, information programs, or others.

The selection of participants in television broadcasts for continuing education requires the same considerations that go into selection of other leaders — the same, but with some "plus factors." These plusses should be kept in mind during the selection of broadcast personnel for lively, interesting, and responsible programing. Public affairs broadcasts are frequently within the province of the continuing education department. These may take the form of presentations of candidates for office, informative broadcasts rising from the need to explain public issues, background documentary programs, and others.

Panels and other programs with live participants require a moderator or host to make introductions; to get into the subject matter of the broadcast; and, in the case of a series, to provide continuity from one broadcast to another. Even filmed or largely taped documentary programs benefit by the presence of a host. Certain questions should be asked in searching for such a person.

1. *Is he articulate?* This is a first consideration for someone working before the cameras and microphones. Many an intelligent citizen, in fact, some of our most reliable community workers, do not have the gift of easy articulation which makes it relatively comfortable for them to appear on television. A person to whom words come easily, who sorts ideas logically and clearly, is likely to soon feel at home with the television medium. To the home audience, it is often uncomfortably evident just who of those before the cameras feels at home and who does not.

2. *Is he reasonably objective?* Does this person have strong ties or well known positions which would prevent objectivity? It is well known, of course, that the people in the community who take action and get things done do often become strongly publicly

identified with these actions. In our efforts to maintain a certain neutrality among our program hosts and moderators, however, we cannot limit ourselves to do-nothings in the community who will offend no one. What we must do is select moderators strong enough to be able to handle situations which arise when often highly motivated participants appear on our programs. Moderators must not be so firmly identified with certain ideas that immediate prejudices spring to the minds of our viewers to becloud the real issues which the programs are designed to illuminate.

3. *Is he knowledgeable in this particular topic?* A discussion leader in a nontelevised group can often do a good job because he has developed good discussion leadership techniques. On the air, however, it is necessary to have someone with enough knowledge of the subject itself to fill gaps in the discussion if need be. He may have to sort quickly in his mind questions pouring in from the public during the broadcast. Many questions which appear innocent to the uninitiated are clearly planted or strongly biased when viewed by someone conversant with the subject matter. The moderator must be able to recognize these even under the pressure of conducting the broadcast.

4. *Is this person usually fair? Has he a good sense of timing?* A constant awareness of others is a quality which contributes to effectiveness on the screen and to good relations among participants themselves. These attributes may be developed in relation to the television medium with experience as a moderator, but often people completely inexperienced in TV carry these qualities over from many other activities and are excellent on the air from their first moment. A wide pool of public talent, of nonprofessional broadcasters who can handle these chores well, is an excellent source of personnel as well as good public relations. An individual's sense of timing is also important — timing from the standpoint of bringing out varying points of view with fairness, and the necessary timing which permits operating effectively within the rigidities of TV's precise timeslots.

These considerations of articulateness, knowledge, and timing apply to participants on programs as well as moderators. In a participant, however, objectivity is frequently more a factor to avoid than to court. Appearance of people with strong points of view and no reticence in expressing them makes lively programs. The channel twirler should be made to want to stay tuned for the fireworks when he idly comes across an educational program, not turn on to find something more interesting. Participants who are by nature articulate and project well are more suitable for educational television when they have something they are really interested in talking about.

Radio

Directors of continuing education should explore the possibility of utilizing radio time that might be available to them—if they have not already done so. This medium has proven very effective for those who have had experience with it. Many of the suggestions indicated above for television apply to radio participants as well.

Community Development

Directors should assume a leadership role in efforts to resolve community problems and concerns. As a matter of fact, they would be remiss in their responsibilities if they did not do so. This is a natural and logical opportunity to be of optimum service. Community development embraces various facets of educating the community through activities other than the traditional classroom situations. Howard Mc-Clusky [7] stated:

> The adult educator is primarily interested in community development as a means of educating the community and the people who live there. For example, if a community sets up a project in improving health and recreational facilities, in the course of doing so there will be an opportunity (often unexploited) to learn a lot of facts about problems of health and recreation. If it conducts a survey of conditions essential for the attraction of new industry, the community should be in a position to acquire a lot of information about town and city planning, and so on for any area of living which it elects to improve. These are the factual learnings which community development may stimulate.

The continuing education program director should be willing to play an active role in working with other community agencies in this endeavor. He is in a position to be of invaluable assistance in joining other local leaders in a united approach toward the consideration and solution of community problems and concerns. Examples might include programs for the aging, urban renewal, the underprivileged, housing, juvenile delinquency, sex education, policy for community relations, traffic safety, the "model city" project, conservation of human and natural resources, mental and physical health, international relations, urbanization, and of course many others. It is strongly suggested that the continuing education director, or a staff member whom he designates, should be a part of the community team selected for this assignment. He will, of course, be a person who is willing to work closely with other agencies and who is more interested in achieving the objective rather than seeking credit for his department!

SOURCES OF TEACHERS AND LEADERS

Good teachers are where you find them! This may seem like an over-simplified statement or to a director a statement that lacks informative direction. However, just as the adult program evidences diversity and variety, the teachers for continuing education are selected from many sources. The adult program depends upon using all possible sources for good teachers and leaders.

Those Engaged in Teaching

A primary source of instructional personnel for the adult program will be those actively engaged in full-time or part-time teaching. This would include regular school teachers in public and private schools, community colleges, technical schools, universities, and other continuing education programs. Those retired from teaching may also provide valuable service to the adult program.

Agencies and Institutions

Many people qualified to be instructors for continuing education are employed in agencies and institutions as paid staff or volunteers. Such agencies and institutions would include churches, libraries, YMCA, YWCA, Red Cross, civic or community centers, Chambers of Commerce, and civic clubs.

Business, Industry, and Trade Organizations

The business, industry, and trade organization groups employ many highly skilled and well trained people who can be identified to teach in adult programs. In addition to programs related to specific occupational competence, many instructors for continuing education come from this group representing a secondary competence or even their avocational area of interest.

Community and Professional Groups

Such community groups as the Parents and Teachers Association, American Association of University Women, and the taxpayers league and such professional groups as the Bar Association, Medical Association, bankers organizations, and engineer associations may be a prime source of outstanding teachers and leaders. Similar to those of business and industry, people from these sources prove valuable in terms of secondary specialty and avocational pursuits as well as in the field of their major competence.

Other Community Resources

The director of the continuing education program must be aware of the fact that teachers and leaders may be obtained from anywhere in the community. It is not uncommon to find a physician leading a philosophy group, an optometrist teaching civics, a receptionist teaching public speaking, or a personnel manager teaching psychology. Good teachers are where you find them, but they must be found.

DISCOVERING TEACHERS AND LEADERS

Inasmuch as good instructors may be obtained from any community source, the director needs to be aware of and utilize all possible techniques for identifying needed teachers and leaders. For the administrator the identification of teachers and leaders is a continuous task.

Assigned responsibility is one technique that will provide a continuous flow of information on instructional resources. All persons involved in the continuing education program can be assigned this responsibility: advisory council, administrative staff, teachers, and the participants.

Acquaintance with key individuals in a community and informal contacts as a line of communication will provide valuable leads on prospective teachers. These key individuals may be identified with the source classifications presented previously or neighborhood coordinators assisting with the total continuing education program as a resource.

Suggestion of others may prove to be valuable for identification of instructors. It is not possible for those directly associated with the program to know about all the teaching resources of a community; however, if there is a general feeling that those involved are "open to suggestion," identification of teachers becomes a natural part of the community relationship.

Application of interested individuals who have talents to offer may be expected when the continuing education program is well recognized in the community.

SELECTION TECHNIQUES

The responsibility of selecting teachers and leaders for continuing education programs is the responsibility of the administrator. Selection of individuals should be based on general characteristics plus the unique talents and skills required for the specific educational task. Some methods of obtaining necessary information by the administrator for selection are—

Application Forms

An application form is most essential for obtaining personal information, educational background, experience background, content areas of specialty, references, and motives for participating as a teacher or leader in continuing education.

Interview

A personal interview with the administrator and members of the staff is a most important part of the selection process. A number of interview techniques may be employed. The application form can be the basis for a general discussion. In a staff type of interview the candidate has a better opportunity to "test himself" against the requirements of the position. A new technique employed as the basis for a selection interview is the "guest lecture" or "invitational presentation" by the candidate in his subject specialty.

Written Report

A technique that has some merit for administrators is to request a report from a prospective teacher or leader. A report may be based upon a series of questions as to understandings about continuing education philosophy, objectives, and instructional goals. Such a report can precede or be subsequent to the interview.

Observation

When a prospective continuing education teacher or leader is normally engaged in an instructional situation, it is most appropriate to observe the person in an actual situation. The inherent danger in "observation" is that brief periods of time may not provide for adequate judgment or the observation period may not be a typical situation. Observation, however, need not be limited to the administrator or supervisory staff, but may include other teachers or students for valid judgment of instructional ability.

Responsibility for Selection

As has been indicated previously, the responsibility for initial selection of teachers and leaders for continuing education is that of the administrator. Through a variety of information-gathering methods and techniques, and with the assistance of other continuing education staff, instructors are selected. The final proof, however, of instructional selection for continuing education must be the relative success of the educational program as felt by the participants.

SELECTION OF ADMINISTRATIVE STAFF PERSONNEL

Continuing education programs vary, of course, in size from the small school where the only administrative staff member is the director to large systems which support a staff of coordinators, counselors, and building principals. Many directors report that they are understaffed and cannot see the forest for the trees. It seems advisable for directors to work toward the employment of adequate staffs in order to be of optimum service to the community. This, of course, may sometimes have to wait until the "market" justifies it, though in some states, like New Jersey, state aid funds are being made available to provide leadership for individual communities.

Coordinators (supervisors) who are responsible for specific subject areas and who are specialists in their field can make a tremendous contribution to the overall program. If financial problems preclude their employment on a full-time basis, part-time persons should be considered for this responsibility. At least directors should explore the possibilities. Staffs vary in size and in organizational structure. One director in a city of 200,000 finds the following combination of part-time and full-time personnel to be quite satisfactory:

Director—full-time
Assistant director—full-time
Coordinators (supervisors)
    Trade and Industrial Training—full-time
    Apprenticeship Training—full-time
    Adult Basic Education—full-time
    Home and Family Life Education—half-time
    Americanization—half-time
    Public Affairs Programing—half-time
    Office Occupations—half-time
    School of Practical Nursing—full-time
    Television Programing—half-time
Counselors—part-time
Adult school principals—part-time
Librarians—part-time
Neighborhood recruiters—part-time

Because of the fact that so many variables stem from local conditions, no attempt will be made to suggest the size of staffs for various communities. The ideal situation is to provide the director with the help he needs to do the complete job.

In selecting his administrative staff, the director will search for well qualified persons who are thoroughly knowledgeable in their field and who can relate to those with whom they work. It is essential that they possess the ability to communicate with key persons in the community and that they can work well with their associates and with those whom they supervise.

In order that the director be free to work throughout the community he should not be confined by administrative responsibilities to an evening school center. This assignment might well be that of an adult school principal. In any school system there can be found daytime teachers who possess the necessary traits to be a building principal. It is far more satisfactory if principals have no teaching responsibilities so they are free to devote all of their time to adminstrative functions which involve supervision, counseling, records, and the many details that must be attended to during class sessions. Counselors might well be chosen from the guidance staff of the school system, assuming that most continuing education activities are scheduled in the evening.

WORKING EFFECTIVELY WITH ADULT EDUCATION PERSONNEL

Not only is the director responsible for the administration of his program but almost equally important is his responsibility as a supervisor. If his is a situation where he does not have a staff of coordinators or supervisors, he will have to do his own supervision of classroom as well as nonclassroom activities or this assignment might well be that of an adult school principal or building supervisor.

Goals of Supervision

The purpose of all supervision, of course, is to improve services of the department whether it is the teaching process or in other areas of activity. The key criterion of effective supervision is the extent to which it inspires the teacher or leader to want to do a better job. The chief administrator of continuing education programs, regardless of the size of the community, must be knowledgeable concerning the quality of service given by his department. This does not necessarily imply that he must be an expert in every area, but he must possess a reasonable fund of pedagogical knowledge. The director should be a democratic and not a dictatorial administrator. If supervision is to be effective, it must be wanted by teachers and it must be helpful, cooperative, and friendly. The supervisor should have broad teaching experience and should be aware that each teacher must work out his own methods and techniques.

Inasmuch as Chapter 15 covers the area of in-service education, we only suggest here that in order to do a good job of in-service training the administrator must know what the needs are. This will come through adequate supervision.

Staff Meetings

One of the essential things to bear in mind is that there must be continuous communication between the director, supervisors, instructors, or leaders. If a director is located in a city large enough to support a supervisory staff, he will find it essential to have staff meetings periodically. This is important for several reasons. First of all, whatever suggestions and directions he wishes to get through to the instructors and leaders can best be channeled through the supervisors who are responsible to him for the various areas of service. Secondly, it is important that "the right hand know what the left hand is doing." Staff meetings will also make it possible for the director to be a listener and get suggestions from his associates.

Teacher Meetings

In some communities supervisors conduct teachers' meetings with those instructors who teach in their particular field. This can be very effective because all of the time is given over to specific problems, concerns, and suggestions of teachers in that specialized area. Other directors find it advisable to have all teachers and leaders meet in general sessions for information and inspiration. The frequency of staff and teachers' meetings will vary from community to community, and the director will need to determine what works best for his particular situation. It might be suggested here that meetings should never be held just for the sake of having meetings. People are too busy to attend any meeting that does not give them the help they want and need. Again it must be stressed that the principle thing to remember is that communication must be continuous between administrative staff and the instructional personnel. By all means, staff personnel must not be forgotten once they begin their activities!

SUMMARY

Adults participate in educational programs because of felt needs or interests, and the increasing diversity and variety of program offerings are evidence of the expansion of these needs or interests. The key to fulfilling educational goals for adults is good instruction through identified teachers for classroom programs and leaders for nonclassroom programs.

Criteria for identifying and selecting teachers and leaders should be based on characteristics applicable to all instruction; however, the criteria should also include the unique characteristics essential for each type of educational opportunity in a diversified, well balanced continuing education program.

Some sources for teachers and leaders have been identified although they represent the entire spectrum of community life. The techniques for identifying teachers and leaders include assigned responsibilities, key individuals, suggestions, and by application. The task of identifying instructional resources is an ongoing responsibility because good teachers for continuing education are where you find them. The selection of teachers and leaders is an administrative responsibility. The validation of the selection process can only be obtained through the felt success of the participants.

Continuing education programs have reached the stage of development where administrative staff (other than the director), supervisory staff, and supporting staff are necessary. The identification and selection of this staff including coordinators for content fields, counselors, principals, librarians, and recruiters is an administrative responsibility. The methods and techniques for identifying and selecting teachers and leaders may be utilized in obtaining administrative and supportive staff for continuing education. In addition, the identification and selection of administrative staff and other personnel should be based upon characteristics supportive of the program and structured to provide the best possible educational opportunities for adults.

A major administrative responsibility is the ongoing process of identification and selection of the best teachers, leaders, and supportive staff for continuing education; however, the administrator must also assume the responsibility of working with the staff to maximize the learning process.

CHAPTER 15

TEACHER TRAINING
AND SUPERVISION

R. Curtis Ulmer

Those of us in the teaching profession have long known that we need to know our students and their individual and collective characteristics. We measure their learning aptitudes, visit their homes to become acquainted with their parents and home environments, read counselors' records to assess motivation and drives, study child growth and development to understand the maturation process — all in an effort to provide better educational opportunities for the child. In short, we make every effort to understand all we can about the student so that our educational program will be appropriate at each developmental stage in his life.

UNDERSTANDING THE ADULT LEARNER

It should not be surprising, therefore, to find that to provide effective adult education, we must also know and understand our adult learners. But, as you learn more about the adult, you will discover that he is not a tall child. His personality and self-image change as he ages, and he brings a lifetime of experiences to the classroom. His motivations, interests, and learning abilities are factors that must be understood and considered as you prepare to teach in adult programs.

There is a growing body of knowledge about adult students — their learning ability, achievement in class, and developmental processes — that will enable the teacher to give better instruction. As you learn more about the adult, you will wish to consider how your approach to teach-

R. Curtis Ulmer is chairman of the Department of Adult Education in the College of Education at the University of Georgia, Athens, Georgia.

ing needs to be adapted to the characteristics of the adult student. Essentially this is what in-service education is all about.

GOALS FOR IN-SERVICE EDUCATION

In-service education in its highest form is grounded in the philosophy and goals of adult education. As a process it should demonstrate these goals and this philosophy. The content of the in-service education program should be developed for each school according to that school's program, purpose, population, and administrative structure. While valuable assistance may be received from federal and state educational agencies, the program must be planned on the local level to meet local requirements. It is the local school district which has the responsibility for planning and conducting preservice and in-service education programs for adult education teachers.

OBSTACLES TO IN-SERVICE EDUCATION

In-service education should be considered a continuing program of learning about actual teaching problems. Any legitimate concern the classroom teacher experiences in the adult program is subject matter for the in-service program, which should be built primarily around topics such as adult learning, methods and techniques of teaching adults, clientele of adult programs, physiological and psychological aspects of aging, the educational program of the school, and the subject matter specialty of the teacher. It is also appropriate to include topics such as group processes, leadership training, and school-community relations in the in-service program. The administrator will not be able to anticipate all teacher concerns, but within the context of a democratic in-service program he will provide a vehicle for dealing with teacher problems and professional concerns as they occur.

Recent federal legislation has made funds available for expanded adult programs. The result has been an unprecedented increase in students with a corresponding increase in the number of new teachers. The survival and expansion of adult education depends on the recruitment and retention of new teachers — effective teachers who bring to adult education professional and vocational skills, and who have (or who acquire) the skills necessary to teach adults. For many years ahead it is likely that the part-time teacher who comes into the profession will depend on local in-service education programs for his orientation and training for working with adults. The in-service program may be the difference between success and failure for the new teacher of adults. And progress will depend, in the final analysis, on a competent, well informed, dedicated faculty.

The part-time nature of the adult program is frequently mentioned as a serious obstacle to in-service education for teachers of adults. Most of the evening faculty members have full-time jobs in addition to their adult classes. Administrators are frequently part-time and have little support for in-service education. In addition, the teacher probably has an active in-service program in connection with his daytime job. Add to these factors a sometimes uninterested day school principal and superintendent, and it would indeed appear difficult to conduct in-service education in many systems.

The part-time nature of adult education is a serious drawback and does present special problems in regard to in-service education. But, as a reasoned enterprise, many adult education programs would not exist at all. The fact that they do indicates a triumph of mind over matter, of determination over circumstance. Similarly, administrators can break free from tradition and create a vital program, individualized for the school and faculty, in spite of the limitations caused by the part-time nature of most programs.

The adult education movement will advance if progressive leadership is provided on the local level — leadership which utilizes every available resource from the state, the regional, and the national level. For example, crash programs of teacher training have been conducted on local and regional levels to develop teaching competencies and teacher trainers for the new programs. These institutes have been helpful in providing a small national core of better prepared adult teachers. But these efforts will have little impact unless the local administrator uses the resources from these institutes — techniques, materials, and training aides — to improve the local program of in-service education.

The adult education enterprise is too vital and too important to lose good teachers just because they do not master the change from teaching children to teaching adults. The large number of adults enrolled in adult education programs throughout the country proves that adult education programs have been successful. But this growing demand for adult education makes in-service training more emphatically necessary for planning adequate, continuous programs to assist faculty in upgrading their professional skills.

If we believe in the adult education process — if we believe that people can and do change through education — then we will stop looking for "born" teachers and will plan adequate, sequential programs of in-service education to assist good teachers of children to become better teachers of adults.

THE PLANNING COMMITTEE FOR IN-SERVICE EDUCATION PROGRAMS

The in-service education program must meet all the training demands of the total adult education program, complex and diverse though they may be. To accomplish this, most administrators will want to form a planning committee, made up of members of the adult education faculty, to assist in planning and conducting a balanced program of in-service education. This creates a democratic situation whereby more support will be given to the final plan, and more expertise will go into all facets of the in-service programs. These added dimensions will more than compensate for the time and effort spent by the administrator in organizing and orienting a faculty planning committee.

GUIDELINES FOR COMMITTEE OPERATION

The committee should include nonprofessional teachers and one or more members of the day school administrative and instructional staff, as well as the director of adult education. Where possible, the committee should be allowed several weeks' lead time before the beginning of the school year to plan a year's program. While the program administrator should be vitally interested in the work of the committee, he must let the committee work in a democratic atmosphere and must carefully define its areas of responsibility. He must give committee members the freedom to plan and to carry out their responsiblities. A committee will not function effectively if its activities are not implemented or if the members see themselves as mere rubber stamps.

Identifying Institutional Goals

The focus of in-service education should be developed within the framework of the purposes and objectives of the adult program. If we do less, we prolong the marginal status of the public adult education program. In planning the in-service program, the committee should have a statement of the philosophy, goals, and objectives of the adult program. This statement should serve to broaden the scope of the in-service program and should foster the idea of a continuing effort utilizing all community resources.

In the event that there is no statement of the philosophy and goals of the adult education program, the committee may wish to develop one as a first order of business. If the committee is working in a community junior college, members might wish to begin with the stated purposes of the college. Nearly every junior college lists its purposes as being three-fold: college-parallel instruction, technical education, and community services. Each of these three functions is, in turn, appropriate subject matter for the adult and evening program. In fact, to the degree that any of these three functions is not available at a time and place convenient to adults employed in the community, to that degree the program is not meeting the stated purposes of the college.

In any case, the philosophy of the adult program must be drawn from the basic philosophy of the institution. Although the objectives may be limited by circumstances, the dream of adult education should never be limited by lack of adequate working aims or lack of vision.

The goals of the adult program can then be translated by the committee into a diversity of activities and programs which will add up to vital, effective in-service education. *In addition to planning the scope and extent of the year's program, the planning committee should have the responsibility for determining the program's content.* All too often the in-service session consists of a speaker whose contribution may not fit the critical needs of the local program.

Using Advisory and Consultant Help

On the other hand, adult educators will certainly wish to utilize the services of advisory committees in planning their in-service program. Several Florida counties have provided summer employment to groups of adult education teachers who planned and wrote courses of study and in-service education material for the coming school year. State department of education consultants and others assisted the teachers in their work. In several instances, the courses of study as well as the in-service education materials were published for state distribution.

In summary, the best in-service education program results when the administration, planning committee, and faculty are all involved in planning and carrying it out. The planning committee, working closely with the administration, can develop a program consistent with teacher needs and, at the same time, build faculty support for in-service education. Such a committee may also strengthen the program by making recommendations to the school board for compensatory time or for faculty participation in the in-service program. All things considered, an interested planning committee is an invaluable asset for gaining administrative and community support for the adult program.

PLANNING THE IN-SERVICE EDUCATION PROGRAM

There are certain activities which are relevant to any in-service education program for adults. These core topics can provide continuity to the program and can be geared to the sophistication level appropriate to the background of individual teachers or the faculty as a whole. Following is a representative, though by no means exhaustive, list of appropriate core topics:

- The instructional program of the adult division
- Adult learning competencies
- Methods and techniques for teaching adults
- Adult interests
- Personal qualities of a successful adult teacher
- Population study of enrolled students
- Differences between teaching children and adults
- Physiological and psychological aspects of aging
- The philosophy of adult education in a technological society
- Leadership training
- Group dynamics
- School-community relations
- The adult counseling process.

Specialized programs, such as adult basic education, will require additional topics in the in-service program. In the case of ABE, for example, the reading program and the culture of the disadvantaged should be added to the list. These specialized topics should be given priority in in-service education for teaching in basic education programs to help faculty members adjust rapidly to a new clientele program. There is also a rapidly growing body of literature devoted to the needs of the educationally disadvantaged.

ADAPTATIONS FOR NEW CLIENTELE

It seems appropriate here to comment further on this specialized aspect of adult education. There was a time when adult educators could predict and describe with some certainty the population they would serve. In the decades of the 1960's and 1970's this is no longer true. Phrases such as "the disadvantaged," "the hardcore poverty groups," "the technologically unemployed," "the job corps," and "manpower development trainees" have become a part of our professional language. These terms often represent groups who have never before been adequately served in educational programs and who are often hostile to the idea of going back to school. To reach and communicate with these people requires skills possessed by very few.

Agencies like the Office of Economic Opportunity and the Departments of Labor and Health, Education, and Welfare are, among others, conducting extensive programs of adult education for these groups. In most cases these agencies are using the public schools to conduct education programs while they provide auxiliary services such as counseling and providing job opportunities. Where this occurs, the preservice and in-service education programs should be planned and conducted jointly with the sponsoring agencies. Their skilled personnel often know the population much better than educators do, and can make a vital contribution to the in-service programs in this respect.

But important though adult basic education may be, we cannot neglect the overall adult program for one segment of the population. High school completion programs, vocational programs, and avocational programs (such as art and music) reflect the needs of the entire community and, as such, are the ingredients of a well balanced program.

CONDUCTING THE IN-SERVICE PROGRAM

Although the activities of the planning committee should not end with the beginning of the in-service education program, the evening school administration should have primary responsibility for implementing the plans made by the committee. Those administrators fortunate enough to have a full-time faculty do not have as much difficulty in scheduling meetings as their colleagues whose faculty is part-time. However, the latter will be able to arrange a schedule which seems best for the individual program, provides continuity, and reflects the purposes of the adult program.

Some administrators schedule workshops on Friday afternoon and Saturday morning several times a year. Others plan monthly meetings in the late afternoon before evening classes begin. Still others schedule programs two evenings a week at times when each faculty member can attend at least one of these meetings.

Regardless of how it is scheduled, each activity in the in-service program should meet the criteria set by the planning committee and should relate to the overall purposes and objectives of the adult education program. Since it is a sacrifice for the adult teacher to spend a day or evening in a meeting in addition to his already full schedule, it would be better to cancel a meeting than to meet without a clear objective.

Effective Use of Resource People

Resource personnel for in-service education programs can be found in many places. Consultants in almost every phase of adult education will be found in the state university, the state department of education, and national organizations such as the U. S. Office of Education and NAPSAE. These consultants will often assist without cost to the local budget. In addition, state and local health and welfare departments have adult educators on their staffs who can make a valuable contribution. And don't forget that psychologists, sociologists, and extension personnel from private agencies or universities can be utilized for specialized topics.

Supervisors and teachers from the local day program are a frequently overlooked source of help in the in-service program. They can often make a particularly valuable contribution because they are acquainted with the community, with local problems, and with school operation and programs.

When resource persons are used in the in-service program, their instructions and assignment should be specific. Materials describing the adult program, the purpose of the in-service program, other consultants used, or topics to be discussed should be sent to consultants in time for them to make appropriate preparations. When the program is scheduled to run for more than a day, it is helpful to have the consultant arrive a day early so that he can observe the program and discuss his presentation with the program chairman.

Involving Boards of Education

Another important resource is the local board of education, which has the basic responsibility for developing a forward-looking policy of in-service education. The local board can be most effective in implementing in-service education for adult programs, if it adopts the following administrative policies and practices in regard to adult education personnel:

- Develops policies with the participation of teachers, administrators, supervisors, and other school officials connected with the adult program
- Makes adequate budgetary provisions to pay the cost of in-service activities and consultants
- Develops salary policies which recognize the desirability of continuous professional growth
- Provides adequate compensatory time.

For example, in one community the local director and a faculty committee developed a policy manual which described the adult in-service education program; gave the personnel policies, purposes, objectives, and administration of the adult program; set salary increments for professional advancement; and provided an administrative organization chart. The policy manual was presented to the school board for study with the recommendation that the board adopt it as official policy.

When the board approved the manual, it was used in the preservice education program, and copies were distributed to all adult teachers at that time. In addition to providing a valuable service to the adult teachers, it served to call the attention of the school board to the scope and importance of the district adult education program.

ACTIVITIES FOR IN-SERVICE PROGRAMS

Meetings and Workshops

The in-service program need not and should not be limited to meetings of the faculty members. Frequently the workshop is a useful activity and is ideally suited to in-service education. Participants actively work on some facet of the curriculum during these workshops which permits them to learn better through participation than they would as passive listeners.

Study Groups

Because of the wide range of subject matter covered in in-service education, the use of committees or study groups is frequently a valuable tool. These groups can work independently, reporting to the entire faculty occasionally. Use of study groups and committees can provide a depth of experience to faculty members which is difficult to achieve in meetings of the faculty as a whole. In addition, flexibility can be achieved through study groups in working with new teachers, subject matter groups, and special projects.

Individualized Approaches

A program of individual instruction should not be overlooked in planning the in-service program. Access to a good adult education library is important in this facet of the program. The administrator may wish to assign new faculty members to experienced colleagues for special help. However, it remains the administrator's responsibility to see that the new teacher is given every opportunity to prepare to work effectively with adults. The new teacher in adult education has, in many respects, the same problems as the new student, and is often uncomfortable in his new role. Close communication and support during the first critical weeks of classes will give the new teacher confidence in his ability to teach adults.

University Extension

As more universities enter the field of adult education, there will be additional resources available for credit courses in adult education. These courses can be offered off campus and can be adapted to meet the needs of a local in-service program. Careful planning on the part of the adult education director and the university professor should be given to the content of the university course if it is to take the place of the local in-service education program. When this is done, it gives the teacher the opportunity to work towards an advanced degree, meet state certificate requirements, and participate in an in-service program.

Field Trips and Joint Agency Meetings

For those teachers who are preparing to teach special groups,such as migrants, seasonal farm workers, or adults from slum areas, it is helpful to schedule visits to the areas where the students live. Many teachers have little concept of the living conditions of their students. A visit will make them more perceptive to the needs and attitudes of this group. Another method of bringing about a better understanding of the problems of disadvantaged students is to schedule joint in-service education sessions with welfare case workers and other social workers. This has the beneficial side effect of achieving better agency cooperation in working with the disadvantaged.

Professional Conferences

Attendance at meetings of local, state, and national organizations provides an important means of communication for the teacher. Teachers have, for example, a unique opportunity to become acquainted with materials and resources when they attend the Teacher's Day and visit the exhibits at the NAPSAE convention. National and state organizations can also perform a service by providing special programs and by inspiring local programs to become active in in-service education.

One example is the Florida Adult Education Association's series of "drive-in workshops" for multicounty areas—a series which covered the state in several months. These workshops, sponsored by the state association, were planned and conducted by university professors, state department of education consultants, local directors of adult education, and teachers from every corner of the state. The state association thereby provided a much needed service by conducting well planned workshops for counties where personnel and resources would not have been available for such programs. In addition, the workshops fulfilled one of the association's objectives.

FACILITIES, EQUIPMENT, AND MATERIALS

As the trend toward day as well as evening programs accelerates in adult education and full-time facilities are constructed or remodeled for adults, thought should be given to the need for a professional library and for meeting places for the in-service programs. An informal setting with comfortable furniture is desirable. Where school facilities are not available for this purpose, in-service programs can be conducted in meeting rooms at local banks, labor organizations, churches, and other public or private organizations. These community facilities are often more centrally located and more comfortable than meeting places in the school.

If school facilities are used, adequate classroom and conference space suitable for adults should be made available. There should be a library of professional books, periodicals, and teaching guides in addition to a library of audiovisual materials. The in-service program should also have access to typing and mimeographing facilities. Finally, teachers should have available files of instructional materials; textbooks, manuals, workbooks, teaching guides, and course outlines in use; standardized and teacher-made tests; and other evaluation materials.

Attention should also be given to demonstrating new instructional materials and equipment developed for use in the adult program. Many adult educators remember the days when there were few instructional materials specifically for adults. Fortunately this is no longer the case. One by-product of federal programs in adult education has been the development of new and better materials. Programed materials and adult education texts are now available from a number of publishers.

However, determining the suitability of available materials is a matter of concern (and an important topic for the in-service program), because publishers' claims for their publications are not always dependable. Readability charts and annotated bibliographies which have been developed for adult educators by several universities are better criteria for evaluating publications. (One such readability scale is contained in *Teaching Reading to Adults*, a NAPSAE publication.) These should be available to teachers in the professional library.

Careful attention should be given to the criteria for selecting materials for the in-service program, as well as the adult program itself. Whenever possible, a faculty committee should be given time during the summer to examine materials and make recommendations about those which might be useful in the adult program. They can then be studied and further evaluated in the in-service program. (Chapter 16 contains more extensive coverage of the problem of evaluating adult education materials.)

In addition, demonstrations to acquaint teachers with videotape recorders, teaching machines, and other new teaching materials are appropriate for in-service sessions, even though it may be some time before the items will be perfected or available for use in the local program.

PRESERVICE TRAINING

Preservice orientation and training should be an essential part of an effectively planned and conducted program of in-service education. In fact, preservice programs are so important that there is little reason for employing a teacher in an adult program without preservice training.

A program of preservice education is required by several adult programs in Florida for prospective teachers before they are employed in the basic education program. Intensive preparation is given in all facets of the instructional program, the culture of the disadvantaged adult, methods and techniques for teaching adults, and characteristics of the adult learner. The preservice program also serves as a valuable screening device. Those teachers who demonstrate a lack of qualifications or potential for teaching adults are not employed.

Ideally, a preservice program for adult teachers should be scheduled for two weeks or more, but it does not seem likely that this ideal situation will come about in the near future. In those systems where there is a two-week preservice program for all teachers before school opens in the fall, the superintendent will often allow parts of several days for the adult teachers to meet. One alternative is to use the first week of school for an in-service education program. While adult students would miss a week of training, this seems preferable to beginning classes with teachers who are unskilled in teaching adults.

As a last resort, the administrator may conduct informal preservice programs individually by giving the new adult teacher reading materials such as *When You Are Teaching Adults, In-Service Training for Teaching Adults, Swap Shop,* and *Teaching Techniques* (all published by the National Association for Public School Adult Education). He can discuss the materials with the teacher before classes begin. Other devices for individualized preservice education will doubtless be designed by the imaginative, innovative director.

IN-SERVICE EDUCATION FOR TEACHER AIDES

A recent development in adult programs across the country is the increasing use of teacher aides in the classroom. There appear to be two philosophical approaches for effective utilization of teacher aides: (a) an instructional aide who has a college degree or some college work and whose function is that of a clerical aide with some responsibility for the instructional program under the supervision of the teacher; and (b) an aide whose primary function is to bridge the social gap between the teacher and the class. This latter aide would be drawn from the same population as the class members and would be selected for leadership qualities with little regard for his educational background. This aide functions as a social interpreter for the teacher while the teacher is gaining experience in working with a new subculture or perhaps with adults in general.

A survey conducted in Palm Beach County, Florida, where aides were used (as social interpreters), gave unqualified support for the use of aides by the teachers questioned. In response to the question, "Would you like to continue to use aides?" the answer was unanimous. Other programs where teacher aides were used reported the same favorable response by teachers.

The in-service education program for teacher aides poses special problems to the adult educator regardless of how they are used in the classroom. Ideally, the state university would conduct extensive training programs, and then refer the aides to a local program. The local program, through a continuing in-service education program, would continue the training process geared to the local needs and circumstances.

Where it is not possible for a university to train aides, the school should plan and conduct a preservice education program before aides are used in the classroom. The rationale for the use of teacher aides should be carefully considered and agreed to by the faculty and administration, and the training program should reflect those objectives. When a teacher is assigned an aide, free time should be scheduled each day for joint planning by the teacher and the aide. This places much of the responsibility for the aide's continuing in-service training program on the adult teacher.

SUPERVISION: THE SUPERVISOR'S ROLE IN THE IN-SERVICE PROGRAM

The supervisor is the person responsible for the total program and is therefore responsible for planning and conducting the in-service education program. And because the entire adult program's success is finally decided in the classroom, the administrator cannot afford to neglect the in-service program. The effectiveness of the in-service program depends to a large degree on his skill in administering the program, even though he may have large numbers of competent people assisting him in its development.

Of course he will need help. Often the supervisor, the program director, the evening school director, and the public relations officer are one and the same person. He will have to depend on the help of faculty committees and consultants in planning and conducting the in-service education program. On the other hand, there are some facets of supervision — the word is used here in the broad, creative sense — which cannot be delegated to others.

Providing Supportive Supervision

Adequate supervision entails a wide range of activities, all of which are designed to create a school climate which will permit the effectiveness of all facets of the program to grow and improve. In terms of the in-service education program, supervision refers to any of those activities which the supervisor instigates to bring about improved instruction.

Although the primary task of the supervisor is that of working with the teacher to stimulate new interest and knowledge, there are other more intangible functions of the educational supervisor. Such diverse activities as meeting with a community group, attending a class party, or going to a national conference are all appropriate in a planned supervision program.

The supervisor must establish a school climate which nurtures freedom of inquiry; an enthusiastic, innovative approach to instruction; and a continuing program of education for teachers as well as students. It is his job to interpret community needs and reflect them in the adult program; to reflect the interests of students and faculty in the instructional program; and to continue to provide for planned change in the curriculum for both teachers and students.

The changes taking place in society occur so rapidly and are so intimately linked with the adult program that no program can afford to become stable. Does the adult typing class use electric or manual typewriters? If they use electric typewriters, are they the latest tape or programed models? Should there be another section for card punch operators? Does the adult program offer a course in the operation of the electronic computer? In 1950 secretaries were trained to operate a manual typewriter, an adding-listing machine, and a mimeograph machine, but these skills no longer qualify a person for employment as a top-flight secretary. The adult program must be sensitive to and prepared for changes of this kind.

Everything the supervisor does or changes in the overall program or the climate for learning in his school will affect (or should affect) the in-service education program. It is through the teachers that his policies will be implemented in the classroom. Besides, the supervisor must work with and through his faculty if he expects to gain the support and understanding of each teacher.

In addition to these broad responsibilities, the supervisor has a more specific role to play in the in-service education program. For example, he must give some time and thought to classroom visits (particularly with new teachers) so that he can assist individual teachers in making the transition from teaching young people to teaching adults. While the teacher can learn the procedures in the in-service education program, he may need some assistance in applying what he has learned.

Necessity of Current Knowledge

To be of maximum assistance to the individual teacher as well as to the total program, the supervisor must be an expert in the theory and practice of adult education. This suggests that he undertake some "self-service" education on his own, especially if he does not already have an academic background in adult education. Even if he has this background, he has a responsibility for continuing his education through professional reading, active participation in local and national adult education associations, attending conferences, and through formal classwork at nearby universities.

EVALUATING THE IN-SERVICE EDUCATION PROGRAM

Adequate evaluation of the in-service program, while difficult to achieve, is necessary for program improvement. In a total approach to in-service education, evaluation should be planned at the time the in-service program is developed. One advantage of such total program planning is an evaluation program based on the purposes and goals of instruction.

The ultimate evaluation of the in-service education program is the success or failure of the adult student in fulfilling the objectives he intended to achieve in the class. Few programs can conduct such a comprehensive evaluation, but short-range evaluation can be effective in determining whether the in-service education program is meeting the criteria set by the planning committee.

Group discussion, observation, and questionnaires can be used to evaluate the effectiveness of the in-service program. A combination of these methods is often used. While evaluation of the total in-service program is vital, it may not be necessary to develop a formal instrument for each segment of the program. The supervisor or administrator can often get a better appraisal of the program through informal discussion and observation than through a formal instrument. Group discussion will often reveal insights about the program that the supervisor or planning group could not otherwise obtain. In addition, a valuable by-product of group discussion is suggestions for program improvement that a more structured instrument may not obtain.

When questionnaires are used to evaluate a program, subjective responses discussing reasons for answers are most effective. An instrument that only elicits a "yes" or a "no" or a mark on a rating scale has little value in improving future in-service programs. And yet this should be the purpose of evaluation. Perhaps a better technique for evaluation would be joint use of the questionnaire and group discussion, where the group discusses the rating of various aspects of the program with a view towards improving the next program. Through his experience in administering programs, his own in-service education, and his knowledge of group processes, the supervisor will then be able to continue to improve the in-service education program along with the total instructional program.

PLANNED DEVELOPMENT OF MASTER TEACHERS

Attention should be given in in-service education programs to the professional preparation of master teachers. However, the master teacher concept has not been an unmixed blessing; the master teacher, according to some literature, seems to be endowed with inborn mystical qualities. He is described as a person who by compassion, knowledge, understanding, and a willingness to work 24 hours a day has achieved greatness.

It seems more appropriate to consider the master teacher in terms of educational objectives. It would be foolish to take the position that the personality of the teacher is not important in the teaching process. It *is* important, but in the development of an in-service program personality growth can occur when a professional teacher gains new competencies in teaching and an understanding of the clientele of adult education.

Perhaps a master teacher is better described as one with specialized subject matter knowledge who can communicate effectively with adults. If this definition could be used as a beginning for discussion, then it seems possible to prepare master teachers through in-service education. A three-phase approach is needed: growth in subject matter knowledge; knowledge of the professional field of adult education; and knowledge of the adult student's interests, aptitudes, and motivations.

The adult education master teacher has learned enough about the particular group he is teaching to be able to communicate effectively with its members. This is a vital link in the learning process. The adult teacher should learn to relate to adults of a different social class or subculture than his own. This is a difficult assignment, particularly for the middle-class teacher in a program for the disadvantaged.

The master teacher is one who has learned to begin the educational process where adults are socially, culturally, financially, and academically. Certainly the adult master teacher has gained knowledge about the adult which helped him develop empathy and understanding. He probably knows that learning depends as much on the adult's motivation and aspirations as on his inborn capacity. He knows that learning is a process of, not for, living.

All of these qualities can be taught in the in-service program. By continuing to learn, adult teachers will remain flexible. By accepting others, they will develop a true concern for their needs, hopes, and aspirations. They will have the ability to be objective and realistic without being cold or showing disapproval. In short, by accepting the process of adult education as a personal philosophy, every teacher (including the master teacher) can be an enthusiastic teacher who continues to work toward becoming a better teacher.

SUMMARY

The ultimate success of an adult education program requires an administration and faculty who are competent and responsible in their professional areas, who are sensitive to adult problems, and who are capable of adjusting to a changing program. The emphasis in in-service education should be on helping the teacher to see his role in the total program and to relate effectively to all aspects of it. This is a vital factor in the success of the program. Few, if any, subject matter specialists can be effective teachers if they are working in semi-isolation from the administration, the counseling program, and the in-service program.

While each adult program should develop its own set of working objectives for its in-service program, generally the following objectives are illustrative. An in-service program strives to—

- Provide systematic orientation to the total adult program.
- Work towards continual improvement and evaluation of the total instructional program.
- Provide a philosophical base for the faculty to develop program objectives and to identify their role in fulfilling these objectives.
- Develop clear concepts and definitions of the expected outcomes of the instructional program.
- Systematically study the adult student in general.
- Study the population served by the adult program.
- Develop a team approach between the teaching faculty and administrative, guidance, and clerical personnel.
- Provide opportunities for continuing professional development in subject matter areas.
- Develop sensitivity to instructional problems unique to adult education.
- Assist the adult teacher to become increasingly sensitive in the use of appropriate classroom teaching techniques.

If adult education is to remain viable and fulfill its role in the years ahead, there must be planned in-service education programs designed to bring effective teachers into the field. No pattern, plan, or model will fit all programs. Inflexible in-service education prescribed by a school board or administration may have little value, especially when carried out in a perfunctory manner. On the other hand, a vital in-service education program will pay rich dividends to a community in terms of an effective adult education program to meet current educational, social, and economic needs.

CHAPTER 16

METHODS AND MATERIALS
FOR ADULT LEARNERS

Monroe C. Neff

INTRODUCTION

With the growing realization of the importance of, need for, and interest in adult education, many organizations such as churches, public schools, charitable institutions, and industries have made a great effort to meet the growing demands of the adult learner. While our country has a record of furnishing education for adults since Colonial days, most of the work has been done with illiterates and the foreign born and in vocational fields.

During World War II, programs were developed to meet the needs of a people in an emergency. Factory workers found they could learn to operate and maintain complicated machinery in order to turn out the war tools needed. Servicemen found they could learn to use and maintain these weapons. Technological change as a result of this period was so great that learning to live in a constantly changing time emphasized even more the need for continuous education and self-development.

ADULT LEARNING IS DIFFERENT

Learning is not limited to formal education. The lack of ability to work with others and make adjustments to change indicates that education should be available throughout the life span. Adult education exists to fill a definite need, and a wide-range curriculum is offered to fill this need. In describing the recent trend in adult education,

Monroe C. Neff is director of the Division of Continuing Education of the New York State Education Department, Albany, New York.

Malcolm S. Knowles says that "participation by the learner in an active role tended to become the dominating concept underlying the new adult educational methodology. Recognition of the fact that adults differ from children in many ways as learners has begun to lead to a differentiated curriculum and methodology for adult education."[1]

Paul L. Essert reminds us that "the educational process among adults is a distinctive educational operation; not an upper layer upon a series of graded levels of schooling, but a separate enterprise closely interwoven with the normal social responsibilities and individual life-tasks of the grown-up American." [2] *Therefore, adult education is no longer an indication of deficiency, but an indication of an awareness of the importance of continuous education.*

Who is the adult learner? He is every adult who is motivated to the extent of using the little spark of curiosity and creativity that is born within each person, that is waiting to be used and cultivated when the individual decides that he wants to use it. These adults, representing every vocational and social level, vary in age from 18 to 80 and in education from the illiterate to the graduate student.

And why? The reasons for their being in continuing education are as varied as the adults themselves. The initial act of the registration is a concrete result of a chain of stimuli and circumstances too numerous to mention. They arrive on registration night accompanied by doubts, fears, inhibitions, ambitions, and persuasions from others, including prodding spouses. After the initial hurdle of completing one course, the interested adult (who in turn is interesting) has no difficulty with finding the time or the opportunity to enroll in another.

Research and Studies on Adult Learning

Adult education publications seem to be on the defensive, continually denying that "You can't teach old dogs new tricks." The same thread of protestations is found woven into the fabric of all articles concerning the adult's capacity to learn. Dwight C. Rhyne is quite emphatic in his criticism of Thorndike's statement that adults could be expected to learn at "*nearly* the same rate and in *nearly* the same manner as they would have learned the same thing at fifteen to twenty."[3] Rhyne makes a minute analysis of the data on Thorndike's experiment in learning Esperanto. As a result, he concludes that mental power is not impaired with age but admits a significant decline in speed or test performance.[4]

As a result of research, we seem to be confronted with questions instead of answers and the constant cry about the need for more research. Some findings, when drawn from actual life situations, show results very different from those gained in experimental situations or mental tests.

Irma T. Hafter studied the performance of women 40 years of age and more who were in direct competition with women 18 to 25. The resulting information questions the ". . . theory of disuse as the cause for decline in ability to learn."[5] Hafter concludes that chronological age is the least valid reason to separate older learners from younger learners. The superior achievements of older women with above the average high school achievement indicate that some intellectual factor remains constant and is possibly improved in the passing of time. She also found that the older learner does not object to comparative evaluations with the young and that modification of previous habits in certain situations is possible. She suggests further study and comparisons of students in a real life situation with an experimental situation. Thus, we conclude that adults *can* and *do* learn.

Learning Theories

Now we ask, How do adults learn? Barton Morgan and Associates have formulated several laws of learning involving readiness, exercise, and effect as a basis for methods used in adult education.[6]

Jack R. Gibb approaches learning theories more cautiously. He mentions that human learning has been an accelerating concern of experimental psychologists since the pioneering work of Ebbinghaus in 1885. Some researchers have centered interest in change which occurs during learning. Others include rewards and punishment, repetition and practice, conditions of readiness, and learning as a social process. After admitting that the adult educator has difficulty in applying any of these learning theories to his practice, he suggests principles for learning in an adult setting that stress the importance of experiences of the adult and his understanding of the goals and the task as a whole.[7]

Principles of Learning

The setting must be provided first: the opportunity and the place to learn. The adult learner, provided with the opportunity, must come of his own volition as he becomes aware of a need. The "dropout" is often the student who attends because of undue pressure from others. So, first, he must have a deep interest in new knowledge or skill, or he will not achieve much. He must *want* to learn.

The adult must be clear as to what he really wants in a course. Unless he understands or is helped to find what ultimate result he is seeking, his progress will be uncertain and meaningless. The learner must be guided by a definite plan leading to a definite goal, which was determined by the learner himself. He should understand that a study of English grammar leads to correct usage. For instance, certain errors in verb forms are pointed out. After a few practice lessons which serve a diagnostic purpose, the student begins to wonder how he can determine the correct answer. Heretofore, he has depended on the way an expression sounded to him. After he realizes he must have some sound guide to correct his errors, he is taken to the rules of using verb forms and asked to understand them, not memorize them. Drill and practice are more effective when used to correct errors; otherwise, they seem pointless and tiresome to adults.

The student is aided by a preview of his textbooks, the general plan of the course, and exactly what the teacher expects of him in the way of course requirements. The material should be on the learner's level of educational background and experience. A level too advanced discourages, and a level that is too low lacks challenge and creates loss of interest. The problem must be suited to the innate capacity to perceive, age, interests, readiness, and capacity to understand.

Activity on the part of the student is essential to learning, and he wants to be actively involved in the learning process. Principles that are memorized do not produce the same retention as those that are reasoned out by the student and actually used. A lesson on reference sources is realistic and meaningful when conducted in the library, having the students actually find material by using the card catalog themselves. Activities involving judgments, reasoning, and creative thinking are the exercises for adults which produce the most favorable results.

The learner must have experiences that relate directly to his problem, data from authorities on the subject, logical argument, or sensory experiences. "Both student and teacher must recognize that the most precious ingredient the adult brings to the classroom is *experience*."[8]

J. W. Powell states that "there is an adult mind, different from those of youth and the undergraduate; that the adult has a qualitatively different way of using his mind, of relating ideas to experience." He further states that the best way for the adult to learn is to try to understand the way his experiences seem to feel to the other person, to state his own uncertainties, clarify his own, thus making an effort to get closer to the meaning that his experience seems to have.[9]

An adult learner brings all his emotions to class with him. Because he appears to have his emotions under control and presents no discipline problems does not mean that he is not affected by all that goes on about him. The learning situation must be satisfying. He must feel a sense of accomplishment after every class. "The individual will tend to persist in a task, no matter how difficult, if he is getting enough satisfaction from it." [10]

He must be interested and stimulated, not annoyed. He must be made aware of the knowledge he does have to build on, not the amount he doesn't have. No learner will respond favorably to a climate that is unpleasant; however, one does learn by unpleasant experiences, because of the impression they make on the individual at the time. The adult educator knows that if he does not create a desirable atmosphere, the student does not have to, and will not, remain.

The adult needs the cooperation of his immediate family and the understanding of his associates. Since many classes are in the evening, it means time spent away from home. An unhappy spouse who begrudges time spent for learning activities and the close friend or neighbor who makes slighting remarks about his pursuit of knowledge can completely deter the student from his course.

A learning experience that is remembered the longest contains interest, vividness, and intensity. A detailed account by the teacher or from the textbook can be dull. It can be brought to life by an outside speaker or material contributed by one of the students. The experience that a student brings to the class is a valuable asset. In a group discussion (which might be an unusual variation from the regular classroom routine) each profits from the other's knowledge. An opportunity to tell what he knows, express an opinion, or even ask a question gives the learner an active part in the class and facilitates his taking an active part in activities outside the class.

Learning is considered an individual process, even though it takes place in a group situation. The individual who adapts to the group has learned a mode of behavior as well as a content. Learners learn from others. The adult learner must be willing to accept the learning situation and the people about him in order to learn. He must *feel* that he can.

Any learner profits from knowledge of results, but the adult must know what progress he is making. Any failure should serve as a challenge and not as a deterrent. Whenever possible, a student should proceed at his own rate of speed, not competing with anyone except himself. Stress should be made on the amount of improvement in relation to his individual ability and not that of the class.

Malcolm S. Knowles says, "The teacher must know whether or not his methods and materials are effective. It is equally important for the student to have some way of measuring his progress, since a sense of achievement is one of the chief motivations for learning."[11] Knowledge of results, evaluation of progress toward goals, indication of success or failure, and achievement compared to aspiration — all are necessary in the functional feedback process.

The processes of learning and teaching are so closely interwoven that they resemble one scene viewed from different angles. An adult educator is aware of learning theories as they apply to adult learning. They are modified to suit the adult learner by methods and techniques. Knowles asks, "How can one identify good teaching? What are the characteristics of the good learning situation?"[12]

Desirable Conditions for Learning

First, the teacher should see that the student understands the goals of the course, what he wants from it, and that he has a part in organizing its procedure. The problem as the center of a learning situation suggests that a solution of the problem is the ultimate goal. The problem must be that of the student and not of the teacher. The teacher's task is to help the student see his problem and direct his activities toward the solution.

Second, the teacher creates an atmosphere which is pleasant and comfortable to the student. Learning in a group can be very effective. The teacher's attitude, acceptance, and respect for personality will be contagious. Every effort should be made, at all times, to avoid any embarrassment on the part of the student.

Third, any physical discomfort of the student is distracting. The furniture and other physical equipment should be suitable for adults. Tables and chairs (instead of the customary student chairs) that can be used in various formations are desirable. Ventilation, heat, lighting, and outside noises should be controlled. A refreshment center should be provided for use during the "break," and a place should be made available for those who smoke.

Fourth, the student will enjoy and receive more from the course if he actively participates in the classroom discussion. In helping plan the activities of the class, he feels some responsibility, and he learns as much as from direct instruction. By using the experience of the students, the generalizations being taught can be applied directly to what they already know.

Fifth, the methods used by the teacher vary. The lecture, group discussion, recitation, demonstration, filmstrips, field trips — all these can introduce variety. These methods, of course, are used according to the subject matter being learned and the type of student being taught; however, methods should vary as much as possible in any course.

Sixth, the student is the center of the adult learning process, but the teacher is the key. His relation to the student is that of a leader or coordinator rather than that of one in authority. He earns respect from his students by knowing his subject and being able to organize the course in a flexible plan toward a definite goal. He does not represent himself as a final authority, but rather as one who can guide the student to a satisfactory goal.

Seventh, the adult educator is aware that adult learning must be voluntary, satisfying, and free of the compulsion of formal education. He uses a blend of the compulsion of formal education. He uses a blend of the theories of learning of Thorndike, Guthrie, and Hill with the theories of the Gestaltists, Lewin, and Tolman. He is aware that these theories apply to adult learning under the conditions most favorable to adult learning. Many of the principles that apply particularly to adult learning have yet to be stated.

In applying Thorndike's theory of readiness, exercise, and effect, he sees that the voluntary student who recognizes a need is actively involved with the learning process and obtains a result that is satisfying. In acknowledging learning by doing and reinforcement by repetition, the teacher recognizes the theories of Hill and Guthrie.

The stress that the adult educator puts on background and experience of the student shows recognition of the field theorists in presenting to the student the course as a whole, giving him an understanding of the purpose, material, and general plan for the course toward a specific goal. The educator also keeps in mind the individual differences in capacity, nature of the task, and variety of presentation as theorized by Tolman.

These theories are applied with the characteristics of the adult student in mind. The adult educator knows that adults can learn if taught under favorable conditions. Efficiency of performance must not be confused with the power to learn. The adult often learns slowly because of disuse and often lacks confidence in his ability to learn new material and adapt to a new social situation. The rate of learning is improved by motivation, and it is the teacher's duty to use methods that apply to a particular situation.

Major Classifications of Learning Theories

One way to achieve an integration of the different learning theories is to classify them into a small number of categories.[13] Many different classifications can be found in the literature of educational psychology. The classification followed here is suggested by Bigge and Hunt [14] and is based on different concepts of the nature of man and of the manner in which he interacts with his environment. The two general classifications of learning theory are (a) stimulus-response associationism and (b) gestalt-field.

Stimulus-response (S-R) associationism theories emphasize the concept of man as a human mechanism who reacts mechanistically to any stimulus situation. The resulting reaction is the only one that could have occurred. No purposing on the part of the individual is necessary. Of course, the advocates of theories in this group differ somewhat among themselves.

Gestalt-field theories hold that man is an active and purposive creature, and they consider the whole greater than the sum of its parts. Environment is what the individual perceives around him; it is psychological and unique to him. Persons in close proximity to environmental stimuli may so structure their perceptions that each individual has a different environment. Thus, man is changed by his environment and his environment is changed by him—by his perception of it.

Learning, according to Gestalt theorists, is a matter of structuring perceptions so that meaning will result. This structuring results in developing insight and is commonly referred to as *insightful learning.*

Recent research into this field of adult learning is minimal. Philosophy of learning research of the Thorndike area is still the major foundation of current operation. There is a critical need for current research in the general areas and also with specific populations, that is, the disadvantaged in the field of continuing education.

METHODS AND TECHNIQUES

Methods of instruction are necessarily limited by administrative organization—historically, class unit administration has duplicated class patterns of the American elementary and secondary school, thereby locking curriculum and methods into traditional patterns. *Accordingly, there is an urgent need for innovative scheduling approaches to encourage use of methods and techniques leading to individualization of instruction.* Methods must be based on the objectives of the program planners, instructors, and enrolled adults to ensure utilization of the best method for the specific content areas and course objectives.

Discussion and Lecture [15]

Sheats explained discussion as the fundamental method in adult education and said that the most significant trend in the field was its increased use.

Perhaps the most significant trend in method as applied to the field of adult education is the increasing use of discussion procedures. This represents a shift from the almost exclusive use of the lecture method and indicates a basic shift of philosophy and direction. The traditional pattern of instruction in colleges and universities and in many public schools has had the effect of casting the teacher in the role of the fountainhead and source of a certain body of subject matter which is to be transmitted to the students. Unfortunately, the processes which developed for informing the student were largely one-way transmission lines with little, if any, opportunity for student participation in the definition of learning objectives or in the learning process itself. The student was on the receiving end and was expected to "soak up" the information handed to him much as a sponge soaks up water.

Unquestionably, there are many situations in which the "informing" procedure is suited to the needs of the group. In many adult education situations, however, "informing" is not the major objective and when this is true the lecture method has been found to be generally less effective than discussion procedures.

Cooperative group discussion as a method of learning casts the teacher or leader in the role of a coequal member of the group, bearing a responsibility with others in the group of bringing personal knowledge and experience to bear on the problem of areas which the group has selected.[16]

Stovall [17] projected the question, "What are the comparative values of the lecture and group discussion for increasing students' knowledge, improving their ability to think critically, and as means of developing more democratic attitudes?" He stated that the problem has been much thought about and discussed by all teachers and that it was of particular concern to those in college programs of general education since the lecture method has been so severely criticized in recent years.

Stovall cited several studies that were completed in the 1930's and 1940's where experimental comparisons of the lecture and group discussion showed that although lecture and discussion produce about equal results in the amount of information acquired by students, knowledge gained in discussion was better retained. Group discussion was found to be distinctly superior to the lecture for stimulating critical thinking and developing problem-solving skills.

Knowles [18] pointed out that whatever the purpose of a group—to teach a subject, to develop ideas, to develop understandings and skills of human relations, or to develop interest and knowledge in international affairs—there was more and more evidence that these goals were most successfully achieved through group processes.

Johnstone [19] projected the number of persons using the discussion and the lecture method. More females use discussion where more males use lecture. Both methods were used equally by the age range 35 to 45. More college people use the lecture method.

Johnstone [20] found that discussion was used most by educational programs in religion, public affairs, and agriculture; also that the method used most in all adult education courses was discussion, with lectures listed second.

A study of the lecture and discussion methods was made by Eglash,[21] in which the emotional climate was similar in two classes, one instructor teaching one elementary psychology class by group discussion and one by lecture. The conclusion was that the method of teaching did not affect achievement on the examinations used in the course.

No difference was found in two types of group discussion by Deignan.[22] In a psychology course taught by discussion and by lecture-discussion, he found no significant difference between the methods.

Authors of six studies have found a difference in the two methods in favor of the group discussion. The first of the six studies cited was by Bond.[23] She compared the effectiveness of lecture and group discussion in a health education program concerned with chronic illness. The problem chosen was breast cancer in women, mainly because criteria of success in that field were fairly amenable to objective measurement. The evidence pointed quite consistently to the superiority of the discussion approach in motivating women toward advocated health practices.

Welch [24] attempted to measure the effectiveness of two precisely defined diffusion processes by a before-and-after measurement of adoption of clearly specified and identified learning. The group method, mass communication method (lecture), and a combination of both were tested. It was found that the group method was significantly better than the communication method.

Leadership in Discussion Groups

Group leaders and members are made, not born. In order to work together with other people in effective groups, people must learn a great number of skills. Anyone who makes a serious attempt to learn these skills can do so. However, one doesn't learn to work with people by reading books on "how to influence others in groups." It is also true that one does not learn to work with people in groups simply by being in groups. One learns by consciously directing his efforts towards change of himself in relation to the group, by intellectual guidance, by specific training, and by the right kinds of experiences.

Effective problem solving is accomplished in groups in one or all of the following ways:

1. Setting up a physical atmosphere conducive to problem solving.
2. Reducing interpersonal tensions that arise in group situations.
3. Setting up procedures that will be conducive to problem solving.
4. Allowing the group freedom to make its own goals and decisions.
5. Teaching group members appropriate decision-making skills.

Democratic leadership does not come about accidentally. It is not the result of a laissez-faire policy on the part of those who occupy positions of authority.

Democratic leaders seem to hold these convictions —

1. The welfare of the group is assured by the welfare of each individual. There should be no conflict between the welfare of the group and the welfare of the individual.
2. Decisions reached through the cooperative use of intelligence are, in general, more valid than decisions made by individuals. A group can take into account more completely than an individual the various considerations relevant to the problem at hand.
3. Every idea is entitled to a fair hearing. Every idea may be examined on its merits by free, informed citizens. When decisions are reached through that process there is nothing to fear.
4. Every person can make a unique and important contribution. Individuality, rather than uniformity, is of value in exploring a problem.
5. Growth comes from within the group rather than from without. People must be allowed to discover things for themselves. People take less initiative when they are told what to do than when they have a part in determining the course of action.
6. Democracy is a way of living. Democratic systems are not perfected systems, but bettering ones. Democratic means are essential for the attainment of democratic ends.
7. Democratic methods are efficient methods. Democracy creates the best plan of action. It helps individuals develop greater creative power. It helps the group use all its resources to solve its problems.
8. Persons merit love. The tender and devout love of all men is the essential component of great personal leadership in a democratic society.

Effective Discussion Groups

The real work in any group takes place in the discussion groups. It is imperative that all leaders recognize that the discussion group is more than a technique or device to lend variety to meetings.

1. Good communication in any meeting is a two-way process.
2. Every participant has something worthwhile to contribute, and he should have an opportunity to do so.
3. Shared thinking in the give-and-take of free and open discussion brings the best results.
4. How we work together is fully as important as what we do.

A good discussion group, then, is focused on the individual, on each group participant as a valued member of the working team. The members give the group its purpose. However, an effective discussion group involves more than simply bringing an aggregation of people together to consider some topic handed to them. Careful planning is required.

1. Topics selected for discussion must be directly related to problems and issues confronting the members.
2. Topics should be specific. Unless they are, group members may flounder in attempting to share their thinking in a fruitful way.
3. The topic should be clearly defined. Frequently, the bare statement of it is not enough. A paragraph or two of explanation, some of the major subpoints, and a short list of questions are helpful. These should not be planned as guides to be slavishly followed, but as thought-provokers and aids to critical thinking by group members before the discussion begins.
4. Ample time should be scheduled for the group to do its work. Too short a period for discussion may short-circuit good group processes.

Successful group activity is revealed by the processes employed. Democratic participation does not take place automatically. Conditions must be right for its emergence. It is here that the predominant role of the group leader comes into the picture.

Effective Lectures

The lecture can be as effective as the teacher makes it. People have and will continue to learn by listening to others. It is a quick way to cover a lot of ground, but it can be misused. The following rules can enhance lectures:

1. Have a specific reason for using the lecture — one that is known and acceptable to adult students.
2. Keep to the subject and avoid talking over the heads of the group.
3. Be as brief as possible; then turn to other methods. Don't lecture all the time; use the lecture method only when the occasion really calls for it.

Adults learn best through participation; so try some of the following in connection with the lecture:

Question and answer periods during the lecture

Group discussions about student experiences

Demonstrations to awaken and maintain interest, thus stimulating individual, intelligent observation of debatable subject matter

Illustrations, through the use of actual uses and visual aids

"Buzz" group discussions.

Buzz Groups

Most people find it easier to talk to a few people rather than to a large group. They find it easier to speak informally than to make an address or even a report. The buzz group is a way of setting up face-to-face communication within a large audience and of getting the general thinking out. It is a subgroup of 4 to 10 people drawn from a larger group or audience. It serves the function of enabling all the people in a large group to participate in planning, in setting a course of action, and in talking something over thoroughly to an extent they could not do if they tried to work in a large group. Buzz groups usually report their thinking or recommendations to the total group by asking one person to summarize their discussion to indicate minority as well as majority opinion. What is said in the reports may be noted on a chalkboard or newsprint and used as a basis for further thinking.

Forum

Sometimes called a lecture-forum or lecture-discussion. A forum is any meeting given over to general public discussion of some particular issue or closely connected group of issues. Its purpose is to air issues, explore ideas, and interpret information. This kind of program presents a greater challenge to the leader than do other types, because more people are taking an active part in the discussion and what happens is more unpredictable.

Film Forum

A forum in which a film is used as the way of presenting information. Someone may explain what the purpose of the film is and suggest how it can be used and may call attention to particular things in the film to watch for. After the film has been shown, audience members may comment or raise questions.

It is absolutely essential to preview any film or filmstrip before it is presented to an audience. Preparations must also be made to prevent mechanical failure of the projector and equipment.

Debate

This technique is suitable only for "either-or" questions. One speaker argues for an issue, and another speaker takes the opposite point of view. A debate is usually followed by a question and answer period from the audience.

Panel

The panel is a discussion by three to six people who sit around a table or in a semicircle and exchange views on some problem or issue. The program is unrehearsed and informal and the discussion has the give-and-take of conversation. Panel members may put questions to one another. They may differ with one another.

Planning in advance exactly what each person will say defeats the purpose of a panel discussion, which is not to give speeches but to explore a subject together. The panel members should have more than a casual knowledge of the subject they discuss.

The chairman or leader of the panel, sometimes called the moderator, opens the discussion with a statement about the problem or topic to be explored. It is his responsibility to introduce the panel members or ask each one to introduce himself. At the close of the discussion, he throws the meeting open to the audience. They may make brief comments, ask questions of the panel in general, or direct their questions to individual members of the panel.

Symposium

Like a panel, a symposium is made up of several speakers. It differs from a panel in that these speakers give short prepared talks on various sides of the same subject. The talks should be short, about 15 minutes. To make the best use of their time, the speakers should know in advance what ground each will cover. The talks may follow one another without any break, and the audience join in a discussion only after the last talk; or there may be both a short question period after each speaker and a general period at the end.

Brainstorming

Brainstorming was designed by Alex Osborn, an advertising executive, to develop radically new ideas. To be successful, it must depend upon an uninhibited atmosphere, spontaneity, and teamwork. This technique may be used with small and large groups, but groups of 12 seem most popular. The problem to be attacked must be important and one of action rather than policy.

The first step is to clearly state the problem. When the problem is satisfactorily defined, the members of the group start reporting any idea that comes to mind regardless of how simple or complex, radical or obvious.

After all ideas offered have been recorded, the group evaluates them in open discussion. Some ideas will be quickly discarded, but many are retained and tried that might never have been advanced under usual conditions because they seem too obvious or too "wild."

Circular Response

The members of the group, 10 to 20 are preferred, are seated in a circle. The chairman or leader proposes the question to be taken up. The discussion begins with the person at his right. That person has the first opportunity to express his views. Then the person at his right has a chance to talk and so on until the discussion has gone around the circle. No member of the group can speak a second time until his turn comes again.

If, for example, you are sitting fourth from the leader's right, you may express your views on the subject or on the opinions advanced by the leader and the three before you. If, however, the person on your right says something that arouses your ire, you have no chance until the next time around.

This technique does wonders toward correcting the bad manners and monopolistic practices that often mar a group discussion. Extreme views presented in a belligerent manner are modified by the restraints imposed. The timid person speaks more freely when he knows that it is his natural right as a member of the group.

Demonstration

The technique of demonstration, in most cases, is quite simple. It is very easy to perform a demonstration before adult classes. The main concern is that demonstrations need a certain amount of advance preparation in order to be worthwhile. This will require time, thought, and gathering of the necessary materials and equipment in advance. A checklist for planning a demonstration follows:

1. Prepare, in advance, by analyzing everything that is to be done.
2. Be ready to begin without delay by having all tools, materials, and supplies in readiness on your desk or table.
3. Have the class gathered around you so that the students can clearly see everything that takes place.
4. Prepare the students by explaining, in advance, what is going to happen, calling attention to the key points to be noticed.

5. Be sure the demonstration is given slowly and deliberately so that each step can be clearly seen and understood.
6. Explain each step after its completion.
7. Provide an opportunity for questions after each step, even if they interrupt the demonstration.
8. Conclude with a final summary; then immediately open the whole demonstration for questions to clear up any confusion and to evaluate.
9. If at all possible, let each student operate the demonstration himself.

MATERIALS

Program planners and administrators must be cognizant of the need to produce and utilize materials best suited for program objectives of each continuing education offering. A multimaterial approach and a multimedia approach should be the concern of teachers and administrators in selecting materials. These two considerations will give a variety of materials and will involve all of the senses. There are many materials and resources available to help enrich teaching and to challenge integrity.

In addition to regular textbooks, resources such as maps, a globe, photographs, scale materials, slides, films, radio and television, recordings, lectures, all types of still pictures, graphs, charts, posters, tape recordings, videotapes, newspapers, manuals, magazines, free and inexpensive leaflets and pamphlets — all these are at hand to make teaching techniques more interesting and effective. How well one learns to use these materials and resources will determine, to a great degree, how successful the teaching will be, because we live in an era of a rapidity of change.

Even though the following is 10 years old, it is a good reference for sources of the various materials mentioned above. *The Handbook of Adult Education in the United States,* 1960 edition, end of Chapter 8, lists a large source of various materials. The source is much the same today, but it would be necessary to request the most up-to-date listing of materials from these sources.

Programed Instructional Materials and Computer-Assisted Instruction

At the present time a number of special and demonstration projects in computer-assisted instruction are under way across the nation. Various materials are taken and programed to fit various computers. Materials from the first-grade level through the college level are available today on a number of computer systems of learning. The programed materials for these computers is, at the present time, extremely limited. The majority of materials, at present, would be for collegiate courses. A few have been developed for use with adults and children at the elementary and secondary level.

In the next few years computer-assisted instruction which includes software, as well as hardware, will be a major approach that will be used by education across the nation. There will be much use of this type of instruction and materials within the coming decade. In many of our urban areas, schools and institutions of learning will be operated 24 hours a day with gymnasium-sized rooms where hundreds of computer terminals will be providing computer-assisted instruction to adults and youngsters. There will be side-by-side studying, where one adult can be learning to read and write while another adult is studying Aristotle on his computer station. Most of the time that is given over to getting factual and lecture-type information will be spent in these computer rooms. Also, time will be spent in small seminar groups discussing what's been learned. At present, software or programed instructional materials are being used very satisfactorily in continuing education programs over the nation.

In the next five-year period many states will become more involved in the use of programed materials in continuing education. This will develop during the interim while the hardware for computer-assisted instruction is designed and is made compatible with the programed materials that are available today. So significant is this development in continuing education that a description of a learning laboratory is given.

The Learning Laboratory: Programed Instruction

The learning laboratories were designed to serve adults in grade levels 1-4. The laboratories also are used to help adults gain educational improvement of their own choosing. The programed instructional materials used are not only for credit toward elementary or high school completion but also for personal improvement.

The fundamentals learning laboratory can best be defined as a systems approach to providing the academic knowledges and skills needed or desired by an individual. It is an accumulation of commercially available materials, used under selected procedures and principles to make them maximally available to, and effective with, adults. It is so organized that any adult can attend at a time convenient to him, stay as long a time as he can, work at his own most efficient pace, use the instructional materials most effective with him, and study only the subjects and skills that serve his own particular purposes. He is never permitted to work beyond his comprehension level and must always master each concept before progressing.

The initial apportionment of materials includes 15 programs and kits in reading; 13 in mathematics; eight in social studies; six in science; three each in business and foreign language; and 10 additional unclassified programs. Forty-nine of these 90 provide instruction typically given to pupils prior to the ninth grade; 32 programs teach high school subjects and skills; and nine of the unclassified programs teach a technical skill or appeal to an adult interest.

Occasionally, additional programed materials, particularly in technical subjects, are supplied to specific laboratories because of individual student needs or interest.

The elementary level materials per "laboratory" account for almost two-thirds of the total cost of three thousand dollars. The number of students that can be accommodated with the initial allocation of materials is almost unlimited. After two to three years of extensive use, a few soiled or worn-out materials have to be replaced.

The physical facilities. The materials require slightly more than 200 feet of 12-inch shelving and a table for reading materials. The shelf case should contain from four to five shelves with the bottom shelf five inches off the floor and the top shelf not more than 45 inches high. The table is used for the reading kits because it makes them more easily and quickly available to the students as well as facilitating traffic flow. The remainder of the materials are shelved "face-up" in subject matter sections and in sequential concept order.

Tables and plastic chairs are provided for student work space. The first arrivals sit one to a table; later arrivals create a trapezoid table top assignment. The tables are arranged to gain maximum use of the room with an attempt to avoid any row or line arrangement. It should be noted that typical school desks have been found to be both inadequate and inappropriate.

A room the size of a typical school classroom will handle 20 to 24 students conveniently and up to one-third more without being frustratingly crowded.

Role of the coordinator. The coordinator is in charge and is present when the laboratory is open. His desk, telephone, file cabinet, student sign-in cabinet, and extra chair for interview of the new enrollee are located near the door. The duties of the coordinator are as follows: test administrator, supervisor, counselor, bookkeeper, observer, and tutor. The work of the coordinator as a tutor is limited, but we have found it necessary in working with the dependent student. The role of the co-ordinator as an observer is very important because frustration results when students are placed in materials above or below their academic levels. Students are moved through the programed materials from subject to subject in relationship to their objective and with the guidance of the coordinator. In summary, his job is to bring together students with the proper materials so that self-instructional progress occurs, to arrange the shortest possible curriculum to attain each student's objective, to inspire each student to reach it, and to give the student necessary assistance when needed.

Student admission and placement. Student admission is preceded by an interview with the coordinator. After establishing rapport the coordinator has a fourfold task to accomplish.

First, he must cause the student to verbalize clearly his purpose or objectives and gain his acceptance of them. Frequently, this is the first time these objectives have been put into words and thus are available as a motivating source. This verbalization has been found to be a valuable aid to student acceptance of low-level assignment in the materials.

Second, on the high school level the coordinator determines reading level placement with the *Adult Basic Education Student Survey.* This is sufficient at this point unless the reading level is sixth grade or above, when the *English 2600* pretest also can be given. Typically, the grammar test is withheld until later because of its verbal level and because some of these skills are taught, directly and indirectly, with the other materials.

Having "sized up" the student and knowing his skill level and his academic objective, the coordinator's third task is to list the materials and programs that will take the student from where he is to where he wants to go. In effect, this gives each student his own curriculum. The student sees the size of the job ahead; and, as happens in many cases, he can establish a deadline by which time he wants to complete it.

The fourth task, then, is for the coordinator to help set up a realistic time schedule for attendance. It cannot be so extensive as to foster its neglect or so infrequent that real progress is not recognizable. Once a time schedule is set, the student is expected to maintain it or to get excused. He is also encouraged to come in early, stay late, or to come in at unscheduled times in order to hasten progress. He is fully warned, and he soon learns, that you cannot make haste in programed materials by hurrying; that progress is made by spending more time at his most efficient pace. In contrast, the program schedule is not fixed. As soon as there is evidence that maximum progress is not being made, program changes are made.

Operating procedures. The student starts to work in the appropriate material before he leaves the enrollment session; thus, he does not come back to start but rather returns to complete a task already started.

For motivational reasons, some students reading at advanced levels begin with arithmetic. Most students, however, are assigned into the *Reading for Understanding Kit* in order to reawaken whatever academic skill they have. They are started at a level just below their placement score, and at least two groups of exercises are completed before they are assigned into the instructional kits and programs. From this point on, each student rotates among the kit-type practice reading, reading skill instruction, and subject matter programs designated for him.

The number of work-type assignments carried by a student varies with the amount of time spent in the laboratory and the student's tolerance span. Work sessions of about one hour usually mean assignment into one program at a time. During two-to three-hour sessions, students frequently work part time in two programs. For a few students who stay longer, sessions frequently alternate among three programs. It is felt that work in more than three programs during a session fragments student effort too greatly and is discouraged.

Progress from one unit or concept to the next is made only by passing each end of course test with a percent score of 85 (90 in some materials or for some students). The coordinator grades the test and assigns the student into the next task. An unacceptable test score brings the assignment of repeating a part, or all, of the previous task. A succession of a few low scores brings reassignment into more appropriate alternate programs or materials.

Low scores are sometimes found to be program selection errors of the coordinator. Either the verbal level of the materials was too high or there were skill deficiencies that first needed elimination. During orientation, students are told, and they learn early in their experience, to either work or loaf and not to try to combine the two. The coordinator is alert to low scores from this cause.

Flexibility. The success experienced with the learning laboratories can probably be attributed to the flexibility and the wide grade-level range of the materials. This new teaching installation has been very popular with adults. The student may work in the laboratory at any convenient time, as many times per week as he wishes, without sacrificing job or home duties. He is limited only by the laboratory's opening and closing hours — usually 9:00 A.M. and 9:30 P.M. A student may work at his own pace, master difficult subjects by taking extra time with materials, miss class because of responsibilities, and resume work exactly where it was left. The student never gets behind.

EVALUATION OF MATERIALS

It is necessary that we have techniques of evaluation so that they may be used on existing materials in continuing education. There are a large number of evaluation forms available from state education departments and commercial sources. These forms are used by professional staffs to evaluate the various types of materials available in the nation. Also, teacher training guides are available from commercial publishers that provide rating charts for evaluation of materials in continuing education. Although the following evaluation example was designed to evaluate reading materials, certain evaluation questions would or could be modified to apply to almost any area of instruction in continuing education. A number rating is given so that a total rating could be given to certain pieces of materials.

EVALUATION OF (READING) MATERIAL

Title _____

Publisher _____

Copyright date _____

Date evaluated _____

Evaluated by _____

		Yes			No
		1	2	3	0

AUTHORSHIP   Are the authors experts in reading as an instructional, psychological, and sociological process? _____

Are the authors experienced writers who understand the needs and interests of the adults? _____

Are the authors able to demonstrate their teaching methods? _____

Are the authors actively engaged today in the teaching of reading on the adult basic level? _____

Have the authors had clinical experience in analyzing reading materials? _____

PHILOSOPHY   Are the objectives of the series clearly defined? _____

	Yes	No
	1 2 3	0

Are these objectives realized? _____

Does the series foster independent reading and the enjoyment of varied reading materials? _____

Does the series foster intellectual growth, social awareness, wholesome attitudes, and sound ethical values? _____

Does the series facilitate the adjustment of content and instruction to the individual adult and his special interests, abilities, and needs? _____

Does the program provide special materials and guidance for slow learners at levels where reeducation is most needed? _____

Does the program recognize the need for and give help in diagnosing and reteaching at frequent intervals? _____

Does the program include professional materials that explain the underlying philosophy and contribute to the effective use of the materials? _____

CONTENT Are the themes well adapted to the interests and needs of adults? _____

Do the themes widen students' interests and knowledge of living in modern society? _____

Is there a balance of reading materials, such as —
    Fiction and fact? _____
    Modern and classical? _____
    Men's and women's interests? _____
    Rural and urban life? _____
    Other cultures? _____

Are the selections written in natural language so that the students can be encouraged to read with realistic expression? _____

	Yes			No
	1	2	3	0

Is the repetition of words natural or have the authors, in an effort to get a high degree of repetition of words with an eye to vocabulary statistics, made the selections artificial and unnatural? _____

Do the plot and subject matter of the stories command the attention of the adults? _____

Will the articles provoke thinking on the part of the student? (Cause and effect, human values, etc.) _____

Would the unit themes widen students' horizons and stimulate interest in the various areas of reading? _____

Are the selections recognized by competent critics as good literature? _____

TEACHER'S GUIDE

Does the teacher's guide outline the organization and philosophy of the program? _____

Does each guide provide an adequate index of skills which identifies the interpretation skills as well as the word perception skills emphasized at that particular level? _____

Does the guide give help for the teacher to use in bringing students to the point of mastery on each skill listed? _____

Is the teacher given on-the-spot suggestions for presenting new words at the exact time they are introduced? _____

Does the guide provide help in developing a complete word perception program? Is there opportunity and guidance for leading students to identify and analyze words while —

Reading the selections in the student's text? _____

	Yes			No
	1	2	3	0

Doing the exercises included with the lessons? _____

Are the words which are to be identified through analysis indicated for the teacher? _____

Is there a clearly defined program for teaching children how to analyze words of more than one syllable? _____

Does the guide include a sequential program for developing the skills needed to use the dictionary efficiently? _____

Do the teaching procedures include specific help in teaching the use of the pronunciation keys of more than one dictionary? _____

Does the guide provide teaching procedures for developing the skills of interpretation? _____

Are there procedures for introducing and motivating reading of the story? _____

Does the guide suggest varied ways of rereading for interesting and different purposes? _____

Are there procedures for leading the students to relate ideas from reading to personal experience? _____

Will the beginning teacher be able to follow the important steps in teaching each lesson to large classes and to groups of varying ability and interest levels? _____

Do the guides serve as helpful stimulating procedures, or are they stereotyped teachers in print? _____

Are the developmental activities in the workbook integrated with the lesson plans? _____

	Yes			No
	1	2	3	0

Is the manual complete enough to help the teacher avoid spending many hours in preparation of the next day's lesson, thus giving time to exercise his initiative in meeting the reading problems of the individual students? _____

Is there a key to the responses desired for each exercise? _____

Is the manual practical? Are exercises and drills prescribed which can actually be carried out by the teacher in a normal teaching period? _____

Does the guide tell the teacher how to group students in order to take care of individual differences? _____

Does the guide contain informal inventories for interest readiness, phonics readiness, thinking readiness, and reading difficulties? _____

Does the guide tell the teacher how to determine the student's independent reading level and the student's instructional level? _____

Does the guide present additional material in the follow-up section for maintaining skills and for meeting the varying needs of the students? _____

PHYSICAL FEATURES

Is the type clear, black, and easy to read? _____

Does the paper have a soft finish which prevents glare? _____

Are the use of color and the general format planned to prevent eyestrain? _____

Are pages pleasing and uncluttered? _____

Does the cover attract the student's interest? _____

SUMMARY

Many possible learning combinations exist to further maximize the effectiveness of adult education methods, techniques, and materials; i.e., small group interaction following lecture or panel, small group interaction to evaluate group and individual experience, small group interaction in the preplanning activities for program and class experiences. Still, any lasting success must begin and continue with meaningful preservice and in-service exploration of program objectives by planners, teachers, and students.

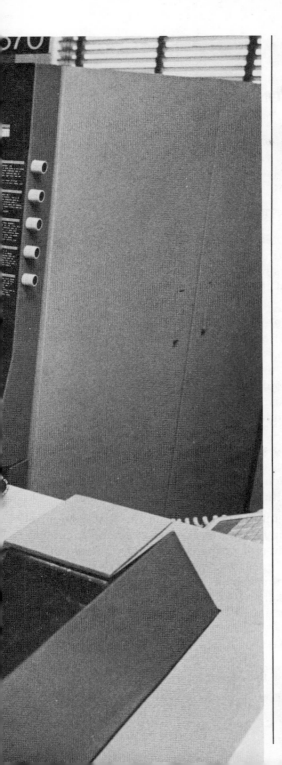

SECTION V

RESEARCH
AND
EVALUATION

CHAPTER 17

RESEARCH FOR ACTION PROGRAMS

George F. Aker and Wayne L. Schroeder

INTRODUCTION

The purpose of this chapter is to describe and clarify the role of research in public continuing adult education. It is the authors' contention that the administrator has a unique and central role in research, and they hope that the following discussion will assist him to —

1. More clearly understand and appreciate the levels and kinds of research which are pertinent to the improvement and effectiveness of his organization.
2. Better understand his unique role in identifying researchable problems and needs, applying research findings, stimulating the conduct of research by others, field testing the findings of basic research, and conducting action research within his own organization.
3. Perfect his competence as an action researcher and become more actively involved in the research process.
4. Develop a plan by which he and his staff can continuously improve their skill and ability as members of a research team.

The chapter is organized into four sections. In the first section research is defined, and its various levels and purposes are differentiated. In the second section an attempt is made to clarify the role of the administrator as stimulator, interpreter, and producer of research. In the third section, through the use of a hypothetical situation, the writers develop and expand the steps involved in conducting action research; and in the last section they identify a series of principles

George F. Aker is professor and head of the Department of Adult and Continuing Education of the College of Education at Florida State University, Tallahassee, Florida.

Wayne L. Schroeder is associate professor in the Department of Adult and Continuing Education of the College of Education at Florida State University, Tallahassee, Florida.

which, when applied, provide the ways and means for personal growth and development as an action researcher.

DEFINING RESEARCH

Definitions of the term *research* have been many, and each has reflected, to some extent, the experientially related basis of the definer. Thus, the biochemist, working in the protective confines of a laboratory with subjects or units upon which he can exert considerable control, tends to define research quite rigidly, although the educational researcher, finding it necessary to work under conditions which are not nearly as subject to his control, tends to define research more loosely. One can find variation even within a single discipline or field. Consider the professor of adult education who may more frequently than not refer to research as activity which results in the generation of broadly applicable principles and generalizations; and compare him with the director of a continuing education program who may refer to research as that activity which results in information leading to the resolution of operational problems.

The crucial question, however, is neither whether differences exist nor why they exist. It is rather the question of what, if anything, is common to all research. The answer to this question cannot be found in what is researched, but rather in how it is researched. Mythology, supernatural explanations, personal experiences, customs and tradition, voices of authority, and syllogistic reason [1] have been and continue to be used frequently as bases for important decisions. They are not, however, the tools of research. Research activity must be scientific, satisfying criteria suggested by such adjectives as precise, systematic, objective, impartial, and verifiable. Indeed it is the how of an exploration (the procedures employed) which makes it research. The scientific procedures which distinguish research from other activity are clearly identified by the following statement from Good and Scates:

> If he questions his explanations, the stage is set for research. If he goes further and challenges the methods by which he arrived at his conclusions; if he critically and systematically repeats his observations; if he devises special tools for taking, recording, and analyzing his observations; and evaluates his data in other ways; if he scrutinizes the thought processes by which he passes from one step of his logic to another; if he gradually refines his concept of what it is he is trying to explain and considers anew the necessary and sufficient conditions for proof; if at every step he proceeds with the utmost caution, realizing that his purpose is

not to arrive at an answer which is personally pleasing, but rather one which will stand up under the critical attacks of those who doubt his answer — if he can meet these criteria and steadfastly hold to his purpose, then he is doing research.[2]

DIFFERENTIATING RESEARCH

Research in General

Numerous dichotomies have been devised in an attempt to identify and clarify different types of research, i.e., theoretical versus nontheoretical, basic versus applied, deductive versus inductive, pure versus institutional, and traditional versus action. Useful though these dichotomies may be for discussion purposes, their practical applications as classification schema are quite limited. Seldom is research either purely theoretical or nontheoretical, basic or applied, and so forth. More frequently than not, research falls somewhere in between these pure forms.

However, these dichotomies indicate extremes of a research continuum. At one end of the continuum appear research projects which may be variously described as theoretical, basic, deductive, pure, or traditional, and at the other end appear research projects described as nontheoretical, applied, inductive, institutional, or action-oriented.

Such a scheme recognizes the extreme variations which may occur in the execution of different steps of the scientific method. Research may start with a practical problem or question generated in the context of a single institution with few, if any, theoretical underpinnings. The findings, however, may subsequently contribute significantly to the development or extension of a theory.

On the other hand, research may spring forth not from a practical workaday problem, but from a theoretical problem. The problem may be that of resolving uncertainty concerning the relationship between two or more concepts of a system of concepts posited to explain or predict some global phenomena. The researcher may proceed by collecting relevant data from a representative sample, analyzing it, and inducing certain principles or generalizations therefrom. These principles may in turn be tested in specific action programs to discern their utility.

Thus, a single research project, although conceived at one end of the continuum, may migrate to the other end where it may stay or may once again return to the starting point. It should be recognized, however, that such movement does not occur in all instances. Many action-applied research projects make little contribution to theory.

Likewise, many traditional-basic research projects make little contribution to problem resolution in the workaday world, at least not immediately.

Action Research in Particular

Since this chapter is devoted primarily to the development of an understanding of the action research process, it is deemed desirable at this point to make a special effort to differentiate action research (variously called applied research, cooperative research, operational research, institutional research, or developmental research) from basic research (variously called pure research, traditional research, or theoretical research). This will be done by examining the two in terms of source of researchable problems, influence on practice, design and analytical procedures employed, and extent of generalization sought.

Source of problem. Problems for action research, be they in continuing education or any other area of education, spring forth from real life situations. A teacher's or group of teachers' uncertainty about the best procedure to employ to achieve a given instructional objective, a program planner's indecisiveness concerning the educational needs of the community, or an administrator's concern with high rates of dropout all define starting points for action research projects. The "grass roots" nature of action research is further revealed in a definition by Smith and Smith: "The process by which practitioners attempt to study their problems scientifically in order to guide, correct, and evaluate their decisions and actions."[3]

By contrast, the problems of basic research usually are not generated by a practitioner's need to know in order to act. As a matter of fact, the pure researcher may be quite unfamiliar and even at times unconcerned with the practical situations to which his findings may relate. The problems of pure research frequently derive from abstract systems (theory) which purport to explain or predict global phenomena in the real world. These problems frequently take the form of hypotheses designed to test relationships between concepts of the theoretical system. Thus the relationship between role definition of the teacher and the achievement of his students, the relationship between dogmatism of an administrator and the interaction patterns that emerge during staff meetings, and the relationship between student expectation and teacher behavior are all examples of problems that typically concern the basic researcher.

Influence on practice. Since action research is conceived primarily as a means by which practitioners scientifically secure information to guide, correct, and evaluate their decisions and actions, then it follows that good action research does indeed result in findings which directly and specifically influence decisions and actions.

The problem for action research is a problem which is really being encountered by practitioners functioning in a specific program or agency, and the data chosen to furnish insight into the problem are collected within the context of that specific program or agency. Assuming that all ramifications of the problem are considered and that valid and reliable data-collecting instruments are employed, then it would appear obvious that the findings generated from action research do relate directly and specifically to the decisions and actions of practitioners of the agencies in question. Moreover, since those who have the responsibility for making decisions and planning actions are deeply involved in the research process, the likelihood of findings generated therefrom actually being considered and thus potentially exerting an influence on decisions and actions is enhanced. In short, there is an ego involvement and a perceived relevance on the part of the researcher-practitioner which is not equally a part of the practitioner who is expected to apply the findings and generalizations of other researchers.

Contrary to action research, the results of basic research seldom relate directly and specifically to the decision and actions of the practitioner. For it is the intent of basic researchers to contribute to the establishment of generalizations that can be stated as observed uniformities, explanatory principles, or scientific laws. With this intent in mind, they design and conduct their research in ways which enable them to draw conclusions extending beyond the populations or situations studied.[4]

However, few pure researchers would admit to the total irrelevance of their findings to the improvement of practice. Most trust that somehow their generalizations and principles will filter down and be finally utilized by the practitioner, but fewer back up that trust with an explicit plan to trigger or facilitate this filtering process. As a matter of fact, many of the generalizations and principles to which the practitioner is somehow exposed are either so obvious as to insult his intelligence or so abstract that he cannot discern their relevance to decisions and actions. In short, since many of the generalizations resulting from pure research never get incorporated in any meaningful way into the experience of the practitioner, they continue to collect dust in professional libraries and exert little, if any, influence on practice.

Design and analytical procedures. Just as the results of action or applied research differ greatly from those of basic or pure research, so also do the designs that produce these results. Action research is normally designed within the context of a single agency, program, or any unit thereof. The size of the population from which data are gathered and to which generalizations are directed usually allows complete involvement; data may be secured from all class enrollees, all program dropouts, etc., rather than from samples thereof. The action researcher generally does not have to be concerned about the representativeness of his study sample, nor does he have to be concerned about the degree to which factors presumed to be related to the problem under investigation are normally distributed. In this regard, he need concern himself only with the degree to which all ramifications of the problem are being considered (conditions other than experimental procedure influencing results or results of a negative nature accompanying the desired results) and the degree to which his data collection devices are reflecting the real situations.

The nature of the action research problem requires relatively simple analytical tools. Most action research data may be handily analyzed by measures of central tendencies (means, mediums, modes, and perhaps standard deviations) or at most rank order correlations.

By comparison, the designs and procedures of the so-called traditional or pure forms of research are quite different from those of action research. Here the research is normally designed within the context of a number of agencies, programs, or situations at one time. This is done to increase the likelihood that the conclusions and generalizations made will be broadly applicable or approach universality. Establishment of such broad-based parameters normally renders the securing of data from all members of the population uneconomical, if not impossible. Thus sampling becomes necessary, as does a concern for the representativeness of the sample and the normality of factors deemed related to the phenomena under study. In addition, of course, the pure researcher shares with the action researcher his concern for the degree to which all important ramifications of the problem have been considered or controlled and for the validity and reliability of his data collecting instruments.

Under conditions alluded to above, the pure researcher frequently must go far beyond measures of central tendency and rank order correlation in an attempt to analyze his data. Frequently, special techniques must be employed to reduce the data to manageable form, to determine if the assumptions of representativeness and normality of the data are satisfied, and to determine if that which has been observed in the data is real or is that which could have been the result of sampling error.

Extension of generalization. From what has been said thus far, it is perhaps clear that generalizing of findings is not as crucial a problem for the action researcher as it is for the basic researcher. The action researcher, however, is concerned with what might be termed vertical extension of his generalizations; that is, a concern for the degree to which the generalizations drawn from current data will indeed be applicable to his future situations. In a sense the action researcher is faced with determining the validity of the assumption that his current population is a random sample of a universe through time.

By comparison the basic researcher is not so concerned with vertical extensions of his generalization, but he is concerned with their lateral extensions; that is, extensions to other institutions or situations existing at a single point in time.

Thus, although the action researcher wishes to generalize to a given institutional situation through time, the pure researcher largely wishes to generalize to a universe of institutional situations at one point in time.

THE ADMINISTRATOR'S ROLE IN RESEARCH

The foregoing discussion implies that the adult education administrator has a vital function in research. In fact, it is frequently the administrator who serves as the bridge or link between the theoretical or basic pole of the research continuum and the applied or practical role of the continuum. In serving this function the administrator fulfills three important roles each of which contributes to the improvement of adult education. These three roles are —

1. Stimulator of needed research
2. Interpreter of research findings
3. Producer of "action" research.

The Administrator as a Stimulator of Research

As a stimulator of research the administrator identifies researchable questions and problems and uses every resource possible to bring about the active study of such questions and problems. To accomplish this task he establishes and maintains a communication network in which the needs, wants, questions, and problems of the individuals, groups, and organizations within the community are continuously directed toward his office.

Through the systematic collection of information relating to the changing community, problems arising within the classroom, evalua-

FIGURE I. – THE COMMUNICATION OF RESEARCH NEEDS

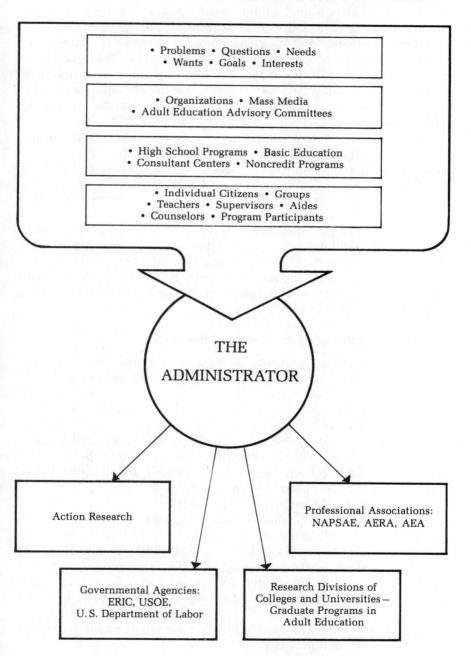

tion of programs, etc., the administrator and his staff can help to clarify and crystalize educational problems and issues which can then be communicated to selected individuals, groups, or agencies that have an interest in or responsibility for educational research in the area.[5]

In taking every opportunity to bring such needs to the attention of researchers the administrator will utilize formal as well as informal means. He will informally discuss his researchable problems with researchers at professional conferences. He will establish working relationships with research faculties and professors of education at nearby colleges and universities, thus making available to them a fertile laboratory for their research which may be highly relevant (or can become relevant) to his problems and needs. On occasion he will develop and transmit research proposals to a USOE Regional Laboratory, a Research and Development Center, or other appropriate research agency.

Frequently, the administrator will discover that the need for new, more, or better information can best be satisfied through action research conducted within the framework of his own organization. This is especially true when the relevance of such information is primarily limited to a specific program, group of students, or unique situation at a given time.

The Administrator as an Interpreter of Research

As an interpreter of research findings the administrator plays the role of consumer analyst. In this role he must perfect his ability to intelligently evaluate, discuss, and apply the results of research to his specific situation.[6] He will strive for both horizontal and vertical development in this regard; e.g., he will establish an ever-widening base of knowledge of all aspects of adult education and adult learning research, and at the same time he will delve deeply into specific areas of research where certain knowledge is central to the resolution of important problems within his institution.

It is not suggested here that the administrator is to keep up with the vast quantity of research that is relevant to adult education — an impossible task as well as one of questionable value.[7] What is suggested is that the administrator should know the pulse and direction of current research, he should spread the responsibility of keeping up with the most useful research throughout the organization, he should incorporate team efforts to distill practical applications from research into an ongoing in-service training program, and most important he should become expert in knowing how to locate and evaluate research findings when such information is needed.[8]

Major References to Adult Education Research

As a minimum it is recommended that the administrator have immediate and direct access to selected volumes which summarize adult education and related research, including —

1. *An Overview of Adult Education Research* [9]
2. *Handbook of Adult Education in the United States* [10]
3. *Adult Education: Outlines of an Emerging Field of University Study* [11]
4. *Handbook of Small Group Research* [12]
5. *Human Behavior: An Inventory of Scientific Findings* [13]
6. *Handbook on Research in Teaching* [14]
7. *Psychological Development Through the Life Span* [15]
8. *Cognitive Processes in Maturity and Old Age* [16]
9. *NSSE Yearbooks* (selected issues on adult teaching and learning) [17]
10. *Handbook of Aging and the Individual* [18]
11. *Contemporary Research on Teacher Effectiveness* [19]
12. Recent volumes of selected journals, including —
    (a) *Adult Education*
    (b) *Adult Leadership*
    (c) *Journal of Cooperative Extension*
    (d) *Training and Development Journal*
    (e) *Review of Educational Research*, Vols. 20, No. 3; 29, No. 3; and 30, No. 3
    (f) Other selected volumes from the literature of the social sciences
13. Recent volumes of other periodical literature including *Techniques, Pulse,* and *Swap Shop*
14. Selected bibliographies of adult education research which are prepared by ERIC clearinghouses, university departments of adult education, NAPSAE, and related agencies.[20]

In addition to having constant and direct access to the foregoing sources of information, the administrator should have access to and be familiar with the nearest social science library where he can quickly search the literature through standard references such as the *Encyclopedia of Educational Research, Psychological and Sociological Abstracts, Dissertation Abstracts,* and the *Education Index.*

Finally, the efficient administrator will adopt or develop an information retrieval system so that research papers, monographs, and reports can be coded and filed within a system which maximizes the probability of retrieving useful information relating to the research problems and questions which are likely to develop within his organization.

In the next section is discussed the third, but by no means the least significant, role of the administrator in research — namely the role of the administrator as a producer of action research within his own institution.[21]

CONDUCTING ACTION RESEARCH

Earlier in this chapter action research was defined as the process by which practitioners attempt to study their problems scientifically in order to guide, correct, and evaluate their decisions and actions.[22] The nature of decisions or actions to which such research relates varies as do the relevant research designs and procedures. In adult education, as in other areas of education, these decisions may be classified as "ends-oriented," "means-oriented," or both "ends- and means-oriented."

An example of the ends-oriented kind of action research is furnished by an adult education administrator who conducts a systematic survey[23] of the felt needs of his adult community — the results of which he intends to utilize in the reformulation of program goals and in decisions concerning precise courses to be offered. Others concerned with the classification of research in general would likely call this example an instance of "descriptive research" in that it is quite clearly an effort to collect data which describe conditions as they currently exist. To be sure, however, the reason for describing the need profile of the example community was to be found in the hypothetical administrator's need to decide about the "ends" of his educational program.

Means-oriented action research can be illustrated by still another example. Consider a group of teachers and supervisors of adult basic education who were pondering the problem of involving the undereducated in their programs. After efforts to brainstorm the problem had run its course, the decision was made to explore accounts of how undereducated immigrants and ethnic groups of the past were encouraged to involve themselves in uplifting educational programs. Such activity may be considered an illustration of both means-oriented action research and historical research.[24]

Finally, there are action research studies designed to investigate means-ends relationships; that is, research to determine the relative effectiveness of a given means or procedure in bringing about a desired end. Consider the supervising teacher who, being uncertain about the effectiveness of the system currently being employed to teach reading to his adult students, designs an experiment to compare the results of the current system with one to which he was recently exposed during a national meeting. Research of this type usually leads to the random assignment of students to groups (experimental and control) for systematically varied treatment and objective observation. It is this kind of procedure that would lead those concerned with general research classifications to label this example of means-ends action research a special instance of "experimental research." [25]

The above efforts to classify action research into three categories should not inhibit recognition that the search for information with which to make all three types of decisions ("means," "ends," and "means-ends") is often inseparably woven into a single action research project.

Furthermore, it should be recognized that action research is not solely dependent for direction on experiential reservoirs of the practitioner. Frequently hypotheses or educated guesses are the products of a marriage between the principles and generalization of a pure researcher and the pending decision and uncertainties of the practitioner. Finally, the future of the marriage is frequently made more secure by the advised practice of securing a professional research specialist to give his counsel before and after marriage.

Steps in the Action Research Process

Although there is reason to expect considerable shuffling back and forth, there are several generally agreed upon steps to action research. The authors now deliver their version:

1. Recognize a problem area or a lack of objective information on which to base a decision or decisions.
2. Select the specific problem and derive researchable hypotheses (relational statements between variables of "means" and "ends") or researchable questions.
3. Specify the data required to test the research hypotheses or answer the research questions.
4. Select the population (or sample thereof) from which data will be collected.
5. Select or develop the data-collecting instrument or technique and actually collect the data.
6. Analyze the data.
7. Generalize concerning relationships between variables under study or concerning answers to research questions.
8. Apply generalization and continue to test.

Admittedly the above eight steps are only vaguely suggestive of the numerous decisions encountered while actually designing and conducting action research, to say nothing of their failure to furnish insights helpful in making such decisions. In an effort to partially correct these shortcomings, the reader is now asked to project himself into a developmental account of a hypothetical action research project.

Illustration of the Action Research Process

The setting for the hypothetical action research project is a large metropolitan public school adult education system (hereafter System X) consisting of several evening school centers each with at least one administrator and several full-time and part-time teachers. In addition, there is an overall system staff consisting of a director and numerous program area specialists.

Recognition of problem. The adult education director of System X had been concerned for some time with what appeared to be a growing discontent on the part of both students and teachers in the system. Complaints from both sources, however trivial, appeared to be on the increase. In addition, enrollment figures were gradually declining and dropout rates were steadily increasing. He decided to take his concern to his program specialists and center administrators.

Defining the problem more precisely. At the next monthly staff meeting, the director expressed his concern and presented supportive evidence in the form of percentage increases in complaints from teachers and students, percentage decline in enrollment, and percentage increase in dropouts. It became clear during subsequent deliberations that most of the program area specialists and center administrators had intuitively arrived at the same conclusion as the director—something was wrong! Furthermore, the support generated by the director's empirical evidence and by the knowledge of a shared concern seemed to spark a great deal of enthusiasm for discovering what indeed was wrong and what could be done about it.

The group agreed to start with the director's definition of their concern—"discontent as measured by complaints, enrollment figures, and dropout rate." This brought them to a decision about how to proceed in their efforts to identify potentially explanatory variables concerning conditions which might be associated with this so-called discontent. One member suggested a short brainstorming session; the suggestion was quickly accepted.

Although the intent of this brief brainstorming session was that of producing variables for study, the actual result was several ideas concerning where to go to look for such variables. These ideas were subsequently reduced to the following three:

1. Review the research and literature. Several areas suggested were employee morale, teacher behavior and student attitude, student dropout, and the nature of adulthood.
2. Analyze more specifically the complaint, enrollment, and dropout data globally presented earlier by the director. More particularly, a quick comparative study[26] of each center was suggested to determine (a) if there were differences between centers in terms of the three discontent criteria and (b) if differences existed, were they associated with still other differences between centers such as quality of faculty, nature of students, qualifications of teachers, etc.?
3. Conduct a survey of teachers and students. It was anticipated that through such a survey the group could secure a more representative and precise indication of both the degree of discontent and reasons for discontent.

Three task forces were then established to perform the preliminary investigations suggested by each of the three ideational sources. In a sense, then, each of the three task forces became involved in conducting a study within a study. Relative to earlier discussions concerning action research classification, all three studies could be considered "means" studies in that each was focused on ultimately deriving a means of ameliorating discontent (the end) by first identifying those conditions which appear associated with it. Furthermore, all of the studies were descriptive in that all purported to describe in some detail the discontent phenomena and those conditions which orbit it.

Each study could be labeled differently, however, in terms of the source of data collected or nature of analysis performed. Thus, the first study (research and literature) is appropriately labeled a library study,[27] the second (center comparisons) a comparative study, and the third (student-teacher survey) a survey study.

Each task force was given two months in which to complete their investigations during which members were to be given a prescribed amount of release time. The efforts and results of each task force are described briefly below.

The library task force immediately mailed a request to the Library for Continuing Education at Syracuse University (the ERIC component for Studies in Adult Education) for leads to studies in the area of employee or adult student morale, teacher effectiveness, adult student attitude, adult student dropout, and the nature of adulthood. The library reacted by mailing letter summaries of research projects in most of these areas or references to findings published elsewhere. Fortunately many of the references cited were found in either System X's professional library or in the library of a nearby university. Individual members of the task force were given an opportunity to explore the research and readings of their choice, so long as this did not result in too much duplication of effort. Every week they came together to share with each other the ideas gleaned from their previous week's reading. This was continued until the last meeting where an effort was made to synthesize and finally sketch out a report for the central committee.

Prominent in their final report were such principles or generalizations as —

1. Adult students are typically better equipped to and more desirous of exerting an influence on the nature and direction of their educational experience than are youthful students.
2. Direct involvement of an individual in the ongoing activities of a group or institution enhances his morale and his identifying with its norms and goals.
3. Teacher behavior which is supportive of student behavior, which draws out the reactions and questions of students, and which permits and even encourages student interaction tends to promote positive attitudes among students.

Fortunately for the *comparative task force*, the director had on file complete records for the past five years relating to the nature and source of every complaint made verbally or in writing relating to system enrollment and finally relating to system dropout. Moreover, the data were arranged in the files in a way which facilitated efforts to compile them by centers.

Once compiled, percentages were computed for each center, being careful that the most sensible and valid base for each percentage was established. All percentages were used to reveal the extent of change experienced by each center over the past five years with reference to the three criterion measures of discontent.

Complaints were expressed as a percent of each year's student enrollment in the case of student complaints or as a percent of the teachers employed each year in the case of teacher complaints. Enrollments were expressed each year as a percentage increase or decrease from the previous year's total. Finally, dropouts each year were expressed as a percentage of the total body of students that year who attended at least two class sessions.

In comparing percentages thus derived, it became obvious that two of the centers were, as defined by the criteria employed, much more "discontent" than were the others. This led the group into a comparative study of these two "discontent" centers and the other four centers judged to be "content" or at least less "discontent."

Here again the task force found all the data it needed in the files of each center. Some years back standard data collection forms were adopted for systematic data collection from all students and teachers. The student data included the typical demographic information plus anecdotal information from the counselor to which each student was assigned. Teacher data included demographic information, information concerning academic and professional experience and periodic evaluation reports from program area specialists.

In addition to these student and teacher data, the task force also conducted interviews[28] with all center administrators to ascertain if there had been any shifts in program emphasis, procedures, etc. over the past five years that could have made any of the centers unique cases. Finally the physical plants were examined systematically with the use of a predesigned check sheet.

Even though the data defined above were either available or easily obtainable, an almost unmanageable compilation job still faced the task force. To reduce this to more manageable proportions, it was decided to draw a 10 percent random sample[29] of students from each center file and thereby reduce the data-handling job by 90 percent.

Once compiled for each center, all the data enabled the group to make cross-center comparisons. Particular interest, of course, was shown in the comparison of the two "discontent" centers with the other four "benchmark" centers. Where the data were highly quantifiable, measures of central tendency[30] (mean, median, and mode) were used as units for comparison. In other instances percentages were used.

With the help of nonparametric tests to determine statistical significance,[31] (where appropriate) the following disclosures were made:

1. Teachers of the "discontent" centers appeared to be somewhat more autocratic or directive than teachers of other centers.
2. A significantly larger proportion of "discontent" center faculty consisted of part-time teachers recently employed from the day school faculty than was the case for "content" center faculty.
3. There was no appreciable difference revealed among centers in terms of the quality of physical plant and the characteristics of students.

The survey task force immediately began developing two separate survey instruments — one for teachers and the other for students. Each instrument consisted of a scale to establish degree of satisfaction with the system (different, of course, for students and teachers) and an open-ended opportunity to explain the "whys" and "why nots" of satisfaction. Help in the development of these scales was secured from a book written by Shaw and Wright [32] in which illustrations of numerous scales developed for researchers in education are given.

Once developed, the scale part of each survey was distributed to a panel of educational experts to check its content validity (degree to which it measures what it purports to measure) and was administered to a subgroup of students twice over a two-week period to check its reliability (degree to which same results are secured on repeated observations using the same subjects). The scales were judged both valid and reliable. [33]

The instruments were then administered to all teachers of each center and to a 10-percent random sample of students in each center. Answers to open-ended questions were then classified, and portions of respondents from each center falling into each category of the classification system were computed. Similarly, responses to the scale were telescoped into a mean score ranging from 0 to 5 for each individual — with zero showing the most dissatisfaction. A one-way analysis of variance [34] was then applied to these mean scale scores to determine differences among centers.

The findings of this investigation appeared to reinforce those made by the comparative task force. They were as follows:

1. The two centers labeled "discontent" by the comparative task force enrolled students and employed teachers who were significantly less satisfied with the system than were those of the so-called "content" centers.
2. Typical comments of the discontent students were —
   "The teachers treat us like kids."
   "Stuff is dull and meaningless."
   "Teacher does all the talking."
   "No time for questions."
   "I just don't need what is being taught."
   "I can't smoke."
3. Typical comments of the discontent teachers were —
   "Administrator is not a good disciplinarian."
   "Students just don't listen."
   "Students talk in class without permission and argue with me when I tell them not to — this must be stopped."
   "Half of the students are just there to have fun, not to learn."

Finally, after two months of study, the three task forces once again came together — this time for the expressed purpose of sharing their discoveries and to arrive at some sort of consensus concerning the predictive variables to employ in the central investigation.

During the discussion following the task force reports, one member referred to what he called a central proposition that appeared in all the reports, namely, that overly directive behavior on the part of a teacher of adults results in a lack of student satisfaction with the educative experience and with the system in general. Positively stated, nondirective teacher behavior or behavior which encourages student questioning results in student satisfaction with the educative experience and with the system in general. One somewhat overzealous member then exclaimed, "It's all clear to me now! The large portion of part-time teachers recently employed by two 'problematic' centers are teaching adults with the directive styles they acquired as day school teachers. That's what's causing all this discontent." Others in the group wisely suggested that further experimentation was needed before any such conclusion could be drawn.

After a long period of interchange, the group finally decided on the following hypotheses:

1. Adult students taught by nondirective teachers are significantly more satisfied with the educational experience and with the system than those taught by directive teachers.
2. Adult students taught by nondirective teachers drop out of school with significantly less frequency than do students taught by directive teachers.

Specification of data. Quantification of the dropout and satisfaction variables was not a difficult decision — the group simply agreed to use the same kind of data as was used by the comparative task force and the survey task force studies. Not so with the teacher behavior variable (directive versus nondirective). What is directive as opposed to nondirective teacher behavior? How does one measure it? These were the questions with which the committee struggled. The questions were finally resolved as a result of a suggestion by one of the members who had served on the research and literature task force. He recalled reviewing the research of Ned Flanders[35] who through the use of an elaborately developed interaction matrix was able to measure the directiveness of teachers' behavior. The system in brief consisted of a trained observer who, at two-second intervals, recorded teacher-student interaction and at the end of an observation period, was able to compute an I/D ratio — a measure of teacher directiveness. Flanders' definitions and observational system were examined at some length and were finally adopted.

Selection of population. There were a number of problems that became apparent when consideration was given to the source of data or the population to be studied. The most crucial of all problems was that of eliminating the influence of outside variables. After all, the group wanted to study alone the influence of teacher directiveness on student satisfaction and dropout.

The first question to be answered of course was "What are these outside variables which, if not adequately eliminated or controlled, could influence undesirably the results?" The three thought to be most crucial were the subject matter, the student, and the institution. Ultimately, all three were controlled by design.

Subject matter was held constant by restricting the study to only 12 classes of an Americanism versus Communism course, all the teachers of which conformed to the state-established curricular plan. Secondly the influence of the institutional variable was thought to be at least reduced by the decision to use classes from only the two centers where "discontent" was the highest. Finally, the student variable through random class assignment was distributed normally and therefore removed from consideration.

The 12 classes to be studied were divided into two groups of six. One was designated as the control group (teachers who conducted class as they always had) and the other the experimental group (teachers who were trained to be nondirective).

The six experimental teachers were then self-trained with the initial help of a person trained in the use of Flanders' interaction recording matrix, and each teacher each day recorded his own behavior (from a tape recording) on a matrix. After each recording session, teachers were helped to analyze their matrix profiles, carefully comparing them with earlier profiles and ideal profiles. This kind of pre-experiment training was continued until the I/D ratios of the experimental teachers were on the average 25 percent higher than were the I/D ratios of the control teachers — with the added condition that there could be no less than a 20 percent differential between any experimental teacher and any control teacher.

Selection of instruments and collection of data.[36] A scale to measure satisfaction was developed earlier and the validity and reliability established. Additional dropout data were to be drawn from records in the center office. And finally, the Flanders observation matrix was to be used to establish teacher directiveness. It was further decided that dropout and satisfaction data would be collected during the last week of the 12 classes.

Analysis of data. It was decided that the significance of differences between mean satisfaction scores recorded for students with directive teachers and those with nondirective teachers would be determined by a one-way analysis of variance. Likewise a simple test determining the significance of differences between percentages was to be applied to the percent dropout figures.[37]

Generalization. Both hypotheses were ultimately supported by the data.

Application. The experimental base was broadened to include all centers, and the data gathering continued. In addition, an in-service teacher training program was initiated, the goal of which was to produce "nondirective" orientations among the teaching staff.

THE CONTINUING EDUCATION OF THE ADMINISTRATOR-RESEARCHER

By now it should be obvious that the competent adult education administrator is a person who not only keeps abreast of pertinent research in adult education and related fields, but he is one who also has the ability to translate and apply specific research findings, principles, and generalizations to the manifold problems and needs of his own organization. At times he will "field test" or replicate the research of others in order to validate certain principles, recommendations, or practices before accepting or adopting them. At other times he will find it desirable or necessary to conceptualize, initiate, and carry forth his own research to obtain the quality of information which is crucial to the success of his decision-making role.

In addition to developing and following a systematic plan or strategy which will enable him to keep updated in the areas relevant to his responsibilities in action research, the effective administrator will also assist his staff in developing a systemwide plan by which all members of the organization will be afforded an opportunity to maintain and improve their respective knowledge and skill in action research.

Recommended Learning Program

How can the adult education administrator best keep abreast of new developments in research? This question is in itself a researchable one. Although there is no simple or direct answer to a question of this kind, certain principles or recommendations which have grown out of studies of adult learning in general and out of studies of the countinuing education needs of professionals in particular can be identified which may be useful in developing one's own program of continuing education. Although limitations of space preclude an elaborate listing of such principles, the following guidelines are considered especially important in this regard.

The adult education administrator should —

1. Identify and budget time to participate in a series of experiences which have been specifically selected to enhance his knowledge about and competence in research.
2. Organize his learning activities to provide involvement in a wide range of methods and techniques.
3. Select learning experiences for a depth examination of one of a few significant areas in particular and for a balanced treatment of action research in general.
4. Sequentially arrange his learning experience as much as possible so that growth and development proceed in an orderly manner.
5. Commit himself to periodically applying new knowledge, such as weighing and using information derived from research in making program decisions, establishing an experimental situation designed to improve teacher training or registration, etc., or applying specific sampling techniques in conducting a community survey for computer analysis.
6. Arrange for feedback so that he has personal and meaningful knowledge of his developing competence in action research.

Program in Action

The following discussion illustrates how a local director might apply the foregoing guidelines in developing a personal program for his own continuing education in action research.

Assume that our adult education director feels he has neglected his responsibilities for or role in action research. After all, he has had more than a full-time job keeping up with the day-to-day routine of administration. Yet, he begins to entertain the following thoughts:

> Perhaps research could provide information which would reduce the magnitude of my problems or strengthen my decisions. Perhaps in the long run, my involvement in research would make my task an easier one, or more interesting, perhaps even exciting. Could it be that action research is one solution to the problem of maintaining a challenging situation in which staff members can develop a deep and continuing commitment to strengthening our program through our mutual efforts?

After undergoing a rather intensive personal assessment of the situation and having sought out the ideas of certain friends and colleagues, our soon-to-be "administrator-researcher" establishes three broad educational goals which he plans to pursue over the coming months:

1. To become aware of current thrusts in adult education research.
2. To recapture and update knowledge and understanding of research methodology.
3. To discover what research says about achievement and dropouts in adult basic education and use this information in strengthening his programs in this area.

On the basis of his own knowledge growing out of past experiences and strengthened by new information acquired through discussions with his staff, neighboring directors, the executive secretary of a professional association of adult education, and a close friend who is deeply involved in adult education research, our director decides that the first goal can best be achieved by combining a planned program of selected reading and participation in the research sessions scheduled for certain state and national conferences. Furthermore, he has arranged to attend a series of weekly luncheons with three of his staff members who share his interest in keeping abreast with current research. Once a month each person in this informal learning group will summarize the latest developments in a particular research area, and the group will discuss the implications of such research for improving the local adult education program.

To achieve the second goal — updating his knowledge of research methodology — our director has decided to review his own personal library to recapture what he had learned 10 years ago, the last time that he had seriously studied the area. Furthermore, after consultation with a professor in educational testing and research he has decided to enroll in a 10-week graduate class which meets one evening each week and which is entitled "Designing Educational Research." To round out this series of experiences he plans to attend the forthcoming National Seminar on Adult Education Research, the members of which will devote three full days to exploring new developments in research methodology.

In developing plans to achieve the third goal — learning what research says about dropout and achievement in adult basic education — our adult education director has consulted with the regional university staff specialist on adult basic education and has obtained several bibliographies from the ERIC Clearinghouses on Adult Education and Cultural Deprivation. He will use this information as a starting point for an intensive library study of the area. He has allotted three months for this activity which will be followed by his participation as an instructor in a two-week regional institute for teacher training in adult basic education.

Program Assessed

Referring to the six guidelines for developing one's own program for continuing education, it can be seen that the director has budgeted time to participate in a wide range of experiences to enhance his knowledge of and competence for research. These experiences have been sequentially arranged for orderly growth and development, and they involve the use of a variety of learning techniques so that pertinent concepts can be examined from several points of view. His learning program provides for both breadth and depth and will be translated into action as he develops his instructional plans for the two-week training institute. Finally, his preliminary review and assessment of what he already knows will provide a base line against which he can measure his own growth and development. It is also expected that our director will become increasingly involved in formulating questions for action research and in initiating and participating in specific information-seeking projects as he acquires the orientation of the action researcher.

Through carefully developed plans for his own continuing education, the administrator-researcher will discover that he is able to keep abreast of new developments in the field, that he is among the first to learn of new sources of useful information, that he is highly regarded as a participant in the affairs of research organizations, that he has learned to read with a greater degree of discrimination, and that he occupies a new and vital role of being an interpreter of knowledge and disseminator of information to his chosen field.

It is our contention that the systematic study of research and periodic involvement in action-research by the adult education administrator will enhance his skill and effectiveness as a planner, manager, and administrator. More importantly, the future quality of adult learning will be significantly related to his future involvement in action research.

CHAPTER 18

CONTINUOUS PROGRAM EVALUATION

Alan B. Knox

CONTRIBUTION OF EVALUATION TO
PROGRAM INPROVEMENT

Victor Balancesheet had arrived at his office an hour early this morning. For the past six months since he was appointed as director of the continuing education division, he had found that the hour before school starts was a good time for planning. Victor Balancesheet was not one to be carried along on the tide without plan or direction.

During the previous year, the superintendent of the Franklin School District had asked Victor if he were interested in becoming the half-time director of continuing education. The state legislature had appropriated funds with which local districts could hire directors of adult and continuing education. Victor was the high school business education teacher, and he had expressed an interest in continuing education from the first day that he taught at Franklin four years ago. His wife insisted that part of his commitment resulted from his father's experience as a university dean of extension. There was, however, no doubt about Victor's dedication to life-long learning. His enthusiastic teaching had made his evening classes on business very popular with adults. And he had been instrumental in the organization of a citizens advisory committee to the continuing education program. One of the other teachers had commented at the time that he had probably picked up the idea in one of his courses at the university where he was working on an administrator's certificate. Even now, the ideas that he wanted to

---

Alan B. Knox is professor of education in the Department of Higher and Adult Education and director of the Center for Adult Education at Teachers College, Columbia University, New York, New York.

try resulted in his spending more time as director than he spent on his half-time position as the business teacher.

Victor privately characterized the course offerings that he had inherited as a hodgepodge. Most of them were either federally reimbursed vocational courses or hobby courses. On the average, about half of those who registered at the beginning of each term had dropped out by the end. Victor believed strongly that substantial program improvement was needed. That was his major concern this morning. What approach could he use that would be most likely to result in program improvement? He had mentioned his concern about program improvement to the superintendent several weeks before, with the result that he had agreed to present a plan for improvement during the following year. The problem was in getting a handle on it. He had thought of evaluation, but the approaches that had been covered in his graduate course on tests and measurements did not seem very relevant. They were aimed at testing students to decide on grades. Few of the continuing education courses gave grades, and having grades for continuing education courses did not seem to be a move in the right direction.

"There must be a more useful approach to program improvement," mused Victor Balancesheet. "There must be a way."

The quandary of the fictional Victor Balancesheet has been shared by many directors of programs of continuing education for adults. Simply testing adult students *does not* seem to be a satisfactory way to improve programs, and yet some procedure is needed to produce evidence upon which to base judgments about program effectiveness. The literature of adult and continuing education abounds with admonitions about the desirability of evaluation. The test and measurement books describe procedures for the collection and analysis of data. What has been substantially missing has been a more general framework, an approach to establishing connections among the goals of evaluation, the functioning of the continuing education programs, and the technical procedures for data collection and analysis. This chapter on continuous program evaluation is an attempt to present and illustrate the major elements of an approach to program improvement.

The purpose of program evaluation is program improvement. The previous chapters of this book have indicated how complex a task it is for a director like Victor Balancesheet to plan and implement an effective continuing education program for adults. If he is to provide leadership on program improvement within the division there must be provision for systematic feedback of information related to program effectiveness to policy makers, administrators, teachers, and learners so that they can make sound judgments regarding program effectiveness. Continuous program evaluation is the process by which evidence regarding program effectiveness is systematically collected, analyzed, and used to improve programs of continuing adult education. The purpose of this chapter is to suggest ways in which the director might strengthen program evaluation procedures.

Purpose of Evaluation

Before suggesting an approach that a director like Victor Balancesheet might take to the program evaluation process, it might be helpful to be more specific about the purposes of the program evaluation process. The general purpose of evaluation is to improve the educational program, facilitating judgments about its effectiveness based on evidence. The specific purposes of program evaluation are—

1. To make more explicit the rationale for the educational program as a basis for deciding which aspects of the educational program are most important to evaluate regarding effectiveness and what specific types of data to collect.
2. To collect evidence or data upon which to base the judgments regarding effectiveness.
3. To analyze the data and draw conclusions.
4. To make judgments or decisions which are based at least in part on the data.
5. To implement the decisions so as to improve the educational program.

Symptoms of Inadequate Evaluation

If Balancesheet's program were small and stable, then program evaluation could occur informally as he, school board members, his teachers, and even the adult learners discussed the program and made decisions about its improvement. Under these conditions, Balancesheet should be able to recognize emerging difficulties and make adjustments as the program proceeds. However, if his program were large, growing, and diversified, then more systematic feedback procedures would be required. There are a variety of symptoms that might indicate to Balancesheet (or to any other director) that evaluation procedures might be inadequate. Although any one symptom may result from other causes, the occurrence of several symptoms together should be recognized by the director as evidence that there are major discrepancies between goals, resources, and procedures that are not being accommodated. Some typical symptoms are as follows:

1. Slow increase in the number of adults enrolled, compared with similar programs.
2. Difficulty in attracting adults from a specified target population.
3. High dropout rate associated with an incompatibility between learning style and teaching style.
4. Low rate of learner persistence from year to year.
5. Limited learner directedness regarding planning, conducting, and assessing of his own educational efforts.
6. Many complaints by learners or teachers regarding a discrepancy among goals, resources, procedures, and learner backgrounds.
7. Unwillingness of the most qualified teachers to accept teaching positions in the division or to continue for another term.
8. Slow improvement of beginning teachers in the division.
9. Difficulty in placing in jobs or further education those participants who successfully complete a course of study in the division.
10. Frequent complaints from employers regarding the obsolescence of the knowledge and skills that their employees have obtained from courses in the division or the inability of the employees to apply what they have learned.
11. Few course sequences.
12. Lack of articulation between courses that are presumably part of a sequence.
13. High incidence of friction in relationships with the youth preparatory education programs of the institution.
14. Lack of support from policy makers regarding budget requests and proposals for new programs.

If a director assesses his division and discovers several of these symptoms, he should review in detail the current procedures for program evaluation to identify points at which they should be improved.

In practice, the range of activities on which program evaluation procedures might focus extends far beyond available time or money. Therefore, one of the most crucial decisions by the director deals with the appropriate extent of evaluation activity within the division, so that the investment of resources for evaluation is sufficient to maximize the other investments but *does not* exceed the anticipated benefits. The director should expect to get his money's worth from evaluation.

AN APPROACH TO EVALUATION

Too often, continuing education evaluation consists of course examinations or learner satisfaction forms or a review of enrollment and income. By contrast, the theme of this chapter is that a more comprehensive approach to the evaluation process must be taken if substantial program improvement is to result. The proposed approach to evaluation which is presented in the remainder of this chapter is divided into the following five sections: (a) important ideas about evaluation; (b) program evaluation data; (c) related agency functions; (d) methods of collecting and analyzing data; and (e) using evaluation results. In each section, the basic steps or ideas are concisely stated and are followed by a brief explanation or example.

Important Ideas About Evaluation

The extensive literature on educational evaluation contains many ideas and principles that can be helpful to adult educators. Many are contained in the Selected Readings for this chapter. The following brief list of important ideas about evaluation were selected because of their special importance and relevance to adult education program improvement.

Evidence. Why bother about formalized evaluation procedures? *People associated with a program will make judgments about effectiveness even without formal evaluation procedures. The function of systematic and continuous program evaluation procedures should be to provide more adequate evidence and to improve the soundness of the judgments.* The learner will decide whether he is receiving enough benefit from a course to warrant his continued investment of time and money. The teacher will decide to try some new instructional methods and to discontinue others. The administrator will decide to rehire some teachers and not others. The school board member will decide whether to vote additional district funds for a proposed expansion of an adult education program. As each person associated with a program makes these and other judgments about program effectiveness, he does so on the basis of the evidence most familiar to him. If the evidence is adequate for making sound judgments which are then used for program improvement, then existing evaluation procedures are probably sufficient. However, if this is not the case, then the director should assess the existing evaluation procedures to identify the major points at which they should be improved so that more adequate evidence and sounder judgments will result. Examples of points at which evaluation procedures might be improved include the use of self-administered diagnostic tests, anonymous end-of-course student opinionnaires, periodic clientele analysis, summary of the characteristics of those who drop out and their reasons for dropping out, a follow-up study of former participants regarding their application of what they learned, and a cost-effectiveness study comparing lecture and discussion methods regarding cost, achievement, application, and motivation.

Benefits. How extensive should the evaluation procedures be? *The extent of the evaluation procedures should depend on the importance of making sounder judgments. There should be a balance between costs of evaluation and the benefits received.* If evaluation procedures are too limited, the anticipated results from the large investments by learner, teacher, and school may not be realized. In this case, a modest increase in evaluation should produce a substantial program improvement. For instance, in a division that uses few formal testing, counseling, or feedback procedures, the introduction of end-of-course opinionnaires for both learners and teachers can inexpensively identify many suggestions for program improvement. However, extensive evaluation procedures aimed at a minor problem may not be worth the effort. The important question is, How important is it to be able to make sounder judgments regarding program effectiveness? If the judgments towards which evaluation efforts are aimed are inconsequential or if satisfactory judgments can be made with less evidence, then a reduction in the extent of evaluation procedures is justified. But, if faulty judgments are being made on important issues related to program effectiveness, then more extensive evaluation efforts are warranted.

Frequency. How often should evaluation data be collected? *The frequency with which evaluation data should be collected depends on the aspect of the program that is being assessed and the anticipated use of the results.* Some information, such as learner achievement related to course objectives, should be collected periodically during each course. Information such as learner expectations or a summary of the dropout rate for each course can be collected once each term. Some information, such as a clientele analysis that compares the characteristics of participants with the adult population that the division is attempting to serve, might be collected every five years. One purpose of the more frequently collected data is to identify *when* to collect more detailed information about selected aspects of the program. For instance, a high dropout rate caused by learner dissatisfaction might lead to an evaluation study of registration and counseling procedures.

Feedback. Who should receive the results of evaluation? *One major function of evaluation should be continuing internal feedback to enable adjustments in the ongoing program.* A major shortcoming of informal evaluation procedures is that evidence of program effectiveness tends not to reach those who could use it. Even though their primary purpose is to facilitate pass-fail decisions, end-of-course examinations in elementary and secondary education tend not to be used as much as they might for program improvement to the benefit of learners in subsequent terms. An example of evaluation for feedback includes periodic brief anonymous tests to provide the learner with evidence of achievement as a basis for adjusting study plans. Summaries each term of participant characteristics to assist both program planning and program promotion might be provided as well as summaries of learner opinionnaires which may assist in the planning and revision of future courses.

Commitment. To what extent should those who are affected by evaluation participate in the process? *Those who are affected by the evaluation and who must use the results if improvements are to occur should participate in the evaluation process so that the likelihood of their using the results will be increased.* This idea differentiates evaluation from research. In social and behavioral science research, one objective is to minimize the extent to which those who are being studied influence decisions that might bias the findings. However, as Corey stressed in his book on action research,[1] when a primary purpose is program improvement, reduced validity and generalizability may be the price paid for a greater commitment to use of the findings. For example, teachers who decide that a study of teaching style is needed and then help to develop the procedures are more likely to read the report and use some of the findings to modify their teaching than would be the case when a similar study is conducted exclusively by an outside consultant.

Objectivity. How then can greater objectivity be achieved? *The outside evaluation specialist can help to increase the objectivity and validity of evaluation procedures.* There is a tendency for persons who evaluate their own program to rationalize. Long-standing conditions such as budget level or personnel tend to be accepted as unchangeable whereas they may constitute the major leverage for program improvement. Also, personal involvement in a program may make candid appraisal difficult. Greater objectivity can be achieved by the assistance of an outside evaluation specialist who may be associated with another part of the institution or with a nearby university. The outside evaluation specialist can help to offset this subjectivity. He can also provide technical assistance regarding procedures of data collection and analysis.

Objectives. How can a clearer statement of objectives be obtained? *The evaluation specialist should assist those who plan the educational* program in making more clear and explicit their intents and objectives as the major basis for judging effectiveness. There are several bases for judging the effectiveness of an educational program, but the major basis should be the extent to which the objectives were achieved. The development of detailed evaluation procedures requires greater clarity and precision in the statement of objectives than do many other aspects of program planning and teaching. For example, the selection of questions for an achievement test, opinionnaire, or follow-up study requires that a decision be made about how the learners are expected to change as a result of the course. In some instances, at least half of the effort of the evaluation specialist is devoted to clarification of program objectives. The resulting statement of objectives contributes not only to evaluation but also to other aspects of program development such as selection of materials and instructional personnel. It is important to recognize, however, that many programs have benefits aside from the stated objectives.

Standards. How can standards of comparison be obtained? The evaluation specialist should also assist in identifying appropriate standards of comparison, both the relative performance of similar programs and absolute standards of excellence. The evaluation specialist should have a familiarity with relevant evaluation studies that will enable him to bring an outside perspective to the development of an evaluation plan. It is in part through the comparison of a program evaluation report with evaluation reports for similar programs and with standards of excellence such as standardized test norms or standards of job performance that the stated objectives of the program are assessed.

Relevance. On what basis should the data to be collected be chosen? Data should be collected and analyzed which are highly relevant to the intents and objectives. This is the question of validity that is so central in writings on educational measurement. Is the teacher testing for what he is teaching? When the focus is shifted from evaluation of learners to program evaluation, somewhat different types of information should be collected. The decisions regarding which information to collect and its subsequent interpretation depends on the rationale for the program. The rationale should include a brief review of the past history of the program being evaluated, its current demands and constraints, and expectations regarding future developments. The statement of intents should include the anticipated outcomes such as learning gain or application of what was learned by the learner in a subsequent job setting. In addition, the statement of intents should describe the anticipated inputs of learners, teachers, materials, and other resources, along with the anticipated transactions between these inputs that are expected to produce the outcomes. Similarly, some information should be collected regarding the actual inputs, transactions, and outcomes of the educational program.

Values. Should evaluation be limited to empirical data? *The process of making judgments should include, in addition to data, appropriate values, consensus, and continuing commitment.* The collection and analysis of data are crucial ingredients in the evaluation process. However, in addition, those who are engaged in the process should be concerned with two other ingredients. One is values. People hold differing convictions regarding desirability. Some people may place emphasis on critical judgment as a priority outcome, although others may stress skillful performance. The second ingredient is consensus and continuing commitment. The success of an educational program depends on the continuing contribution made by various persons. The process of making judgments regarding effectiveness should include provision for achieving consensus and a commitment to use the findings to improve the educational program.

Program Evaluation Data

Each continuing education program has broad goals, one of which is the long-term benefits that participation brings to the learner. For the purpose of evaluation, however, it is necessary to focus on specific educational objectives, the achievement of which will substantially assist the learner to move towards the long-term goals. In addition to specific educational objectives, there are often other program outcomes in the form of benefits to the community or sponsoring institution. Community benefits may include a reduction in the numbers of people on welfare or who are unemployed and an increase in productivity or greater survival of small businesses. Institutional benefits include greater plant utilization, increased citizen support for preparatory education, and increased teacher familiarity with adult life settings within which preparatory education students will later have to function. Part of the purpose of program evaluation is to collect data regarding the extent to which the intended program *outcomes* and other unanticipated benefits are achieved. In addition to outcomes, educational program development includes attention to intended *inputs* and transactions. Intended inputs include the characteristics of learners, teachers, materials, and other needed resources. Intended *transactions* include the activities in which learners and teachers engage together with instructional materials that are intended to transform the inputs into the intended outcomes. In the total process of evaluation of an effective continuing education program, data are collected regarding the actual or observed *inputs, transactions,* and *outcomes.* Because it is never possible to collect data on all of the variables related to a functioning program, evaluation efforts must be selective. One basis for deciding variables for data collection is the *rationale* of the program including its history, current demands and constraints, and expectations regarding future developments. These four aspects of the program from which to collect data *(rationale, inputs, transactions,* and *outcomes)* provide a framework which the director can use in assessing current evaluation procedures and in developing more satisfactory procedures for continuous program evaluation. Listed below are the four aspects of the program from which to collect data, along with examples of the specific data that might be collected.

Rationale. The rationale within which a continuing education program is developed and evaluated typically has three parts — its history, the current demands and constraints, and expectations regarding future developments. If the program to be evaluated is entirely new, it would be helpful just to note what led to establishment of the program. Otherwise, a brief program history might record the number of years that it had been operating, trends in size and emphasis, and major influences that helped or hindered. Current demands and constraints such as legal mandates and budget limits may emanate from the national or community setting of the division or from the sponsoring institution. Community influences include the level of supply and demand of the competence that the program would develop; the competitive position of the program for resources; the relation to the program of preparatory education; and relevant social, economic, and political trends. Institutional influences include the locus of decision making between the division and the remainder of the school system and the competitive position of the program for resources. Expectations regarding future developments may relate to the program itself or to related activities. An example of a program expectation is that the program is a demonstration project in preparation for the development of many similar programs, in comparison with a single course that is to be offered once each year as long as demand warrants. An example of an expectation regarding related activities is that many other continuing education agencies are developing similar courses on a topic that has had a relatively stable demand, in comparison with a course in response to an emerging demand for which the division has unique resources.

If the evaluator has a familiarity with the program rationale, he will be better able to decide on the scale on which the evaluation of the program should be occurring and on the aspects of the program which should receive primary attention. For example, a greater investment in evaluation would be warranted when the program is a demonstration project on a new topic of growing importance than when the program has been offered satisfactorily for years. Also, an understanding of situational demands and constraints may explain limited results that might otherwise be attributed to the performance of learners and teachers. Examples include inadequate published instructional materials or severe budgetary restrictions.

Inputs. This type of program data includes descriptions of both the intended inputs that are planned and the observed inputs that are actually achieved. Part of the evaluation process is a comparison of the description of the intended inputs with a description of the observed inputs to ascertain the extent to which they are congruent. A finding of incongruence would indicate an adjustment in either or both. Four major inputs are learners, teachers, materials, and administrators. Illustrative data regarding learners include the number and their characteristics, such as estimated learning ability, competence related to objectives that the learner has at the outset of the program, educational level, age, occupation, and community size. Illustrative data regarding mentors (persons who participate in the teaching-learning transaction by virtue of their being teachers, counselors, and writers) include the number and their characteristics such as educational level, subject matter competence, experience teaching adults, and teaching style. Illustrative data regarding materials, equipment, and facilities include their availability both in general and to individual learners and the procedures that are used for acquiring or developing them. Illustrative data regarding administrators and support staff include the number and their characteristics such as their previous experience and their relationship with the program development process. In the evaluation process, inputs should be compared with both absolute standards of excellence and similar programs. The resulting analysis can indicate which portion of the outcomes is attributable to the input of resources and which portion is attributable to what is done with them.

Transaction. The teaching-learning transaction includes the activities that produce changes in the learner's knowledge, skills, and attitudes that achieve the educational objectives. Some activities are shared by the teacher and learner, although for some the teacher or the learner works alone reading or writing or working with equipment. Each teaching-learning transaction occurs within one of four settings — individual, temporary group, organizational, and community. The *individual* setting includes correspondence study and ETV courses. The *temporary group* setting includes the typical evening class in which adults without previous contact assemble for the class each week and at the end of the course go their separate ways. The *organizational* setting includes in-service training for work groups in which the prior and subsequent working relationships between the learners have a major influence on the program. The *community* setting emphasizes working relationships between different organizations and segments of a neighborhood or community. Within each of these four settings the balance of responsibility for planning and directing the learning experience may rest with the mentor or with the learner or at some intermediate point of shared responsibility. In combination, these two dimensions of setting and locus of responsibility provide a basis for the classification of types of teaching-learning transactions. One type of program data that should be provided regarding the teaching-learning transaction is a classification regarding setting and balance of responsibility. For programs that include two or more settings, such as a combined correspondence study and evening class, information should be included regarding the amount of time devoted to each segment. Additional information should be collected regarding learner activity, teacher activity, and outside support. Illustrative data regarding learner activity include amount of time spent in each type of activity in a group and hours spent in each type of activity by himself. Illustrative data regarding teacher activity include amount of time spent giving information, obtaining information, and guiding learner search. Illustrative data regarding outside support include contributions by institutional support staff such as a librarian and extent of encouragement by persons in the learner's reference groups, such as an employer or a spouse. In many continuing education programs, the major ways to improve an educational program relate to the teaching-learning transaction. Therefore, a major purpose of program evaluation is to identify aspects of this transaction that can be improved.

Outcomes. The purpose of a continuing education program is to produce the intended outcomes. These outcomes or objectives are typically stated in several stages of impact which serve as the criteria for assessing effectiveness. The more immediate stage describes direct changes in the learner's knowledge, skills, and attitudes. Ways of assessing this change include achievement level on a test, gain in competence from the beginning to the end of a program, performance in a simulated situation, and application in life through change in practices. The more remote stage of outcome is stated as a benefit to the community. As an objective it may relate to specific institutions such as employers, families, or organizations, or it may be more generalized and refer to productivity, economic growth, cultural level, or social participation. This set of variables from individual educational achievement through application, benefit to specific institutions, and generalized benefit to the community constitutes a type of continuum. At the more specifically individual end the emphasis is on the benefits to the individual, and it is somewhat easier to collect valid data. At the more generalized end the emphasis may still be on the benefits to the individual, but it is more difficult to collect valid data. This is partly because of influences other than the educational program, such as opportunities related to neighborhood, ethnic background, or personality. Of special usefulness is performance in a simulated situation such as a driver training car or a computer-based decision-making game. This type of simulation allows the learner to show how he would perform in a real life situation without the distractions of outside influences such as a supervisor who might not allow the learner to try a new practice. One aspect of the evaluation process is to ascertain the extent of congruence between the intended outcomes and the observed outcomes, that is, to discover the extent to which the objectives have been achieved.

In stating the intents of an educational program, the primary test for adequacy is logical contingency. Does it seem reasonable that with the intended inputs the intended transactions could produce the intended outcomes? The primary test in comparing the intended with the observed is congruence. Did they do what they planned? The primary test for the relationships between the observed inputs, transactions, and outcomes is empirical contingency. To what extent did the inputs contribute to the transactions, and the transactions to the outcomes? These six aspects of program evaluation can be compared with two outside standards in the process of making specific judgments regarding effectiveness. One standard is descriptive data from other programs. This yields conclusions such as, the performance in the program being evaluated was better than for half of the similar programs for which evaluation reports are available. Another standard is general hallmarks of excellence, such as the statement that at least 90 percent of the eligible voters should vote in each election. The relationship between these aspects of the program evaluation process is presented schematically in Figure I.

Related Agency Functions

Depending on the aspect of the program that is the focus of evaluation efforts, it is typically necessary to include in the evaluation procedures

FIGURE I.–
PROGRAM EVALUATION PROCESS*

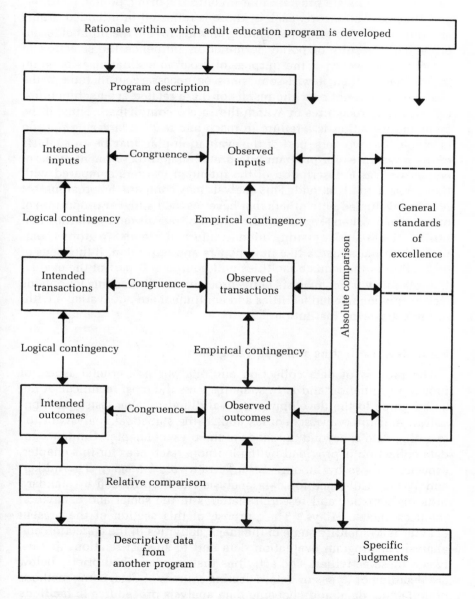

*Adapted from Stake, Robert E. "The Contenuance of Educational Evaluation." *Teachers College Record* 68: 523-540; April 1967.

the collection of data that extend beyond variables that are directly related to the teaching-learning transaction. Examples of these related agency functions are program interpretation, staffing, policy, facilities, and finance. To be sure, each of these is reflected in intended inputs and outcomes. The results of staffing efforts provide the input of teachers and the results of policy formulation influence the selection of objectives. However, if the purpose of program evaluation is program improvement, then it will sometimes be necessary to include in the evaluation plan not only the results of these related agency functions, but also the procedures by which they are accomplished. Thus, if the focus of evaluation is a failure to reach and teach a larger proportion of blue-collar workers, part of the evaluation plan may be an analysis of the procedures for program interpretation and recruitment of learners, as well as a description of the intended learners compared with those who actually attend. This analysis may compare the program that is being evaluated with others that have reached a higher proportion of blue-collar workers, regarding the extent of recruitment activities that utilize face-to-face communication in informal friendship groups compared with mass media like newspapers and television. If the focus of evaluation is inadequate facilities and equipment, part of the evaluation plan may be an analysis of the procedures for arranging for outside facilities when needed facilities and equipment are not available within the sponsoring institution.

Methods of Collecting and Analyzing Data

The process of data collection and analysis is a crucial aspect of program evaluation and is in some respects the most technical. A detailed guide to the development of valid and reliable tests, questionnaires, and interview schedules and to the statistical analysis of the resulting data is beyond the scope of the present chapter. Guidance for data collection is provided by the footnote references for this chapter, especially those by Bloom,[2] Bryn,[3] Krathwohl,[4] Mager,[5] Thorndike,[6] and Webb.[7] Guidance for data analysis can be provided by standard tests on statistics and research methods in the social and behavioral sciences such as Hays.[8] The purpose of this section of the present chapter is to identify some of the major activities in the collection and analysis of program evaluation data and to suggest relationships between these activities. The activities that are described briefly below are deciding on types of data, selecting sources of data, using methods of collecting data, and choosing data analysis procedures to facilitate arriving at conclusions.

Deciding on types of data. In the evaluation of a specific continuing education program, the types of data that should be collected depend very much on the purposes and anticipated use of the results. Those who develop an evaluation plan have many types of potential data from which to select. The most familiar types of data result from the use of verbal paper-and-pencil multiple-choice tests to assess level of knowledge, attitude, and skill. Categories of knowledge objectives along with illustrative test questions are provided by Bloom[9] and comparable materials regarding attitudes are provided by Krathwohl.[10] A comparable taxonomy has been developed recently for skills by Simpson,[11] and there are numerous brief skill tests that have been developed for use in the appraisal of employee aptitudes. Attitude scales and opinion poll questions yield additional types of attitudinal data. In addition to the verbal paper and pencil tests, there are nonverbal tests that are used for assessing ability and achievement in fields such as mathematics, art, music, and use of equipment. The data may focus on the content of the topic being studied or on the process of doing something with the content, such as understanding of relationships or using critical judgment. This type of data may be collected at the beginning and at the end of an educational program to assess progress. In some instances it may be satisfactory to find out afterwards from the learner or from someone close to him such as a supervisor, his opinion of how much was learned. A more convincing but less accessible type of data is based on the ability of the learner to perform either in an actual or a simulated situation. This type of data would typically result from the report or the observation of the learner regarding how well he was able to apply what he learned. Examples include computer programs written following a programing course, skill in play following bridge lessons, reduction in erosion following a soil conservation course, and estate plans prepared following an estate planning course. In some respects, the simulated situation such as the link trainer for pilot training or the computer-based decision-making game for the preparation of administrators provides a more satisfactory basis for assessing the extent to which the course has prepared the learner to apply what he has learned. This is because it eliminates the interference of the actual situation, such as a supervisor who blocks the efforts of the learner to apply ideas gained from a course.

Selecting sources of data. Data should be collected from the most valid sources that are feasible, given the purposes of a specific evaluation plan. Pre- and posttesting of learners provide a more valid indication of learning gain than the opinions of administrators regarding learner progress, but, for some purposes, administrator opinions may be satisfactory. Observations of teaching style and consensus by class members are equivalent sources of data, each of which may be preferable in a specific instance. Both participant observers and outside observers can record information about the teaching-learning transaction. In addition to learners, teachers, administrators, and observers, records provide an important source of data. The records may be agency records such as student registration forms or lists of methods that were used to inform the community about available courses, or community records such as voting figures by precinct or categories of people on welfare or unemployed. The important point is to attempt to collect data from the appropriate source, which depends upon the type of data to be collected and the purposes for which the data are to be collected.

Using methods for collecting data. The most familiar method of collecting evaluation data in preparatory education is the test that is administered under controlled conditions in the classroom. In addition, there are several other major methods of collecting data for continuing education program evaluation. One typical method is the questionnaire or opinionnaire, which may be either signed or anonymous. The signed questionnaire may be necessary when it must be combined with other information for each learner or teacher. If the frank expression of possibly unpopular views is important, the anonymous opinionnaire may be preferable. An intermediate procedure, when it is desirable to combine information that is collected from the same participants on several occasions, is to ask each person to assign a familiar number (such as telephone, social security, license, or house) to the first questionnaire that is completed, and to make a record of the number that was selected so that it can be assigned to the subsequent questionnaires. The following two items illustrate the types of questions that can be included in brief end-of-session opinionnaire forms. Other items might collect data on how time was spent, especially useful ideas that were gained, and suggested program improvements. The tabulations from a session can be compared by the teacher with similar tabulations, and a substantially less positive reaction can be a cue for a more detailed appraisal. For brief evaluation interviews, an interview schedule can be prepared that contains the sequence of questions to be asked, and spaces for the interviewer to record the responses. A similar schedule can be prepared for observers.

1. How important was this subject and discussion topic for you?
   (Check one)   Most important .... 1 ☐
                        Very important .... 2 ☐

Some importance .... 3 ☐
Little importance .... 4 ☐
No importance .... 5 ☐

2. Did the presentations have clear and to the point explanations? (Check one)

Exceptional .... 1 ☐
Very good .... 2 ☐
Good .... 3 ☐
Fair .... 4 ☐
Poor .... 5 ☐

Another method of collecting evaluation data is consulting public records or accessible private records (such as registration forms) that may have been prepared for other purposes but which contain valuable data that can be appropriately used for evaluation purposes. Examples of registration form items include occupational type, educational level, age and experience, and interests related to the program topic. Detailed suggestions for the use of unobtrusive measures are provided by Webb.[12] Again, both desirability and feasibility are criteria in deciding which methods are most appropriate given the types and sources of data to be collected.

Choosing data analysis procedures. The purpose for analyzing the evaluation data that are collected is to be able to draw conclusions from the evidence that can provide a major basis for making judgments regarding program effectiveness and improvement. The elegance of the data analysis procedures that should be used largely depends on the precision of the conclusions to be drawn. A basic analysis procedure is coding, in which someone may read all of the responses to a question and prepare a list of all of the different types of responses that occur. The resulting inductive classification categories can be used to code the original responses for data processing purposes. A similar but more elaborate procedure is content analysis in which a transcript, tape recording, or videotape recording is analyzed regarding the occurrence of predetermined ideas or themes. A standard procedure for presenting coded data or the responses to test or questionnaire questions is the frequency distribution in which the number of persons in each category is noted. It is sometimes helpful also to compute the percentage of persons in each category. The same applies to cross tabulations in which a table is prepared that may, for instance, present the number of persons in each of four age categories who had achieved each of four levels of preparatory education. An illustration of such a table containing both frequency distributions and percentages is presented in Figure 2. When tests or attitude scales are used, it is sometimes necessary to use item analysis and other procedures to increase the reliability and validity

FIGURE II.–
NUMBER AND PERCENTAGE OF CONTINUING EDUCATION
PARTICIPANTS IN FOUR AGE CATEGORIES
WITHIN FOUR EDUCATIONAL LEVELS

AGE	YEARS OF FORMAL EDUCATION								Total No.
	−9		9-11		12		13+		
	No.	Percent	No.	Percent	No.	Percent	No.	Percent	
−25	(2)	20	(4)	20	(8)	16	(3)	12	(17)
25-34	(4)	40	(6)	30	(25)	50	(15)	60	(50)
35-44	(2)	20	(6)	30	(10)	20	(4)	16	(22)
45+	(2)	20	(4)	20	(7)	14	(3)	12	(16)
TOTAL	(10)	100	(20)	100	(50)	100	(25)	100	(105)

of the set of items. In some instances it is important to obtain a more precise understanding of the extent to which distributions of data differ significantly from what would be expected by chance in a larger population. When the data are in table form, significance tests can be used such as Chi Square. When the difference between two distributions is to be tested, a parametric procedure such as analysis of variance or a nonparametric procedure such as Mann-Whitney U can be used. Parametric procedures are appropriate when the distribution is similar to the normal bell-shaped curve, with most persons in the middle of the range and fewer persons at the extremes. Many more elaborate statistical procedures are available for use when warranted, such as the correlation coefficient, which indicates the extent to which a high degree of one variable (such as intelligence) is associated with a second variable (such as achievement). The important point about all of these data analysis procedures is that the purpose is to place the data in a form that will enable the most valid conclusions to be drawn.

Using the Results

The basic criterion for the effectiveness of a plan for continuous program evaluation is the extent to which the results are used. There are several ways in which a director can assist in increasing the likelihood that the results of program evaluation will be used for program improvement.

Validity. The best assurance that evaluation findings will be used is evaluation procedures that are well planned and implemented to produce valid results.

Communication. The results of evaluation efforts should be communicated to those who can use them in a form that they can readily understand. Included here are learner, teacher, administrator, and policy maker.

Commitment. Those who would use the results of evaluation should be sufficiently involved in the evaluation process so that not only are the results valid, but also through involvement they develop a commitment based on understanding. Special efforts may be required to use evaluation findings to justify programs to policy makers such as institutional administrators and boards, legislators, and state education department personnel.

Timing. The evaluation results should reach those who can use them during a time period in which their use is feasible. The ideal time is often just before a decision is to be made. Earlier the results have sometimes not become relevant, and later they are sometimes obsolete.

Implications. The major implications of the findings should be included in both the evaluation report and the discussion of it.

Time. Ways should be found to allocate time for the study and utilization of evaluation findings. This time allocation should be reflected in planning for both program development and staff schedules.

Assistance. Technical assistance should be available for both additional analysis and interpretation of findings.

SUMMARY AND APPLICATION

The application of the foregoing ideas about continuous program evaluation by a director like Victor Balancesheet might proceed in the following way. Imagine that Victor decided to prepare an evaluation plan for just one course and to discuss this plan with the superintendent and several others before proceeding to prepare a plan for a more extensive evaluation of courses in the division. He wanted his preliminary effort to go well because he recognized that the improvement of program evaluation procedures is one of the major ways in which he can help to increase program effectiveness. He felt that it was especially important to develop a feasible evaluation plan and to encourage the use of results to improve the selected course. The course that he selected was one on business law that showed declining initial enrollments in recent years and a high dropout rate. Following is an outline of the kind that Victor Balancesheet might have prepared for his course evaluation plan:

I. *Background regarding the anticipated contribution of evaluation to program improvement*
   A. *Primary purpose of evaluation for this course.* To provide evidence on which to base sound judgment regarding the effectiveness of the course and the reason for the high dropout rate.
   B. *Symptoms that indicated that the existing evaluation procedures were inadequate*
      1. An apparent decline in initial enrollments in recent years, although accurate enrollment records had not been maintained. Enrollments in other business courses were increasing.
      2. A higher dropout rate than for most other courses.
      3. Little information from the teacher, present or former participants, or from employers regarding course effectiveness.
II. *The approach to the evaluation plan*
   A. *Ideas about evaluation to keep in mind*
      1. *Evidence.* Especially if the conclusions indicate that the course should be substantially changed or dropped, or that the current instructor should not be rehired, then the evidence on which the decision is based should be convincing to those affected.
      2. *Benefits.* The cost in time and money should be justified by the anticipated benefits of the program evaluation.
      3. *Frequency.* Existing evaluation data for the course are sparse. The results of moderate evaluation procedures should indicate which data to collect each term, which data to collect in a more detailed study in a year or two, and which data do not appear relevant.
      4. *Feedback.* The evaluation plan should provide for feedback of appropriate information to learners, teacher, and to the administrator.
      5. *Commitment.* The way in which the evaluation procedures are conducted should encourage the instructor to use the results constructively to improve the course, if possible. This suggests that he should become involved in the planning and conducting of the evaluation procedures as soon as possible.
      6. *Objectivity.* It might be helpful to have someone skilled in program evaluation from outside the division assist in conducting the evaluation.
      7. *Objectives.* An early step should be the preparation of a

clear set of objectives that describe what the learners should know, feel, and be able to do at the conclusion of the course if it is successful. These objectives will provide a basis for assessing effectiveness.

8. *Standards.* It would be useful to obtain descriptions of similar courses in similar institutions and communities, with an indication of enrollment trends, dropout rates, and major outcomes.

9. *Relevance.* Care should be taken to collect data relevant to what the teacher is attempting to accomplish and to the course objectives.

10. *Values.* In arriving at conclusions, value judgments should be identified, and an effort should be made to achieve consensus on the conclusions and next steps by those who are affected.

B. *Types of evaluation data to be collected*

1. *Rationale regarding the setting of the course.* The course has been offered in the division about once a year for about 20 years. It has usually been taught by the person who also teaches it in the daytime for the preparatory education students. The participants have been young adults entering the business field. Outside governmental funds reimburse the division for part of the costs. Employers in the community have indicated that such a course is useful to their personnel development efforts and should continue to be in the future.

2. *Inputs.* The most readily specified input is the teacher who has taught the course during the past two years since he started teaching. There is little information on hand about the characteristics of the learners or of the instructional materials.

3. *Transaction.* The instructional setting consists of a two-hour class session once a week for 12 weeks, plus homework. It would seem useful to find out how teacher and learners spend their time related to the program.

4. *Outcomes.* There appear to be no statements of intended outcomes, beyond the broad course purpose of teaching principles of business law. It is assumed that teacher and learners could identify the objectives that are implicit in the current course. One intended outcome seems to be to assist employers in personnel development.

C. *Functions of the division that may relate to course effectiveness.* It would appear that the functions that might be related to course effectiveness are publicizing courses, working relationships between the division and employers, and procedures for staff selection and supervision.

D. *Probable methods of data collection and analysis*

1. *Types of data.* Primarily factual information about personal characteristics and course procedures, opinions regarding course objectiveness and effectiveness, and test results regarding learner achievement.

2. *Sources of data.* At this stage, the data would be collected primarily from teacher, current participants, and former participants (separated by those who completed the course and those who dropped out).

3. *Methods of collecting data.* An informal interview with the teacher and an anonymous opinionnaire for participants.

4. *Data analysis procedures.* The forms would be tabulated separately for the teacher and the three categories of participants.

E. *Using the results.* The following procedures will be employed to increase the likelihood that the findings will be used.

1. *Validity.* Working closely with both the teacher and the outside evaluation specialist should increase the validity of the findings.

2. *Communication.* Make sure that the teacher is involved or informed at each step of the process.

3. *Commitment.* Endeavor to establish and maintain the constructive interest of the teacher in the process.

4. *Timing.* Plan to complete the project so that the results can contribute to planning for next year.

5. *Implication.* Include implications for action in the report.

6. *Time.* Recognize the extra time that the teacher and participants will be spending on the evaluation process.

7. *Assistance.* Make provision for the needed technical assistance for designing evaluation procedures and data processing.

The foregoing outline of an evaluation plan would provide a starting point for Victor's conversation with the superintendent. It is likely that the plan would be modified substantially after conversations with the superintendent, the teacher of the business law course, and an outside evaluation specialist. Information gained in the early stages of the process would contribute to detailed planning of later stages. If all goes well with the course evaluation, Victor would probably explore with his teachers the points at which more widespread evaluation procedures would be most useful. In this way, over several years, it would be possible to set up procedures for continuous program evaluation that would contribute to the achievement of increasingly effective programs of continuing education for adults.

A LOOK AHEAD—PATTERNS AND TRENDS

This, then, is continuing adult education today—a natural growth of what adult education was yesterday. It is a confusing mixture of both raw and well-worn programs, of separate and overlapping programs, of programs that work together and programs that work at cross-purposes. It is a mixture of adults who are scarcely students and of students who are scarcely adults. It is a mixture of education for jobs that are disappearing and for jobs yet to appear. All of this may appear to be a swirling maelstrom through which the adult educator can pick his way only with difficulty. Certain strengths, however, are emerging from this mixture.

First, adult educators now talk less about operating on a "fourth level" of education that is unrelated to elementary, secondary, and higher education and, instead, strive to closely coordinate their educational efforts with those of their colleagues on other levels of education. Increasingly, the goal is to build programs which provide useful educational experiences for a continuation onward from whatever level at which the adult may have discontinued formal schooling.

Second, there is a steadily increasing awareness on the part of both school authorities and the general public that a closer relationship must exist between the school dropout and his opportunities for a "second chance" education. What was once an "it's too bad it has to happen" attitude on the part of schoolmen and community leaders toward the dropout has, over the years, changed first to a serious endeavor to improve the holding power of the school and then broadened to include cooperative programing on the part of secondary school officials and of adult education in behalf of both the potential and actual dropout.

Translated into curriculum terms this means that our present concept of literacy is being revised; it is generally understood within the education profession and among members of the general public as a capability of an individual to become a responsible member of the community, a productive worker, and a successful participant in family life experiences. In most cases, this modern literacy level is understood to be at least a high school education or its equivalent.

Third, school superintendents, community college presidents, and their board members are showing an increasing awareness of and commitment to continuing adult education. Recognizing a need for more community and individual development programs, they are showing a growing acceptance of the necessity of employing well trained men. With this acceptance of the responsibility for providing adequate leadership there comes a concomitant realization that a whole range of supportive services is called for, each of which makes some contribution to a needed redefinition of the adult program director's role.

Fourth, the role of the director of public adult education has been evolving for more than a century, and interacting forces assure that the process will accelerate. Community and legislative leaders will continue to see adult education as a positive response to social ills and they will provide financial support in increasing quantities for public education programs to alleviate those ills. Adult program and community service directors, because they stand to gain or lose more than any other group, are demonstrating an active concern in the redefinition of their role. By their efforts to set academic standards for their profession; by their development of criteria to judge the adequacy of programs; by their growing commitment to adult education as a profession rather than a stepping-stone; by their willingness to try new approaches; by their acceptance of the posture of a leader rather than simply a manager; by their efforts to overcome any parochial single-institutional viewpoint; by their acceptance of responsibility for influencing the drafting, passage, and interpretation of adult education legislation; and by their eagerness to work with adult educators from a variety of institutions, they have shown that they intend to play a major part in this redefinition.

Today more than ever before resources are being made available to adult education leaders who have visions of new and increasingly effective institutional forms and programs. Now in the last third of the twentieth century, the opportunities for professional adult educators as active community change agents have never been brighter. ONLY TIME WILL TELL IF ADULT DIRECTORS HAVE BEEN EQUAL TO THE CHALLENGE.

APPENDIX A

FOOTNOTE REFERENCES

CHAPTER 2

1. National Education Association, Research Division. *Opinions of School Superintendents on Adult Education.* Research Report 1964-R4. Washington, D. C.: the Association, 1964. p. 8.

2. National Education Association, *op. cit.,* p. 9.

3. Harris, Norman C. *Technical Education in the Junior College/ New Programs and New Jobs.* Washington, D. C.: American Association of Junior Colleges, 1964. p. 27.

4. Kerner, Otto, and others. *Report of the National Advisory Commission on Civil Disorders.* New York: Bantam Books, 1968. 608 pp.

5. McClusky, Howard. "The Educative Community." *The Community School and Its Administration.* Midland, Mich.: Mott Program of the Flint Board of Education. Vol. 5, No. 9. May 1967.

6. Kerner and others, *op. cit.*

CHAPTER 3

1. Johnstone, John W. C., and Rivera, Ramon J. *Volunteers for Learning: A Study of the Educational Pursuits of American Adults.* Chicago: Aldine Publishing Co., 1965. 624 pp.

2. Johnstone and Rivera, *op. cit.,* p. 61. Adapted from Table 3, 14: "Estimates of Courses Attended at Different Sponsoring Institutions."

3. Adapted from Macomb Association of School Administrators. *Macomb Occupational Education Survey.* Warren, Mich.: the Association, 1966. p. 132.

4. American Library Association. *Libraries and Adult Education.* New York: Macmillan Co., 1926. p. 9.

5. Johnstone and Rivera, *op. cit.*

6. Houle, Cyril. "Development of Leadership." *Liberal Adult Education.* White Plains, N.Y.: Fund for Adult Education, n.d. p. 58.

7. Kleis, Russell J., editor. *An Area Approach to Continuing Education.* East Lansing: Educational Publication Services, Michigan State University, 1967.

CHAPTER 4

1. Johnstone, John W. C., and Rivera, Ramon J. *Volunteers for Learning: A Study of the Educational Pursuits of American Adults.* Chicago: Aldine Publishing Co., 1965. p. 61.

2. Olds, Edward B. *Financing Adult Education in America's Public Schools and Community Councils.* Washington, D. C.: National Commission on Finance, Adult Education Association of the U.S.A., 1954. p. 16.

3. Woodward, Marthine V., and Mason, Ward S. *Statistics of Public School Adult Education.* U. S. Office of Education Circular No. 660. Washington, D. C.: Government Printing Office, 1961. p. 22.

4. Dorland, James M., and Baber, Gaye M., editors. *Public School Adult Education Program Study.* Washington, D. C.: National Association for Public School Adult Education, a department of the National Education Association, 1967. p. ii.

5. National Education Association, Research Division. *Opinions of School Superintendents on Adult Education.* Research Report 1964-R4. Washington, D. C.: the Association, 1964. pp. 6, 9.

6. Kempfer, Homer. *Adult Education.* New York: McGraw-Hill Book Co., 1955. p. 293.

7. Chase, Francis S. "School Changes in Perspective." *The Changing American School.* (Edited by John I. Goodlad.) Sixty-Fifth Yearbook, Part II, National Society for the Study of Education. Chicago: University of Chicago Press, 1966. pp. 305-306.

8. Lee, Gordon C. "The Changing Role of the Teacher." *The Changing American School.* (Edited by John I. Goodlad.) Sixty-Fifth Yearbook, Part II, National Society for the Study of Education. Chicago: University of Chicago Press, 1966. p. 29.

9. *Ibid.,* p. 22.

10. See National Association of Public School Adult Educators. *Adult Education in the Public Schools.* Statement by a Joint Committee of the American Association of School Administrators, Council of Chief State School Officers, National Association of Public School Adult Educators, and National Congress of Parents and Teachers. Washington, D. C.: the Association, a department of the National Education Association, 1961.

American Association of School Administrators and National Association for Public School Adult Education. *Impact.* A brochure published as part of a project to advance public school adult education supported by the Fund for Adult Education. Washington, D. C.: the Associations, departments of the National Education Association, 1964.

Regional Committee on Adult Education of the American Association of School Administrators. *Now . . . In Our Time.* Washington, D. C.: the Association, a department of the National Education Association, and the Institute for Adult Education, Teachers College, Columbia University, 1945.

11. Bailey, Thomas D. *The School Administrator's Responsibility for Providing an Adequate Program of Continuing Education.* Official Report, 1959. Washington, D. C.: American Association of School Administrators, a department of the National Education Association, 1960. p. 202.

12. See Luke, Robert A. "What Is So Different About the Secondary Curriculum for Adults?" *Bulletin of the National Association of Secondary School Principals* 49: 196-202; March 1965.

Martin, Arthur G. "What Educational Opportunities Can the School Offer to Adults in the Community?" *Bulletin of the National Association of Secondary School Principals* 40: 238-40; April 1956.

13. Hoffman, Fred W. "Personnel Services for Adults." *Bulletin of the National Association of Secondary School Principals* 52: 60-61; January 1968.

14. North Central Association of Colleges and Secondary Schools, Criteria Revision Committee. *Proposed Policies and Criteria for the Approval of Secondary Schools.* Chicago: the Association, May 1968. pp. 41-42.

15. Mueller, Felix. "A Report on an Adult Education Program." *Continuous Learning* 6: 119-24; May-June 1967.

16. Curtis, B. E. "Public Responsibility and the School Trustee." *Continuous Learning* 4: 90-92; March-April 1965.

17. Des Champs, Allen. "The Role of School Boards in Continuing Education." *Continuous Learning* 4: 261-67; November-December 1965.

18. Griffith, William S. "Public School Adult Education – A Growing Challenge." *Administrator's Notebook* 13: 4; March 1965. (Chicago: Midwest Administration Center, University of Chicago.)

19. Clark, Burton R. *Adult Education in Transition.* University of California Publications in Sociology and Social Institutions, Vol. 1, No. 2. Berkeley: University of California Press, 1958. p. 60.

20. London, Jack. "The Career of the Public School Adult Administrator." *Adult Education* 10: 5; Autumn 1959.

21. Clark, Burton R., *loc. cit.*

22. London, Jack, *loc. cit.*

23. Griffith, William S., and others. *Public School Adult Education in Northern Illinois.* Circular Series A-192. Springfield, Ill.: Office of the Superintendent of Public Instruction, 1966. p. 41.

24. "A profession is a specialized, high-status career which serves a socially acceptable function of benefit to society by means of a theoretical body of knowledge and an esoteric technique and terminology which have been secured through a long, extensive period of formal training, and for the skillful application of which the professional person receives remuneration. It is composed of autonomous practitioners who, subject to various controls by the state and/or a professional association, administer their services in such a manner that the client's interests are placed above and before those of the professional, and abide by a code of ethics enforced by the professional organization to protect the public interests."

Allen, Lawrence A. *The Growth of Professionalism in the Adult Educational Movement, 1928-1958, A Content Analysis of the Periodical Literature.* Doctoral dissertation. Chicago: Department of Education, University of Chicago, 1961. p. 20.

25. Luke, Robert A. "What Is So Different About the Secondary School Curriculum for Adults?" Address given at the annual convention of the National Association of Secondary School Principals, Miami Beach, Fla., January 17, 1965. p. 9. (Mimeo.)

26. Spalding, Willard B. *The Superintendency of Public Schools—An Anxious Profession.* Cambridge: Harvard University Press, 1954. p. 1.

27. Griffith and others, *op. cit.,* p. 39.

28. Committee on Evaluation and Professional Standards. "Professional Standards for Administrators of Public School Adult Education Programs." *Public School Adult Education 1967 Almanac.* Washington, D. C.: National Association for Public School Adult Education, a department of the National Education Association, 1967. p. 15.

29. Griffith and others, *op. cit.,* p. 42.

30. Ingham, Roy J. *An Addendum to the Preliminary Report on "A Comparative Study of Graduate Programs in Adult Education."* Tallahassee: Department of Adult and Continuing Education, Florida State University, 1967. Table I. (Mimeo.)

31. Griffith and others, *op. cit.,* p. 47.

32. *Ibid.*

33. Xerox Corporation, Special Projects Section. *Federally-Funded Adult Basic Education Programs: A Study of Adult Basic Education Programs in Ten States.* New York: the Section, June 1967. p. 227.

34. Griffith and others, *op. cit.,* pp. 33, 37.

35. *Ibid.,* pp. 75-76.

36. Gordon, Paul J. "Objectives for Education in Administration." *Management International Review* 7: 27; 1967.

37. *Ibid.,* pp. 29-30.

38. Erickson, Donald A. "The School Administrator." *Review of Educational Research* 37: 420; October 1967.

39. Essert, Paul L., and Repole, Frank R. "The Adult Education Administrator." *Public School Adult Education, A Guide For Administrators and Teachers.* Washington, D. C.: National Association of Public School Adult Educators, a department of the National Education Association, 1956. pp. 144-45.

Mann, George C.; Essert, Paul L.; and Repole, Frank R. "The Administration of Adult Education." *Public School Adult Education, A Guide for Administrators.* (Edited by John H. Thatcher.) Revised edition. Washington, D. C.; National Association of Public School Adult Educators, a department of the National Education Association, 1963. pp. 33-36.

40. Committee on Evaluation and Professional Standards, *op. cit.,* pp. 15-18.

41. Lipham, James M. "Leadership and Administration." *Behavioral Science and Educational Administration.* Sixty-Third Yearbook, Part II, National Society For the Study of Education. (Edited by Daniel E. Griffiths.) Chicago: University of Chicago Press, 1964. p. 122.

42. *Ibid.*

43. *Ibid.*

44. *Ibid.*

45. Harlacher, Ervin L. *Effective Junior College Programs of Community Service: Rationale, Guidelines, Practices.* Occasional Report No. 10. Los Angeles: Junior College Leadership Program, School of Education, University of California, 1967. p. 23.

46. *Ibid.,* p. 14.

47. *Ibid.,* p. 19.

48. Gleazer, Edmund J., Jr., and Houts, Paul L., editors. *American Junior Colleges.* Seventh edition. Washington, D. C.: American Council on Education, 1967. p. 32.

CHAPTER 5

1. Miner, Jerry. "Financial Support of Education." *Designing Education for the Future, No. 2: Implications for Education of Prospective Changes in Society.* (Edited by Edgar L. Morphet and Charles O. Ryan.) Denver: Designing Education for the Future, an Eight-State Project, 1967. Chapter 16, p. 317.

2. *Ibid.,* p. 318.

3. California Bureau of Adult Education. *Handbook of Adult Education in California.* Sacramento: State Department of Education, 1966. p. 45.

4. Sworder, Stanley, chief, Bureau of Adult Education, California State Department of Education.

5. National Association for Public School Adult Education. *National Association for Public School Adult Education 1968 Almanac.* Washington, D. C.: the Association, a department of the National Education Association, 1968. pp. 15-23.

6. California Bureau of Adult Education, *op. cit.,* pp. 25-34.

7. "Recommendations for Improving Federal Grants to Public Schools." Prepared by the Joint Committee on Federal Aid to Education Consultant Erick Lindman, professor of education, UCLA—CASA, CASSA, CESAA, CAAEA, CAPSBO.

8. Brunner, Edmund deS., and others. *An Overview of Adult Education Research.* Chicago: Adult Education Association of the U.S.A., 1959. p. 116.

9. Kempfer, Homer. "Financing Adult Education." *Public School Adult Education: A Guide for Administrators.* (Edited by John H. Thatcher.) Washington, D. C.: National Association of Public School Adult Educators, a department of the National Education Association, 1963. p. 44.

10. Campbell, Alan K. "Financing Education: Matching Resources to Needs." Paper presented to the National Conference of State Legislators, sponsored by the National Conference for Support of Public Schools. December 5, 1966. p. 1.

11. National Education Association, Research Division. *Opinions of School Superintendents on Adult Education.* Research Report 1964-R4. Washington, D. C.: the Association, 1964. pp. 15-17.

12. See NAPSAE's *Public School Adult Education: A Guide for Administrators,* 1963 edition.

13. Miner, *loc. cit.*

14. Bell, Wilmer V. "Finance, Legislation, and Public Policy for Adult Education." *Handbook of Adult Education in the United States.* (Edited by Malcolm S. Knowles.) Chicago: Adult Education Association of the U.S.A., 1960. Chapter 12, p. 138.

15. Shetler, Richard L. "Major Problems of Society in 1980." *Designing Education for the Future, No. 1: Prospective Changes in Society by 1980.* (Edited by Edgar L. Morphet and Charles O. Ryan.) New York: Citation Press, 1967. Chapter 16, p. 266.

16. "Inquir," Demonstration Data File with Computer-Assisted Instructions in Its Use, prepared by Frank A. Yett, chairman, Computer Sciences Department, Pasadena City College.

17. "Operating Personnel Information System" by Robert L. Griner, administrative analyst, Controlling Division, Los Angeles City Schools.

18. Weller, George A., account representative, International Business Machines Corporation.

19. McMullen, George, administrative coordinator, Budget Division, Los Angeles City Schools.

20. "Inquir," *loc. cit.*

21. Southern California Research Council. *Crisis in School Finance, the Next Ten Years in Southern California.* Report No. 14. Los Angeles: Occidental College, 1966. p. 31.

22. *Ibid.,* p. 34.

23. Shetler, *op. cit.,* pp. 261-68.

24. Southern California Research Council, *op. cit.,* p. 10.

25. *Ibid.,* p. 267.

CHAPTER 6

1. National Association of Public School Adult Education. *Public School Adult Education 1968 Almanac.* Washington, D. C.: the Association, a department of the National Education Association, 1968. 158 pp.

2. Public Law 87-415; Title II, Part A, Section 202(1); Manpower Development and Training Act of 1962.

3. Public Law 88-210; Part A, Section I; Vocational Education Act of 1963.

4. Public Law 88-452; Title II B, Section 212; Economic Opportunity Act of 1964.

5. Public Law 89-329; Title I, Section 102; Higher Education Act of 1965.

6. Public Law 89-754; Statement of Purpose, Demonstration Cities and Metropolitan Development Act of 1966.

CHAPTER 7

1. Lindeman, Edward C. *The Community.* New York: Association Press, 1921. pp. 1-10.

2. McClenhan, Bessie Averne. "The Nature of a Community." *How To Know and How To Use Your Community.* Washington, D. C.: Department of Elementary School Principals, National Education Association, 1942. p. 14.

3. Hart, Joseph K. *Community Organization.* New York: Macmillan Co., 1927. p. 3.

4. Hillery, George A., Jr. "Definitions of Community: Areas of Agreement." *Rural Sociology* 20: 111-23; June 1955.

5. Lindeman, Edward C. "Community." *Encyclopedia of the Social Sciences* 4: 102-105; 1948.

6. *Ibid.*, p. 103.

7. Stroup, Herbert Hewitt. *Community Welfare Organizations.* New York: Harper and Brothers, 1952. p. 7.

8. *Ibid.*, p. 9.

9. Park, Robert Ezra. *Human Communities.* Glencoe, Ill.: Free Press, 1952. p. 13.

10. Tönnies, Ferdinand. *Fundamental Concepts of Sociology.* (Translated by Charles P. Loomis.) New York: American Book Co., 1940.

11. Hobbes, Thomas. *Leviathan.* Oxford: Clarendon Press. 1909. p. 132.

12. Homans, George C. *The Human Group.* New York: Harcourt, Brace and Co., 1950. p. 317.

13. *Ibid.*, pp. 319-20.

14. Bernard, Jessie. *American Community Behavior.* New York: Dryden Press, 1949. p. 558.

15. *Ibid.*, pp. 558-59.

16. Hart, Joseph K. *Adult Education.* New York: Thomas Y. Crowell Co., 1927. pp. 82-83.

17. *Ibid.*, p. 294.

18. Llao, Ken Kwei. *The Individual and the Community.* London: Kegan, Paul, Trench, Trubner and Co., 1933. p. 2.

19. *Ibid.*, p. 1.

20. See Taylor, Griffith. *Urban Geography.* New York: E. P. Dutton and Co., 1946.

21. See Harris, Chauncey. "A Functional Classification of Cities in the United States." *Geographical Review* 33: 86-99; 1943.

22. Kinneman, John A. *The Community in American Society.* New York: F. S. Crofts and Co., 1947. pp. 18-35.

23. Melby, Ernest O. "Education and the Defense of America." *Saturday Review of Literature* 33: 48; September 9, 1950.

24. Biddle, William W. *The Cultivation of Community Leaders.* New York: Harper and Brothers, 1953. p. 45.

25. Rogers, Maria. "Autonomous Groups and Adult Education." *Adult Education Journal* 6: 177; October 1947.

26. Doddy, Hurley H. *Informal Groups and the Community.* New York: Bureau of Publications, Teachers College, Columbia University, 1952. p. 32.

27. See references for this Chapter in Appendix B.

28. For a more definitive breakdown of each element, see Hand, Samuel E. *An Outline of a Community Survey for Program Planning in Adult Education.* Bulletin No. 71F-2. Revised. Tallahassee: State Department of Education, 1968.

CHAPTER 8

1. Johnson, Lyndon B. Address given at the annual conference of the American Association of School Administrators, a department of the National Education Association, Atlantic City, New Jersey, February 16, 1966.

2. Goodlad, John I. *School, Curriculum, and the Individual.* Waltham, Mass: Blaisdell Publishing Co., 1966. p. 125.

3. Hott, Leland, and Sonstegard, Manford. "Relating Self-Conception to Curriculum Development." *Journal of Education Research* 58: 348-51; April 1965.

4. Spencer, Herbert. "What Knowledge Is of Most Worth?" *Education.* New York: Appleton, 1960.

5. Commission on the Reorganization of Secondary Education. "The Cardinal Principles of Secondary Education." *Bureau of Education Bulletin* 35, 1918.

6. National Education Association, Educational Policies Commission. *The Purposes of Education in American Democracy.* Washington, D. C.: the Commission, 1938.

7. French, Will, and Ransom, William L. "Evaluating the Curriculum for Meeting the Imperative Needs of Youth." *NASSP Bulletin* 32: 48-49; April 1948.

8. Havighurst, Robert J. *Developmental Tasks and Education.* First edition. Chicago: University of Chicago Press, 1948.

9. *A Report to the President.* Washington, D. C.: Government Printing Office, 1956.

10. Bloom, Benjamin S. *Taxonomy of Educational Objectives.* New York: David McKay Co., 1956.

11. American Association of School Administrators, Council of Chief State School Officers, National Association for Public School Adult Education, and National Congress of Parents and Teachers. *Adult Education in the Public Schools.* Washington, D. C.: the Association, a department of the National Education Association, 1961.

12. Havighurst, Robert J. *Developmental Tasks and Education.* Second edition. New York: David McKay Co., 1952. 100 pp.

13. Houle, Cyril O. *The Inquiring Mind.* Madison: University of Wisconsin Press, 1961. p. 87.

14. Kempfer, Homer H. *Identifying Educational Needs of Adults.* U. S. Office of Education, Federal Security Agency, Circular No. 330, 1951. Washington, D. C.: Superintendent of Documents, Government Printing Office, 1951. p. 64.

15. Goodlad, John I. "The Educational Program to 1980 and Beyond." *Designing Education for the Future, No. 2: Implications for Education of Prospective Changes in Society.* (Edited by Edgar L. Morphet and Charles O. Ryan.) Denver: Designing Education for the Future, an Eight-State Project, 1967. pp. 48-49.

16. Johnstone, John W. C. *Sociological Backgrounds of Adult Education.* Chicago: Center for the Study of Liberal Education for Adults, 1964. 126 pp.

CHAPTER 11

1. Fried, Barbara. *The Middle-Age Crisis.* New York: Harper & Row, 1967.

2. Blair, Glenn Myers; Jones, R. Stewart; and Simpson, Ray H. *Educational Psychology.* Second edition. New York: Macmillan Co., 1962. p. 168.

3. Kuhlen, Raymond G., editor. *Psychological Backgrounds of Adult Education.* Papers presented at a Syracuse University Conference. Chicago: Center for the Study of Liberal Education for Adults, 1963. 148 pp.

4. Erikson, Erik H. *Childhood and Society.* Second edition. New York: W. W. Norton and Co., 1963. pp. 266-68.

5. Fried, Barbara, *op. cit.,* p. 116.

6. Erikson, Erik H., *op. cit.,* p. 266.

7. Pearl, Arthur, and Riessman, Frank. *New Careers for the Poor: The Nonprofessional in Human Service.* New York: Free Press, 1965. 273 pp.

8. Kerner, Otto, and others. *Report of the National Advisory Commission on Civil Disorders.* New York: Bantam Books, 1968. p. 2.

9. Blair, Jones, and Simpson, *op. cit.,* p. 208.

10. U. S. Department of Commerce, Bureau of the Census. *U. S. Censuses of Population and Housing: 1960.* Washington, D. C.: Government Printing Office, 1961.

11. Harrington, Michael. *The Other America: Poverty in the United States.* New York: Macmillan Co., 1962. 191 pp.

12. U. S. Department of Labor. *The Negro Family.* Washington, D. C.: Government Printing Office, 1965.

13. May, Edgar. *The Wasted Americans.* New York: Harper & Row, 1965. 227 pp.

14. Kerner and others, *op. cit.*

15. Verner, Coolie, and Newberry, John S., Jr. "The Nature of Adult Participation." *Participants in Adult Education.* Washington, D. C.: Adult Education Association of the U.S.A., 1965.

16. Harrington, Michael, *op. cit.*, p. 185.

17. *Ibid.*, p. 185.

18. Kerner and others, *op. cit.*, p. 175.

19. Myrdal, Gunnar. *An American Dilemma: The Negro Problem and Modern Democracy.* New York: Harper & Row, 1962. 1,483 pp.

CHAPTER 14

1. Roberts, T. Hewiston, director of Adult Education, Western Australia University, Perth—formerly professor of Adult Education, University of Iowa, Iowa City.

2. Overstreet, Harry A., and Overstreet, Bonaro W. *Leaders for Adult Education.* New York: American Association for Adult Education, 1941. 202 pp.

3. California State Department of Education. *Development of Adult Education in California.* Bulletin Vol. 22, No. 6. Sacramento: the Department, June 1953. p. 68.

4. National Association for Public School Adult Education. "Teacher-Student Relationships." *Techniques for Teachers of Adults.* Vol. 1, No. 2. Washington, D. C.: the Association, a department of the National Education Association, October 1960. 4 pp.

5. National Association for Public School Adult Education. *Adult Basic Education, A Guide for Teachers and Teacher Trainers.* Washington, D. C.: the Association, a department of the National Education Association, May 1966. pp. II 16-II 17.

6. Redfield, Robert. *The Educational Experience.* Pasadena: Fund for Adult Education, 1955. p. 41.

7. McClusky, Howard. *Handbook of Adult Education in the United States.* (Edited by Malcolm S. Knowles.) Chicago: Adult Education Association of the U.S.A., 1960. p. 419.

CHAPTER 16

1. Knowles, Malcolm S. "Background Historical Development." *Handbook of Adult Education in the United States.* (Edited by Malcolm S. Knowles.) Chicago: Adult Education Association of the U.S.A., 1960. p. 25.

2. Essert, Paul L. "A Proposed New Program in Adult Education." *Adult Education* 10: 131-40; Spring 1960.

3. Thorndike, Edward L., and others. *Adult Learning.* New York: Macmillan Co., 1928. pp. 177-78.

4. Rhyne, Dwight C. "Variations on a Theme by Thorndike." *Adult Education* 12: 91-97; Winter 1962.

5. Hafter, Irma T. "The Comparative Academic Achievement of Women." *Adult Education* 12: 106-15; Winter 1962.

6. Morgan, Barton; Holmes, Glen; and Bundy, Clarence. *Methods in Adult Education.* Danville, Ill.: Interstate Printers & Publishers, 1960. pp. 14-18.

7. Gibb, Jack R. "Learning Theory in Adult Education." *Handbook of Adult Education in the United States.* (Edited by Malcolm S. Knowles.) Chicago: Adult Education Association of the U.S.A., 1960. pp. 54-64.

8. Siegal, Peter E. "The Adult Learner." *Leader's Digest* 3: 11-13; 1956.

9. Powell, J. W. *Learning Comes of Age.* New York: Association Press, 1956. p. 15.

10. *Ibid.*, p. 257.

11. Knowles, Malcolm S. *Informal Adult Education.* New York: Association Press, 1950. p. 52.

12. *Ibid.*, p. 33.

13. Neff, Monroe C. *Adult Basic Education Seminar Guide, A Study Program for Teacher Training.* Chicago: Follett Publishing Co., 1966. pp. 103-105, 118-19, 127-28.

14. Bigge, Morris L., and Hunt, Maurice P. *Psychological Foundations of Education.* New York: Harper and Brothers, 1962. p. 256.

15. Neff, Monroe C. *A Study of Liberal Adult Education Discussion Groups in Wyoming.* Doctor's thesis. Laramie: University of Wyoming, 1964. pp. 44-51.

16. Sheats, Paul H.; Jayne, Clarence D.; and Spence, Ralph B. *Adult Education: The Community Approach.* New York: Dryden Press, 1953. p. 328.

17. Stovall, T. F. "Lecture vs. Discussion." *Social Education,* January 1956. pp. 10-12.

18. Knowles, Malcolm S., and Bradford, Leland P. "Group Methods in Adult Education." *Journal of Social Issues* 3:11-21; 1952.

19. Johnstone, John W. C., and Rivera, Ramon J., *Volunteers for Learning: A Study of the Educational Pursuits of American Adults.* Chicago: Aldine Publishing Co., 1963. p. 88.

20. *Ibid.*, p. 51.

21. Eglash, Albert. "A Group Discussion Method of Teaching Psychology." *Journal of Educational Psychology,* May 1954. pp. 257-67.

22. Deignan, Francis James. "A Comparison of the Effectiveness of Two Group Discussion Methods." Doctor's thesis. Boston: School of Education, Boston University, 1955. *Microfilm Abstracts,* pp. 1110-11, 1956.

23. Bond, Betty Wells. "The Group Discussion—Decision Approach—An Appraisal of Its Use in Health Education." Doctor's thesis. Minneapolis: University of Minnesota, 1955. *Microfilm Abstracts,* pp. 903-904, 1956.

24. Welch, John M., and Verner, Coolie. "A Study of Two Methods for the Diffusion of Knowledge." *Adult Education* 12: 231-36; Summer 1962.

CHAPTER 17

1. Good, Carter V. *Essentials of Educational Research.* New York: Appleton-Century-Crofts, 1966. p. 2.

2. Good, Carter V., and Scates, Douglas E. *Methods of Research: Educational, Psychological, Sociological.* New York: Appleton-Century-Crofts, 1954. p. 11.

3. Smith, Henry L., and Smith, Johnny R. *An Introduction to Research in Evaluation.* Bloomington, Ind.: Educational Publications, 1959. p. 7.

4. Corey, Stephen M. *Action Research To Improve School Practice.* New York: Teachers College, Columbia University, 1953. p. 4.

5. Knox, Alan B. *Research Arrangements Within University Adult Education Divisions.* Chicago: Center for the Study of Liberal Education for Adults, 1963.

Office of Economic Opportunity. *Catalog of Federal Assistance Programs.* Washington, D. C.: the Office, June 1, 1967.

Adult Education Association of the U.S.A. *Federal Support for Adult Education, A Directory of Programs and Services.* Washington, D. C.: the Association, 1966.

6. Galfo, Armand J., and Miller, Earl. *Interpreting Education Research.* Dubuque, Iowa: Wm. C. Brown Co., 1965. 369 pp.

7. Wandt, Edwin. *A Cross-Section of Educational Research.* New York: David McKay Co., 1965. 301 pp.

8. Draper, James A. "A Proposal for Systematically Collecting and Reporting Research Relating to Adult Education in Canada." *Continous Learning* 6: 211-14; September-October 1967.

9. Brunner, Edmund de S., and others. *An Overview of Adult Education Research.* Chicago: Adult Education Association of the U.S.A., 1959. 275 pp.

10. Knowles, Malcolm S., editor. *Handbook of Adult Education in the United States.* Chicago: Adult Education Association of the U.S.A., 1960. 640 pp.

11. Jensen, Gale; Liveright, A. A.; and Hallenbeck, W., editors. *Adult Education: Outlines of an Emerging Field of University Study.* Chicago: Adult Education Association of the U.S.A., 1964. 334 pp.

12. Hare, A. Paul. *Handbook of Small Group Research.* New York: Free Press, 1962. 512 pp.

13. Berelson, Bernard, and Steiner, Gary A. *Human Behavior.* New York: Harcourt, Brace, and World, 1964. 712 pp.

14. Gage, N. L. *Handbook on Research in Teaching.* Chicago: Rand-McNally, 1963. 1,218 pp.

15. Pressey, S. L., and Kuhlen, R. G. *Psychological Development Through the Life Span.* New York: Harper and Brothers, 1957. 654 pp.

16. Botwinick, J. *Cognitive Processes in Maturity and Old Age.* New York: Springer Publishing Co., 1967. 212 pp.

17. National Society for the Study of Education. *The Psychology of Learning.* Forty-First Yearbook, Part II. Chicago: the Society, 1942.

National Society for the Study of Education. *Learning and Instruction.* Forty-Ninth Yearbook, Part I. Chicago: the Society, 1950.

National Society for the Study of Education. *The Integration of Educational Experiences.* Fifty-Seventh Yearbook, Part III. Chicago: the Society, 1958.

National Society for the Study of Education. *The Dynamics of Instructional Groups.* Fifty-Ninth Yearbook, Part II. Chicago: the Society, 1960.

18. Birren, James E., editor. *Handbook of Aging and the Individual.* Chicago: University of Chicago Press, 1959. 939 pp.

19. Biddle, Bruce J., and Ellena, William J., editors. *Contemporary Research on Teacher Effectiveness.* New York: Holt, Rinehart and Winston, 1964. 352 pp.

20. Department of State Agency for International Development. *Community Development Abstracts.* New York: Sociological Abstracts, 1964. 281 pp.

Carpenter, William L., and Kapoor, Sudarshan, compilers. *Graduate Research in Adult Education.* Tallahassee: Department of Adult Education, Florida State University, June 1966.

Aker, George F., compiler. *Adult Education Procedures, Methods and Techniques, A Classified and Annotated Bibliography.* Syracuse,

N.Y.: University of Syracuse, 1965. 163 pp.

Knox, Alan B., and others. *Adult Learning, Abstracts and Bibliography of Research Related to Adult Learning.* Lincoln: University of Nebraska, 1961.

Knox, Alan B., and Janory, D. *Adult Affiliation, Abstracts of Research Related to the Need for Affiliation of Adults.* Lincoln: University of Nebraska, 1961.

Knox, Alan B., and Sjorgren, Douglas. "Motivation To Participate and Learn in Adult Education." *Adult Education* 12: 238-42; Summer 1962.

Knox, Alan B., and others. *Adult Motivation To Participate.* Abstracts of Research on Relationships Between Motivation and Participation. Lincoln: University of Nebraska, 1962.

Ontario Institute for Studies in Education. *Research and Publication in Adult Education.* Ontario, Canada: the Institute, n.d.

DeCrow, Roger, editor. "Research and Investigations in Adult Education." *Adult Education* 17: 195-258; Summer 1967.

Stott, Margaret M., and Verner, Coolie, compilers. *A Trial Bibliography of Research Pertaining to Adult Education.* Vancouver: Extension Department, University of British Columbia, June 1963.

21. Guba, Egon, and Elam, Stanley, editors. *The Teaching and Nurture of Educational Researchers.* Sixth Annual Symposium on Educational Research. Bloomington, Ind.: Phi Delta Kappa, 1965. 297 pp.

22. Smith and Smith, *loc. cit.*

23. See also Young, Pauline V. *Scientific Social Surveys and Research.* Third edition. New York: Prentice-Hall, 1956. 540 pp.

24. See also Travers, Robert M. W. *An Introduction to Educational Research.* Second edition. New York: Macmillan Co., 1967. pp 110-35.

25. See also Campbell, Donald T., and Stanley, Julian C. *Experimental and Quasi-Experimental Designs for Research.* Chicago: Rand McNally & Co., 1966. 84 pp.

26. Galfo and Miller, *op. cit.*, pp. 15-16.

27. *Ibid.*, pp. 52-73.

28. See also Kahn, Robert L., and Connell, Charles F. *The Dynamics of Interviewing: Theory, Techniques, and Cases.* New York: John Wiley & Sons, 1957. 368 pp.

29. See also Johnson, Palmer O. *Statistical Methods in Research.* New York: Prentice-Hall, 1949. pp. 184-209.

30. See also Downie, N. M., and Heath, R. W. *Basic Statistical Methods.* Second edition. New York: Harper & Row, 1965. pp. 6-77.

31. See also Siegel, Sidney. *Nonparametric Statistics in the Behavioral Sciences.* New York: McGraw-Hill Book Co., 1956. 312 pp.

32. Shaw, Marvin E., and Wright, Jack M. *Scales for the Measurement of Attitudes.* New York: McGraw-Hill Book Co., 1967. 604 pp.

33. See also Garrett, Henry E., and Woodworth, R. S. *Statistics in Psychology and Education.* New York: David McKay Co., 1958. pp. 337-70.

34. See also Ferguson, George. *Statistical Analysis in Psychology and Education.* New York: McGraw-Hill Book Co., 1959. pp. 227-41.

35. See also Flanders, Ned A. *Interaction Analysis: A Technique for Quantifying Teacher Influence.* Published privately by the Author, 1961. pp. 1-10. (Mimeo.)

"Using Interaction Analyses in the In-Service Training of Teachers." *Journal of Experimental Education* 30: 313-16; June 1962.

U. S. Department of Health, Education, and Welfare, Office of Education. *Teacher Influence, Pupil Attitudes and Achievement.* Cooperative Research Monograph No. 12. Washington, D. C.: Government Printing Office, 1965. 126 pp.

36. See also Shaw and Wright, *op. cit.*, pp. 15-32.

Good, Carter V., *op. cit.*, pp. 190-280.

37. See also Garrett and Woodworth, *op. cit.*

CHAPTER 18

1. Corey, Stephen M. *Action Research To Improve School Practices.* New York: Bureau of Publications, Teachers College, Columbia University, 1953. 161 pp.

2. Bloom, Benjamin S., and others. *Taxonomy of Educational Objectives: Handbook 1: Cognitive Domain.* New York: David McKay Co., 1955. 207 pp.

3. Byrn, Darcie, and others. *Evaluation in Extension.* Prepared by U. S. Federal Extension Service, Division of Extension Research and Training. Topeka, Kans.: H. M. Ives, 1959. 107 pp.

4. Krathwohl, David R., and others. *Taxonomy of Educational Objectives: Handbook 2: Affective Domain.* New York: David McKay Co., 1964. 196 pp.

5. Mager, R. F. *Preparing Objectives for Programmed Instruction.* San Francisco: Fearon Publishers, 1962. 62 pp.

6. Thorndike, Robert L., and Hagen, Elizabeth. *Measurement and Evaluation in Psychology and Education.* New York: John Wiley & Sons, 1961. 602 pp.

7. Webb, Eugene J., and others. *Unobtrusive Measures.* Chicago: Rand McNally & Co., 1966. 225 pp.

8. Hays, William L. *Statistics for Psychologists.* New York: Holt, Rinehart & Winston, 1963. 719 pp.

9. Bloom and others, *op. cit.*

10. Krathwohl and others, *op. cit.*

11. Simpson, Elizabeth J. "The Classification of Educational Objectives, Psychomotor Domain." *Illinois Teacher of Home Economics* 10: 110-44; Winter 1966-67.

12. Webb and others, *op. cit.*

APPENDIX B

SELECTED READINGS

CHAPTER 1

Griffith, William S., and others. *Public School Adult Education in Northern Illinois.* Circular Series A-192. Springfield, Ill.: Office of the Superintendent of Public Instruction, 1966.

Harlacher, Ervin L. *Effective Junior College Programs of Community Services: Rationale, Guidelines, Practices.* Occasional Report No. 10. Los Angeles: Junior College Leadership Program, School of Education, University of California, 1967.

Harlacher, Ervin L. *The Community Dimension of the Community College.* Report to the American Association of Junior Colleges. Oakland, Calif.: the Author (Oakland Community College), November 1967.

Houle, Cyril O. "The Obligation of the Junior College for Community Service." *Junior College Journal* 30: 502-16; May 1960.

Johnstone, John W. C., and Rivera, Ramon J. *Volunteers for Learning: A Study of the Educational Pursuits of American Adults.* Chicago: Aldine Publishing Co., 1965. 624 pp.

Knowles, Malcom S. *Adult Education Movement in the United States.* New York: Holt, Rinehart & Winston, 1962. 335 pp.

Luke, Robert A. "The Signs of Revolution in Public School Adult Education." *Adult Leadership* 13: 203-4, 237-8; January 1965.

Mann, George C. "The Development of Public School Adult Education." *Public School Adult Education: A Guide for Administrators.* Washington, D. C.: National Association for Public School Adult Education, a department of the National Education Association, 1963. pp. 1-18.

Michigan Department of Education. *The High School Completion Program for Adults and Out-of-School Youth.* Bulletin No. 370, revised. Lansing: the Department, 1967.

National Education Association, Research Division. *Opinions of School Superintendents on Adult Education.* Research Report 1964-R4. Washington, D. C.: the Association, 1964. 27 pp.

Reynolds, James W. "Community Services." *The Public Junior College.* Fifty-Fifth Yearbook of the National Society for the Study of Education, Part I. Chicago: University of Chicago Press, 1956. pp. 140-60.

Richmond Public Schools, Division of Vocational and Adult Education. *Comparative Policies on High School Diplomas for Adults, U.S.A.* Richmond: the Division, n.d.

Zerox Corporation, Special Projects Section. *Federally-Funded Adult Basic Education Programs: A Study of Adult Basic Education Programs in Ten States.* New York: the Section, June 1967. p. 227.

CHAPTER 3

Beal, George M., and others. *Social Action and Interaction in Program Planning.* Ames: Iowa State University Press, 1966. 510 pp.

Bergevin, Paul E., and McKinley, John. *Design for Adult Education in the Church.* Greenwich, Conn.: Seabury Press, 1953.

Biddle, William W., and Biddle, Loureide J. *The Community Development Process: The Rediscovery of Local Initiative.* New York: Holt, Rinehart & Winston, 1965. 334 pp.

Carey, James T. *The Development of the University Evening College as Observed in Ten Urban Universities.* Chicago: Center for the Study of Liberal Education for Adults, 1961. 73 pp.

Clark, Harold F., and Sloan, Harold S. *Classrooms in the Factories.* Rutherford, N.J.: Farleigh Dickinson University, 1958. 139 pp.

Clark, Harold F., and others. *Classrooms in the Stores.* Sweet Springs, Mo.: Roxbury Press, 1962. 123 pp.

Clark, Harold F., and Sloan, Harold S. *Classrooms on Main Street.* New York: Teachers College Press, Columbia University, 1966. 162 pp.

Dyer, John P. *Ivory Towers in the Market Place: The Evening College in American Education.* Indianapolis: Bobbs-Merrill Co., 1956. 205 pp.

Eddy, Edward D. *Colleges for Our Land and Time: The Land Grant Idea in American Education.* New York: Harper & Row, 1957. 328 pp.

Freedman, Leonard, and Power, Hilton. *The Few and the Many: Two Views on Public Affairs Education.* Chicago: Center for the Study of Liberal Education for Adults, 1963.

Gardner, John W. *Self Renewal: The Individual and the Innovative Society.* New York: Harper & Row, 1964. 141 pp.

Harlacher, Ervin. *Effective Junior College Programs of Community Services: Rationale, Guidelines, Practices.* Occasional Report No. 10. Los Angeles: Junior College Leadership Program, School of Education, University of California, 1967.

Harper, Ernest B., and Dunham, Arthur, editors. *Community Organization in Action.* New York: Association Press, 1959.

Haygood, Kenneth, editor. *A Live Option: The Future of the Evening College.* Brookline, Mass.: Center for the Study of Liberal Education for Adults, 1965.

Ingham, Roy J., editor. *Institutional Backgrounds of Adult Education.* Brookline, Mass.: Center for the Study of Liberal Education for Adults, 1966. 115 pp.

Johnson, Eugene I. *Metroplex Assembly: An Experiment in Community Education.* Brookline, Mass.: Center for the Study of Liberal Education for Adults, 1965.

Johnstone, John W. C., and Rivera, Ramon J. *Volunteers for Learning: A Study of the Educational Pursuits of American Adults.* Chicago: Aldine Publishing Co., 1965. 624 pp.

Keppel, Francis. *The Necessary Revolution in American Education.* New York: Harper & Row, 1966. 201 pp.

King, Clarence. *Working with People in Community Action: An International Casebook for Trained Community Workers and Volunteer Community Leaders.* New York: Association Press, 1965. 192 pp.

Kleis, Russell J., editor. *An Area Approach to Continuing Education: Report of Study and Recommendations for a Coordinated System of Continuing Education.* East Lansing: Educational Publication Service, College of Education, Michigan State University, 1967.

Knowles, Malcolm S., editor. *Handbook of Adult Education in the United States.* Chicago: Adult Education Association of the U.S.A., 1960. 640 pp.

Kreitlow, Burton; Alton, E. W.; and Torrence, Andrew P. *Leadership for Action in Rural Communities.* Second edition. Danville, Ill.: Interstate Printers & Publishers, 1965.

Lee, Robert Ellis. *Continuing Education for Adults Through the American Public Library, 1833-1964.* Chicago: American Library Association, 1966. 158 pp.

Lemke, Antje B., editor. *Librarianship and Adult Education: A Symposium.* Syracuse: Syracuse University School of Library Science, 1963. 54 pp.

Liveright, Alexander A. *Adult Education in Colleges and Universities.* Chicago: Center for the Study of Liberal Education for Adults, 1965.

Mial, Dorothy, and Mial, Curtis, editors. *Our Community.* New York: New York University Press, 1960. 269 pp.

Olson, Edward G., editor. *The School and Community Reader: Education in Perspective.* New York: Macmillan Co., 1963.

Rossi, Peter H., and Biddle, Bruce J. *The New Media and Education: Their Impact on Society.* Chicago: Aldine Publishing Co., 1966.

Sanders, Irwin T. *Making Good Communities Better.* Revised edition. Lexington: University of Kentucky Press, 1953. 197 pp.

Shannon, Theodore J., and Schoenfeld, Clarence A. *University Extension.* New York: Center for Applied Research in Education, 1965. 115 pp.

Sheats, Paul H.; Jaynes, Clarence D.; and Spence, Ralph B. *Adult Education: The Community Approach.* New York: Dryden Press, 1953. 503 pp.

CHAPTER 4

Drucker, Peter F. *The Effective Executive.* New York: Harper & Row, 1967. 178 pp.

Harlacher, Ervin L. *Effective Junior College Programs of Community Service: Rationale, Guidelines, Practices.* Occasional Report No. 10. Los Angeles: Junior College Leadership Program, School of Education, University of California, 1967.

Jensen, Gale; Liveright, A. A.; and Hallenbeck, W., editors. *Adult Education: Outlines of an Emerging Field of University Study.* Washington, D. C.: Adult Education Association of the U.S.A., 1964. 334 pp.

Journal of Cooperative Extension. "Administrative Climate." *Journal of Cooperative Extension 5.* Spring 1967.

Knowles, Malcolm, editor. *Handbook of Adult Education in the United States.* Chicago: Adult Education Association of the U.S.A., 1960. 624 pp.

Lipham, James M. "Leadership and Administration." *Behavioral Science and Educational Administration*. Sixty-Third Yearbook of the National Society for the Study of Education, Part II. (Edited by Daniel E. Griffiths.) Chicago: University of Chicago Press, 1964. Chapter 6, pp. 119-41.

Miller, Harry L. *Teaching and Learning in Adult Education*. New York: Macmillan Co., 1964. 340 pp.

CHAPTER 6

Deakin, James. *The Lobbyists*. Washington, D. C.: Public Affairs Press, 1966. 309 pp.

Elementary and Secondary Education Amendments of 1966. *Hearings Before the General Subcommittee on Education of the Committee on Education and Labor*. House of Representatives. Part I. March 7, 9, 10, 11, and 14, 1966.

Enactments by the 88th Congress Concerning Education and Training 1963-1964. Committee on Labor and Public Welfare, United States Senate. October 1964.

Enactments by the 89th Congress Concerning Education and Training, Second Session, 1966. Committee on Labor and Public Welfare, United States Senate. Part I, March 1967.

Kerner, Otto, and others. *Report of the National Advisory Commission on Civil Disorders*. New York: Bantam Books, 1968. 608 pp.

CHAPTER 7

Colcord, Joanna C. *Your Community: Its Provision for Health, Education, Safety, and Welfare*. Third edition. New York: Russell Sage Foundation, 1947, 263 pp.

Gilson, Winifred, and others. *A Community Looks at Itself*. Lincoln: Nebraska Council on Children and Youth, Graduate School of Social Work, University of Nebraska Bureau of Community Service, Extension Division, University of Nebraska, 1952.

Hand, Samuel E. *An Outline of A Community Survey for Program Planning in Adult Education*. Bulletin No. `71 F-2. Tallahassee: Florida State Department of Education, 1968.

Hayes, Wayland J., and Netboy, Anthony. *The Small Community Looks Ahead*. New York: Harcourt, Brace & World, 1947. 276 pp.

Hoiberg, Otto G. *Exploring the Small Community*. Lincoln: University of Nebraska Press, 1955.

Matthews, Mark S. *Guide to Community Action: A Sourcebook for Community Volunteers.* New York: Harper & Brothers, 1954. 434 pp.

Poston, Richard Waverly. *Democracy Is You: A Guide to Citizen Action.* New York: Harper & Brothers, 1953. 312 pp.

Warren, Roland L. *Studying Your Community.* New York: Russell Sage Foundation, 1955. 385 pp.

CHAPTER 11

Bergler, Edmund. *The Revolt of the Middle-Aged Man.* New York: Grosset & Dunlap, 1957.

Erikson, Erik H. *Identity and the Life Cycle.* Psychological Issues, Vol. I, No. 1. New York: International Universities Press, 1959. 176 pp.

Fried, Barbara. *Middle-Age Crisis.* New York: Harper & Row, 1967. 141 pp.

Harrington, Michael. *The Other America: Poverty in the United States.* New York: Macmillan Co., 1962. 191 pp.

Kerner, Otto, and others. *Report of the National Advisory Commission on Civil Disorders.* New York: Bantam Books, 1968. 608 pp.

Kuhlen, Raymond G. *Psychological Backgrounds of Adult Education.* Chicago: Center for the Study of Liberal Education for Adults, 1963.

May, Edgar. *The Wasted Americans.* New York: Harper & Row, 1964. 227 pp.

Myrdal, Gunnar. *An American Dilemma: The Negro Problem and Modern Democracy.* Twentieth anniversary edition. New York: Harper & Row, 1962. 1,483 pp.

Neugarten, Bernice, and others. *Personality in Middle and Late Life.* New York: Atherton Press, 1964.

Pearl, Arthur, and Riessman, Frank. *New Careers for the Poor: The Nonprofessional in Human Service.* New York: Free Press, 1965. 273 pp.

Pearson, G. H. J. *Adolescence and the Conflict of Generations.* New York: W. W. Norton & Co., 1958. 186 pp.

Thorndike, E. L. *The Psychology of Wants, Interest, and Attitudes.* New York: Appleton-Century Co., 1935. 301 pp.

Verner, Coolie, and White, Thurman, editors. *The Nature of Adult Participation, Participants in Adult Education.* Washington, D. C.: Adult Education Association of the U.S.A., 1965. 48 pp.

Warren, Virginia B. *How Adults Can Learn More — Faster.* Washington, D. C.: National Association of Public School Adult Educators, a department of the National Education Association, 1961. 52 pp.

CHAPTER 12

Allen, L. S. "Counseling Adults Poses Different Problems than Counseling Day Students." *Personnel and Guidance Journal* 42: 622-23; February 1964.

Bay, A. V., and Pine, J. "The Counseling Process: A Perspective on Information and Advice." *Vocational Guidance Quarterly* 14: 201-204; Spring 1966.

Buros, Oscar Krisen, editor. *The Sixth Mental Measurements Yearbook.* Highland Park, N.J.: Gryphon Press, 1965. 1,714 pp.

Calia, V. F. "The Culturally Deprived Client: A Reformulation of the Counselor's Role." *Journal of Counseling Psychology* 13: 100-105; Spring 1966.

McGowan, John F., and Schmidt, Lyle D. *Counseling: Readings in Theory and Practice.* New York: Holt, Rinehart & Winston, 1962. 623 pp.

National Association of Public School Adult Educators. *Counseling and Interviewing Adult Students.* Washington, D. C.: the Association, a department of the National Education Association, 1959. 24 pp.

Patterson, C. H. *Theories of Counseling and Psychotherapy.* New York: McGraw-Hill Book Co., 1966. 518 pp.

Remmers, H. H.; Gage, N. L.; and Rummel, J. Francis. *A Practical Introduction to Measurement and Evaluation.* Second edition. New York: Harper & Row, 1965. 390 pp.

Wolfbein, S. I. "Role of Counseling and Training in the War on Unemployment and Poverty." *Vocational Guidance Quarterly* 13: 50-52; Autumn 1964.

CHAPTER 13

Adult Education Association of the U.S.A., Commission on Architecture. *Architecture for Adult Education.* Cincinnati: Berman Printing Co., n.d. 74 pp.

Florida State Department of Education. *Let's Teach Adults.* Tallahassee: the Department, 1954. 55 pp.

Hunsicker, Herbert C., and Pierce, Richard, editors. *Creating a Climate for Learning.* Report of a conference. Lafayette, Ind.: Division of Adult Education, Purdue University, and Adult Education Association of the U.S.A., 1959. 116 pp.

Jensen, Gale; Liveright, A. A.; and Hallenbeck, W., editors. *Adult Education: Outlines of an Emerging Field of University Study.* Washington, D. C.: Adult Education Association of the U.S.A., 1964. 334 pp.

Knowles, Malcolm, editor. *Handbook of Adult Education in the United States.* Chicago: Adult Education Association of the U.S.A., 1960. 624 pp.

Loomis, William P., editor. *The Operation of a Local Program of Trade and Industrial Education.* Office of Vocational Education Division Bulletin No. 250. Washington, D. C.: Government Printing Office, 1953. 166 pp.

Miller, Harry L. *Teaching and Learning in Adult Education.* New York: Macmillan Book Co., 1964. 340 pp.

National Association of Public School Adult Educators. *Public School Adult Education: A Guide for Administrators.* (Edited by John H. Thatcher.) Washington, D.C.: National Association of Public School Adult Educators, a department of the National Education Association, 1963. 199 pp.

Prosser, Charles A. *Evening Industrial Schools.* Chicago: American Technical Society, 1951. 372 pp.

Struck, F. Theodore. *Vocational Education for a Changing World.* New York: John Wiley & Sons, 1950. 550 pp.

Zahn, Jane C. "Differences Between Adults and Youth Affecting Learning." *Adult Education* 17: 67-77; Winter 1967.

CHAPTER 14

Debatin, Frank M. *Administration of Adult Education.* New York: American Book Co., 1938. 486 pp.

Essert, Paul L. *Creative Leadership of Adult Education.* New York: Prentice-Hall, 1951. 333 pp.

Kempfer, Homer. *Adult Education.* New York: McGraw-Hill Book Co., 1955. 433 pp.

Knowles, Malcolm S. *Informal Adult Education: A Guide for Administrators, Leaders, and Teachers.* New York: Association Press, 1950. 272 pp.

National Association of Public School Adult Educators. *Public School Adult Education: A Guide for Administrators.* (Edited by John H. Thatcher.) Washington, D.C.: the Association, a department of the National Education Association, 1963. 199 pp.

Miller, Harry L. *Teaching and Learning in Adult Education.* New York: Macmillan Co., 1964. 340 pp.

CHAPTER 15

General References for In-Service Training

Adult Education Association of the U.S.A. *How To Teach Adults.* Leadership Pamphlet No. 5. Chicago: the Association, 1955. 48 pp.

Cantor, Nathaniel. *The Teaching-Learning Process.* New York: Dryden Press, 1953. 350 pp.

Miller, Harry L. *Teaching and Learning in Adult Education.* New York: Macmillan Co., 1964. 340 pp.

National Association of Public School Adult Education. *Adult Basic Education: A Guide for Teachers and Teacher Trainers.* Washington, D. C.: the Association, a department of the National Education Association, 1966. 212 pp.

National Association for Public School Adult Education. *When You're Teaching Adults.* Washington, D. C.: the Association, a department of the National Education Association, 1966. 24 pp.

Saylor, J. Galen, and Alexander, William M. *Curriculum Planning for Better Teaching and Learning.* New York: Rinehart and Company, 1954. 624 pp.

Warren, Virginia B. *How Adults Can Learn More — Faster.* Washington, D.C.: the Association, a department of the National Education Association, 1966. 52 pp.

Clientele or Participants

Brunner, Edmund deS., and others. *An Overview of Adult Education Research.* Chicago: Adult Education Association of the U.S.A., 1959. pp. 89-118.

Holden, John B. "A Survey of Participation in Adult Education Classes." *Adult Leadership* 6: 258-60, 270; April 1958.

Houle, Cyril O. "Who Stays and Why?" *Adult Education* 14: 225-33; Summer 1964.

Johnstone, John W. C. "The Educational Pursuits of American Adults." *Adult Education* 13: 217-22; Summer 1963.

Newberry, John S., Jr., and Verner, Coolie. "The Nature of Adult Participation." *Adult Education* 8: 208-22; Summer 1958.

Adult Learning

Brunner and others, *op. cit.,* pp. 8-26.

Kidd, James Robbins. *How Adults Learn.* New York: Association Press, 1959. 324 pp.

Miller, Harry L. *Teaching and Learning in Adult Education,* New York: Macmillan Co., 1964. 340 pp.

Owens, William A., Jr. "Age and Mental Abilities." *Genetic Psychology Monographs* 48. 1953.

Sorenson, Herbert. *Adult Abilities: A Study of University Extension Students.* St. Paul: University of Minnesota Press, 1938. 190 pp.

Thorndike, E. L. *Adult Learning.* New York: Macmillan Co., 1928.

Zahn, Jane C. "Differences Between Adults and Youth Affecting Learning." *Adult Education* 17: 67-77; Winter 1967.

Methods for Adult Teachers

Brunner, Edmund de S., *op. cit.*, pp. 142-62.

Miller, Harry L. *Teaching and Learning in Adult Education.* New York: Macmillan Co., 1964. 340 pp.

Verner, Coolie, and Booth, Alan. *Adult Education.* New York: The Center For Applied Research in Education, 1966.

CHAPTER 17

Adult Education Association of the U.S.A. *Federal Support for Adult Education: A Directory of Programs and Services.* Washington, D. C.: the Association, 1966. 111 pp.

Aker, George F., compiler. *Adult Education Procedures, Methods and Techniques, A Classified and Annotated Bibliography.* Syracuse, N.Y.: University of Syracuse, 1965. 163 pp.

Berelson, Bernard, and Steiner, Gary A. *Human Behavior: An Inventory of Scientific Findings.* New York: Harcourt, Brace & World, 1964. 712 pp.

Birren, James E., editor. *Handbook of Aging and the Individual: Psychological and Biological Aspects.* Chicago: University of Chicago Press, 1959. 939 pp.

Botwinick, J. *Cognitive Processes in Maturity and Old Age.* New York: Springer Publishing Co., 1967. 212 pp.

Brewer, A. L. "Classroom Teachers in Action Research." *Michigan Education Journal* 42: 15; October 1964.

Brunner, Edmund de S., and others. *An Overview of Adult Education Research.* Chicago: Adult Education Association of the U.S.A., 1959. 275 pp.

Campbell, Donald T., and Stanley, Julian C. *Experimental and Quasi-Experimental Designs for Research.* Chicago: Rand McNally & Co., 1966. 84 pp.

Carpenter, William L., and Kapoor, Sudarshan, compilers. *Graduate Research in Adult Education.* Tallahassee: Department of Adult Education, Florida State University, June 1966.

Corey, Stephen M. *Action Research To Improve School Practices.* New York: Bureau of Publications, Teachers College, Columbia University, 1953. 161 pp.

Devault, M. V. "Research and the Classroom Teacher." *Teachers College Record* 67: 211-16; December 1965.

Department of State Agency for International Development. *Community Development Abstracts.* New York: Sociological Abstracts, 1964. 281 pp.

DeCrow, Roger, editor. "Research and Investigations in Adult Education." *Adult Education* 17: 195-258; Summer 1967.

Downie, Norville M., and Heath, R. W. *Basic Statistical Methods.* Second edition. New York: Harper & Row, 1965. 325 pp.

Draper, James A. "A Proposal for Systematically Collecting and Reporting Research Relating to Adult Education in Canada." *Continuous Learning* 6: 211-14; September-October 1967.

Ebel, Robert L. "Some Limitations of Basic Research in Education." *Phi Delta Kappan* 49: 81-84; October 1967.

Ferguson, George. *Statistical Analysis in Psychology and Education.* New York: McGraw-Hill Book Co., 1959. 347 pp.

Gage, N. L. *Handbook on Research in Teaching.* A project of the American Educational Research Association, a department of the National Education Association. Chicago: Rand McNally & Co., 1963. 1,218 pp.

Galfo, Armand J., and Miller, C. Earl. *Interpreting Education Research.* Dubuque, Iowa: William C. Brown & Co., 1965. 369 pp.

Garrett, Henry E., and Woodworth, R. S. *Statistics in Psychology and Education.* Fifth edition. New York: David McKay Co., 1958. 478 pp.

Good, Carter V. *Essentials of Educational Research: Methodology and Design.* New York: Appleton-Century-Crofts, 1966. 429 pp.

Good, Carter V., and Scates, Douglas E. *Methods of Research: Educational, Psychological, Sociological.* New York: Appleton-Century-Crofts, 1954. 920 pp.

Glassow, R. B. "Research and You." *Journal of Health, Physical Education, Recreation* 31: 81-82; March 1965.

Guba, Egon, and Elam, Stanley, editors. *The Training and Nurture of Educational Researchers.* Sixth Annual Symposium on Educational Research. Bloomington, Ind.: Phi Delta Kappa, 1965. 297 pp.

Hain, J. "Research in the Classroom." *National Elementary Principal* 44: 49-51; November 1964.

Hare, A. Paul. *Handbook of Small Group Research.* New York: Free Press, 1962. 512 pp.

Jensen, Gale; Liveright, A. A.; and Hallenbeck, W., editors. *Adult Education: Outlines of an Emerging Field of University Study.* Chicago: Adult Education Association of the U.S.A., 1964. 334 pp.

Johnson, Palmer O. *Statistical Methods in Research.* New York: Prentice-Hall, 1949. 377 pp.

Kahn, Robert L., and Cannell, Charles F. *The Dynamics of Interviewing: Theory, Techniques, and Cases.* New York: John Wiley & Sons, 1957. 368 pp.

Knowles, Malcolm S., editor. *Handbook of Adult Education in the United States.* Chicago: Adult Education Association of the U.S.A., 1960. 640 pp.

Knox, Alan B., and others. *Adult Learning.* Abstracts and Bibliography of Research Related to Adult Learning. Lincoln: University of Nebraska, 1961.

Knox, Alan B., and Janory, D. *Adult Affiliation.* Abstracts of Research Related to the Need for Affiliation of Adults. Lincoln: University of Nebraska, 1961.

Knox, Alan B. *Research Arrangements Within University Adult Education Divisions.* Chicago: Center for the Study of Liberal Education for Adults, 1963.

Knox, Alan B., and Sjorgren, Douglas. "Motivation To Participate and Learn in Adult Education." *Adult Education* 12: 238-42; Summer 1962.

Knox, Alan B., and others. *Adult Motivation To Participate.* Abstracts of Research on Relationships Between Motivation and Participation. Lincoln: University of Nebraska, 1962.

MacDonald, J. B. "Thoughts About Research in School." *Educational Leader* 23: 601-604; April 1966.

National Society for the Study of Education. *The Psychology of Learning.* Forty-First Yearbook, Part II. Bloomington, Ill.: Public School Publishing Co., 1942. 502 pp.

National Society for the Study of Education. *Learning and Instruction.* Forty-Ninth Yearbook, Part I. Chicago: University of Chicago Press, 1950. 352 pp.

National Society for the Study of Education. *The Integration of Educational Experiences.* Fifty-Seventh Yearbook, Part III. Chicago: University of Chicago Press, 1958. 278 pp.

National Society for the Study of Education. *The Dynamics of Instructional Groups.* Fifty-Ninth Yearbook, Part II. Chicago: University of Chicago Press, 1960. 285 pp.

Pressey, S. L., and Kuhlen, R. G. *Psychological Development Through the Life Span.* New York: Harper & Row, 1957. 654 pp.

Ontario Institute for Studies in Education. *Research and Publication in Adult Education*. Toronto, Ontario, Canada: the Institute, n.d.

Scandura, J. M. "Educational Research and the Mathematics Educator." *Mathematics Teacher* 58: 13-18; February 1965.

Shaw, Marvin E., and Wright, Jack M. *Scales for the Measurement of Attitudes*. New York: McGraw-Hill Book Co., 1967. 604 pp.

Siegel, Sidney. *Nonparametric Statistics in the Behavioral Sciences*. New York: McGraw-Hill Book Co., 1956. 312 pp.

Smith, Henry L., and Smith, Johnny R. *An Introduction to Research in Evaluation*. Bloomington: Educational Publications, 1959. 287 pp.

Stott, Margaret M., and Verner, Coolie. *A Trial Bibliography of Research Pertaining to Adult Education*. Vancouver: Extension Department, University of British Columbia, June 1963.

Straham, R. D., and Todd, E. A. "Educational Improvement Through Research." *Education* 86: 281-85; January 1966.

Travers, Robert M. W. *An Introduction to Educational Research*. Second edition. New York: Macmillan Co., 1967.

U. S. Office of Economic Opportunity. *Catalog of Federal Assistance Programs*. Washington, D. C.: the Office, June 1, 1967. 701 pp.

Wandt, Edwin. *A Cross-Section of Educational Research*. New York: David McKay Co., 1965. 301 pp.

Young, Pauline V. *Scientific Social Surveys and Research*. Third edition. New York: Prentice-Hall, 1956. 540 pp.

CHAPTER 18

American Educational Research Association. *Perspectives of Curriculum Evaluation*. AERA Monograph Series on Curriculum Evaluation, No. 1. Chicago: Rand McNally & Co., 1967. 102 pp.

Cook, Desmond L. *An Introduction to PERT*. Columbus, Ohio: Bureau of Educational Research and Service, 1964. 15 pp.

Knox, Alan B. "Adult Education Agency Clientele Analysis." *Review of Educational Research* 35: 231-39; June 1965.

Lee, Doris M. "Teaching and Evaluation." *Evaluation as Feedback and Guide*. 1967 Yearbook. Washington, D. C.: Association for Supervision and Curriculum Development, a department of the National Education Association, 1967. Chapter 4, pp. 72-100.

Miller, Harry, and McGuire, Christine. *Evaluating Liberal Adult Education*. Boston: Center for the Study of Liberal Education for Adults, 1961. 184 pp.

Stake, Robert E. "The Countenance of Educational Evaluation." *Teachers College Record* 68: 523-40; April 1967.

APPENDIX C

BIBLIOGRAPHY FOR FURTHER READING

The following selections are offered as a continuing introduction to literature which is considered pertinent for the administrator of publicly supported education for adults. Readings have been divided into nine sections: one for each of the five major divisions of this book, plus Periodicals, Basic References, Other Bibliographies, and Clearinghouses for Adult Education and Community Services.

THE ORGANIZATION AND ADMINISTRATION OF CONTINUING EDUCATION

Adams, Dewey. *An Analysis of Roles of the Community College in Continuing Education in Conjunction with Other Organizations Which Provide Education for Adults.* Doctoral dissertation. Gainesville: University of Florida, 1966. 262 pp.

Adult Education Association of the U.S.A. *Federal Support for Adult Education: A Directory of Programs and Services.* Washington, D.C.: the Association, 1966. 111 pp.

Bergevin, Paul E. *A Philosophy for Adult Education.* Greenwich, Conn.: Seabury Press, 1967. 176 pp.

Borus, Michael E. *The Economic Effectiveness of Retraining the Unemployed Based on the Experience of Workers in Connecticut.* Doctoral dissertation. New Haven, Conn.: Yale University, June 1966. 228 pp.

Burns, Robert W. *Sociological Backgrounds of Adult Education.* Notes and Essays on Education for Adults, No. 41. Chicago: Center for the Study of Liberal Education for Adults, 1964. 169 pp.

Changing Times. "The Fantastic Growth of the Two-Year College." *Changing Times* 22: 35-38; September 1968.

Engleman, Finis E.; Cooper, Shirley; and Ellena, William J. *Vignettes*

This Appendix was prepared by Richard W. Cortright, who is director of the Adult Education Clearinghouse, National Education Association, Washington, D. C. Grateful acknowledgment is made to the professors of adult education, and the following adult educators—Patrick G. Boyle, Eugene I. Johnson, Russell J. Kleis, Ernest E. McMahon, Carl E. Minich, Lynn Mock, Bernadine H. Peterson, Nathan C. Shaw, David F. Shontz, Sara M. Steele, Allen Tough, and to Roger DeCrow of the ERIC Clearinghouse for Adult Education—for their assistance in compiling this Bibliography for Further Reading.

on the Theory and Practice of School Administration. New York: Macmillan Co., 1963. 237 pp.

Fretwell, E. K., Jr. "Issues Facing Community Colleges Today." *Today's Education* 57: 46-48; October 1968.

Hallenbeck, Wilbur C., and others. *Community and Adult Education: Adult Education Theory and Method.* Chicago: Adult Education Association of the U.S.A., 1962. 40 pp.

Houle, Cyril O. "Back to New Francisco." *Adult Leadership* 15: 261-62; February 1967.

Kidd, James R. *Financing Continuing Education.* New York: Scarecrow Press, 1962. 209 pp.

Kreitlow, B. W. *Relating Adult Education to Other Disciplines.* Cooperative Research Project E012. Washington, D.C.: Office of Education, U.S. Department of Health, Education, and Welfare, 1964. 106 pp.

Liveright, Alexander A. *A Study of Adult Education in the United States.* Boston: Center for the Study of Liberal Education for Adults at Boston University, 1968. 138 pp.

McMahon, Ernest E.; Coates, Robert H.; and Knox, Alan B. "Common Concerns: The Position of the Adult Education Association of the U.S.A." *Adult Education* 18: 197-213; Spring 1968.

New Jersey Department of Education, Bureau of Adult Education, Division of Higher Education. *Directing the Adult Program.* Trenton: the Department, n.d. 34 pp.

New York State Education Department, Bureau of Adult Education and Bureau of Educational Finance Research. *Adult Education, The Relationship of Program Development to State Fiscal Policy.* Albany: the Department, October 1964. 24 pp.

Olds, Edward B. *Financing Adult Education in America's Public Schools and Community Councils.* Chicago: National Commission on Adult Education Finance, Adult Education Association of the U.S.A., 1954. 124 pp.

Ulich, Mary E. *Patterns of Adult Education: A Comparative Study.* New York: Pageant Press, 1965. 205 pp.

Verner, Coolie, and White, Thurman, editors. *Administration of Adult Education.* Washington, D.C.: Adult Education Association of the U.S.A., 1965. 52 pp.

PROGRAM DEVELOPMENT AND OPERATION

Bloom, Benjamin S. *Educationally Disadvantaged — Conferences.* New York: Holt, Rinehart & Winston, 1965. 179 pp.

California Department of Education. *Directory of Occupation Centered Curriculum in California Junior Colleges and Schools for Adults.* Sacramento: the Department, 1964.

California Department of Education, Division of Instructional Services. *Catalog of Authorized Subjects for Adult Schools, Graduation Requirements and Curricula.* Revised edition. Los Angeles: the Department, 1967. 145 pp.

Davis, Alvin Russell. *An Institutional Approach to a Study of Community Needs with Special Reference to the Community College.* Doctoral dissertation. Austin: University of Texas, 1964. 191 pp.

Ferguson, Clyde C. *Community Education—Methods, Techniques.* Washington, D.C.: U.S. Department of Health, Education, and Welfare, Welfare Administration, Office of Juvenile Delinquency and Youth Development, 1964. pp. 105-31.

Florida Department of Education, Division of Vocational, Technical and Adult Education. *Organization and Administration of Distributive Education Programs for Adults.* Bulletin 74 H-5. Tallahassee: the Department, July 1966. 85 pp.

Harris, Norman C. *Technical Education in the Junior College/New Programs for New Jobs.* Washington, D.C.: American Association of Junior Colleges, 1964. 102 pp.

Knox, Alan. *The Audience for Liberal Adult Education.* Chicago: Center for the Study of Liberal Education for Adults, 1962.

Lanning, Frank W., and Many, Wesley A., editors. *Basic Education for the Disadvantaged Adult: Theory and Practice.* New York: Houghton-Mifflin Co., 1966. 411 pp.

McCloskey, Gordon. *Education and Public Understanding.* Second edition. New York: Harper & Row, 1967. 622 pp.

National Association for Public School Adult Education. *IMPACT.* Washington, D.C.: the Association, a department of the National Education Association, 1964. 33 pp.

National Association for Public School Adult Education. *IMPACT Filmograph.* A 13-minute filmograph based on the IMPACT brochure. Washington, D.C.: the Association, a department of the National Education Association, 1964.

National Association for Public School Adult Education. *It Can Be Done.* Washington, D.C.: the Association, a department of the National Education Association, 1964. 60 pp.

National School Public Relations Association. *The Schools and the Press.* Washington, D.C.: the Association, a department of the National Education Association, 1965. 112 pp.

New York Department of Education, Bureau of Continuing Education.

Curriculum Development. Bulletin No. 98. Albany: New York State Bar Association, 1966. 104 pp.

Riendeau, Albert J. *The Role of the Advisory Committee in Occupational Education in the Junior College*. Washington, D.C.: American Association of Junior Colleges, 1967. 75 pp.

Rindt, Kenneth E. *Handbook for Coordinators of Management and Other Adult Education Programs*. Madison: University Extension, University of Wisconsin Commerce Department Management Institute, 1968. 120 pp.

Rodgers, Florestine B. *Home Economics Education*. Norman: University of Oklahoma, 1964. 88 pp.

Scott, Carl A., and others. *Family Life Education*. New York: Child Study Association of America, 1965. 27 pp.

Stern, Milton. *People, Programs, and Persuasion: Some Remarks About Promoting University Adult Education*. Notes and Essays No. 33. Chicago: Center for the Study of Liberal Education for Adults, 1961. 101 pp.

Willcox, Wanda Marie. *A Survey of the Present State of Public School Adult Elementary Education in the United States and a Formulation of Programs for Use in Adult Elementary Education*. Doctoral dissertation. Coral Gables: University of Miami, June 1963. 134 pp.

THE ADULT PARTICIPANT

Colorado Department of Education. *Migrants—Educational Needs*. Denver: the Department, 1965. 83 pp.

Cook County Department of Public Aid. *Poverty*. Chicago: Science Research Associates, 1963. 167 pp.

Dannenmaier, W. D. "Counseling Adults: A New Horizon or an Old Vista?" *Adult Education* 14: 96-99; Winter 1964.

Dobbs, Ralph C. "Self-Perceived Educational Needs of Adults." *Adult Education* 16: 92-100; 1966.

Draper, James Anson. *A Study of Participant Objectives in Selected Management Institute Programs*. Doctoral dissertation. Madison: University of Wisconsin, 1964. 237 pp.

Green, Alan C., editor. *Educational Facilities with New Media*. Washington, D.C.: Department of Audiovisual Instruction, National Education Association, 1966. 230 pp.

Houle, Cyril O. *Continuing Your Education*. New York: McGraw-Hill Book Co., 1964.

Hurlburt, E. V. "Adult Teachers Are Counselors." *Adult Leadership* 10: 263-64; March 1962.

Kamrath, W. A. "El Camino by Night." *Junior College Journal* 34: 32-38; May 1964.

Knox, Alan B., and Videbeck, Richard. "Adult Education and Adult Life Cycle." *Adult Education* 13: 102-21; Winter 1963.

Knox, Alan B. "Adult Education Clientele Analysis." *Review of Educational Research* 35: 231-39; June 1965.

London, Jack; Wenhert, Robert; and Hagstron, Warron O. *Adult Education and Social Class.* Coop. Res. Proj. No. 1017, U.S. Office of Education. Los Angeles: Survey Research Center, University of California, 1962. 246 pp.

Modesto Junior College. *Study of Characteristics of Adult Part-Time Students Enrolled in the Adult Education Program in Modesto.* Modesto, Calif.: the College, March 1968. 78 pp.

North Carolina Agricultural Extension Service. *Home Economics Education — Negroes.* Raleigh: the Service, 1964. 120 pp.

Northern Illinois University. *Speaking About Adults and the Continuing Educational Process.* Adult Basic Education Workshop. DeKalb: the University, June 1966. 163 pp.

Verner, Coolie. "Patterns of Attendance in Adult Night School Courses." *Canadian Education and Research Digest.* September 1966. pp. 230-40.

Wolfe, Lloyd A. *A Study of the Relationship Between Life Long Learning and the Adjustment of Older People.* Doctoral dissertation. Ann Arbor: University of Michigan, 1962. 119 pp.

IMPROVEMENT OF INSTRUCTION

Adult Education Association of the U.S.A. *Supervision and Consultation.* Leadership Pamphlet No. 7. Chicago: the Association, 1960. 48 pp.

Beck, Kenneth N. *Retention of Part-Time Teachers in Public School Adult Education Programs.* Master's thesis. Chicago: Chicago University, June 1965. 61 pp.

Bergevin, Paul; Morris, Dwight; and Smith, Robert M. *Adult Education Procedures: A Handbook of Tested Patterns for Effective Participation.* Greenwich, Conn.: Seabury Press, 1963. 245 pp.

Dale, Edgar. *Audio-Visual Methods in Teaching.* New York: Holt, Rinehart & Winston, 1965. 534 pp.

Erickson, Clifford G., and others. *Eight Years of TV College.* Chicago: Chicago City Junior College, 1964. 40 pp.

Florida State University. *Leadership Training Institute for Public School Adult Basic Education.* Report. Tallahassee: the University, 1965. 135 pp.

Gommersall, Earl R., and Myers, M. Scott. "Breakthrough in On-the-Job Training." *Harvard Business Review* 44: 62-72; July-August 1966.

Gordon, George N. *Educational Television.* New York: Center for Applied Research in Education, 1965. 113 pp.

Heinberg, Sylvester. *Procedures for the Supervision and Evaluation of the New Part-Time Evening-Division Instructors in California Junior Colleges.* Doctoral dissertation. Los Angeles: University of Southern California, 1966. 311 pp.

Lorge, Irving, and others. *Psychology of Adults.* Chicago: Adult Education Association of the U.S.A., 1963. 36 pp.

McBride, Wilma, editor. *Inquiry: Implications for Televised Instruction.* Washington, D.C.: Division of Audiovisual Instruction Service and Center for the Study of Instruction, National Education Association, 1966. 64 pp.

National Association for Public School Adult Education. *A Treasury of Techniques for Teaching Adults.* Washington, D.C.: the Association, a department of the National Education Association, 1964. 48 pp.

National School Public Relations Association. *Technology in Education.* Washington, D.C.: the Association, a department of the National Education Association, 1967. 24 pp.

National School Public Relations Association. *The Conference Planner: A Guide to Good Education Meetings.* Washington, D.C.: the Association, a department of the National Education Association, 1967. 72 pp.

Oates, Stanton C. *Audio Visual Equipment Self-Instruction Manual.* Dubuque, Iowa: William C. Brown Book Co., 1966. 155 pp.

Rufsvold, Margaret, and Guss, Carolyn. *Guides to Newer Educational Media: Films, Filmstrips, Kinescopes, Phonodiscs, Phonotapes, Programmed Instruction Materials, Slides, Transparencies, Videotapes.* Chicago: American Library Association, 1967. 62 pp.

Stenzel, A. K. "Guidelines for Evaluating Leadership Training in Community Organizations." *Adult Leadership* 13: 254-56, 269; February 1965.

Torrence, Preston E. "The Tuskegee Experiment in Adult Training." *Adult Leadership* 15: 83-84; September 1966.

Verner, Coolie, and White, Thurman, editors. *Processes of Adult Education: Adult Education Theory and Method.* Washington, D.C.: Adult Education Association of the U.S.A., 1965. 62 pp.

Verner, Coolie, and White, Thurman, editors. *Adult Learning.* Washington, D.C.: Adult Education Association of the U.S.A., 1965. 48 pp.

RESEARCH AND EVALUATION

Aker, George F., and Carpenter, William L. *What Research Says About Public School Adult Education.* Tallahassee: Department of Adult Education, Florida State University, November 1966. 33 pp.

Brooks, Deton J., Jr. *A Study To Determine the Literacy Level of Able-Bodied Persons Receiving Public Assistance.* Chicago: Cook County Department of Public Aid, 1962. 166 pp.

Clifford, Virginia I. *Educationally Disadvantaged — Research Reviews.* New York: Auburn Library, Union Theological Seminary, 1964. 32 pp.

DeCrow, Roger, and Grabowski, Stanley, editors. *A Register of Research and Investigation in Adult Education.* Washington, D.C.: Adult Education Association of the U.S.A., 1968. Sec. 6B, no. 41, p. 13.

Johnson, R. L.; Cortright, R. W.; and Cooper, J. V. "Attitude Changes Among Literacy Teachers Coincident with Training and Experience." *Adult Education* 18: 71-80; Winter 1968.

Kahn, Louis. *An Appraisal of Practices of Adult Evening Programs of Community Colleges in Washington State.* Doctoral dissertation. Pullman: Washington State University, 1966. 102 pp.

Knox, Alan B. *Adult Education Methods: Abstracts of Research on Relative Effectiveness of Teaching Methods.* Lincoln: Adult Education Research, University of Nebraska, 1962. 26 pp.

Los Angeles City School Districts, Division of College and Adult Education. *Criteria for Evaluating Instruction in Adult Education.* Los Angeles: the Division, 1963. 46 pp.

Modesto Junior College, Adult Division. *Depleting Welfare Rolls: A Study of Welfare Recipients.* Modesto, Calif.: the Division, March 1967. 69 pp.

Rawlinson, Howard E. *Evaluating Community Service in Public Junior Colleges.* Doctoral dissertation. Carbondale: Southern Illinois University, 1963. 175 pp.

U.S. Department of Labor. *Report of the Secretary of Labor on Research and Training Activities Under the Manpower Development and Training Act.* Washington, D.C.: Government Printing Office, February 1963. 135 pp.

PERIODICALS

Adult Education Association of the U.S.A. *Adult Education.* Washington, D.C.: the Association, published quarterly.

Adult Education Association of the U.S.A. *Adult Leadership.* Washington, D.C.: the Association, monthly except July and August.

Adult Services Division, American Library Association. *Adult Services Division Newsletter.* Chicago, Ill.: the Division, published quarterly.

American Association of Junior Colleges. *Community Services Forum.* Washington, D.C.: the Association, published monthly.

American Association of Junior Colleges. *Junior College Journal.* Washington, D.C.: the Association, published monthly from September through May (December-January issue combined).

American Association of Junior Colleges. *Occupational Education Bulletin.* Washington, D.C.: the Association, published on an occasional basis.

American Vocational Association. *American Vocational Journal.* Washington, D.C.: the Association.

Campbell, Clyde M., editor. *The Community School and Its Administration.* Midland, Mich.: Ford Press, published monthly.

Canadian Association for Adult Education. *Continuous Learning.* Toronto, Ontario: the Association, published bimonthly.

Kidd, J. Roby, editor. *Convergence.* Toronto, Ontario: Ontario Institute for Studies in Education.

National Association for Public School Adult Education. *The Pulse of Public School: Adult Education.* Washington, D.C.: the Association, a department of the National Education Association, published eight times a year.

National Association for Public School Adult Education. *Swap Shop for Administrators.* Washington, D.C.: the Association, a department of the National Education Association, published bimonthly.

National Association for Public School Adult Education. *Techniques for Teachers of Adults.* Washington, D.C.: the Association, a department of the National Education Association, published eight times a year.

National Association of Educational Broadcasters. *Journal of NAEB.* Urbana, Ill.: the Association, published monthly.

National Education Association, Department of Audiovisual Instruction. *Audiovisual Instruction.* Washington, D.C.: the Department, published monthly except July and August.

National Home Study Council. *NHSC News.* Washington, D.C.: the Association, published monthly.

National School Public Relations Association. *Education U.S.A.* Washington, D.C.: the Association in cooperation with the American Association of School Administrators, Department of Elementary School Principals, and National Association of Secondary School Principals, published weekly September-May, plus two summer issues.

National University Extension Association. *NUEA Spectator.* Minneapolis, Minn.: the Association, published bimonthly except August-September at the University of Minnesota.

BASIC REFERENCES

Aker, George F. *Adult Education Procedures, Methods and Techniques. A Classified and Annotated Bibliography, 1953-1963.* Syracuse, N.Y.: Library of Continuing Education at Syracuse University and University College of Syracuse University, 1965. 163 pp.

Brunner, Edmund deS., and others. *An Overview of Adult Education Research.* Chicago: Adult Education Association of the U.S.A., 1959. 273 pp.

Essert, Paul L. *Creative Leadership of Adult Education.* Englewood Cliffs, N.J.: Prentice-Hall, 1951. 333 pp.

Gleazer, Edmund J., Jr., and Houts, Paul L., editors. *American Junior Colleges.* Seventh edition. Washington, D.C.: American Council on Education, 1967. 957 pp.

Harlacher, Ervin L. *The Community Dimension of the Community College.* Report to the American Association of Junior Colleges. Bloomfield Hills, Mich.: Oakland Community College, November 1967. 196 pp.

Jensen, Gale; Liveright, A. A.; and Hallenbeck, W., editors. *Adult Education: Outlines of an Emerging Field of University Study.* Chicago: Adult Education Association of the U.S.A., 1964. 334 pp.

Johnstone, John W. C., and Rivera, Ramon J. *Volunteers for Learning: A Study of the Educational Pursuits of American Adults.* National Opinion Research Center Monographs in Social Research, No. 4. Chicago: Aldine Publishing Co., 1963. 624 pp.

Kempfer, Homer H. *Adult Education.* New York: McGraw-Hill Book Co., 1955. 433 pp.

Kidd, James R. *How Adults Learn.* New York: Association Press, 1959. 324 pp.

Knowles, Malcolm S., editor. *Handbook of Adult Education in the United States*. Chicago: Adult Education Association of the U.S.A., 1960. 624 pp.

Knowles, Malcolm S. *The Adult Education Movement in the United States*. New York: Holt, Rinehart & Winston, 1962. 335 pp.

Miller, Harry L. *Teaching and Learning in Adult Education*. New York: Macmillan Co., 1964. 340 pp.

National Association of Public School Adult Educators. *Public School Adult Education: A Guide for Administrators*. Revised edition. Washington, D.C.: the Association, a department of the National Education Association, 1963. 199 pp.

Sheats, Paul H.; Jayne, Clarence D.; and Spence, Ralph B. *Adult Education: The Community Approach*. New York: Dryden Press, 1953. 530 pp.

Snow, Robert H. *Community Adult Education*. New York: G. P. Putnam's Sons, 1955. 170 pp.

Verner, Coolie, and Booth, Alan. *Adult Education*. New York: Center for Applied Research in Education, 1964. 118 pp.

OTHER BIBLIOGRAPHIES

American Association of Colleges for Teacher Education. *Teacher Education and Media — 1964: A Selective Annotated Bibliography*. Washington, D.C.: the Association, a department of the National Education Association, 1964. 49 pp.

American Association of Junior Colleges. *The Junior and Community College: A Bibliography of Doctoral Dissertations, 1964-66*. Washington, D.C.: the Association, 1967. 17 pp.

American Educational Research Association. *Review of Education Research*. 1931 — . (Five times a year. Special issues on Adult Education in June of 1950, 1953, 1959, 1965). Washington, D.C.: the Association.

Byrn, Darcie, compiler. *Home Economics Education — Bibliography*. Washington, D.C.: Federal Extension Service, U.S. Department of Agriculture, 1965. 12 pp.

ERIC Clearinghouse on Adult Education. *Adult Basic Education #1 (Bibliography)*. Syracuse, N.Y.: Syracuse University, 1967. 17 pp.

ERIC Clearinghouse on Adult Education. *Higher Adult Education #1: Current Information Sources*. Syracuse, N.Y.: Syracuse University, 1967. 20 pp.

ERIC Clearinghouse on Adult Education. *Public School Adult Education #1*. Syracuse, N.Y.: Syracuse University, 1968. 11 pp.

Illinois, Superintendent of Public Instruction, Department of Adult Education. *Bibliography: Curriculum Materials for Adult Basic Education.* Springfield: State of Illinois, 1966.

Little, Lawrence C. *A Bibliography of Doctoral Dissertations on Adults and Adult Education.* Revised edition. Pittsburgh: University of Pittsburgh Press, 1963. 163 pp.

National Education Association, Department of Audiovisual Instruction and National Association of Educational Broadcasters. *Audio Cardalog.* Washington, D.C.: the Department, 1967. 102 pp.

National University Extension Association. *Bibliography Materials for the Adult Basic Education Administrator and Teacher.* Washington, D.C.: the Association, 1967. 49 pp.

Potts, Alfred M., compiler. *Educationally Disadvantaged — Bibliography.* Alamosa, Colo.: Center for Cultural Studies, Adams State College, 1965. 460 pp.

Sheffield, Sherman B., and Buskey, John H., compilers. *Annotated Bibliography on Residential Adult Education (Conferences and Institutes).* Project of the Research Committee, Conference and Institute Division, National University Extension Association. College Park: Conference and Institute Division, University College, University of Maryland, 1968. 22 pp.

University Microfilms. *Dissertation Abstracts:* Ann Arbor, Mich.: University Microfilms. Complete dissertations may be ordered as microfilm or as enlargements.

U.S. Department of Health, Education, and Welfare, Office of Education. *Sources of Information on Educational Media.* Prepared by John A. Moldstad for the Educational Media Council. Washington, D.C.: Government Printing Office, 1963. 29 pp.

U.S. Office of Education, Adult Education Branch and the National University Extension Association. *Bibliography Materials for the Adult Basic Education Student.* Washington, D.C.: the Association, 1967. 129 pp.

CLEARINGHOUSES FOR ADULT EDUCATION AND COMMUNITY SERVICES

ERIC Clearinghouse on Adult Education (Roger DeCrow, director, Syracuse University, 107 Roney Lane, Syracuse, N.Y. 13210). Sponsored by the Library of Continuing Education of Syracuse University and the Educational Resources Information Center of the U. S. Office of Education, the clearinghouse is responsible for acquiring, indexing, abstracting, and disseminating research information in the following areas: informal adult education carried on by national or community voluntary and service agencies; adult education in the formal educational system, such as public schools, junior and community colleges and universities; in-service training in business, industry, unions, and the armed forces; church-sponsored adult education; educational aspects of community development, and rural and urban extensions; fundamental and literacy education for adults; educational media programs involving adults; correspondence study; and continuing education in the professions. Adulthood is defined not only by chronological age, but also by the assumption of mature responsibilities such as marriage or full-time employment.

The NEA Adult Education Clearinghouse (Richard W. Cortright, director, 1201 16th Street, N.W., Washington, D.C. 20036). The NEA Adult Education Clearinghouse (NAEC) has been established by the National Education Association (NEA) to provide easier access to information useful in the education of adults and out-of-school youth. NAEC obtains, processes, and disseminates information about all aspects of adult education. Particular attention is placed on elementary level and high school completion programs for adults. NAEC supplies written answers to requests for information about adult education (a) by citing references; (b) by providing copies of documents, when possible; and (c) by providing summaries of information. In addition to supplying written responses to requests, NAEC makes its services available (a) by conducting workshops on information utilization, (b) by distributing multimedia programs on resources and research information, (c) by maintaining a referral system of consultants on adult education, (d) by publishing broadsides of adult education information, and (e) by preparing professional articles. NAEC cooperates with all organizations which are interested in adult education. Arrangements for collaboration with the ERIC Clearinghouse on Adult Education have been developed so that the two services complement and reinforce each other.

AAJC Clearinghouse on Community Services (J. Kenneth Cummiskey, director, American Association of Junior Colleges, 1225 Connecticut Avenue, N.W., Washington, D.C. 20036). The AAJC Clearinghouse on Community Services (ACCS) is a product of the American Association of Junior Colleges' Project in Community Services funded by the W. K. Kellogg Foundation of Battle Creek, Michigan. Through the AAJC Clearinghouse, policies, programs, and procedures in community services are compiled and made available to the community college.

Publications to assist community colleges and their community services coordinators are produced and distributed. Information on consultant services, conferences and workshops, sources of financial support, innovative programs, graduate study opportunities, and research projects is transmitted to the community colleges. The AAJC Clearinghouse (ACCS) responds to requests from community colleges for information on community service activities by providing (a) information of general interest to community colleges through a newsletter and special publications, (b) regional and national conferences to further the sharing of information on community college policies and programs in service to their communities, and (c) a referral service for institutions desiring consultant services. The AAJC Clearinghouse utilizes the services of the ERIC Clearinghouse for Junior College Information at UCLA and the ERIC Clearinghouse on Adult Education at Syracuse University, when the information desired can be provided from these sources.

APPENDIX D

INDEX

A

Accrediting associations, 23-24, 84-85
Administrative staff selection, 294-95
Administrators, school, 80-81, 83-84, 294-95
Adult basic education, 182-84, 283-84
Adult education
  Agencies, 13, 46-47
  Centralized plan, 264-65
  Cost, 81
  Curriculum, 16, 161-73, 175-79, 181-93
  District plan, 265-66
  History, 14-16, 28-30
  Enrollment statistics, 16, 17-18, 46-47
  Evaluation, 93, 368-91
  Evening high school, 4, 21, 188
  Leadership, 21-23
  Model, 93-97, 98-101
  Public support, 12-26, 82-83
  Research, 344-66
Adult Education Act, 123-25, 134
Adult education administrator, 76-101, 196-98, 223-25

Change agent, 150-51, 393
Consultant, 190
Employment statistics, 81, 119
Legislative role, 78-80, 134-35
Practical concerns, 196-98
Research role, 363-66
Staff relations, 42-45, 213-15
Adult Education Association of the U.S.A., 24-25, 85
Adult Education Demonstration Project, 122, 176
Adult education programs, 29-30, 42-45, 80-84, 93-95, 98-101, 133-34, 200-201, 226, 304
Adult learning, 9, 316-41
Adult participant. See Students
Advisement programs, 252-53
Advisory committee
  Functions and types, 173-75, 210
  Organization, 203-205, 212
  Value, 93-94, 153-54, 158
Aging process, 194-95, 272
Aides, teaching, 285-86

Aker, George F., 344-66 (chapter on research)
American Association for Adult Education, 24
American Association of Junior Colleges, 25
American College Testing Program, 250
American Society for Training and
   Development, 64
Americanization program, 182, 284
Appalachian Regional Development Act, 126
Apprenticeship Information Centers, 126
Area occupational education centers, 53-54
Arts and Humanities Act, 66

B

Boards of education, 305-306
Brainstorming, 329-30
Budget development, 107-112, 115-17
Bureau of Adult, Vocational, and Library
   Programs, 22
Bureau of Educational Personnel Development,
   128
Business, role of, 63-64
Business education, 192
Butcher, Donald G., 46-74 (chapter on roles
   and interrelationships)
Buzz groups, 328

C

Canadian Adult Education Association, 84-85
Catalogs, 206-208
Churches, role of, 66-67
Cincinnati Public Schools, 4-5, 15
Civil defense education, 62
Clancy, Peter L., 28-45 (chapter on community
   schools)
Classrooms, 272-74
Cognitive skills, 164
College Entrance Examination Board, 250
Communications media, 69-70
Communications skills, 163
Community
   Advisory committee. See Advisory committee
   Agencies, 61
   Council, 72-74, 154-55
   Needs and resources, 138-58, 200-203
   Problems, 132-34, 160, 226
   Programs, 123, 126-28, 253-54, 290
   Relations, 34-35, 41-42, 84-85, 201-206,
      213-14
   School model (see also Flint community
      school model), 35-37, 38-45
Community action agencies, 61
Community colleges, vii, 13, 16-17, 20,
   49-53, 92, 98-99, 193-94, 301-302
Community development, 51-52, 290
Community services, 16, 25, 39, 51, 52, 53,
   122-23
Computation skills, 163-64
Computer, advantages of, 110-111
Computer-assisted instruction, 331-32
Confidentiality in student records, 240, 244
Continuing education, 6, 8-9, 42-48, 368-91
Cooperative Extension Service, 58-59
Coordination, See Program, coordination
Correspondence courses, 271
Cost of adult education program, 81

Council of Continuing Education
   Administrators, 72-74
Counseling services, 236-62, 267-68
Cultural enrichment, 192, 285
Curriculum, 16, 161-73, 178-79, 181-93

D

Dade Co. (Fla.) Public Schools, 271
Debates, 329
Demonstration Cities and Metropolitan
   Development Act, 127
Demonstration techniques, 330-31
Department of Adult Education, 24, 25
Department of Immigrant Education, 24, 25
Detroit Public Schools, 224, 230
Disadvantaged populations, vii, 183-84, 209,
   226-29, 232-35, 303-304
Discussion groups, 254-55, 287-88, 325-30
Discussion and lecture, 323-25
District system, 265-66
Division of Adult Education Programs, 22
Division of Adult Education Service, 25
Dorland, James, 118-35 (chapter on legislation),
   134
Drive-in workshops, 307
Dropouts, 195-96, 261

E

Economic Opportunity Act, 17, 23, 120-21, 182
Education Professions Development Act, 79,
   127-28
Educational placement service, 257-58
Educative community, vi, 38-39
Elementary and Secondary Education Act,
   122-25
Employment security agencies, 61
Enrollment statistics, 16, 17-18, 46-47, 81
Evaluation of program. See Program evaluation

F

Facilities, 5-6, 33-34, 264-76
Federal legislation (see also names of federal
   agencies and legislative acts), 19, 119-26
Ferrier, D. Ray, 218-35 (chapter on recruitment)
Financial support (see also names of federal
   agencies and legislative acts), 4, 6-7, 18-20,
   34-35, 39-42, 57, 62, 103-107
Finch, Robert E., ii, v, vii, 1, 12
Flint (Mich.) Board of Education, 30
Flint (Mich.) community school model, 35-36,
   40-41, 42-43, 44-45
Florida Adult Education Association, 307
Forums, 328
Foundations, private, 21-22, 23, 25, 44, 90
Future trends, 175-79, 390-91

G

General Educational Development (GED) test,
   23-24, 189, 250
Ghettoes, 6, 31, 39
GI Bill of Rights, 106, 118
Government agency. See under United States
Griffith, William S., 76-101 (chapter on adult
   education director)
Guidance services, vii, 236-62, 267

H

Hand, Samuel E., 138-58 (chapter on needs and resources)
Handicapped adults, 195
Hanna, Mark C., ii, v, viii
Health education, 187
Health agencies, 60-61
High school completion, 8, 187-89, 285
Higher adult education, 57-60
Higher Education Act, 122-23
History of adult education, 14-16, 28-30
Holden, John, 13
Home study courses, 270-71
Human Resources and Development Centers, 125
Human rights groups, 67-68

I

Individualized instruction, 7, 331-35
Industry, 63-64
Informal groups, 152-53
Information services, 252-57
In-service education, 299-313
Instruction improvement, 295-96, 298-315
Instructional methods, 7, 69-70, 179, 270-71, 323-25, 327-35
Intermediate school district, 54-55
Inventories, 245-50

J

Job Opportunities in the Business Sector (JOBS), 126
Johnston, William J., 102-117 (chapter on finance)
Junior colleges, 16-17, 49-53, 92, 98-99, 193-94

K

Kleis, Russell J., 46-74 (chapter on roles and interrelationships)
Knowles, Malcolm, 13
Knox, Alan B., 368-91 (chapter on program evaluation)

L

Labor unions, 62-63
Langdon, Golden I., 236-62 (chapter on counseling)
Leaders, 21-24, 286-93
Learning, 317-41
Laboratory, See Programed instruction
Lecture and discussion, 323-25
Lectures, 327-28
Legislation (see also names of federal acts and agencies), 19, 79-80, 119-35
Library services, 55-56, 274-75
Los Angeles City Schools, 111-12, 176
Luke, Robert A., ii, v, viii, 12-26 (chapter on public support), 25

M

McCall, Raymond T., 160-79 (chapter on curriculum)
Mann, George C., 13
Manpower Development and Training Act, 4, 119-20, 125, 191
Mass media, 69-70, 208-212
Master teachers, 313-14

Materials, sources and evaluation, 331, 336-40
Minich, Carl E., 180-99 (chapter on curriculum)
Model Cities, 127
Model Neighborhoods in Demonstration Cities, 127
Motivation of students, 218-27

N

National Advisory Commission on Civil Disorders (quoted), 132-33
National Advisory Committee on Adult Basic Education, 124
National Alliance of Businessmen, 126
National Association for Public School Adult Education, 24-25, 85, 90, 134
National Community School Education Association, 30
National Defense Education Act, 119, 132
Neff, Monroe C., 316-41 (chapter on methods and materials)
Neighborhood Facilities Grants, 127
North Central Association of Secondary Schools and Colleges, 8, 23, 84

O

Occupational training, 53-54, 190-92
Occupations in the U.S., 31, 32
Off-campus facilities, 270
Office etiquette, 205-206
Orientation programs, 252-53

P

Panels, 329
Parent and family life education, 185-87
Partnership for Learning and Earning Act, 134
Personnel relations, 280-96
Peters, Floyd N., 264-76 (chapter on facilities)
Physical differences between youth and adults, 271-72
Physical facilities, 266-76
Placement service, 257-59
Practical crafts, 192
Preservice training, 309
Printing, arranging for, 207-208
Private schools, 56-57
Professional associations, 24-25
Professional schools and seminaries, 57-58
Professional and technical societies, 63
Program
    Budgeting, 111-12
    Coordination, vii, 5, 6, 36-37, 49, 70-74, 126-27
    Development, 40, 41, 42, 51-57, 93-101, 149, 157, 170-78
    Evaluation, 368-91
    Promotion, 206-215, 252-53
Programed instruction, 331-35
Public affairs education, 189-90, 286-87
Public agencies with auxiliary education functions, 60-62
Public library, 55-56
Public relations, 205-215
Public schools, 29-30, 32-45
Publications, 206-208

R

Rauch, David B., 200-215 (chapter on public relations)
Record keeping, 240, 244, 261-62
Recreation departments, 61
Recruitment. *See* Students
Referral service, 259
Registration facilities, 269-70
Research, 345-66
Richmond (Va.) Public Schools survey, 23
Riot Commission (quoted), 132-33

S

Safety education, 187
Schenz, Robert F., vii, 122, 160-79 (chapter on curriculum)
Schroeder, Wayne L., 344-66 (chapter on research)
Secondary school administrators, 80-81, 83-84
Senior citizens, 194-95, 272
Servicemen's Readjustment Act, 106, 118
Shaw, Nathan C., ii, v, viii
Sheldon, James A., 280-97 (chapter on staff)
Smith-Bankhead Act, 118
Smith-Hughes Act, 118, 132
Smith-Lever Act, 58, 77, 118
Social functions, 255-56
Special interest groups, 68-69, 194-96
Staffing adult programs, 280-95
State aid, 14-15, 18-19, 19-20, 128-29
Students, vi, 4, 17-18, 21, 46-47, 170, 177-78, 194-95
    Dropouts, 195-96, 261
    Fees, 4, 6, 20, 106
    Follow-up, 259-61
    Motivation, 219-27
    Recruitment, 205-213, 220-24, 227-35
Supervision, 295-96, 299-313
Symposia, 329

T

Teachers
    Aides, 285-86
    Facilities, 268

Guides, 338-40
In-service education, 299-315
Master, 313-14
Selection, 281-86, 291-93
Supervision and training, 299-315
Technical institutes, 17, 193-94
Television, 209-210, 270-71, 288-90
Testing service, 245-51
Tests, 245-50

U

Ulmer, R. Curtis, 298-315 (chapter on teacher training)
U.S. Department of
    Defense, 126
    Health, Education, and Welfare, 126
    Housing and Urban Development, 126-27
    Labor, 2, 119, 125-26
U.S. Office of
    Economic Opportunity, 121-23
    Education, 17, 22, 121-24, 125, 126, 128, 134-35
University evening college, 58
University extension, 58, 62, 307
Urban universities, 58

V

Vocational education, 190-92, 284-85
Vocational Education Act, 120, 132, 134, 272
Vocational placement service, 258-59
Voluntary associations, 64-66

W

Wasinger, Gordon B., 280-97 (chapter on staffing)
Welfare agencies, 60-61
Women, second careers for, 196
Work Experience Program, 125
Work-related institutions, 62-64
Workshops, drive-in, 307

Y

Young adults, 195-96, 271-72
Youth Opportunity Centers, 125